AF574911

HENNA
SOURCEBOOK

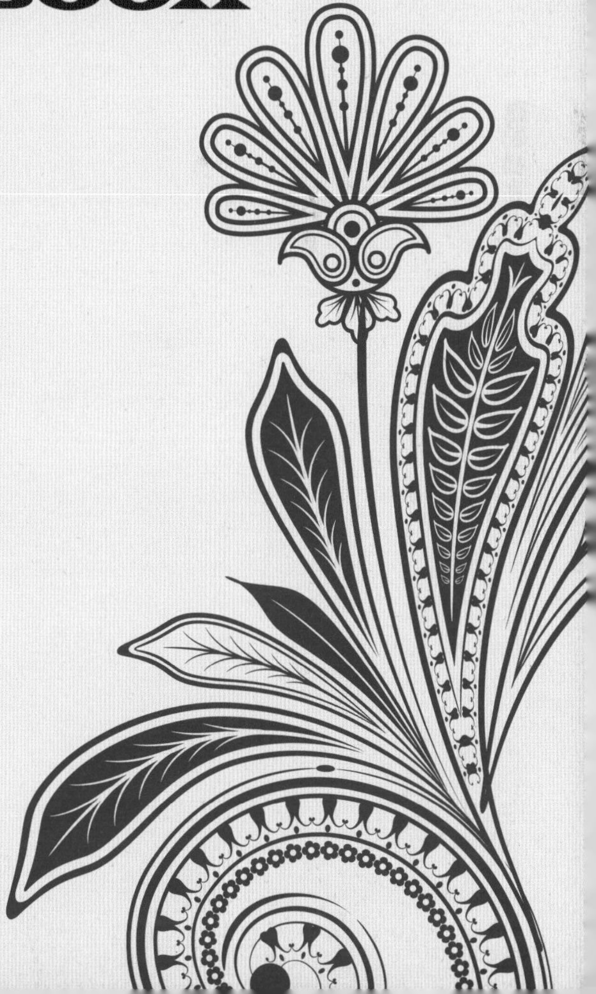

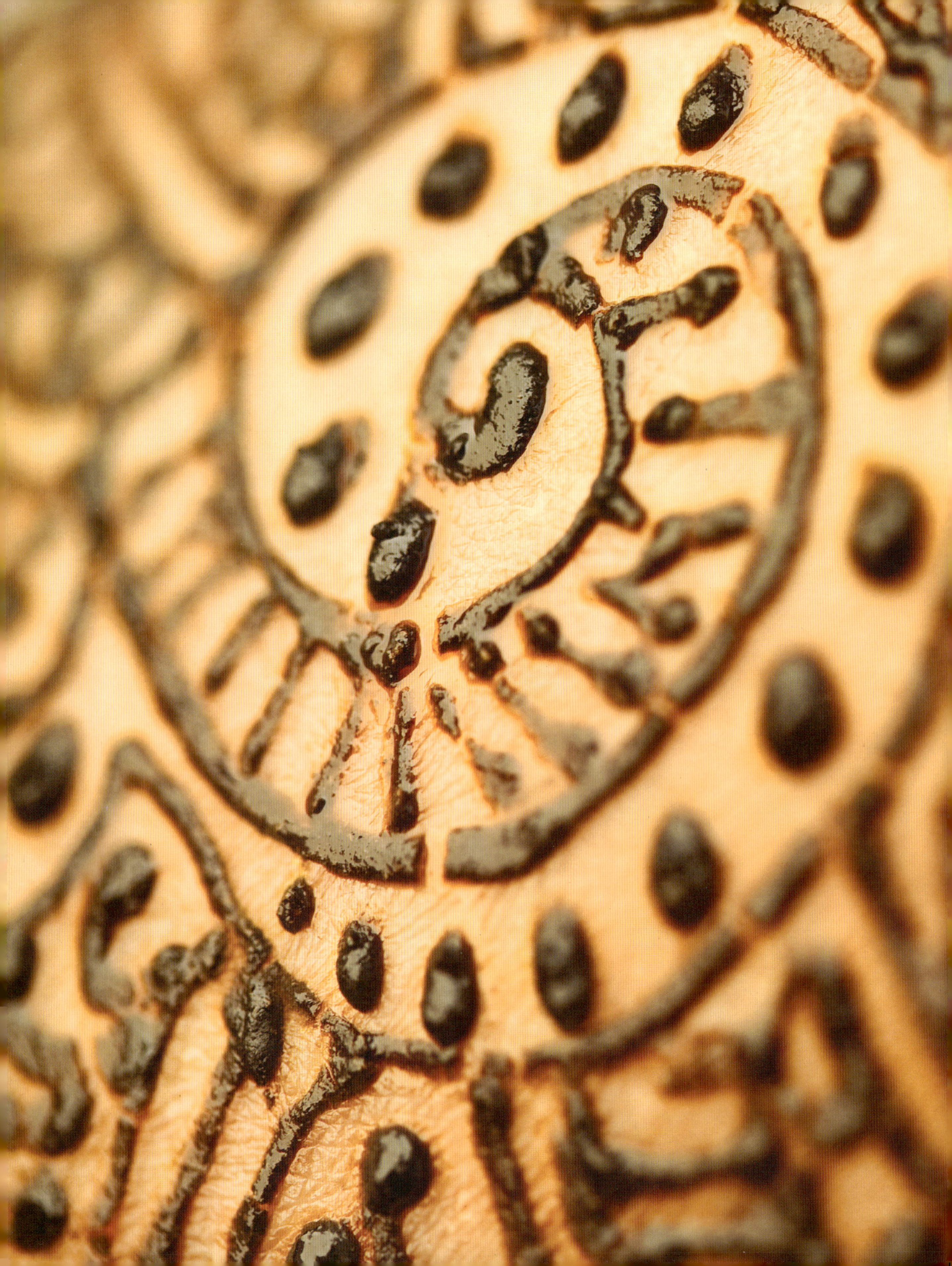

HENNA SOURCEBOOK

Mary Packard

Patterns collected and adapted by
Eleanor Kwei

Race Point
PUBLISHING
www.racepointpub.com
New York, NY

A division of Book Sales, Inc.
276 Fifth Avenue Suite 206
New York, New York 10001

This 2012 edition published by Race Point Publishing by arrangement with The Book Shop, Ltd.

EDITOR Sherry Gerstein
DESIGN Tim Palin Creative

ISBN-13: 978-1-937994-08-2

Printed in China

2 4 6 8 10 9 7 5 3 1

www.racepointpub.com

TABLE OF CONTENTS

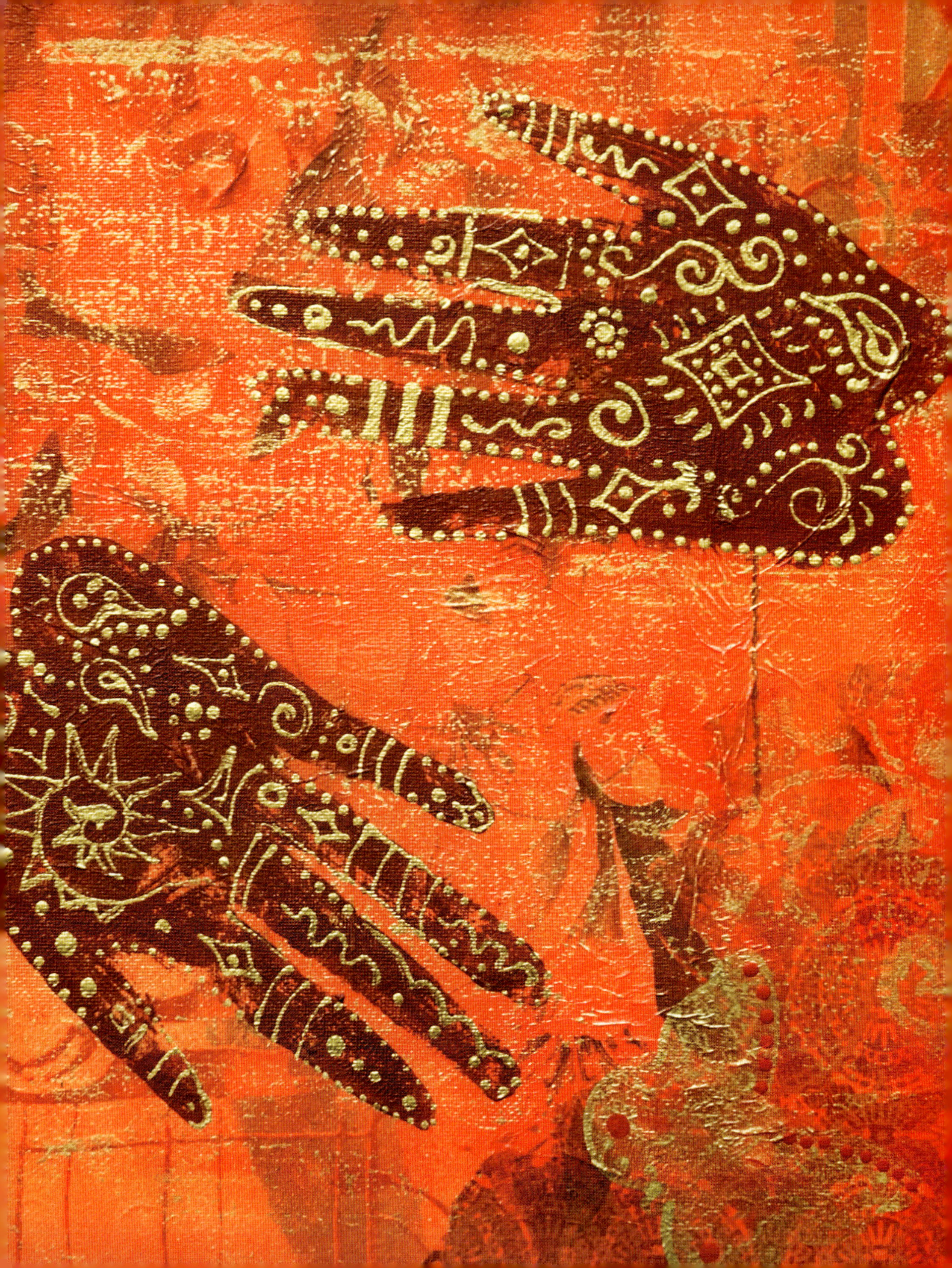

THE HISTORY AND USES OF HENNA

Henna body art has been a part of traditions surrounding love and fertility, luck and celebration for over 3,000 years. The leaves of the henna plant—dried, crushed to a powder and mixed into a paste with a mildly acidic liquid—can be used to make safe, beautiful, temporary body art. Henna paste can also stain skin, fingernails, and hair a reddish-orange to dark brown color, in much the same way as a wet teabag can stain white cloth.

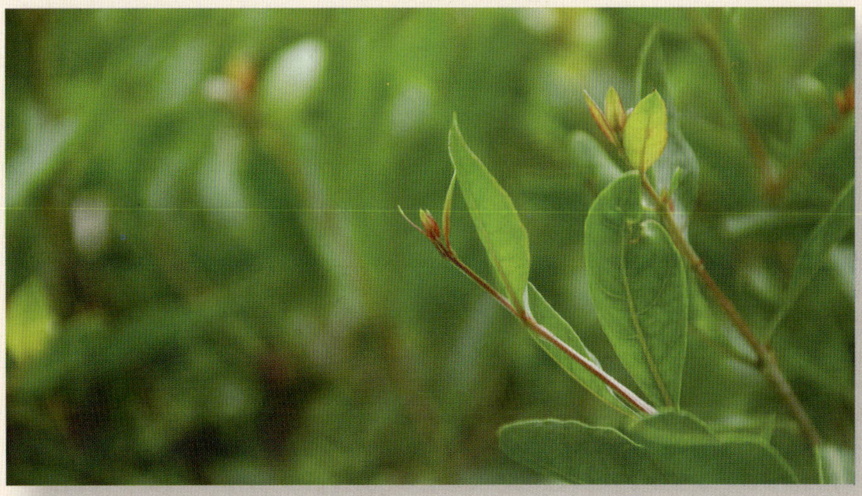

The henna plant, *Lawsonia inermis*, is a small tree that grows in frost-free, semi-arid climates. There is no single origin of henna art and traditions, and no single discovery of henna, though the use of henna worldwide falls into three general categories: hair coloring, use in folk medicine, and skin markings. These uses are based on the red-orange dye molecule that occurs naturally in henna leaves: *lawsone*. This molecule has two characteristics useful to humans. Lawsone will readily stain keratin (the protein found in hair and nails) and it is anti-fungal.

The Evolution of Henna

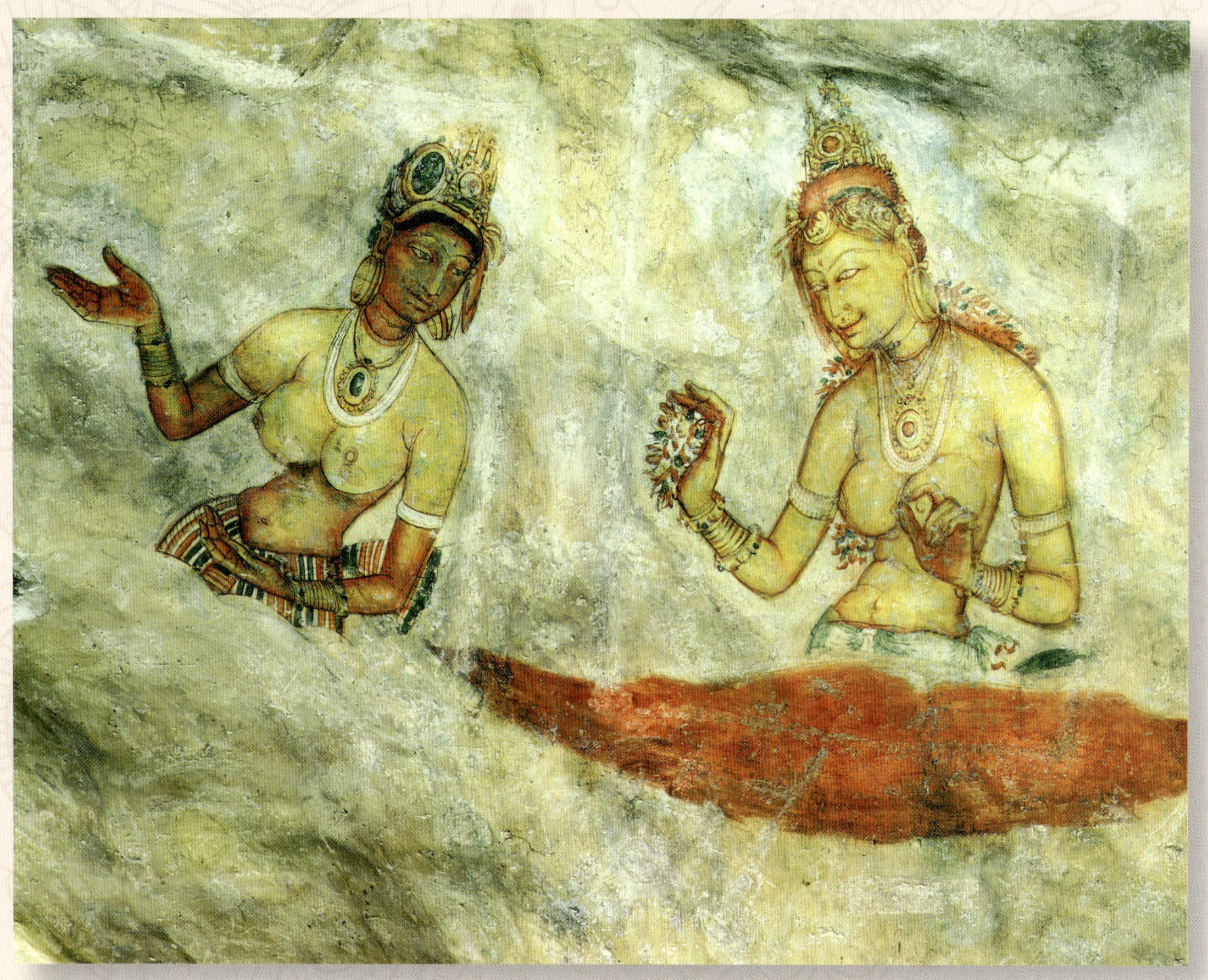

Fresco of courtesans or nymphs offering flowers from court of King Kassapa on rock of Sigiriya, Sri Lanka, ca. 485 CE

It is believed that the earliest uses of henna were probably in Africa during the last ice age, between 7500 and 3500 BCE, when the Sahara region was greener than it is today. The theory goes something like this: humans herded livestock through the warm savannahs during this period, and some of their animals browsed on the henna plants growing there. The animals' mouths would have been stained red-orange by chewing the henna leaves. If the herdsman saw the stains and worried that an animal was bleeding and then tried to pull the chewed leaves from the animal's mouth, the herdsman's hands would have been stained red. This may have been the "Aha" moment, the recognition that crushed henna leaves can stain skin, and though the stain color resembles blood, the stain is not harmful. People would have learned by continued observation that henna leaves, crushed and mixed with a slightly acidic liquid, would stain hair, fingernails, and skin. They would also have learned that this stain relieved them and their animals of some nuisances such as head lice and fungal infections of the skin, nails and hooves. This anti-fungal effect of henna probably gave rise to the cultural belief that henna had *baraka*—baraka being the Arabic word for luck or blessing.

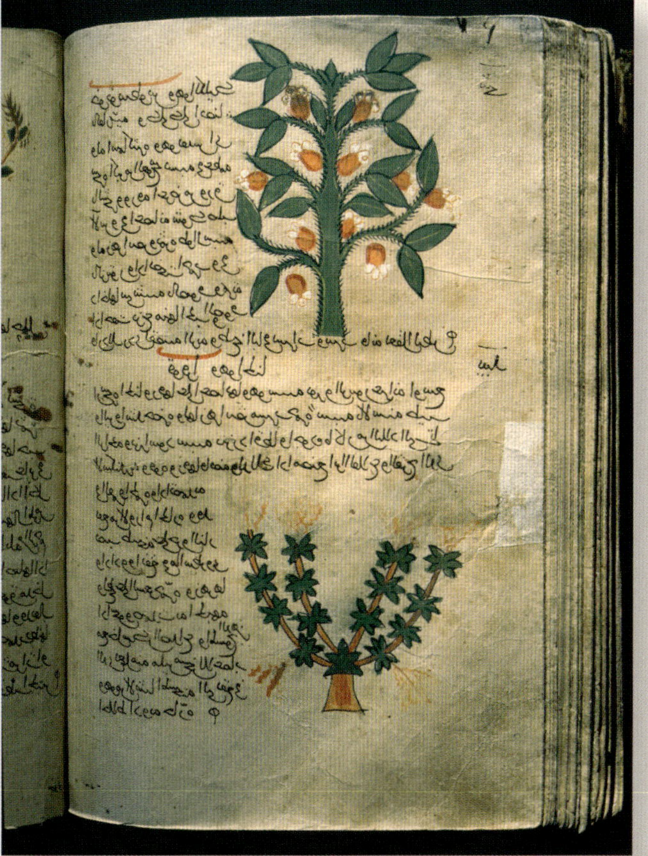

Folio 37r of the Arabic version of *De Materia Medica* by the Greek physician, Dioscorides, shows a henna plant in the lower right corner. Islamic, 987–990 CE

Birds likely helped the geographical spread of henna along. Assuming that henna was indigenous to North Africa during the most recent ice age, birds could have consumed the berries and left the seeds in their droppings as they flew northward and eastward along the river valleys and coasts, farther and farther seasonally as the climate warmed, into henna's present habitats. Henna now grows along the southern and eastern coasts of the Mediterranean, in Africa north of the rainforests from the Atlantic coast to the Red Sea, east Africa from Egypt south to Zanzibar, the Arabian Peninsula, the Persian Gulf region, Pakistan,

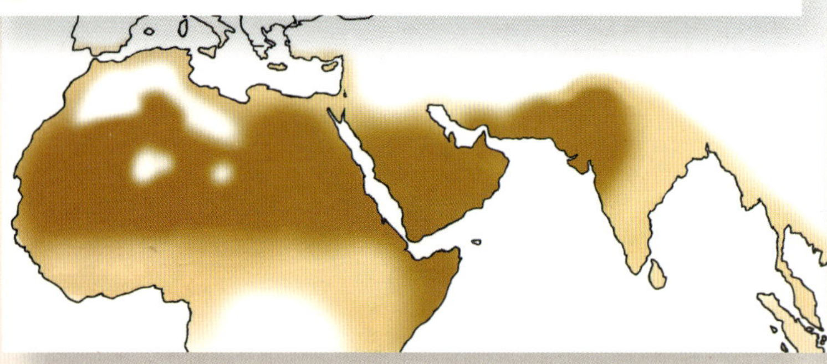

India and Indonesia. It grows most easily in frost-free areas where there are long periods of drought.

There is physical evidence of early henna use in Egypt dating to 3400 BCE. In several mummies, including the mummy of Ramses II, the gray hair is dyed with henna. There is no evidence of patterned henna body art during the Egyptian dynastic period, so henna may only have been used to mask graying hair or for therapeutic use at this time.

In the Bronze Age, on the eastern coast of the Mediterranean near Syria, Cyprus, and the Aegean Islands, there are artifacts that may be interpreted as evidence of the origins of henna body art traditions associated with women. Between 2000 BCE and 800 BCE, there are statuettes of women with markings on their hands consistent with henna, as well as fragments of ancient texts from the city of Ugarit that mention henna used for marking women's bodies to celebrate fertility, betrothal, sacrifice, and victory. These early connections between women and henna are the beginnings of the "Night of the Henna," the ritual application of henna patterns to a bride in preparation for her wedding, which is still celebrated throughout henna-using cultures today. There is similar evidence of henna used for body markings in customs celebrating betrothal, sacrifice, and victory in the pre-monotheistic groups of Syria and Cyprus, the Arabian Peninsula and the southern Mediterranean, particularly in the areas populated by the cultures that worshipped deities such as Baal and Anat or Tanit. The Assyrians were using henna as part of women's wedding preparations by 800 BCE. Some of these cultural uses of henna appear to have been adapted from the pre-monotheistic religions into the cultures of early Judaism. Henna was indigenous to Israel during the Biblical period and is mentioned fondly in the Song of Solomon as *camphire* (the Latin transliteration of *kopher*, ancient Hebrew for henna). The imperial Romans were familiar with henna, and used it as a hair dye, but do not seem to have used it widely for body marking. It was more associated with the cultures of their eastern provinces.

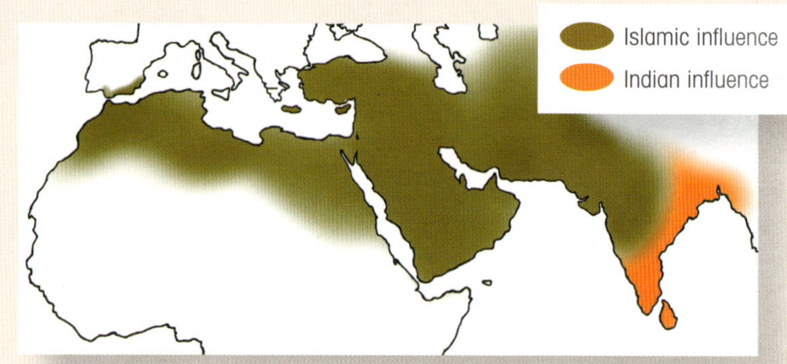

Henna Traditions

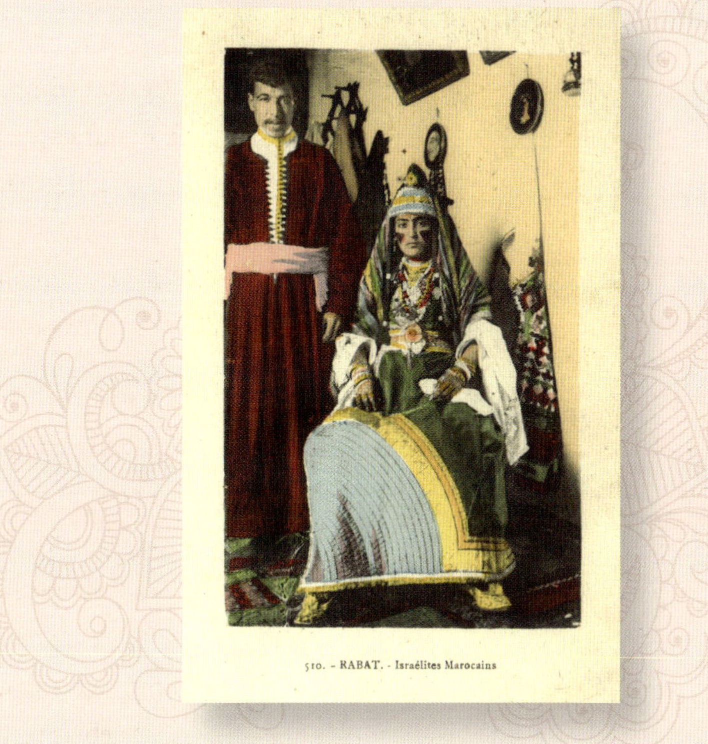
510. - RABAT. - Israélites Marocains

The Night of the Henna has been a tradition since 1000 BCE, at least. In the Night of the Henna, a girl is purified, dressed and bejeweled for her wedding, and marked with henna. The markings are done at a party held by the bride and groom's families, and the guests are often marked as well. The girl's mother or the groom's mother marks the bride with henna, unless there is a local professional henna artist for hire. The party includes traditional songs, dancing, and feasting. The bride may be placed on a dais and displayed in her finest clothing and jewels, often completely veiled except for her hennaed hands and feet. Friends and relatives bring her gifts and money; the money is often dabbed with a bit of henna to take off the "Evil Eye." Henna is believed to attract good luck and dispel bad luck. The Night of the Henna can last for many hours or all night, and is one of the most beloved, widespread folk traditions in the world.

Henna has always been more associated with women than men, especially with women who are in their reproductive years, rather than children or elders. One of the reasons for this is that henna can be harmful to infants and children who have *homozygous G6PD deficiency*, a genetic blood enzyme disorder

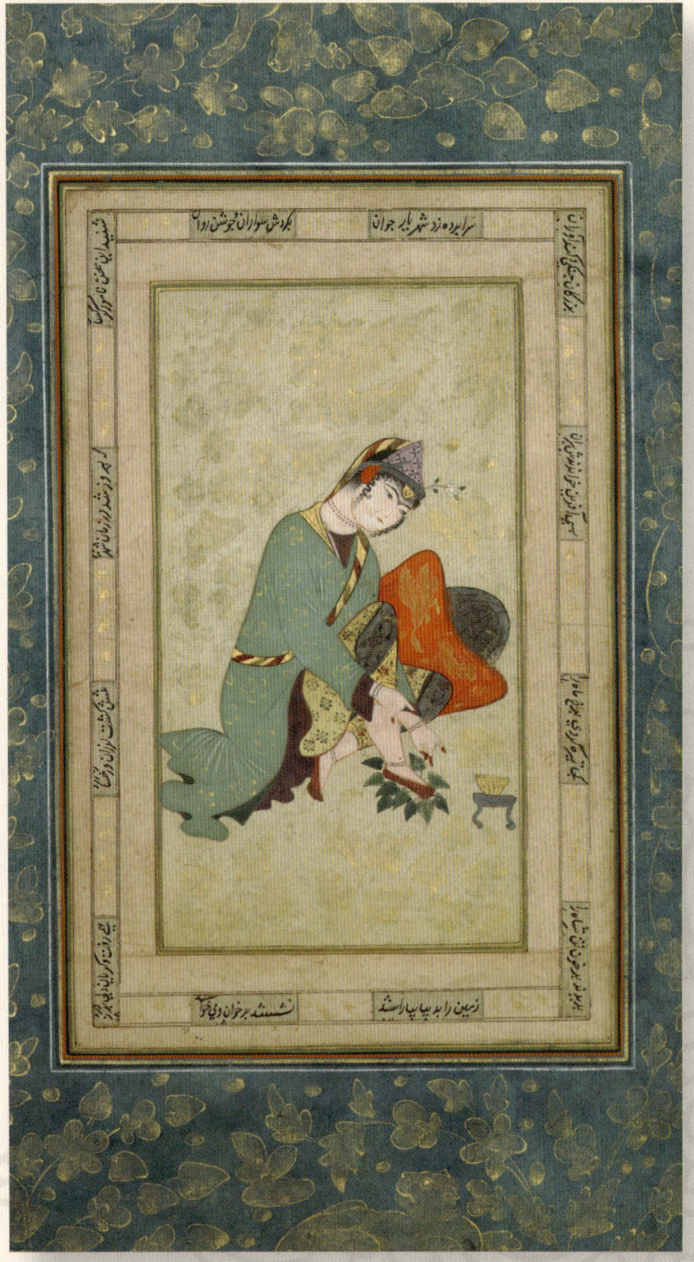

Woman Applying Henna is a rare depiction of a young woman applying henna to her feet, a ritual associated with rite of passage celebrations, paticularly marriage, in Iran and surrounding regions. Iran, late sixteenth century

that is mainly found in areas where malaria is endemic. This genetic deficiency affects males more than females for the same reason that men have hemophilia—because it is transmitted on their single X chromosome. The simple observation that henna never seemed to harm postpubescent females, and occasionally harmed juvenile males shaped the practice that henna was appropriate for women, and not men. Men did use henna in some instances, but always less so than women. Men often had a "Night of the Henna" before marriage, but with simpler patterns, and fewer of them. In many times and places, men had a little henna for luck before they went into battle, and to celebrate Eid, festival days in Islamic cultures.

Henna was indigenous to Israel when Christianity was forming, and early Christians maintained the use of henna for fertility and celebration, though often to a lesser extent than their neighbors who were Jewish, or who were devotees of earlier religions who used henna for their special occasions. When Jewish populations spread outward from Israel after the first century CE, henna use did not follow beyond the plant's natural growing zone, although Jews from Sephardic and Mizrahi (Arabian or African) communities often maintained Night of the Henna traditions, and continued to use henna to mark girls at Purim, and lambs for Passover. As Christian beliefs spread outward through the Roman Empire and beyond, henna use again did not move beyond the availability of the plants, though Egyptian Coptic and Armenian Christians maintained Night of the Henna traditions into the twentieth century.

Henna was part of wellness and social celebrations in Arabia during the period of the formation of Islam, and henna was adapted into Muslim cultural practices. Henna was integrated particularly into Muslim women's cultural life. In Islam, every observant person must wash before prayer. In addition, women are required to have a purifying wash before prayer to remove reproductive blood and fluids (from menstruation, birth, and sexual activity). As Muslim culture spread, the culture of bathing spread with it, and benefactors constructed public baths for the health and well being of the community. In the women's baths, henna was an integral part of the bathing process, and was used to dye hair, fingertips and soles for beautification and for wellness. As Islam spread, so did ritual ablution and the application of henna as part of bathing for purification. Women learned from other women how to use henna (if they weren't familiar with it already) and the Muslim cultural use of henna spread outward from Arabia, west to Spain and the Atlantic shore of Africa, north to the Ottoman and Persian empires, as well as to Muslim communities in western China and Russia, and eastward through India and Malaysia.

In medieval Sicily, during a period of Muslim influence, women hennaed their fingertips for Christmas. There is evidence that Muslims, Christians and Jews all used henna for hair, soles, fingernails and fingertips, as well as ornamental body marking for celebrations in medieval Spain during years of Moorish influence. The Catholic Church forbade the use of henna in Spain on penalty of death in the sixteenth century as part of the expulsion of Muslims, Jews, and their culture. In Armenia, Christian women continued to henna their hands for weddings until recent times. Jewish Kurdish women had rich henna traditions for Purim, betrothal, and for weddings. In Yemen and North Africa, Jewish women had similar henna traditions, and very elaborate bridal henna, paralleling their Muslim neighbors.

Between the tenth and seventeenth centuries, wealthy Persian women wore some of the most elaborate henna work in history, displaying complex, beautiful henna patterns on their hands and feet for the Persian New Year celebration, Nowruz, weddings, Eid, and other social celebrations. They also ornamented their bodies, indulging in henna patterns of flowers and birds to beautify their bodies for their husbands. Women in the Ottoman Empire also regularly used henna for beautification and celebration.

As Persian and Arabic influences spread into western India through trade and conquest, their religions and henna traditions spread as well, including the Night of the Henna. From as early as 500 BCE, people in India marked their hands and feet with red dyes and pigments, but not necessarily with henna, and not in the same way as henna. Some red body markings were made with vivid red alkalized turmeric, and others were done with *lac*, a scarlet dye made from *Laccifer laca*, an insect indigenous to southeast India. The colors of both alkalized turmeric and lac are true reds, not the orange or brown color of henna. Lac and turmeric can be removed from the skin surface, but henna cannot—henna stains the skin through its layers. Men rarely used henna, but in southern and southeast Asia, both men and women used lac to tint their palms and soles, and this can be seen in many paintings of the Buddha. Both men and women also painted a neat red line around the soles of their feet, and sometimes painted small patterns on their skin. This skin painting was part of daily grooming and not reserved for celebrations, though people often painted more elaborate designs on their skin for festivals. Lac production is indigenous to the tropical rainy areas of Southeast Asia, and henna is indigenous to the tropical semi-arid areas.

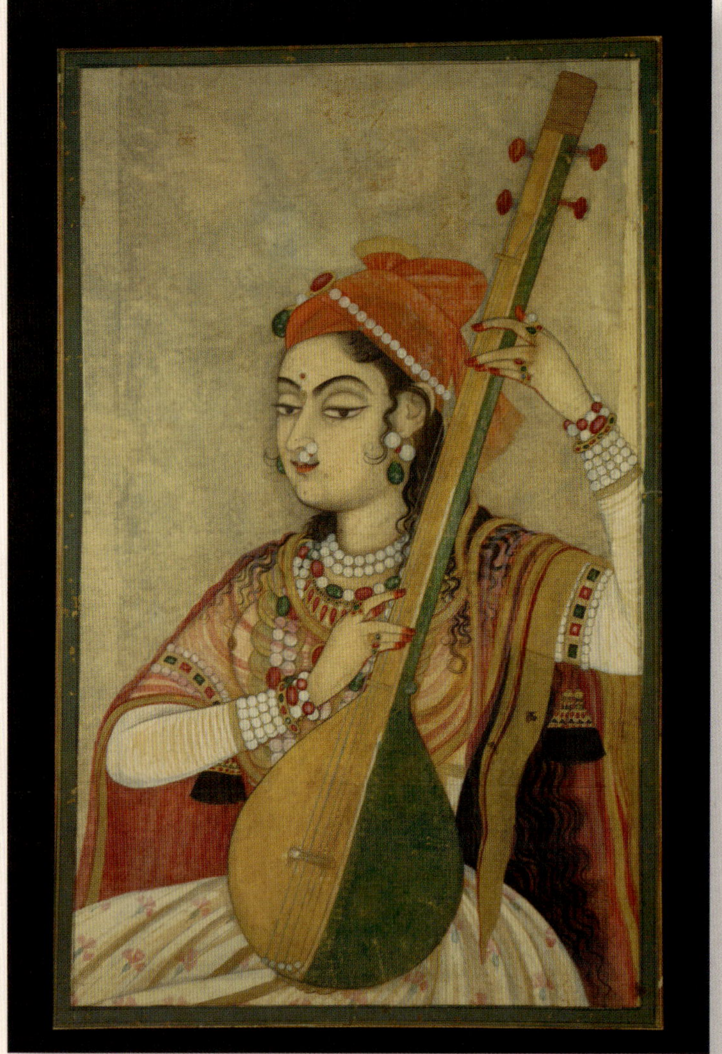

A Lady Playing the Tanpura portrays an entertainer adorned in courtly costume and jewels with henna-dyed fingertips. India, ca. 1735

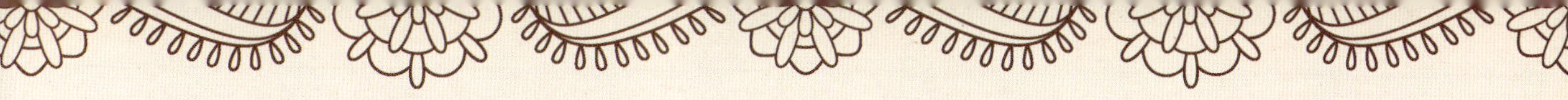

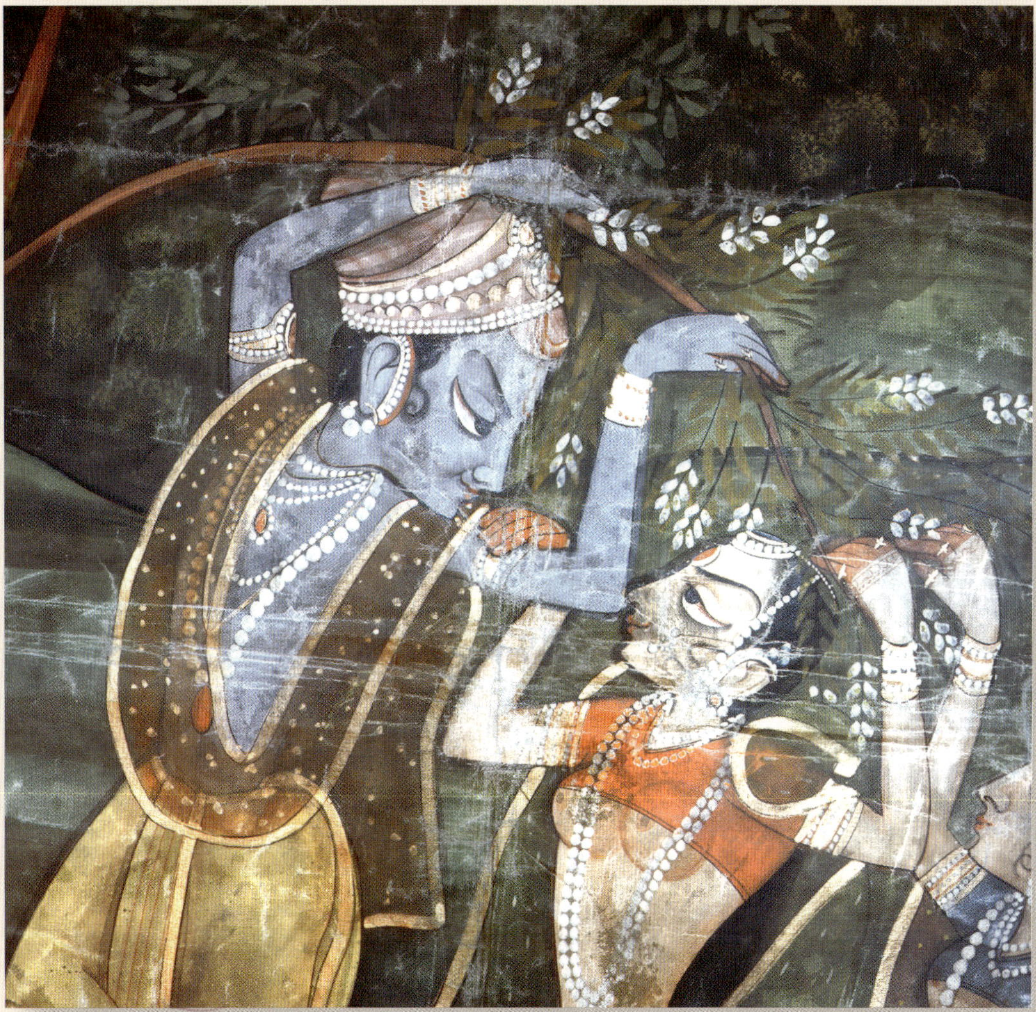

Detail from a nineteenth century Hindu wall hanging with scenes from the legend of Krishna

Much of the traditional body art in Hindu India, done with turmeric, alkalized turmeric, and blue and white pigments was applied for devotional, ritual, and religious purposes. Muslim India adopted the Arabic and Persian cultural traditions of Night of the Henna for weddings, and betrothals, henna for victory and sacrifice, but henna body marking was always secular, and connected with luck and celebration; it was not sacred. Friends, family, or a local artist with a steady hand applied henna. The Night of the Henna didn't become popular in Hindu Indian culture until relatively recently, crossing over from Muslim culture to be part of Hindu bridal parties and social celebrations.

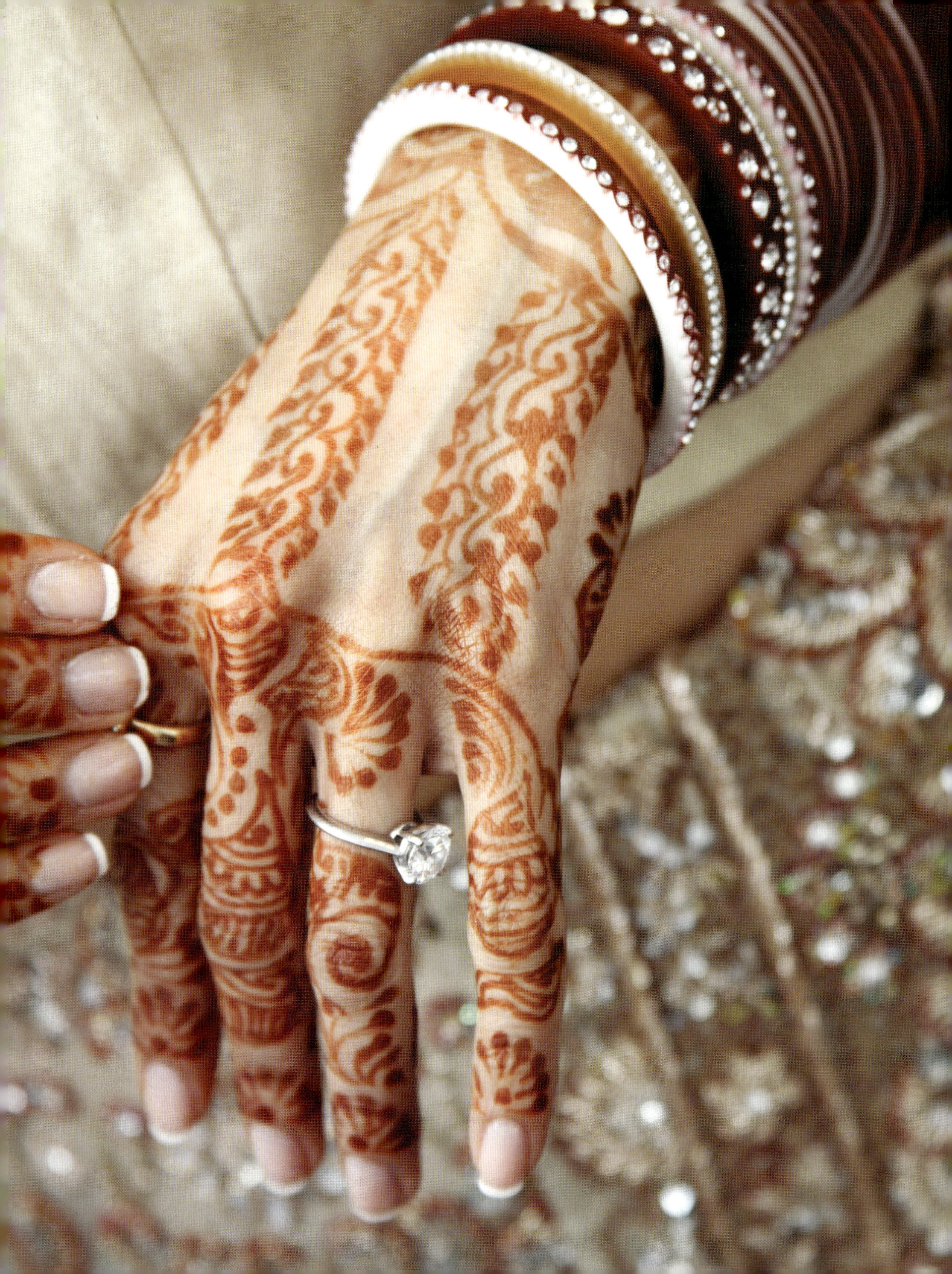

The Craft of Henna

In the last thirty years, the craft of henna has changed rapidly, driven by changes in production, application techniques, and cultural cross-pollination. Improved milling and sifting of henna leaves has bolstered the quality of henna powder and paste, making more complex artwork possible. In previous centuries, henna was applied with a wire or toothpick, or spread on and then quickly scraped into patterns with a small stick (similar to the process of finger-painting). Other artists used resist techniques, such as making patterns with flour paste or first-aid tape that's stuck to the skin, and applying henna over them. These simple techniques can be used to make beautiful henna patterns, but the process is slow.

When snacks and drinks in plastic packaging became widely available, women taught themselves to recycle the bags, and roll them into cones like tiny pastry tubes. When henna artists apply paste with these little cones, they can make delicate patterns, do shading, and fill the skin surface quickly with beautiful, complex patterns. Artists now add glitter, gilding, and glued rhinestones onto henna patterns for extra dazzle.

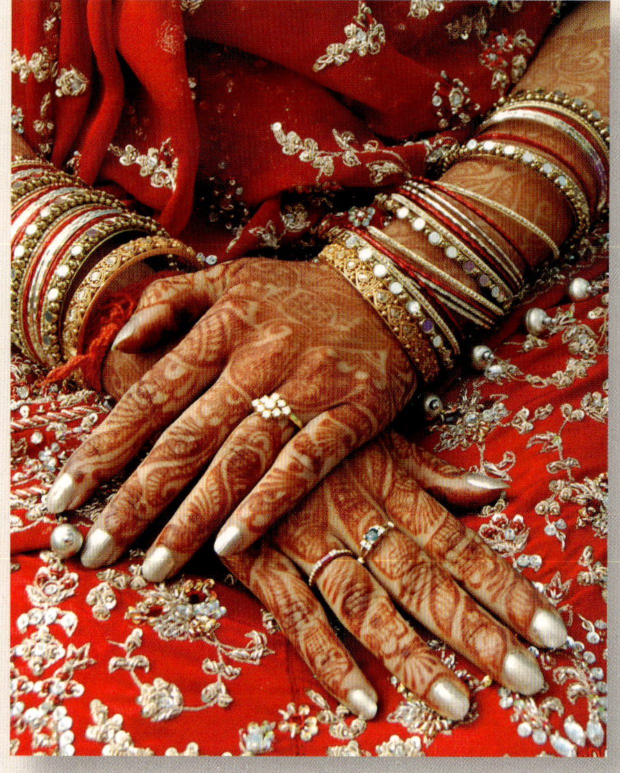

In the last twenty years, people in Europe and the Americas have been introduced to henna body art through the Internet, through Bollywood movies, and through their friends and neighbors who have migrated from henna-using countries. Though traditional henna culture has not always traveled with the product of henna, the new artists brought enthusiasm and innovation to henna, and the art has evolved rapidly in the West. Henna artists everywhere now imitate traditional henna styles and innovate with western pictorial art forms.

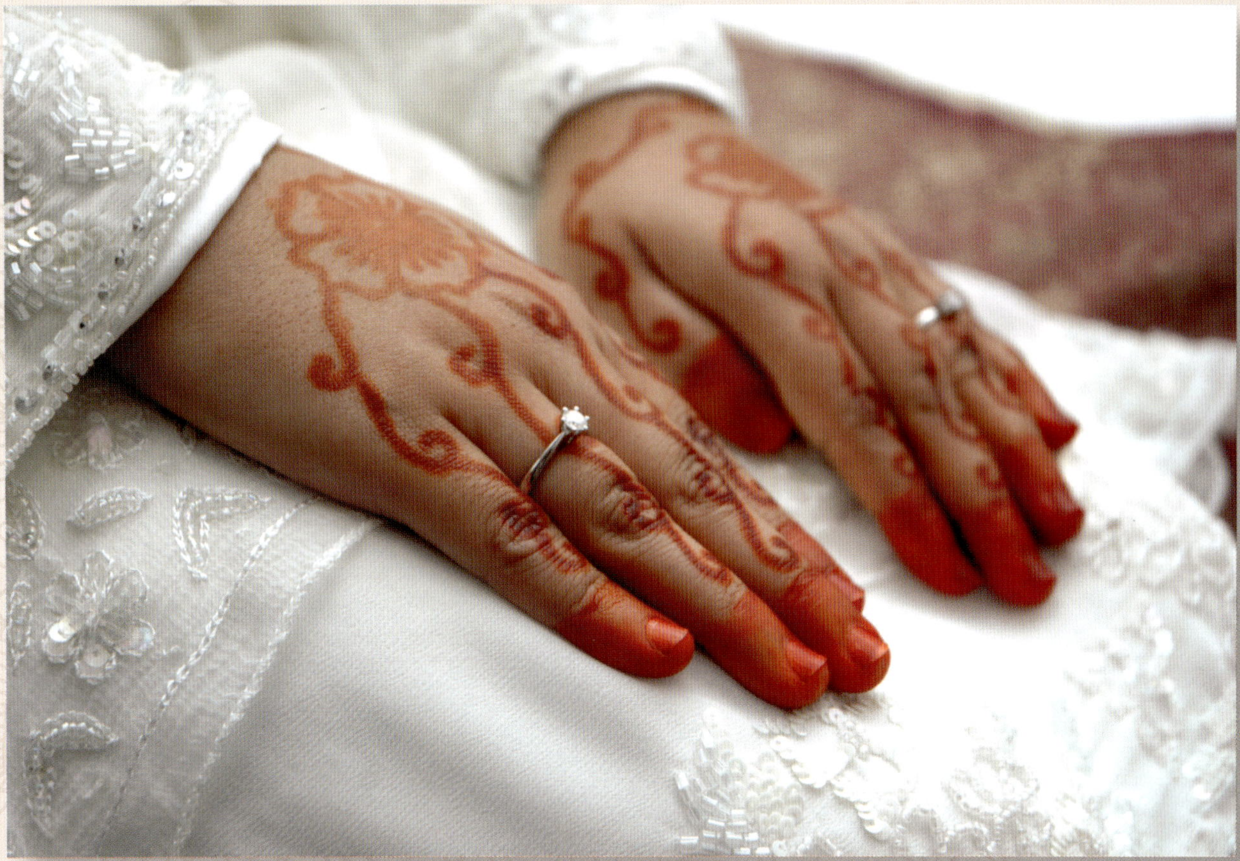

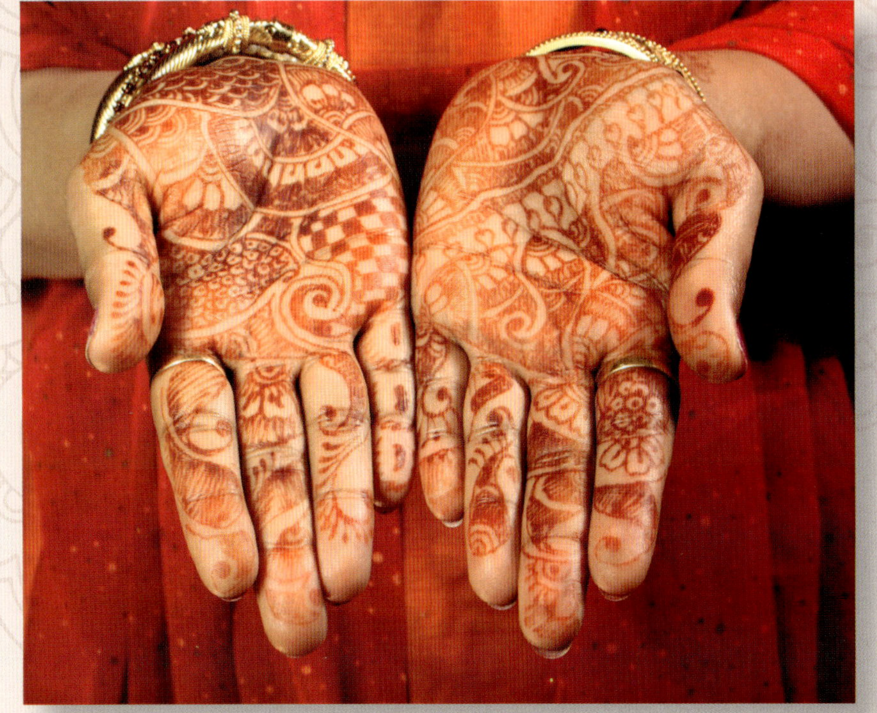

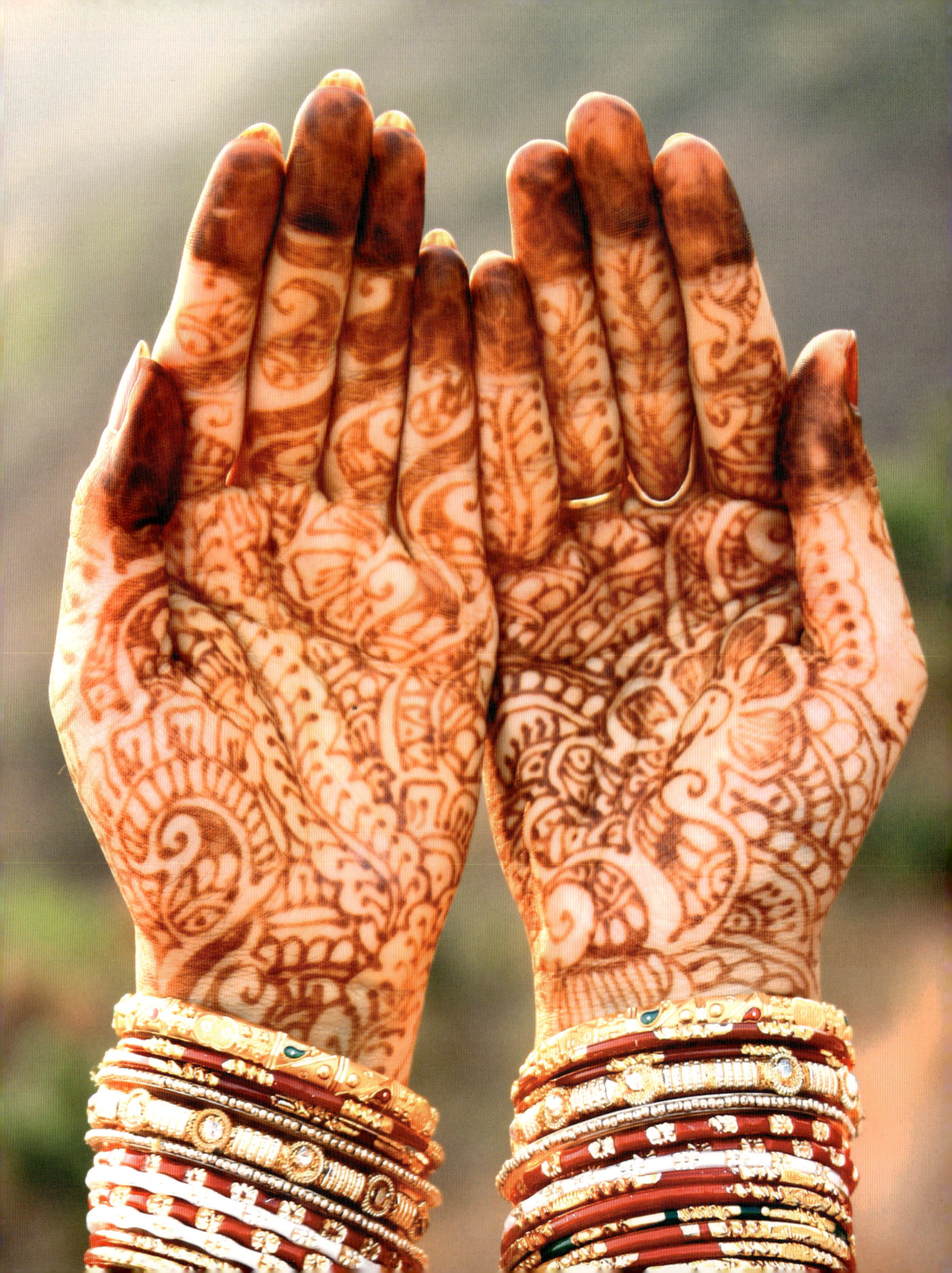

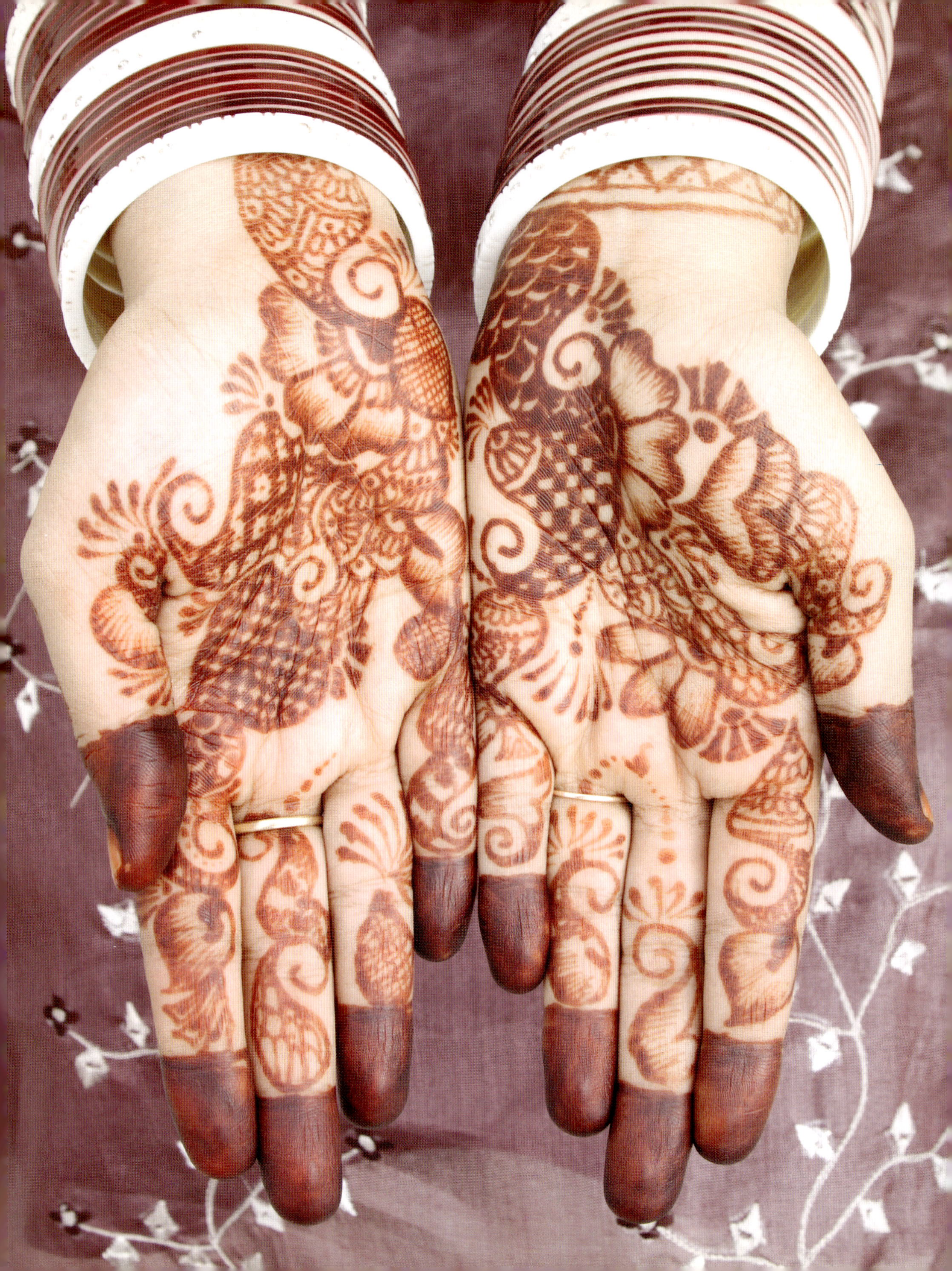

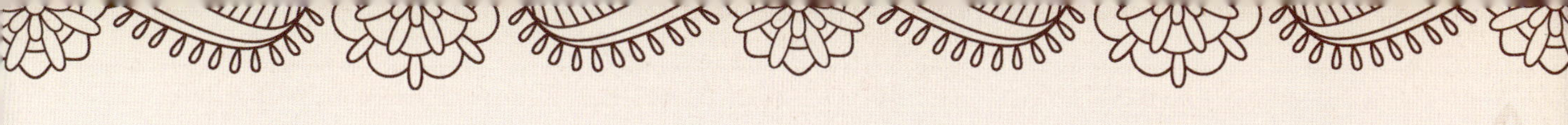

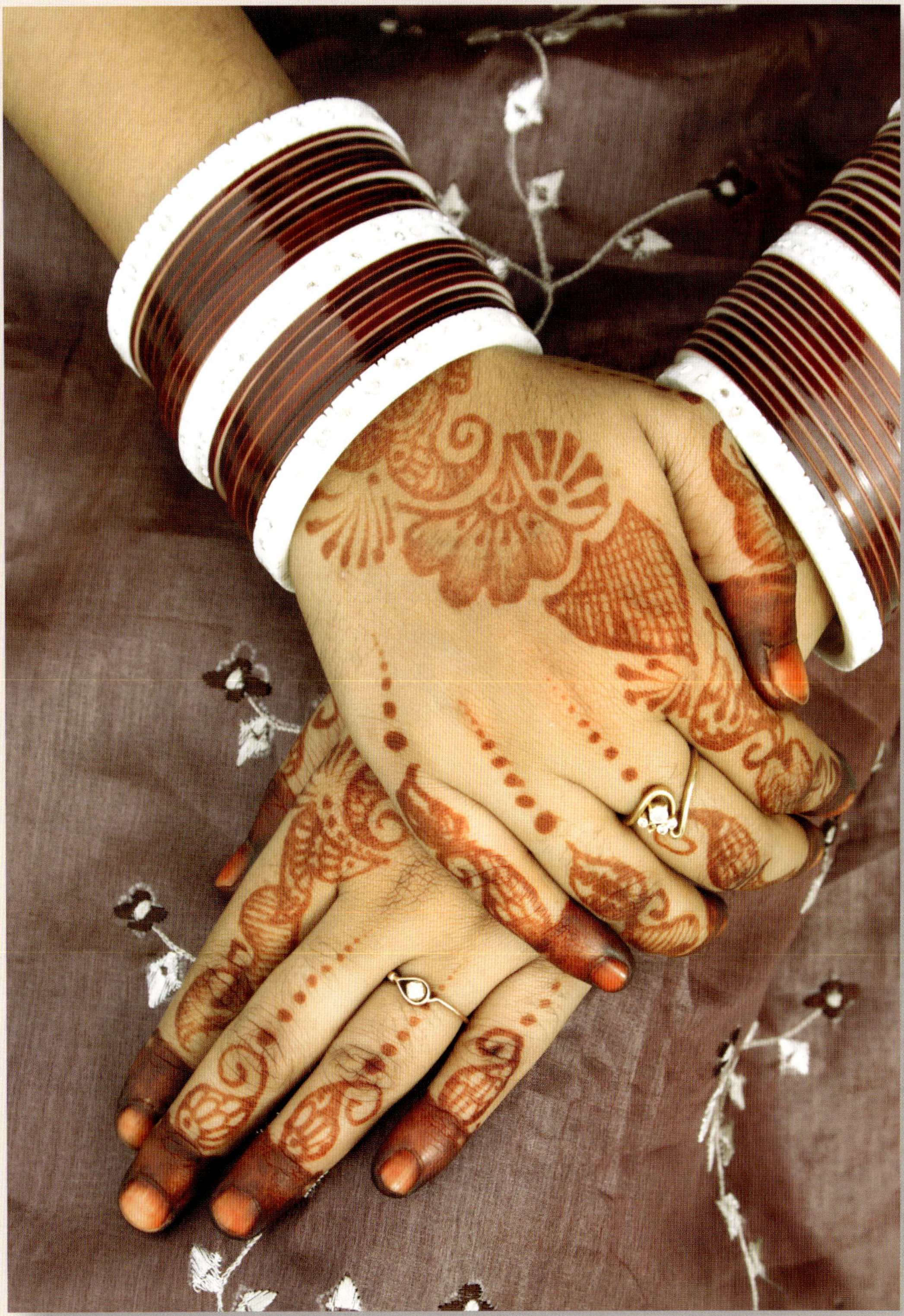

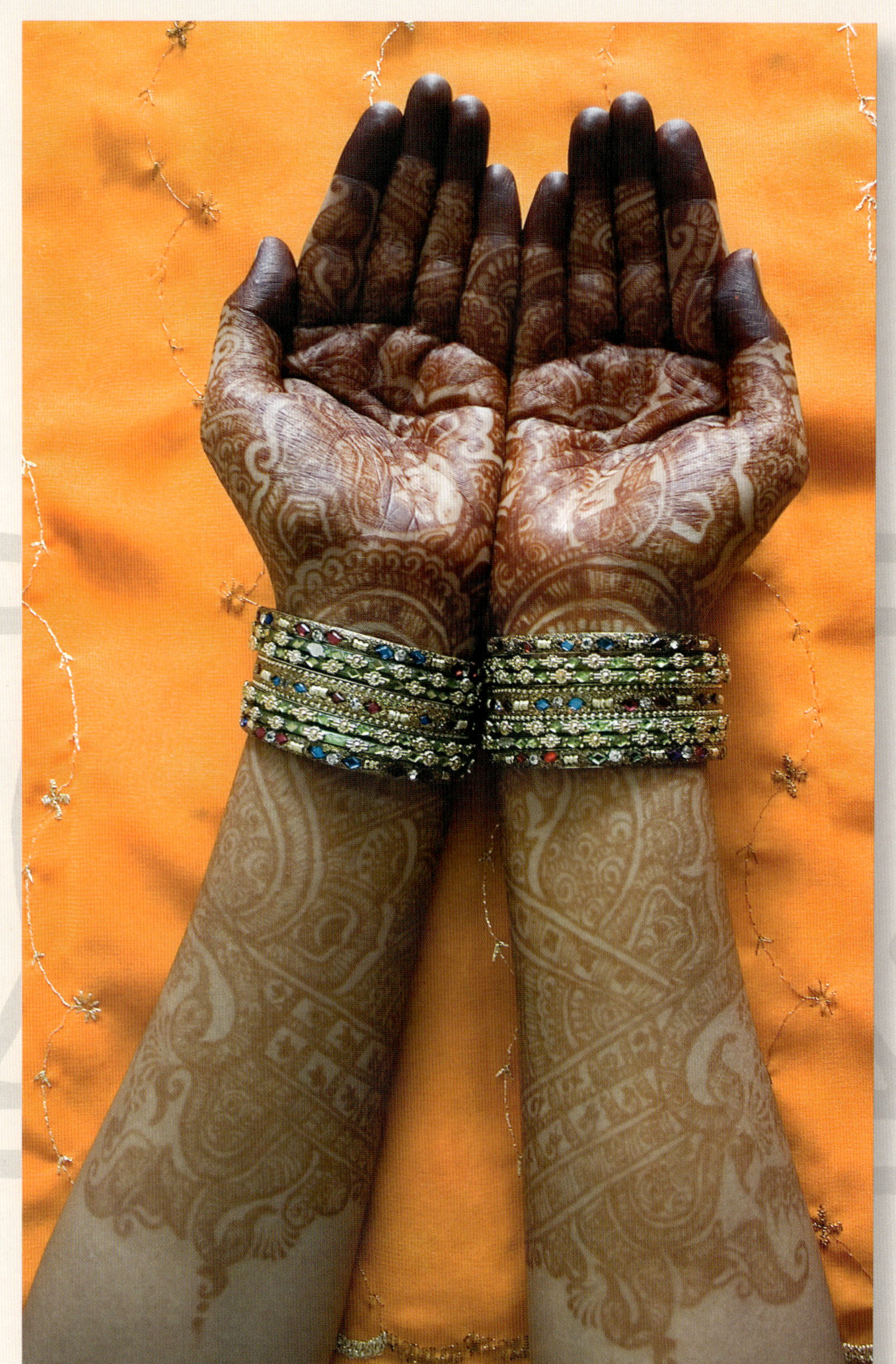

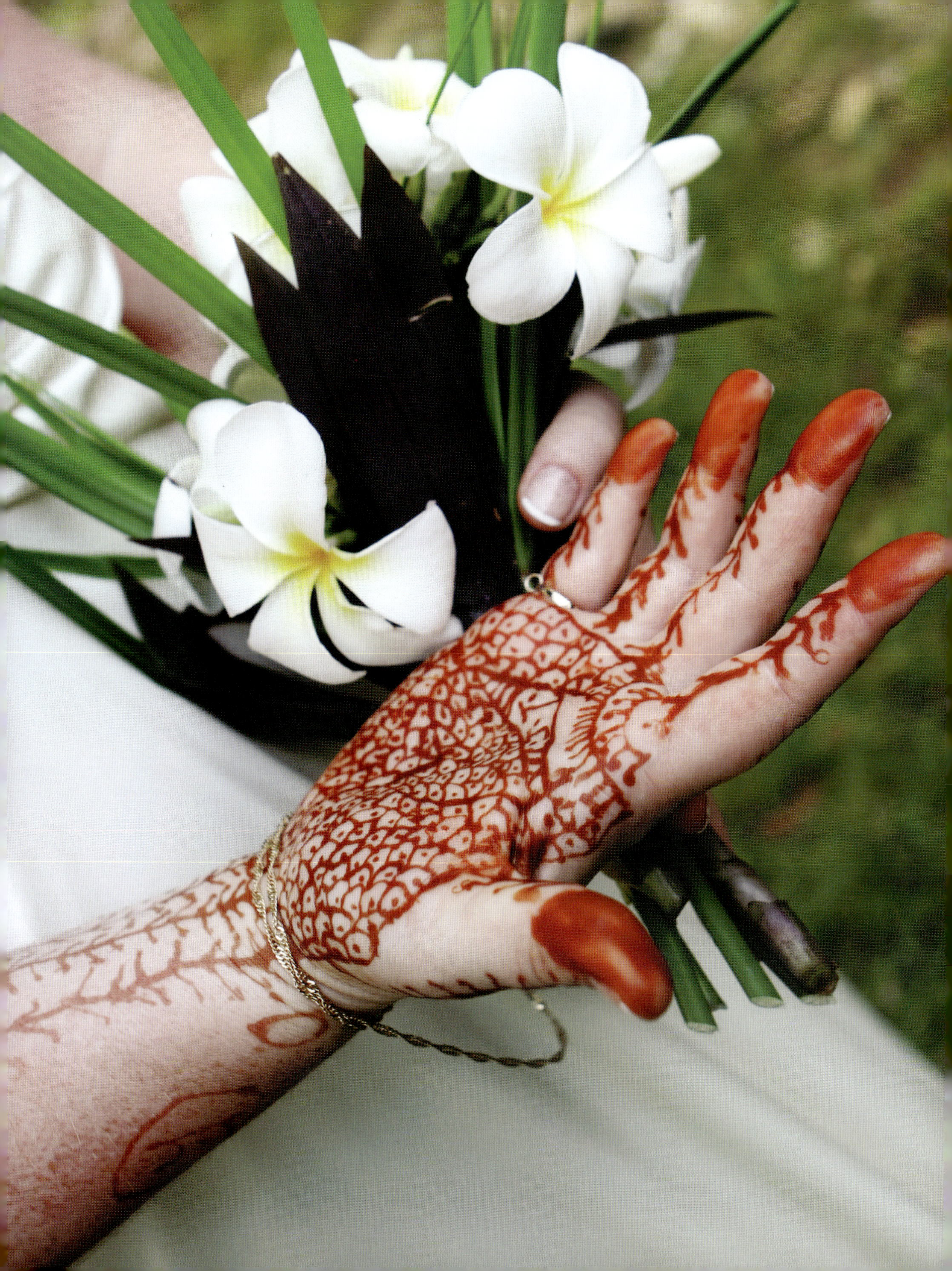

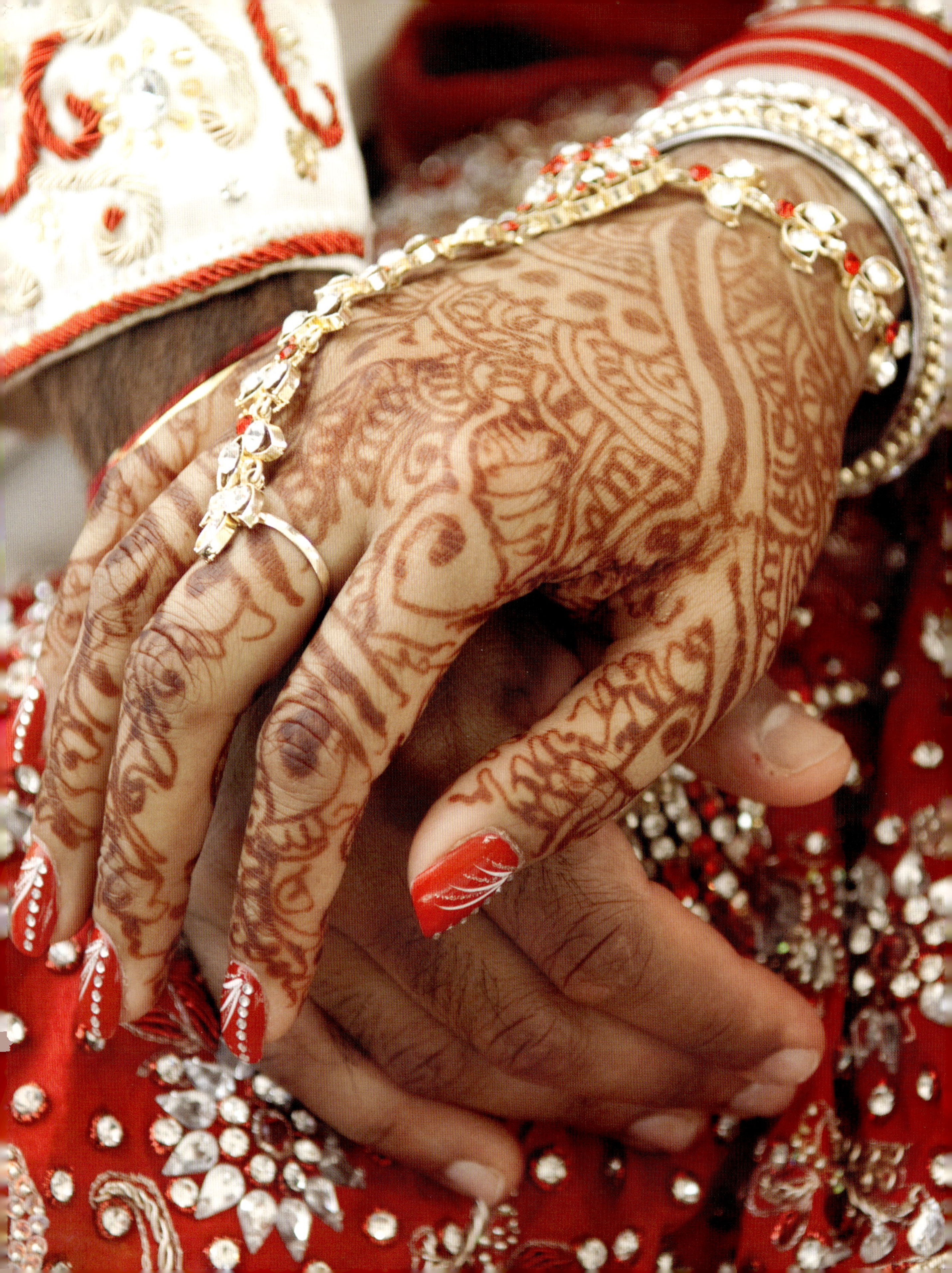

Black Henna Warning

Natural henna is very safe, and has a long history of being a symbol of celebration, luck and love, but its application takes time. That's why there is growing interest in a dangerous, fast-acting product called "black henna." Do not confuse black henna with natural henna. Henna is not black. Any product that will stain the skin black in less than 20 minutes is not natural and is not safe. The only thing that will quickly stain the skin black is *paraphenylenediamine* (PPD). This is a chemical used in hair dye, and it is not approved for use on skin. PPD—black henna—painted on skin as body art can cause blisters, severe allergic reactions, scars, and life-long damage to a person's health. Never use any product on your skin that is labeled black henna. If the product is powdered indigo leaf, a green powder sometimes marketed as black henna, the stain will be a rather ineffective pale bluish-gray. But if the black henna powder is very dark brown or black, it probably contains the chemical PPD and you should not use it.

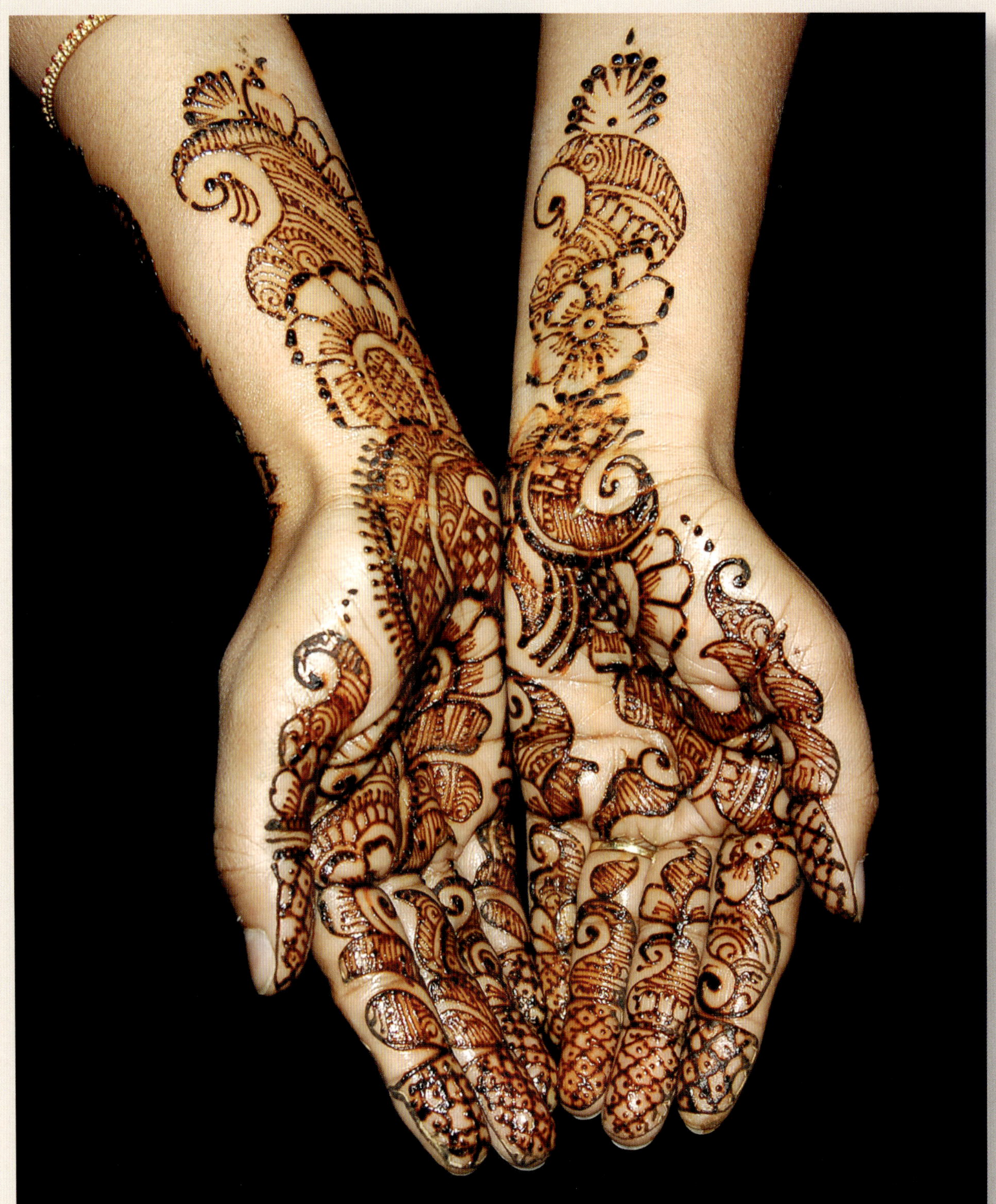

HENNA BASICS

Once you've chosen a beautiful design or symbol, you'll want to wear it as soon as possible. Before you get started, though, here are a few helpful tips.

You can purchase fresh henna at most health food and Asian markets. Natural henna is completely safe, since the dye penetrates only the top layers of the skin. Just be sure to avoid a powder that goes by the name of "black henna." As mentioned earlier, this product contains very little henna and most likely contains a toxic chemical called paraphenylenediamine or PPD. PPD has been known to cause severe allergic reactions in people who have used it in the hope of achieving a look that resembles a permanent black tattoo.

Henna comes in powder form, so you will have to mix it into a paste before you apply it. The color does not take as well on some body parts as it does on others. It penetrates best on the palms and backs of hands, feet, abdomen, and inner arms. Once the stain has had time to sink in, the paste is scraped off the skin.

Henna takes time to darken. So, for optimum effect, it's best to have it applied two days in advance of a special occasion. You can make sure that your henna will continue to look lovely for several weeks if you follow these simple steps.

- Do not use lotion or sunscreen for at least 24 hours before the henna is applied.
- Henna should remain on the skin for at least six hours before removing it. A period of twelve hours is better. Some people leave it on overnight.
- If you are applying henna to your hands, you will not be able to put them in water, and use of your hands will be restricted while the henna is curing. It's a good idea to make arrangements ahead of time to have someone around to help with simple tasks.

Recipe

It's a good idea to wear latex gloves while preparing your henna to avoid staining your hands before you are ready. This recipe makes enough paste to create one large design or several small ones.

Ingredients

2 teaspoons finely sifted henna powder
2 tablespoons lemon juice
1 teaspoon sugar
1 teaspoon eucalyptus or lavender essential oil
1 cup water

Directions

- Pour the henna powder into a bowl.
- Add the lemon juice (fig. 1), sugar, and essential oil (fig. 2).
- Add the water a little at a time, stirring constantly with a spoon (fig. 3).
- If the mixture is too thin, add a bit more henna until the mixture reaches the consistency of cake frosting or toothpaste.
- Cover the bowl with plastic wrap and store it in a dark place for at least 12 hours.
- Keep away from light.
- Do not use henna paste that has been left at room temperature for three days; it loses its ability to stain. If you freeze it, however, it will last for up to a year.

Remember, mixing henna paste is far from an exact science. You might consider adding other ingredients, such as tea, rose petals, beet or berry juice. If you are sensitive to the effects of caffeine, don't use tea, since caffeine can be absorbed through the skin. One of the ingredients, however, must be a mildly acidic liquid. Use only 100% pure essential oil without additives that may irritate skin or prevent the henna from staining skin properly. Experiment and create your own special brew.

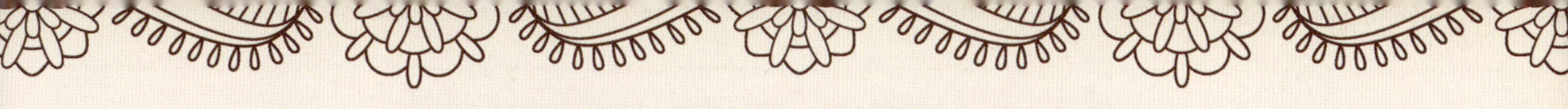

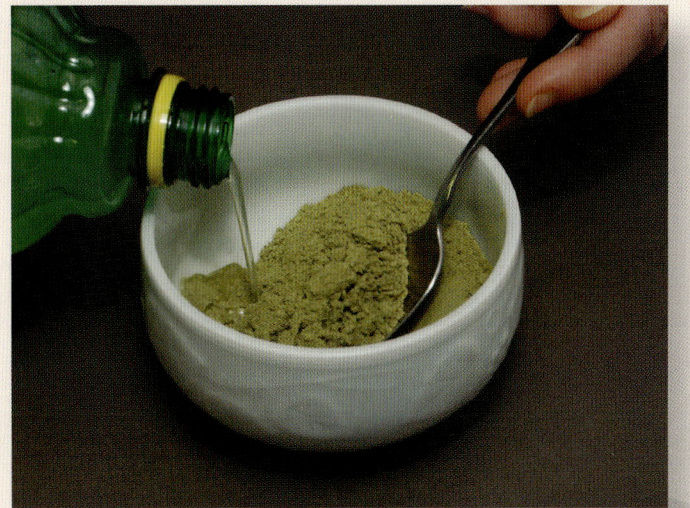

fig. 1

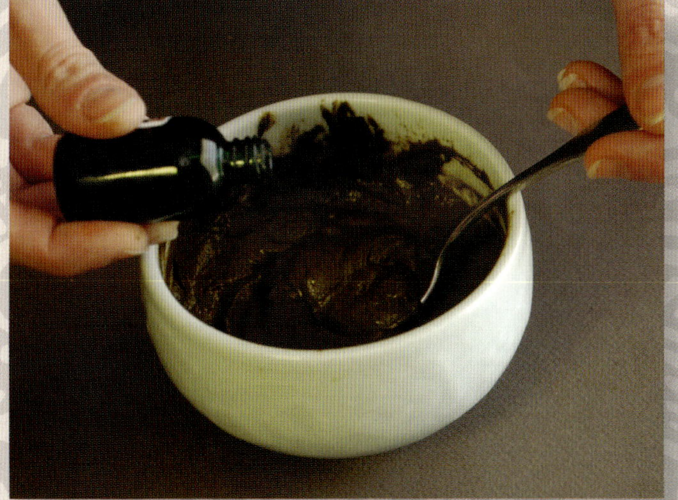

fig. 2

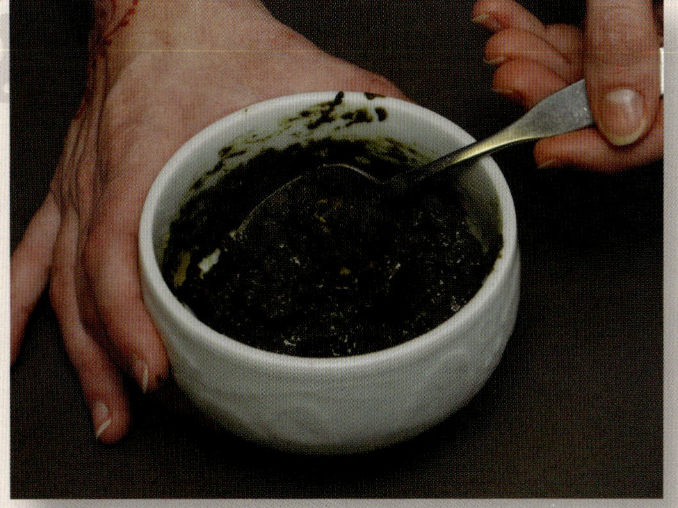

fig. 3

Tools of the Trade

There are several methods of applying henna to the skin. In the past, artists dipped twigs into henna to paint their designs. A jacquard squeeze bottle with a metal tip is a good option for beginners, as are transfers. But by far the most traditional method for applying henna is with a cone. In fact, some henna powders come packaged with one. You can also make a cone out of a sheet of Mylar wrapping paper:

- Cut a right triangle from the Mylar paper. The length of the sides can be 5 to 10"; whatever you are comfortable with.
- Roll the triangle into a cone, taping the ends in place.
- Leave a very small hole at the tip, about the width of a straight pin.
- For an even quicker DIY tube, use a small plastic freezer bag. Pierce a hole in one corner after filling to make the tip.

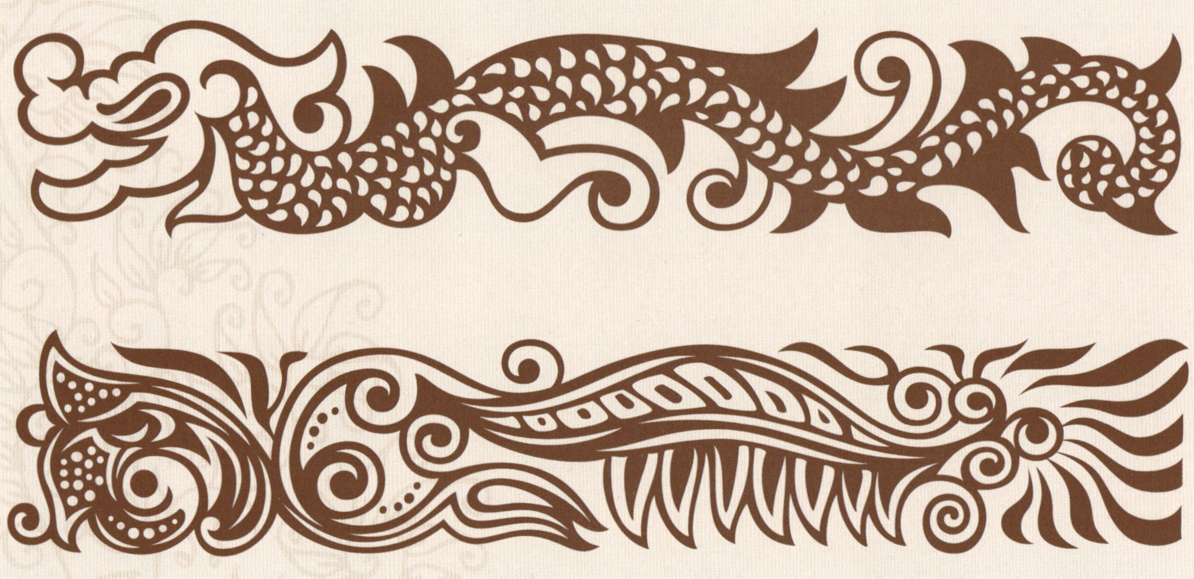

Once you've prepared your application device, be it a squeeze bottle, a cone or a makeshift tube, follow these steps:

- Strain out all the lumps from your prepared henna paste.
- Spoon paste into your application device.
- If it is a cone or tube, squeeze the paste to the tip from above to eliminate air pockets.
- When the cone or tube is half filled, fold the top over and tape it shut.
- Be prepared to clear clogs—have straight pins handy.
- Have a sugar-and-juice glaze ready (see the recipe on page 34). Daub on the finished design to keep the paste moist until it has finished curing.

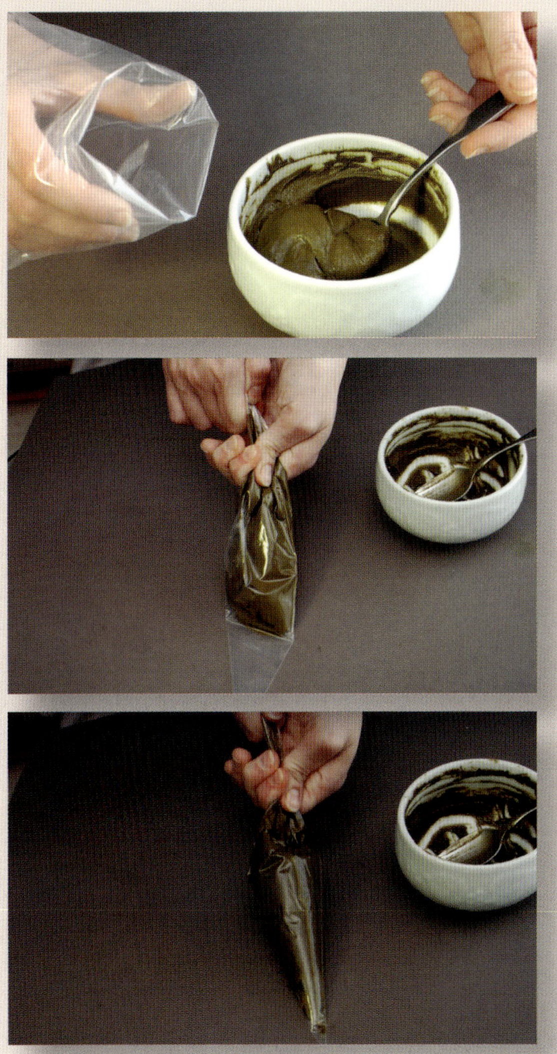

Practice, Practice, Practice

Now you are ready to work with the henna. Remember that no one produces perfect lines right away. It takes a while to get comfortable using any new tool. Think back to when you were first learning to use a pencil!

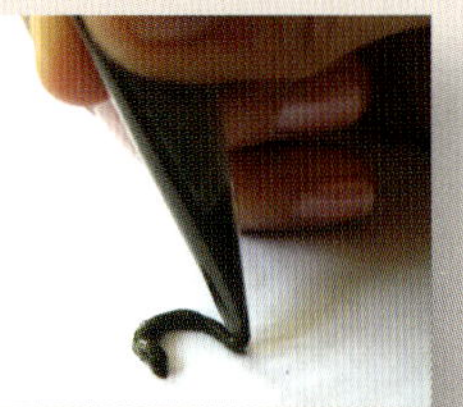

Try squeezing fine lines of henna onto sheets of graph paper until you find the position that works best for you. Some artists hold the cone in a vertical position; others find holding it at a slant is easier.

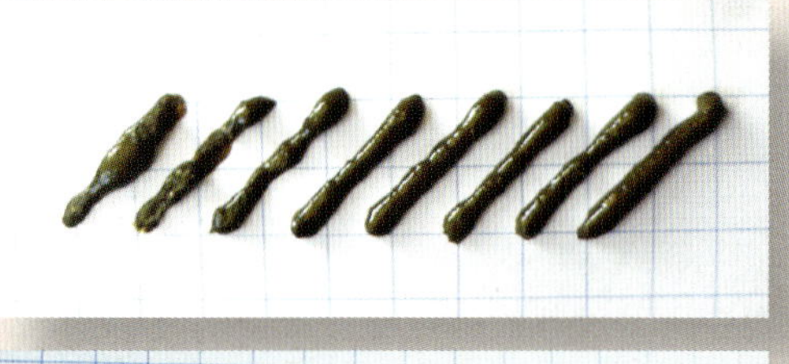

To prevent smudging, try not to squeeze out too much paste at one time. When you have mastered making thin straight lines, try doing some slanted ones.

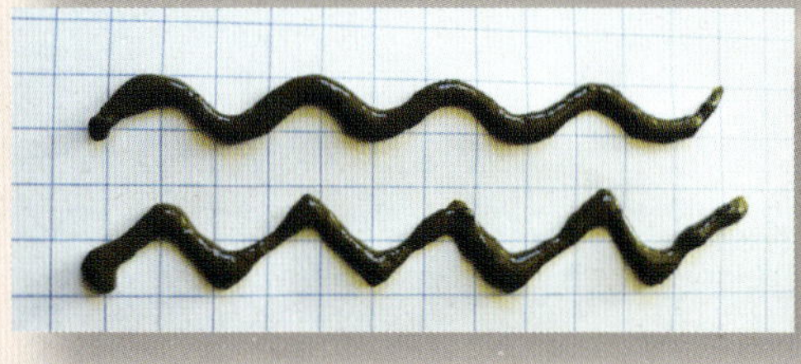

Try making zigzags.

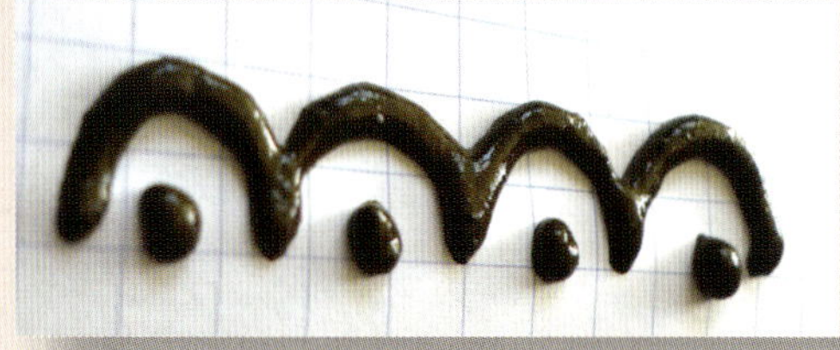

Now make some scallops with decorative dots.

When you become more proficient, you'll be ready to progress to some actual henna design elements. But you still need to practice these on paper before you are ready to tackle application on skin.

The pages of this book have lots of traditional and modern design elements. Practice drawing them over and over again. Then try combining them in creative ways. When you feel confident in your ability to copy the intricacies of these designs, try coming up with some fun designs of your own.

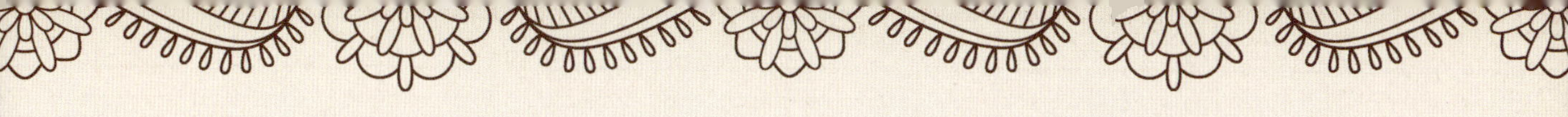

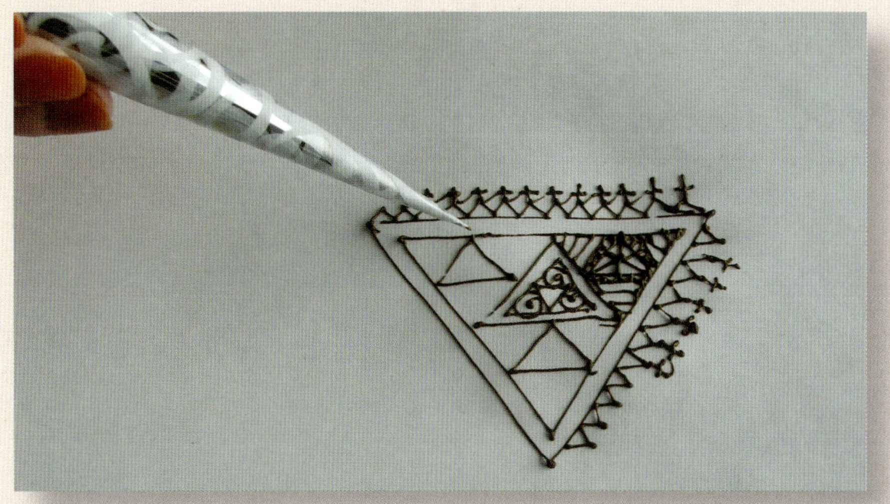

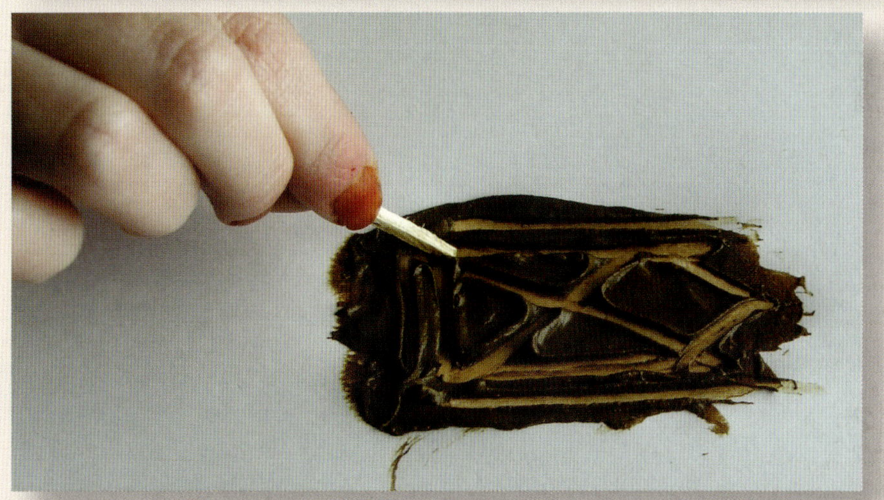

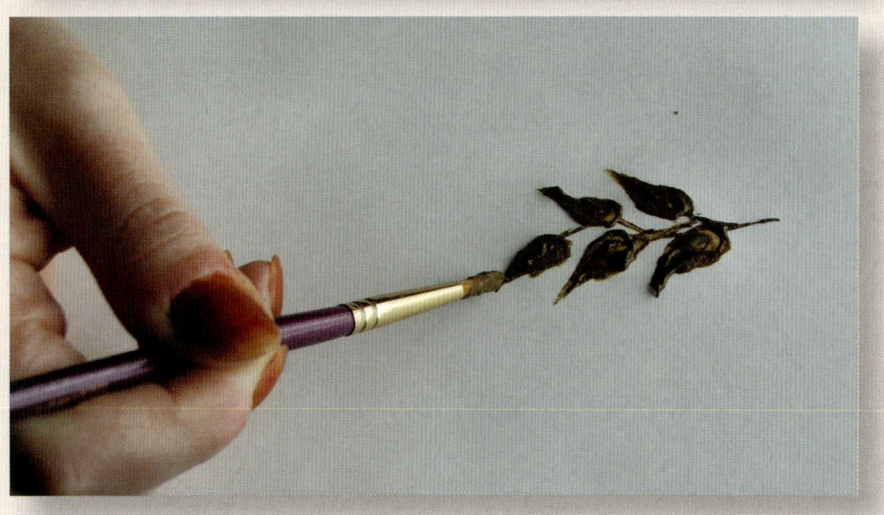

Some Skin in the Game

When you feel ready to paint henna designs on skin, it will help to have the following supplies on hand:

- Aquarellable pencil, optional
- Cotton swabs
- Glaze (3 teaspoons lemon juice mixed with 1 teaspoon sugar)
- Toothpicks or an orange wood stick
- A butter knife
- Paper towels
- Rubbing alcohol
- Straight pins for clearing clogs in your cone

Some artists like to sketch designs on skin with an aquarellable pencil first. These pencils are available in craft stores and online. They do not interfere with the henna stain at all. They work well on moist skin and wipe off easily with a damp cloth.

Before you get started, be sure there is no oil or suntan lotion on the skin, which will keep the henna from penetrating. If there is oil, wash with soap and water. If there are no lotions on the skin, it is not necessary to wash before applying henna.

Remember to keep your design moist as you work by daubing at it with the sugar-and-lemon-juice glaze. If you make a mistake, you can erase it with a cotton swab (or an orange wood stick or a toothpick) dipped in alcohol.

After the design has cured for at least six hours, scrape off the hardened paste with a dull butter knife.

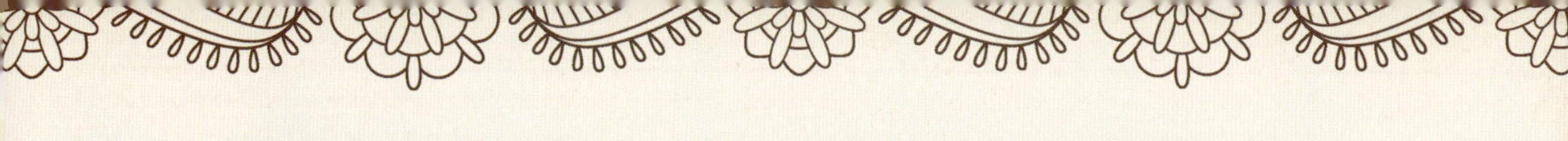

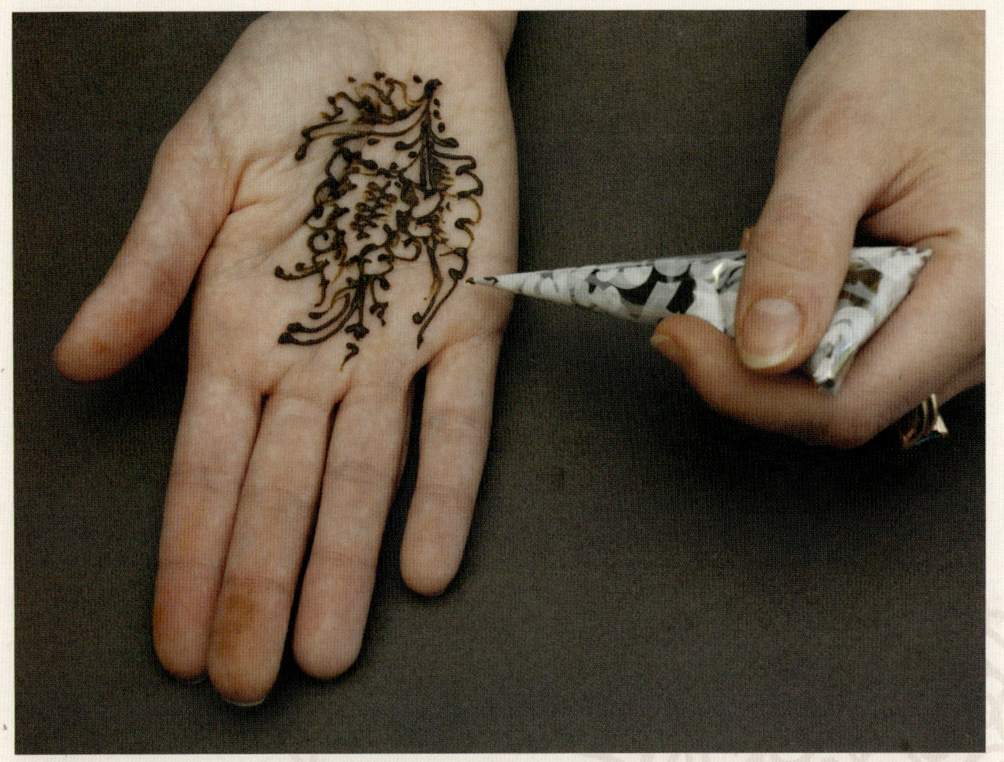

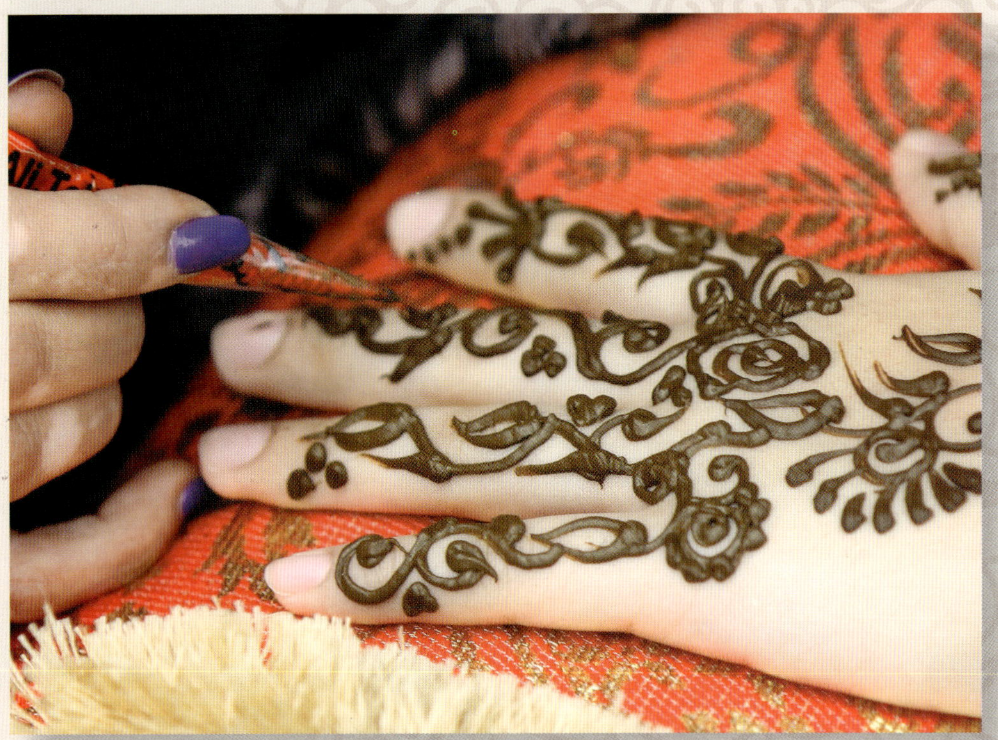

A much easier method of applying henna is to use transfers to create guides. They work well for beginners or for those who lack a steady hand. Transfers are also particularly good for applying delicate designs made of many fine lines because the ink does not show through the henna. You can buy transfers, but it is quite easy to make them yourself. You will need the following supplies:

- Special tattoo transfer paper (available from tattoo shops and office supply stores)
- Deodorant stick
- Pencil
- Typing paper

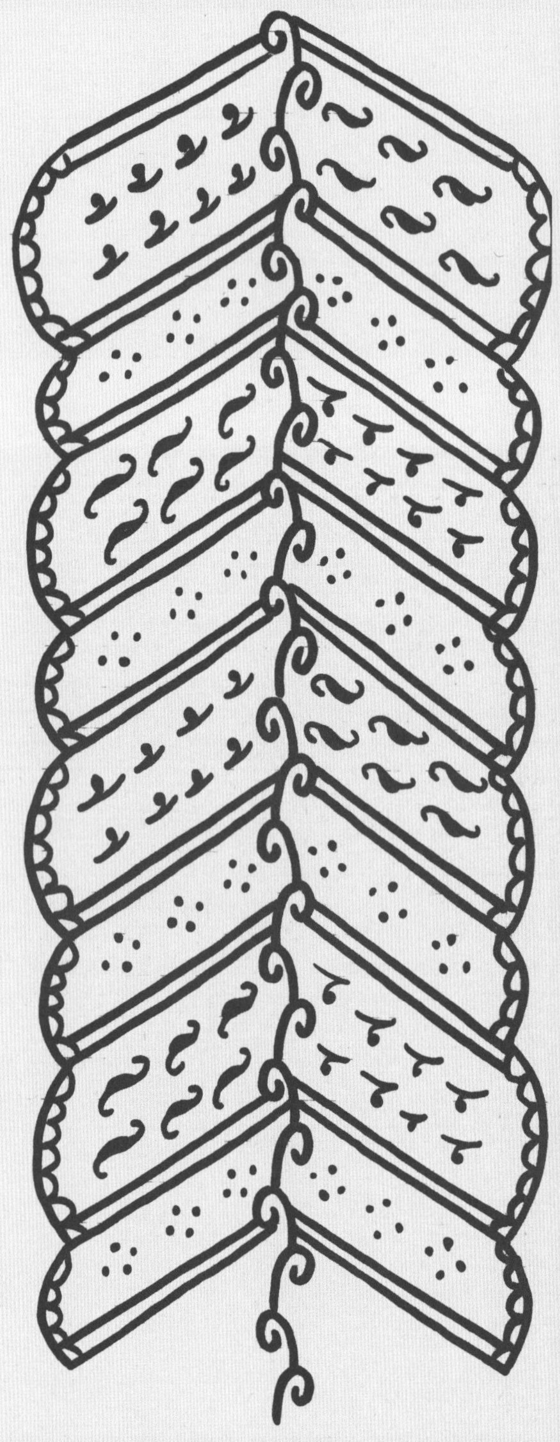

To create your transfer:

- Just photocopy a design that you've chosen from these pages in a size you want to appear on your skin.
- With the transfer paper ink side up, lay your design printed side up on top of it.
- Trace over the design printed on the photocopy with a pencil. This will transfer the ink to the back of the photocopy.
- Apply stick deodorant to your skin.
- Press your transfer, ink side down, onto the treated area.
- Remove the transfer and presto—the design will appear on your skin!

To complete your design, use a cone or jacquard squeeze bottle to apply the henna paste, following the directions on page 34.

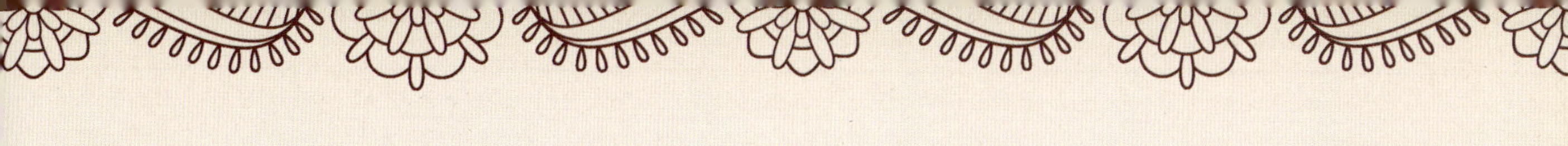

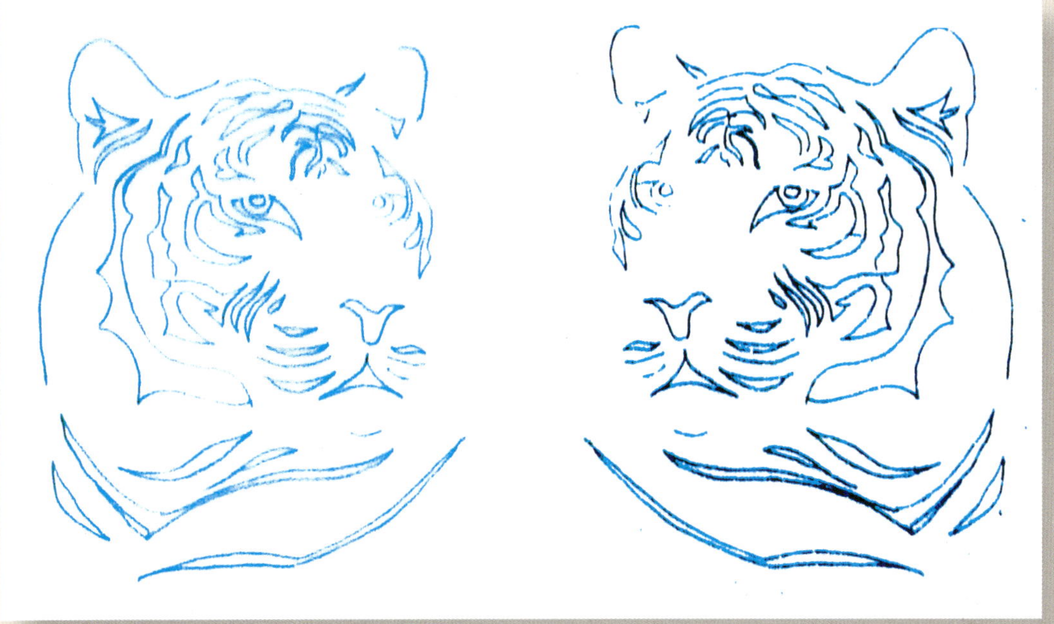

The chosen design is outlined (l). The completed transfer (r) will be placed ink-side down on the skin.

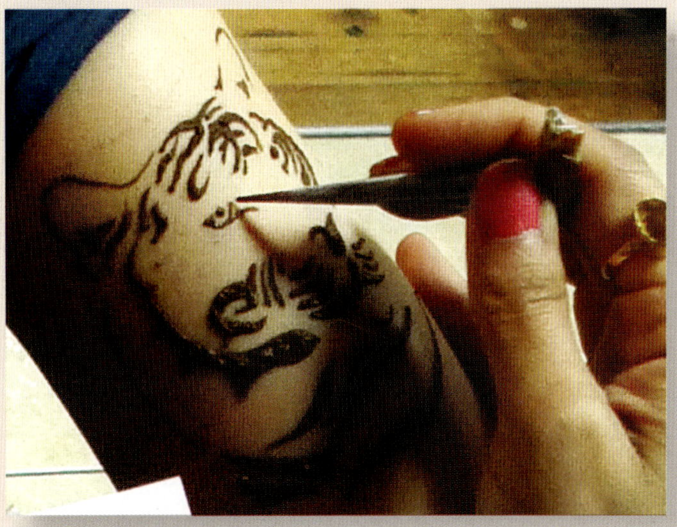

Apply the paste over the faint lines on the skin.

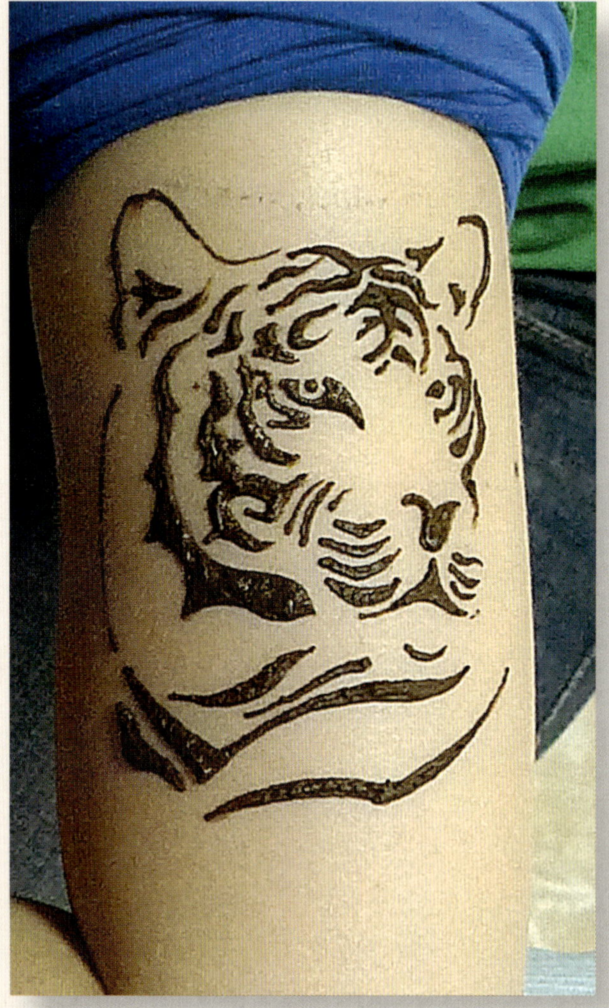

The completed application must dry for several hours.

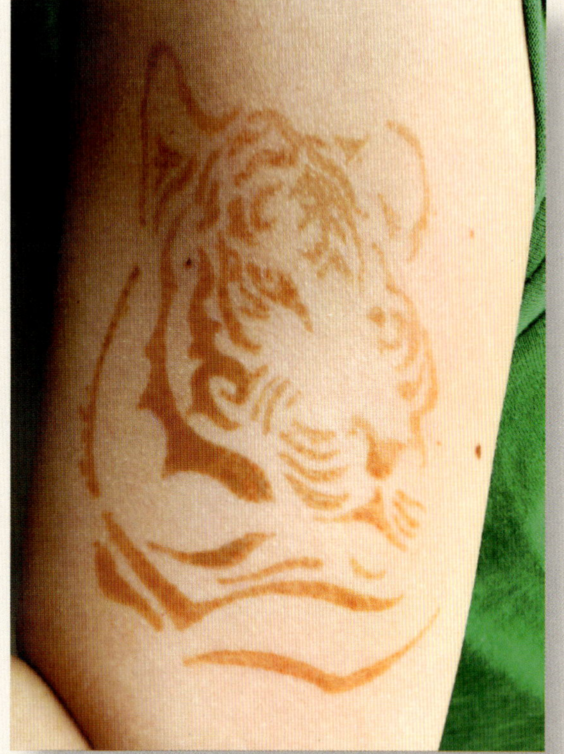

The henna paste has been scraped off. The design is light at first, but it will darken over time.

PARTY ON

To make your beautiful artwork last, moisturize with vegetable oil twice daily. Avoid using anything abrasive on your henna tattoo and stay away from chlorine and any beauty products that contain petroleum.

Now that you have mastered the henna process, the next time you adorn yourself, why not consider inviting some friends over to share in the fun? Create the mood for your henna party by lighting aromatic candles, playing Indian or Pakistani music, and setting out some spicy snacks with an Asian theme.

Display the henna paste in decorative bowls scattered about the room. Then choose designs that best express each person's individuality. You might find that there is no better way to bring a little beauty to your life and to nurture the bonds of friendship at the same time!

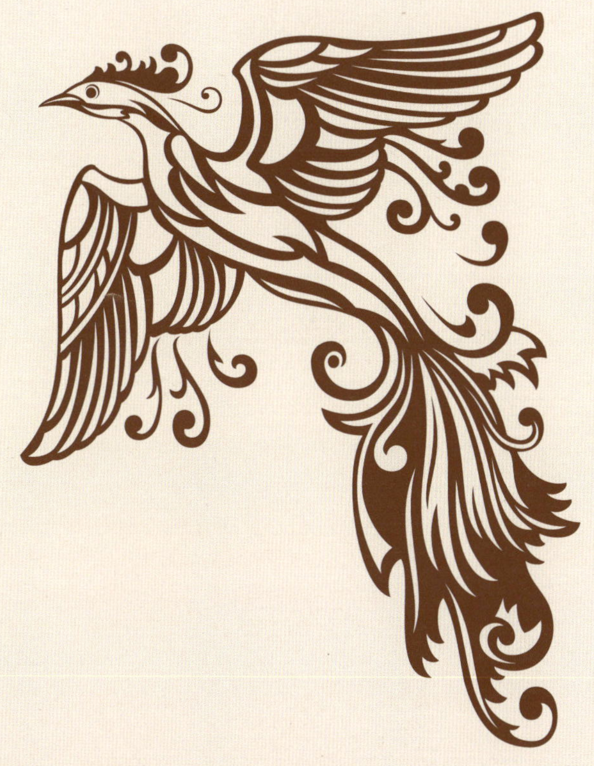

THE INDIAN SUBCONTINENT

The word for henna in Hindi is *mehndi*. But now that the art form is so popular, many people use this term to refer to henna body art in general. Although henna first came to the region through Muslim influences, the art was eagerly adopted by other resident women. Now symbols from many of the region's cultures feature largely in henna. Lakshmi, the Hindu goddess of wealth and good fortune was said to prize henna's blossoms for their fragrance, and its crushed leaves for their power to adorn. Both Lakshmi and the henna plant are associated with good luck. In fact, many believe that one who wears henna will be greatly blessed and that the prayers of the wearer will be more readily heard.

When traditional symbols from this region are applied by an accomplished henna artist, the result is nothing short of breathtaking. Meandering fine lines connect a variety of graceful floral, paisley, and other fanciful motifs, each of which is imbued with its own special meaning. The finished design is an interlacing work of art covering hands, feet, wrists and/or ankles in complex patterns that are as delicate as the finest lace.

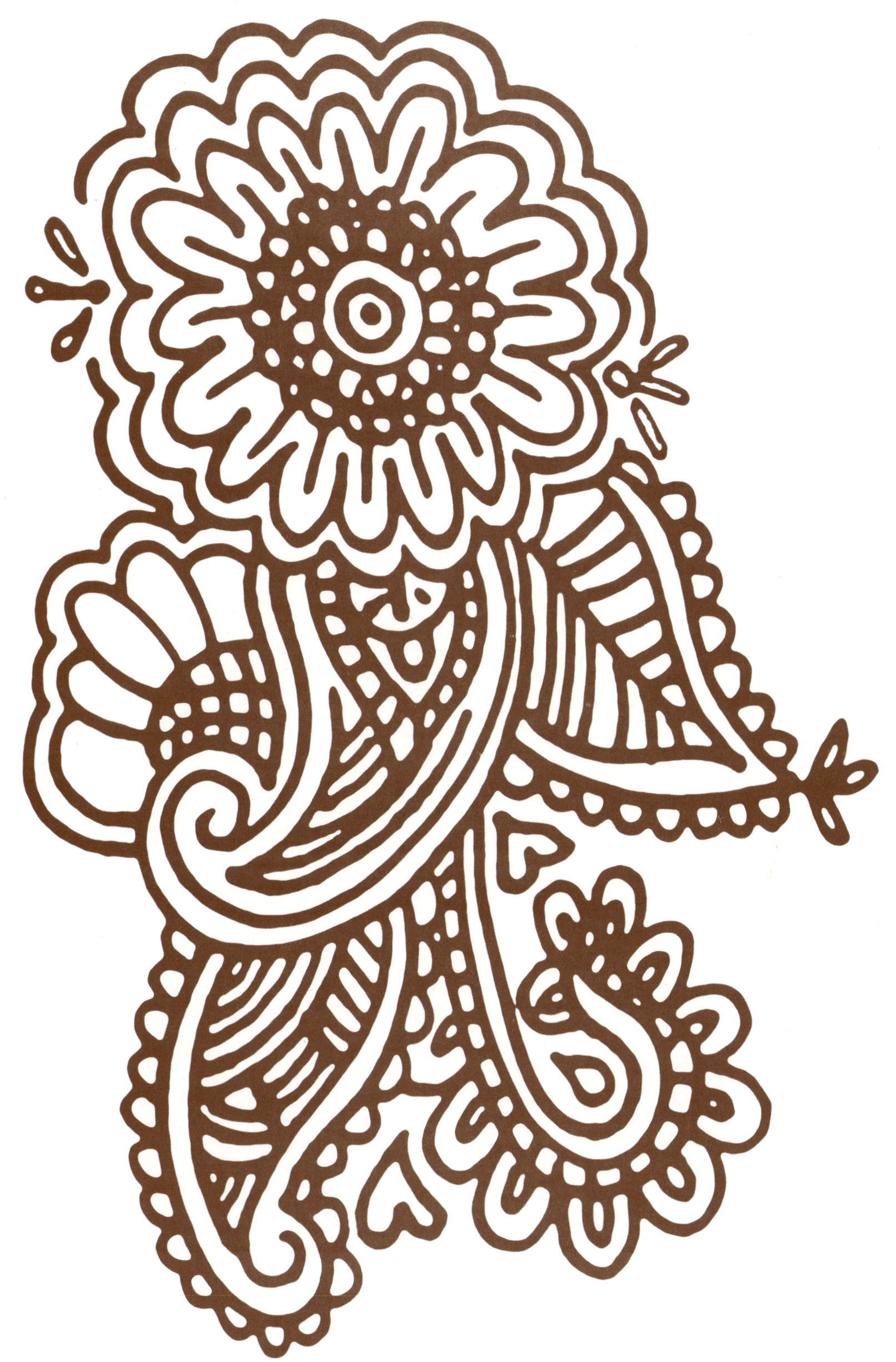

The Circle

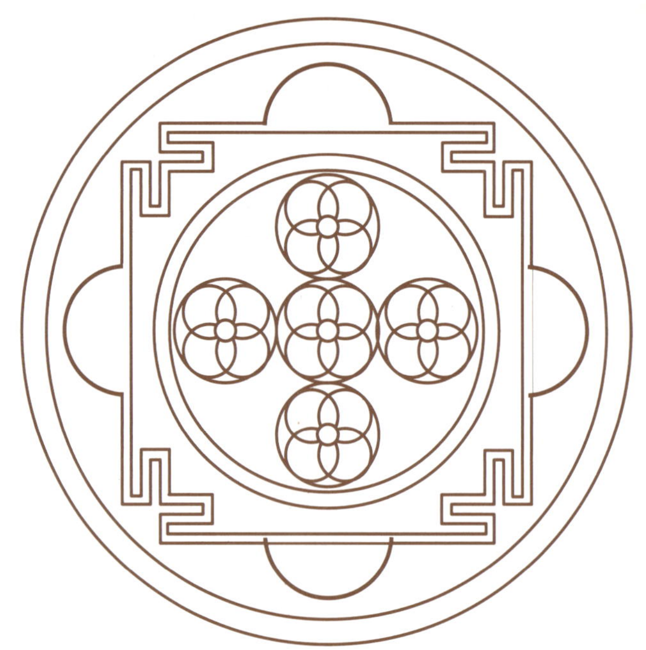

Circular designs can be found in the art of ethnically and geographically diverse civilizations, centuries before it would have been possible for them to have contact with one another. In Buddhism, there is the mandala (from the Sanskrit word for "circle"); in Christianity, there are rose windows and the Celtic cross; in Native American cultures, there is the *Ojo de Dios*, or "the Eye of God." These symbols may be sacred in origin, but their meaning—wisdom, balance and the expression of self—finds application in every aspect of life.

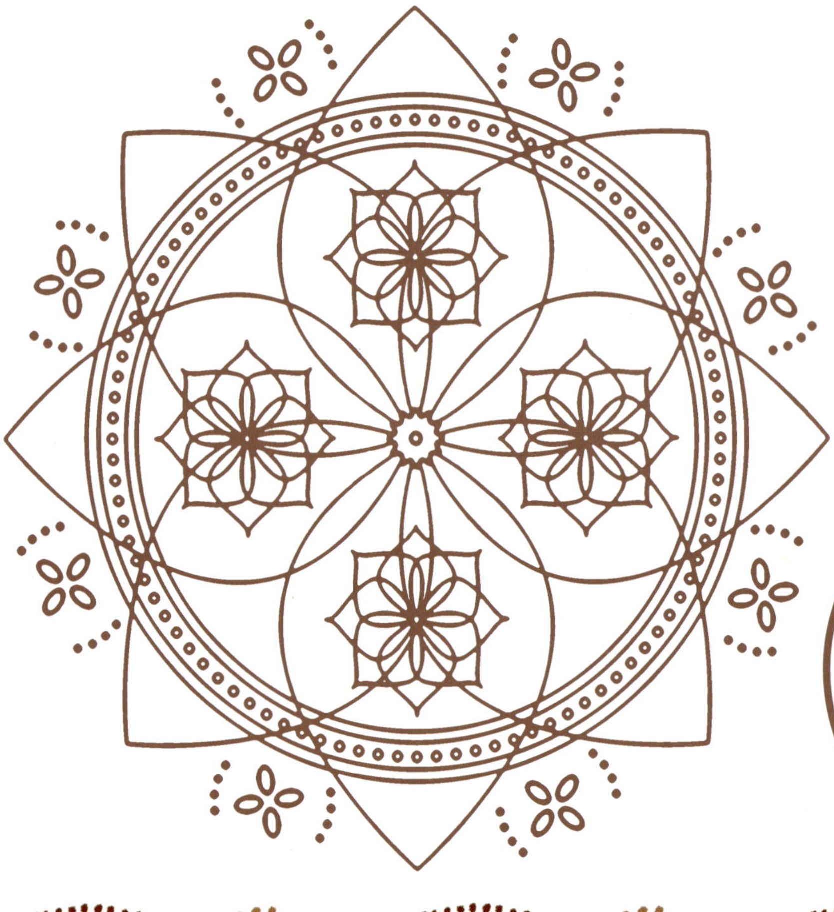

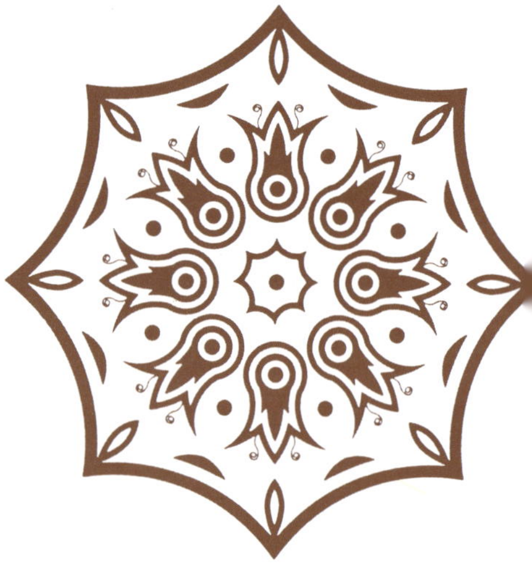

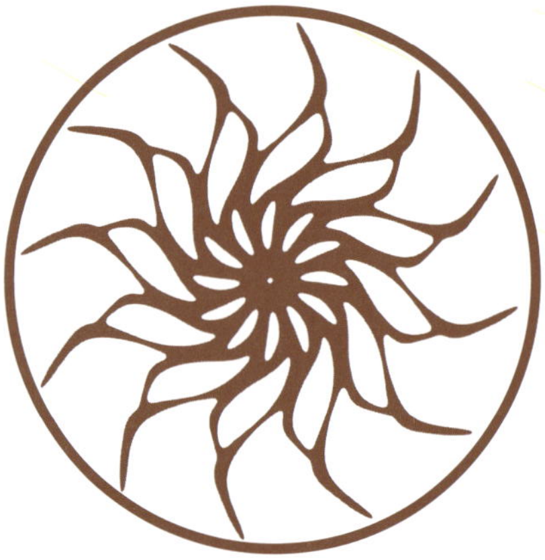

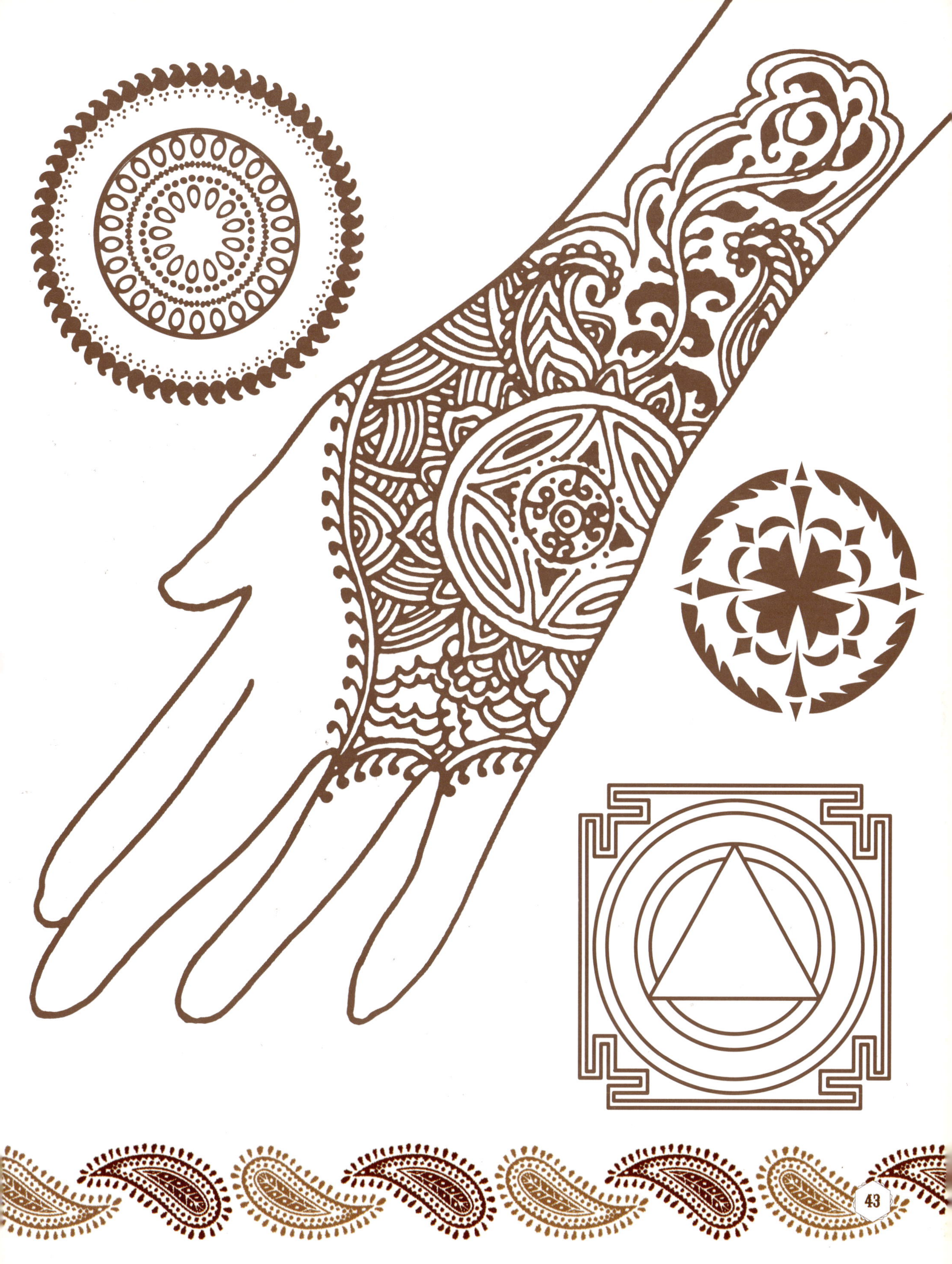

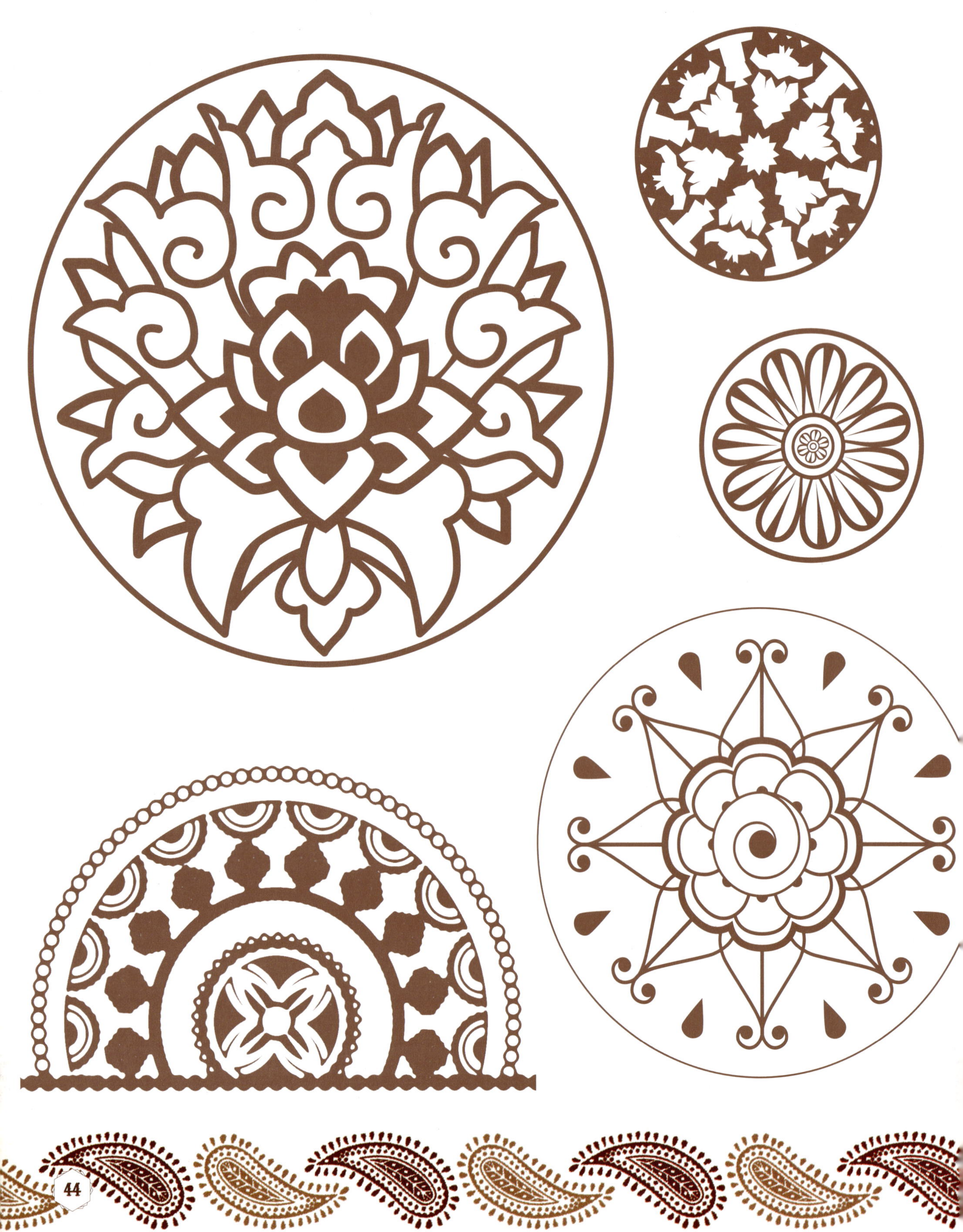

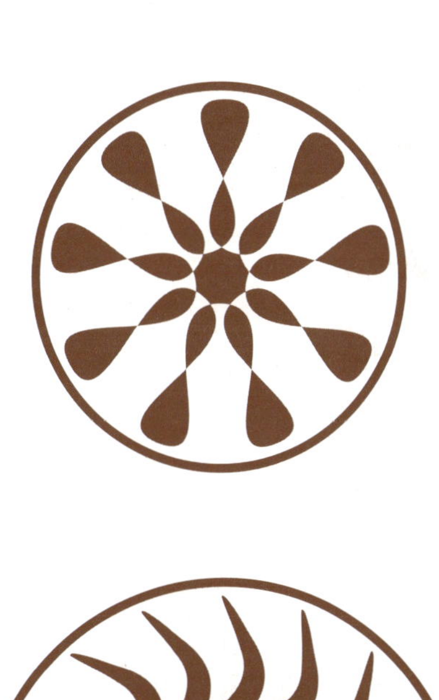
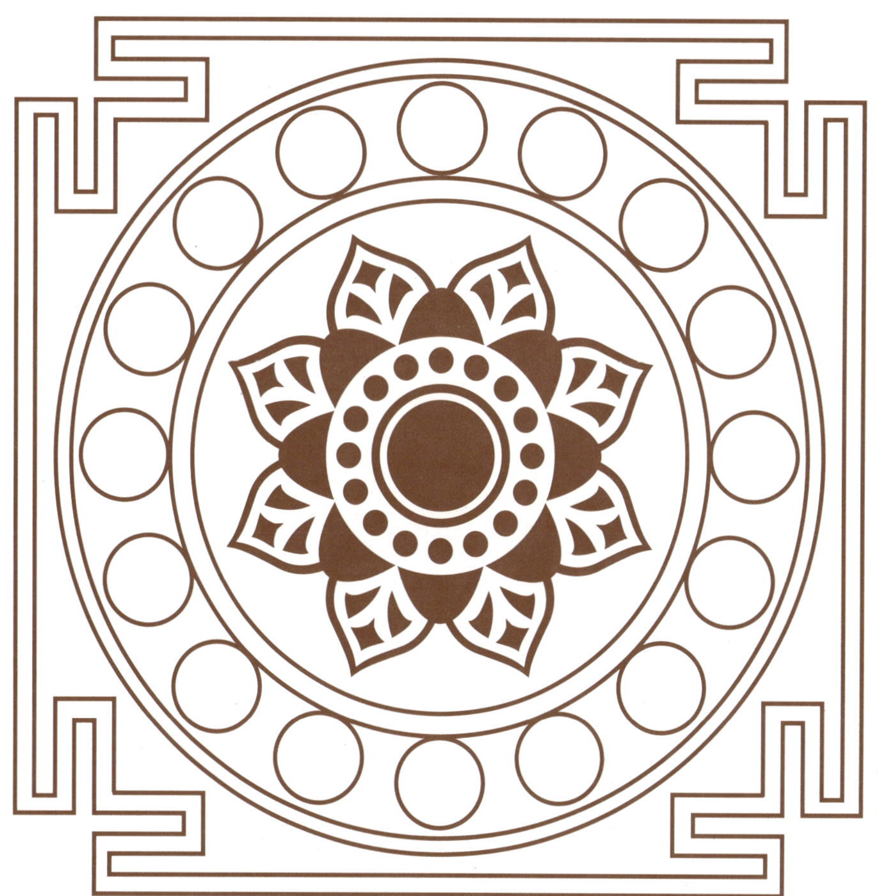
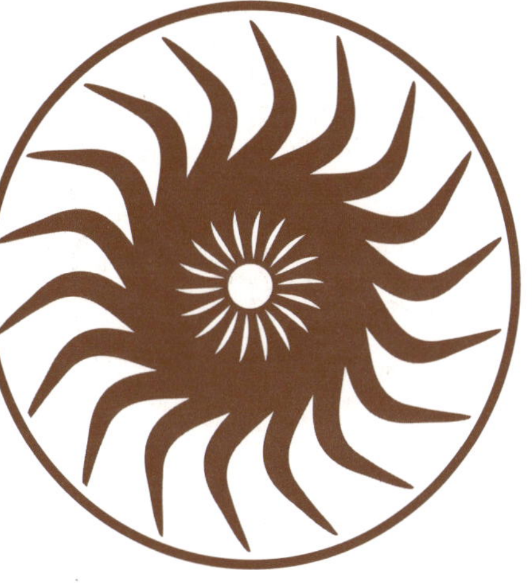
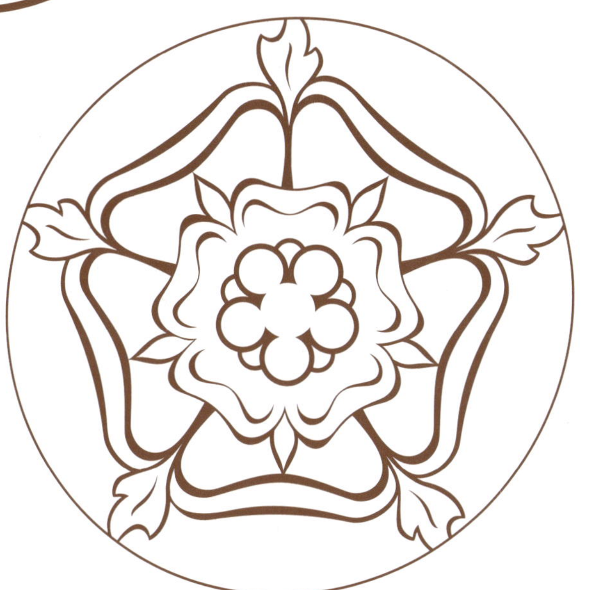
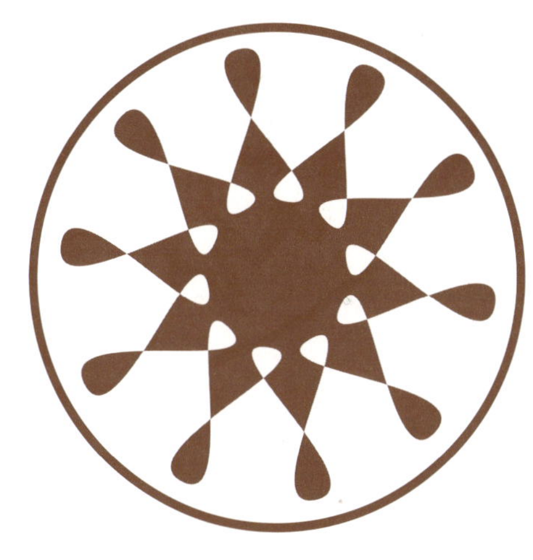
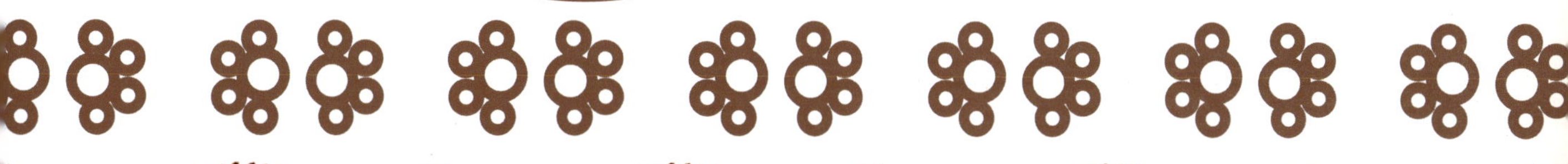
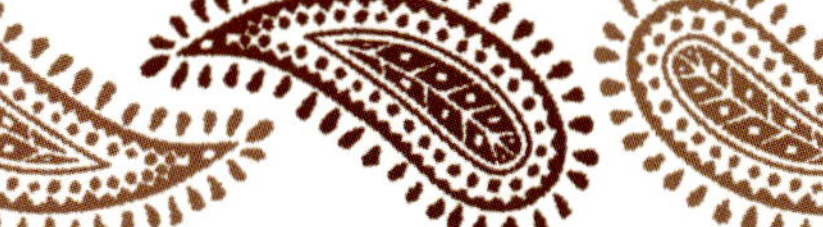
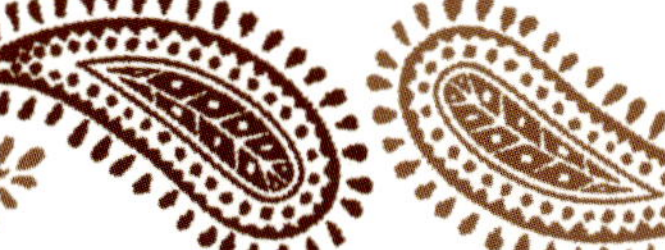
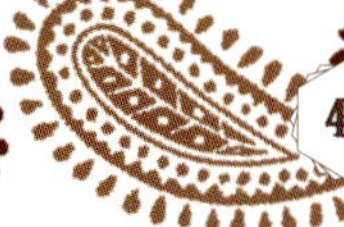

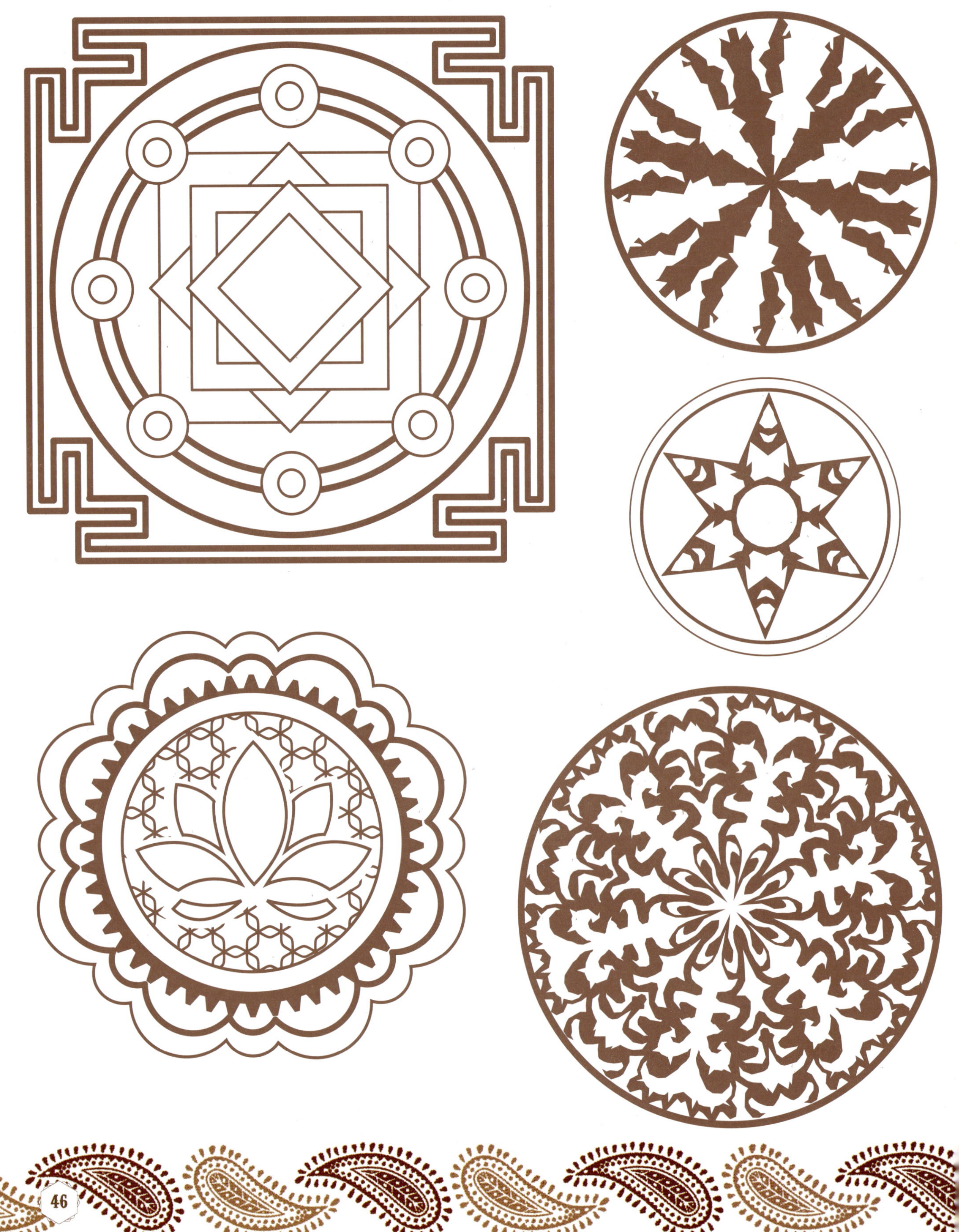

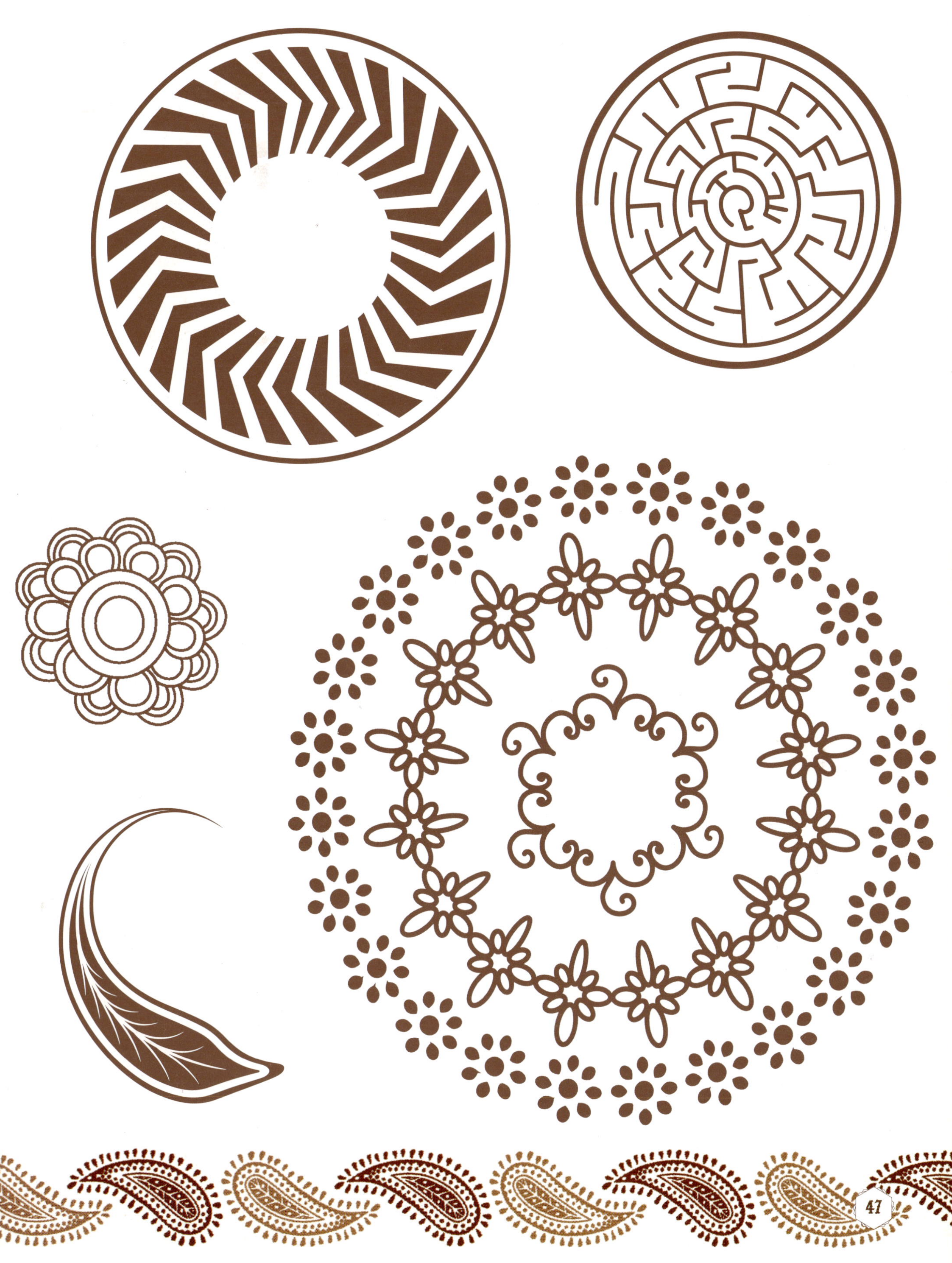

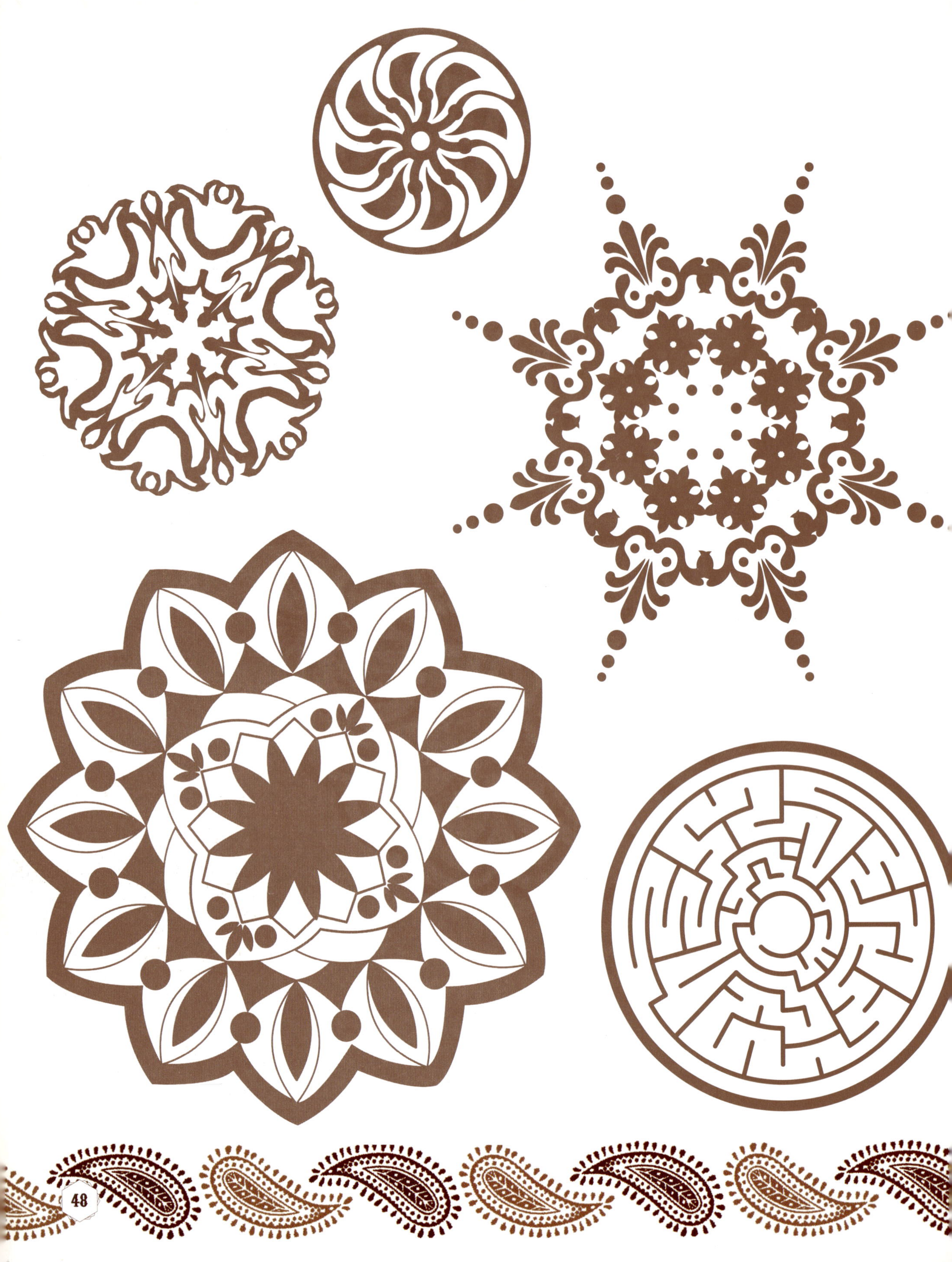

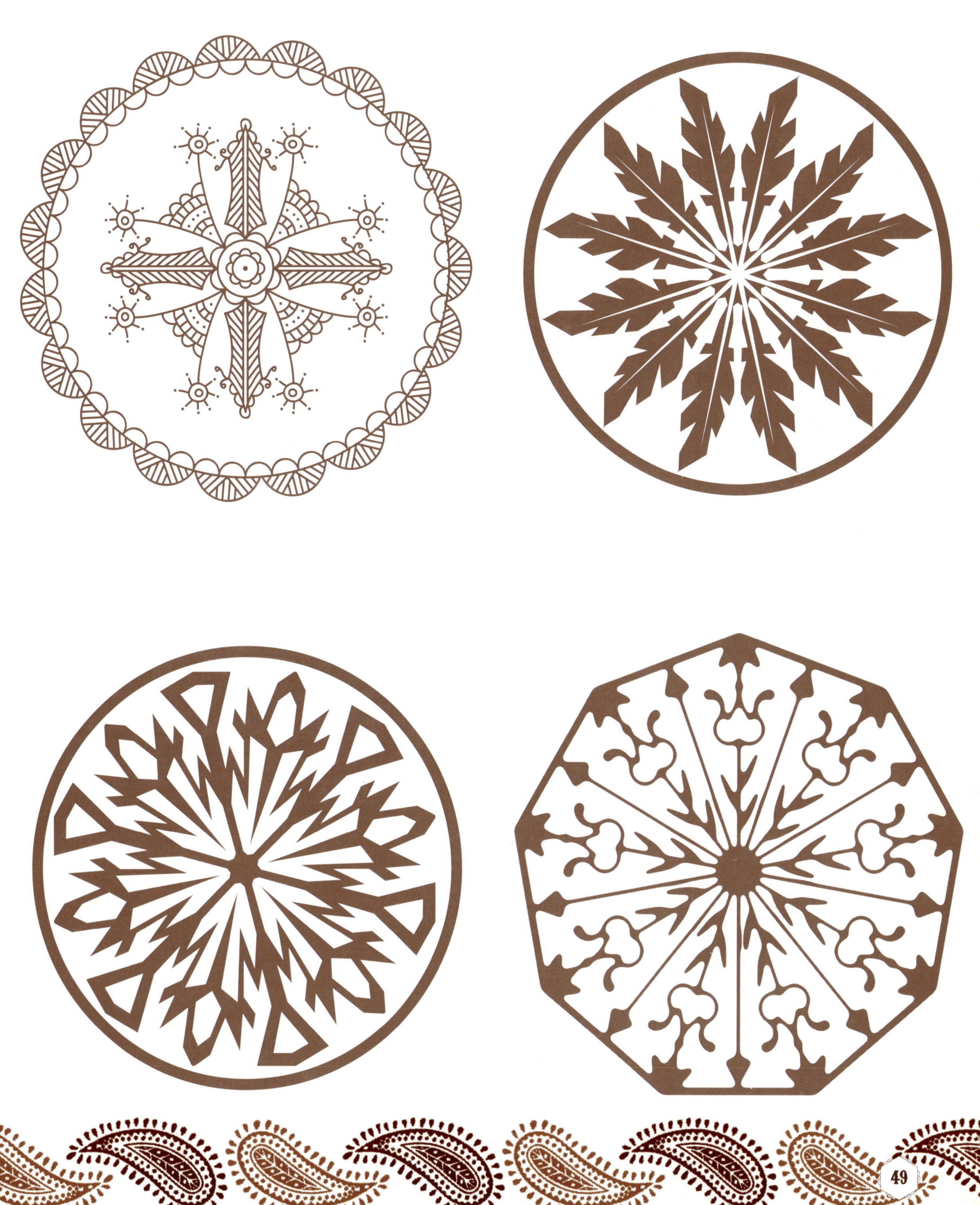

Paisley

The paisley pattern is a very popular shape that abounds in the art of this region. While the shape originates from Asia, the name "paisley" comes from the Scottish town of Paisley, where cloth using the pattern was first made. Some see an unripe mango in the paisley shape and compare it to a young girl's breasts. Others associate the shape with a cedar tree (the Tree of Life) or a flame. It also symbolizes the wasp, whose sting inflames like falling in love.

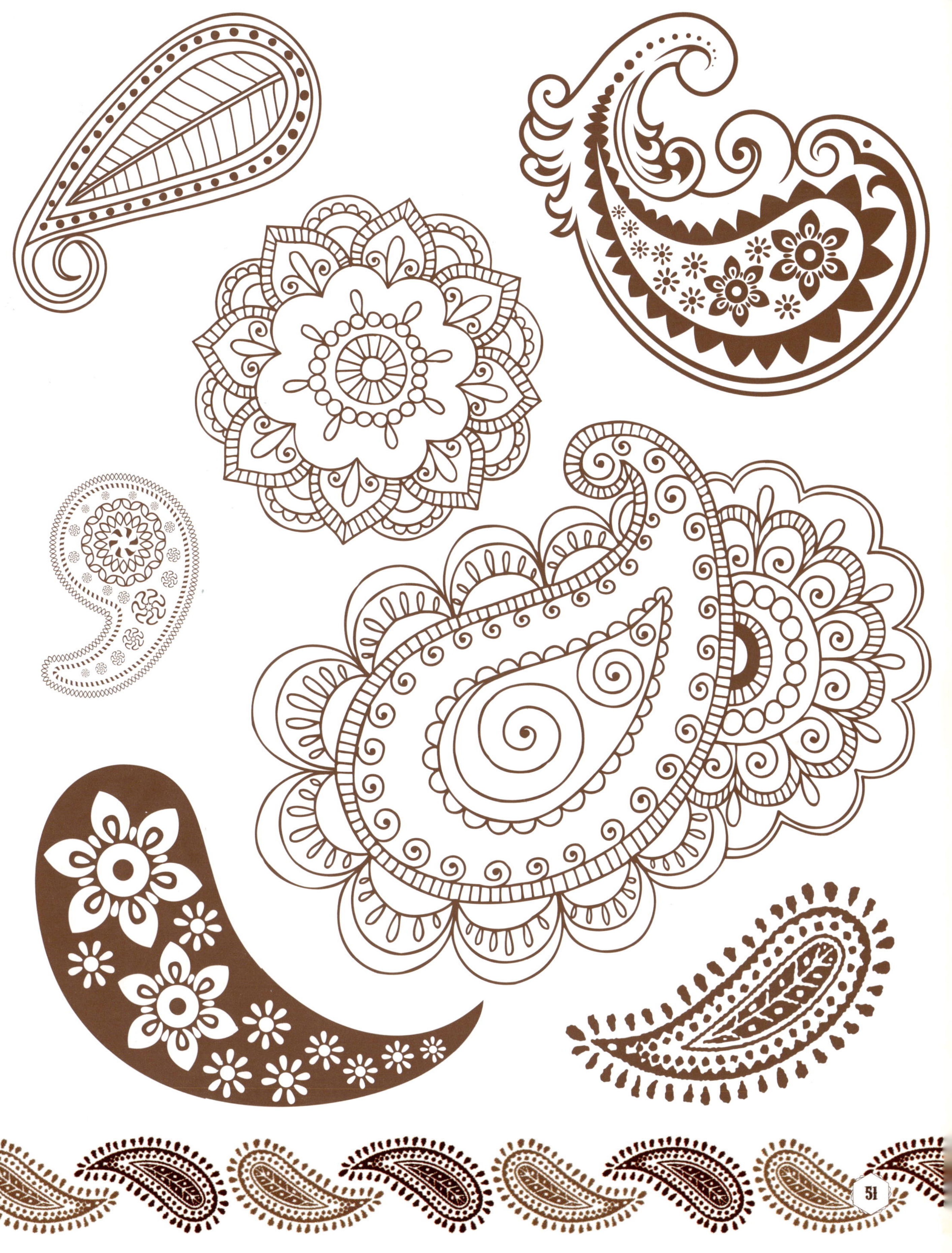

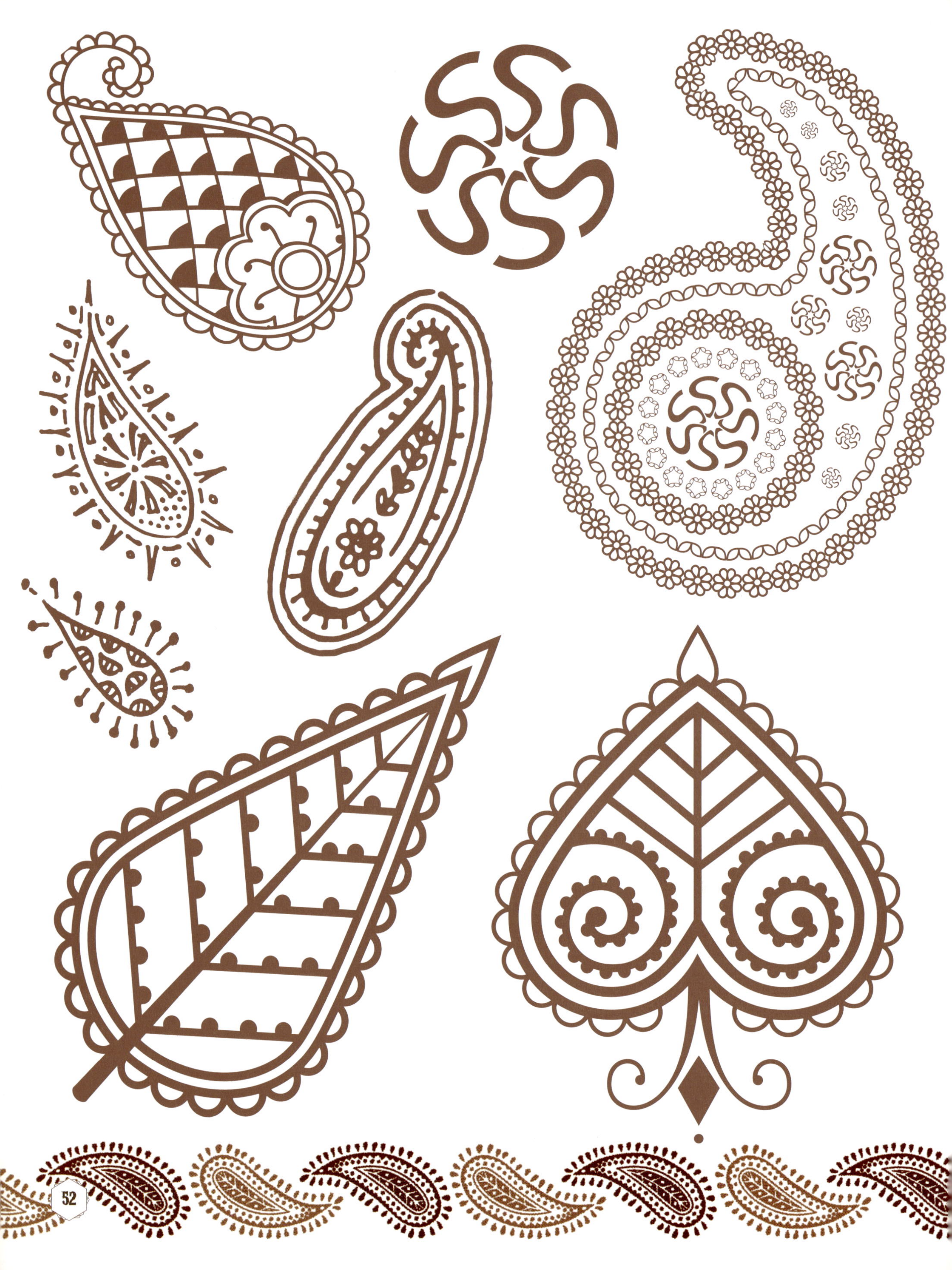

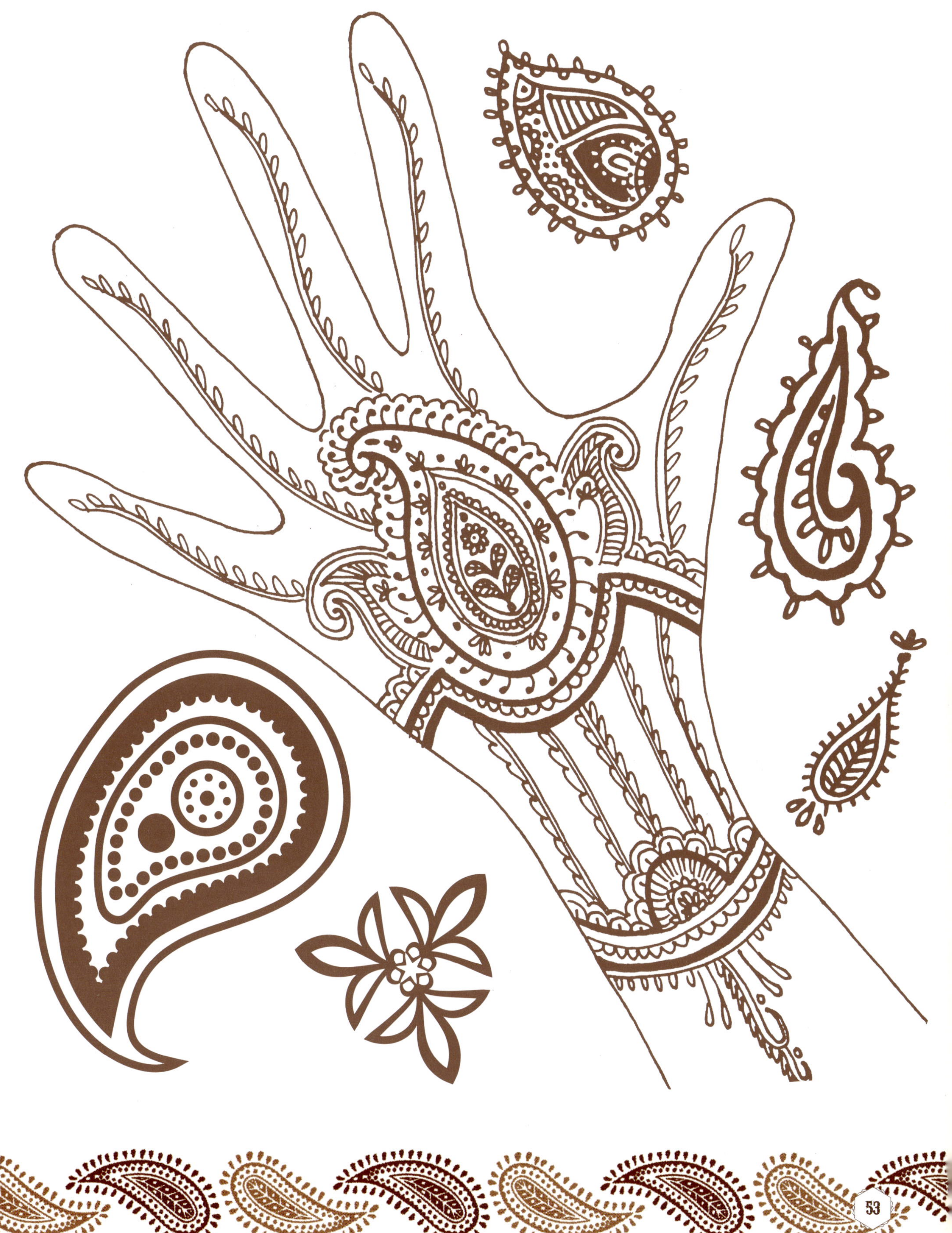

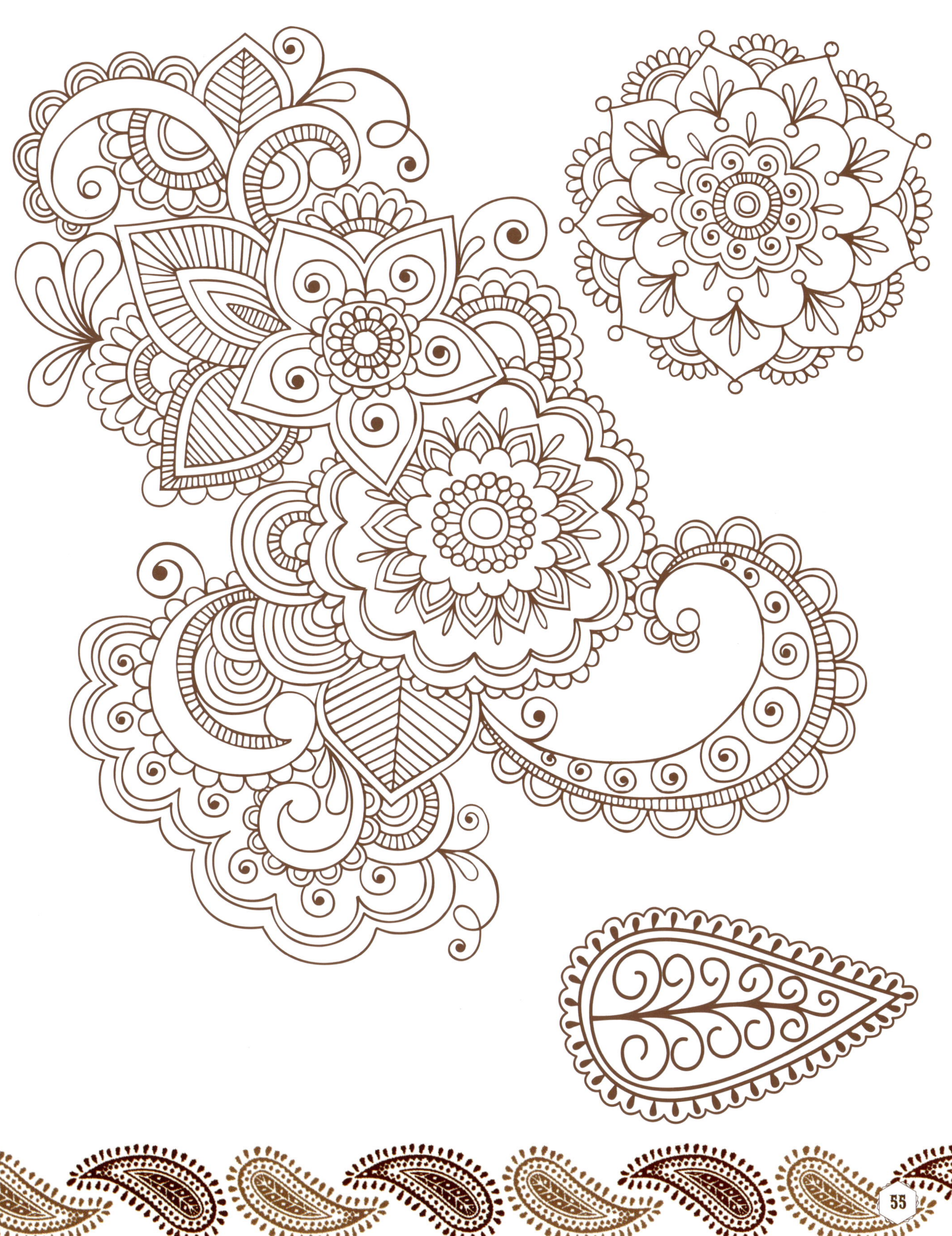

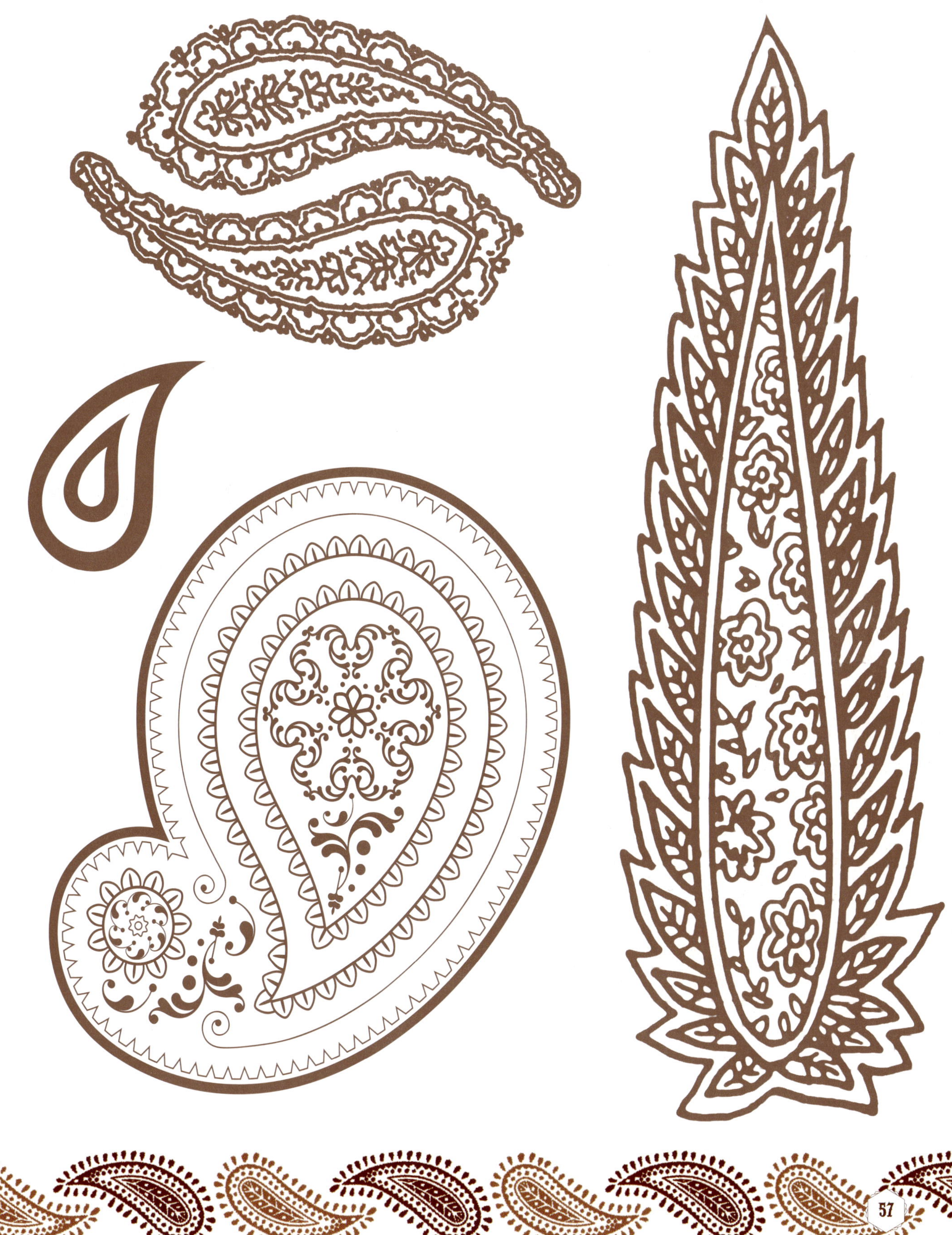

FLORALS

Few things suggest joy more than flowers in full bloom. And as celebratory symbols, flowers abound in henna designs. They include the lotus, sunflowers, roses, daisies, lilies of the valley, and irises. In bud form, flowers are symbols of renewal, fertility, and of happiness to come.

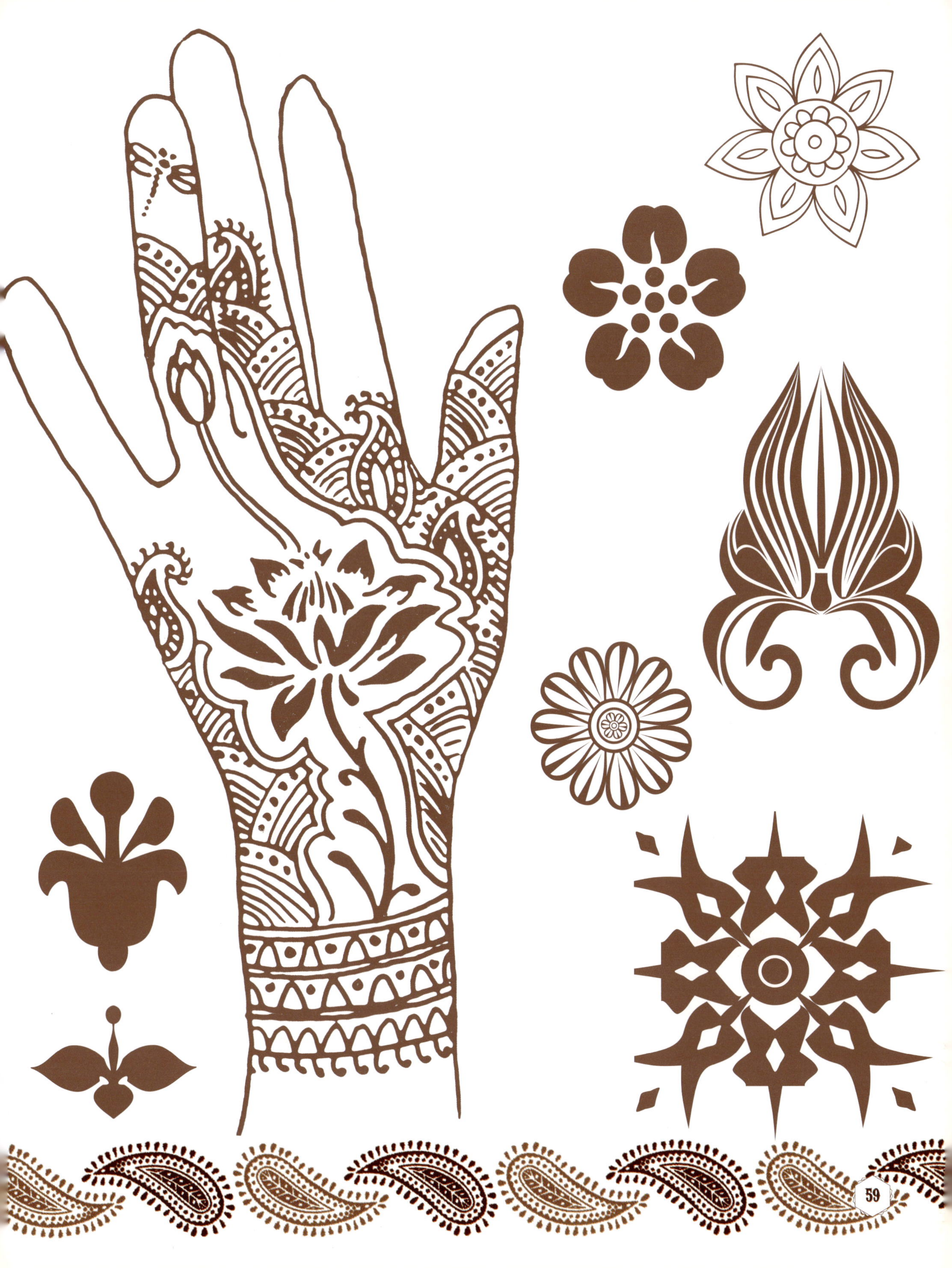

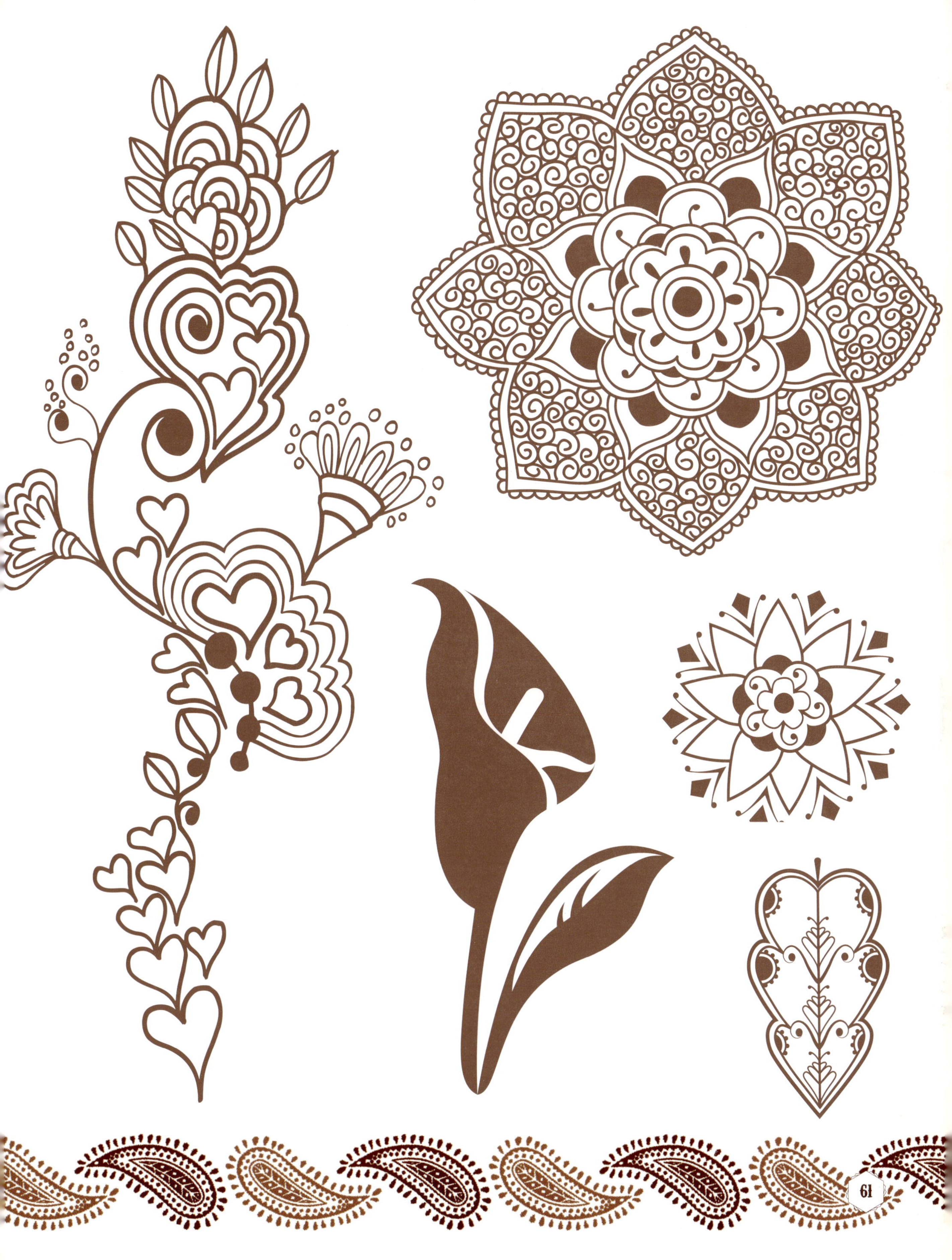

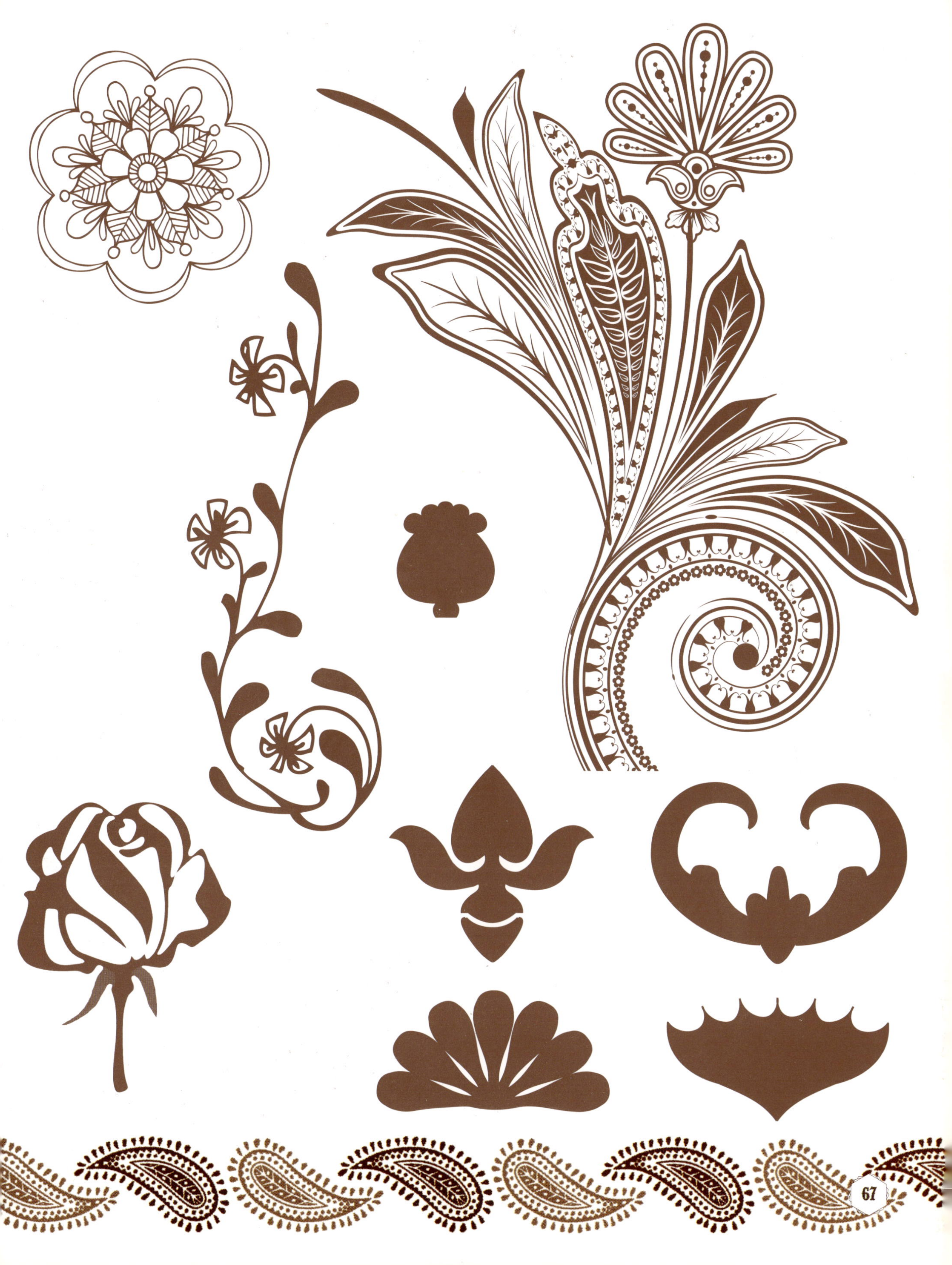

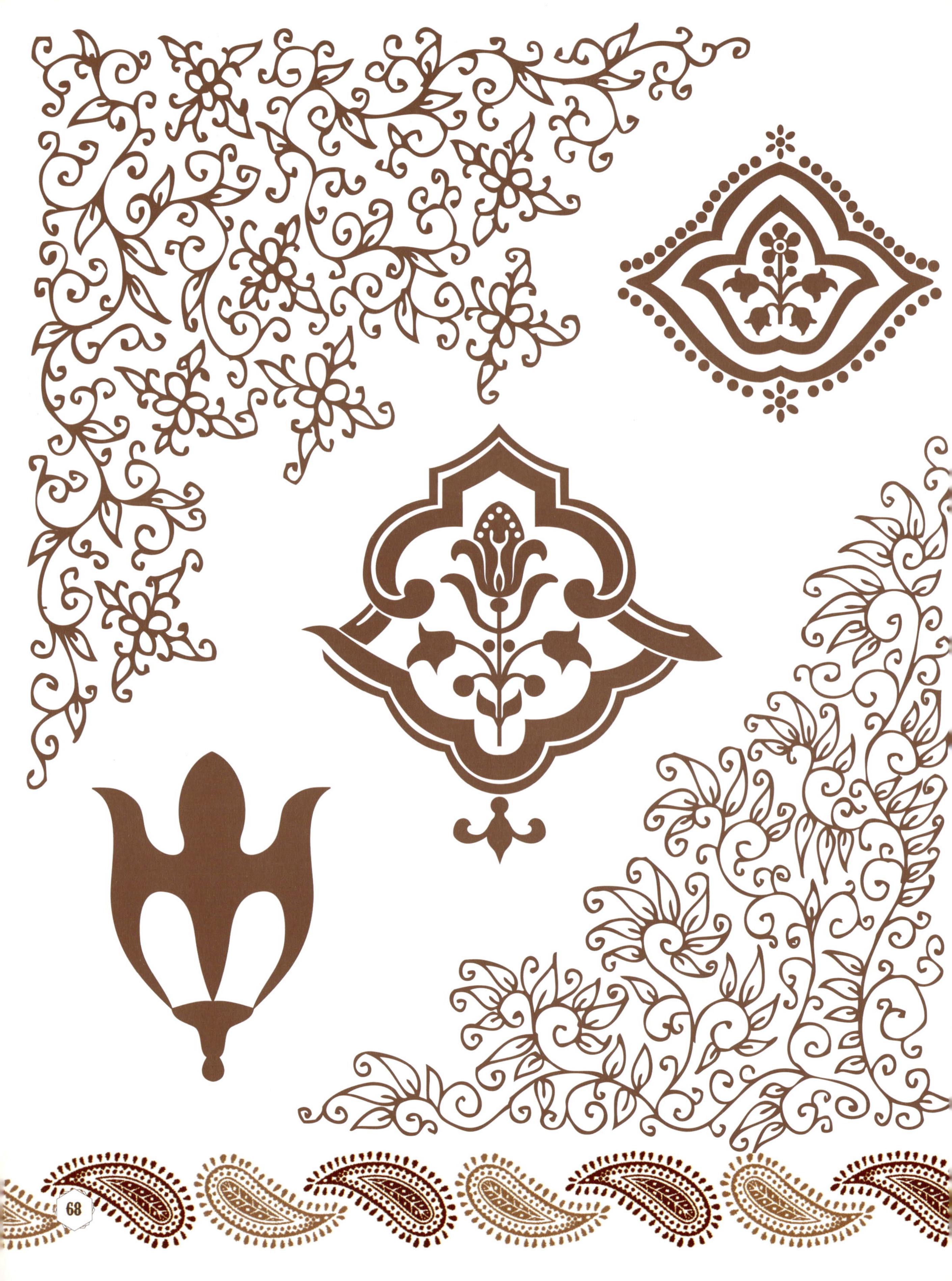

The Lotus

For Hindus, the lotus flower is closely associated with Lakshmi, the goddess of prosperity, wisdom, and fertility. On their wedding day, Indian women make sure that the lotus is prominently featured in their henna as a symbol of good luck, secure in the belief that Lakshmi will forever protect them from infertility and money woes.

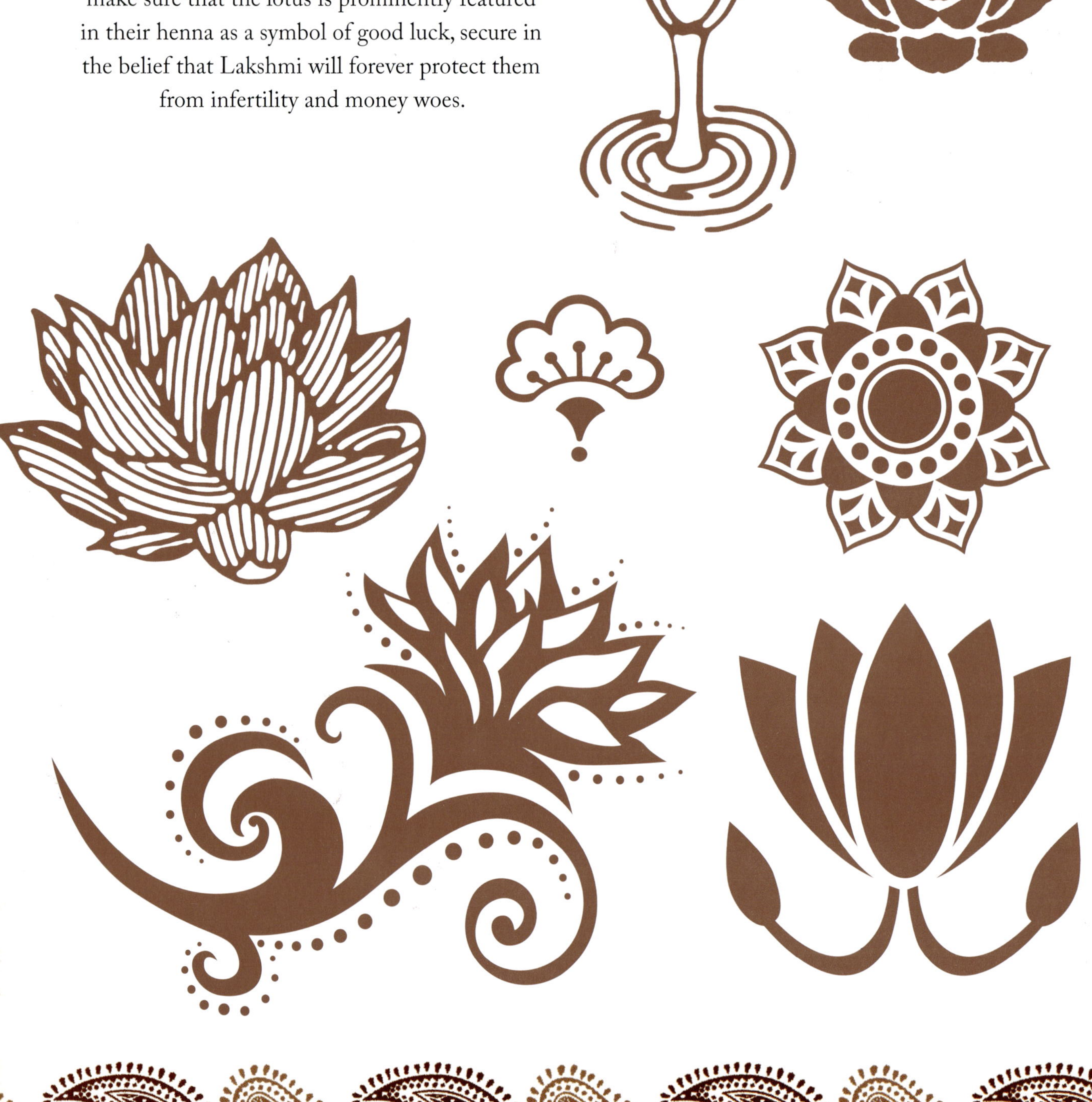

The Peacock

The national bird of India, the peacock appears quite often in henna designs. As a symbol of love and desire, it is a popular choice for brides on their wedding day. Women also seek out this pattern when they are to be separated from their husbands for any length of time. Known for its snake-killing ability, the peacock also symbolizes protection from evil.

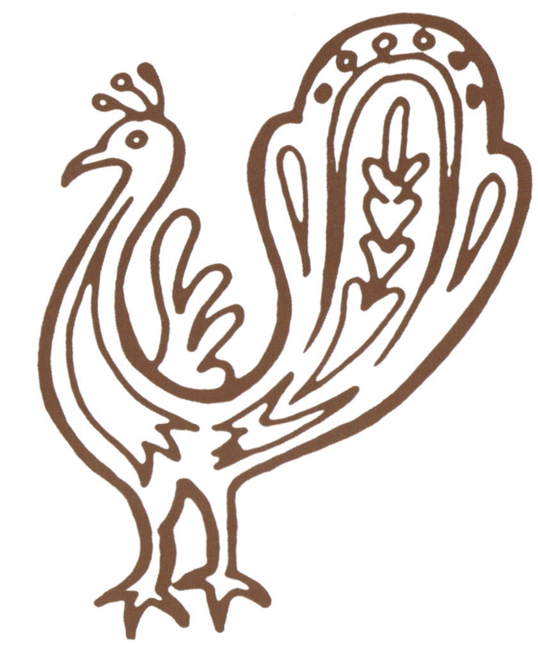

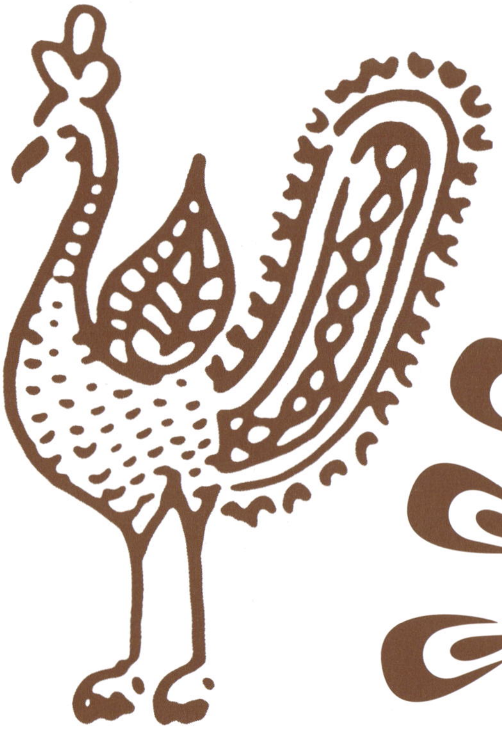

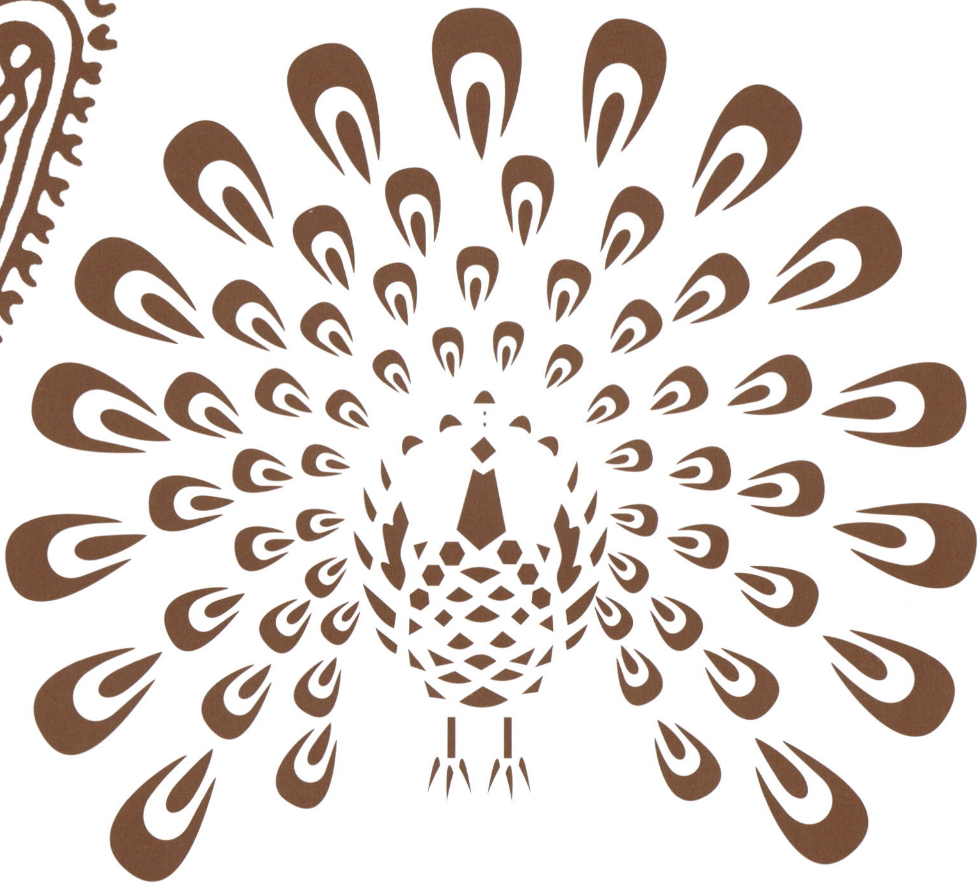

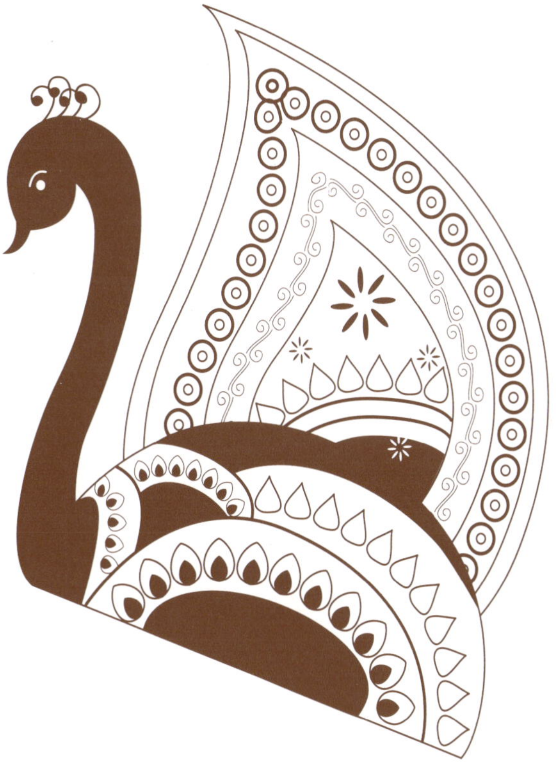

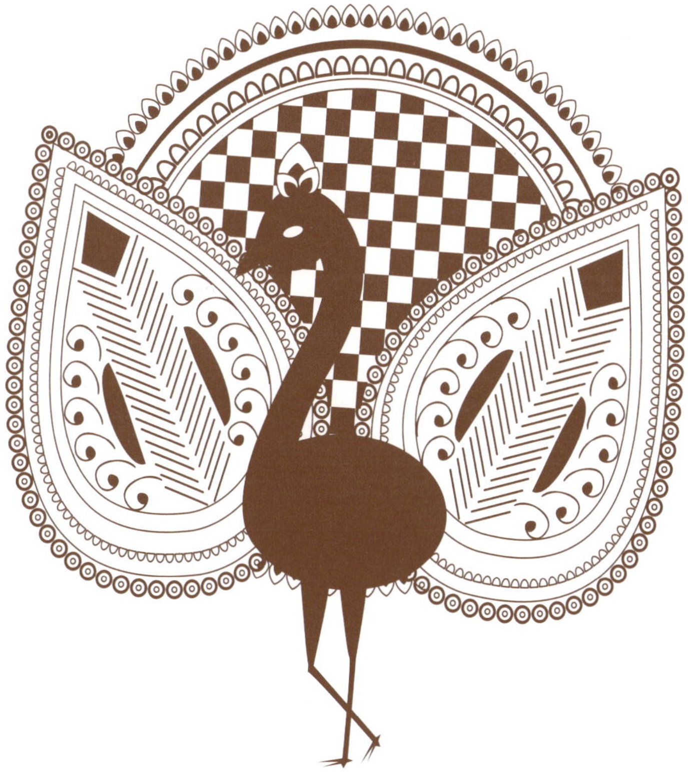

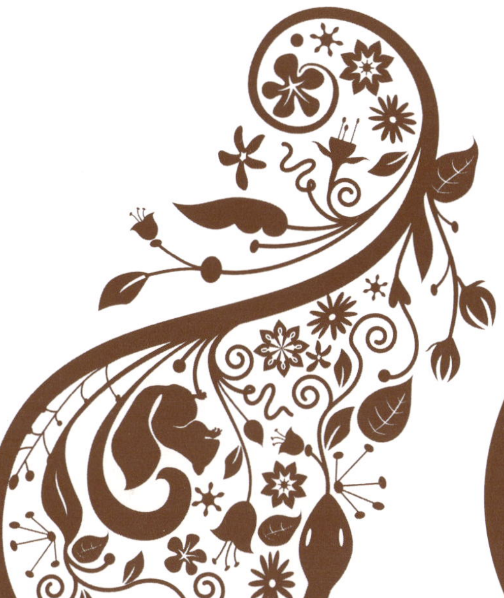

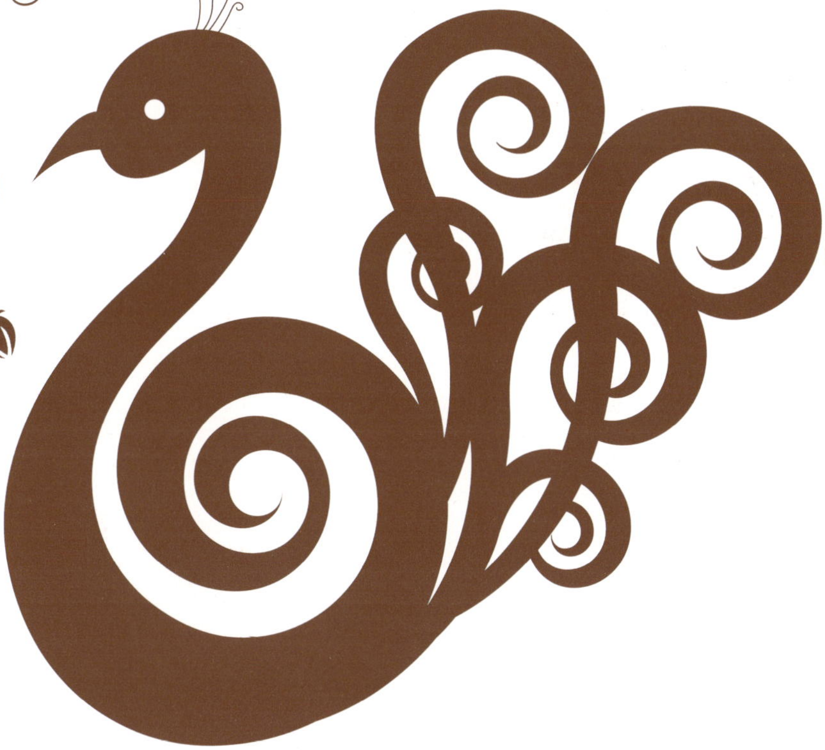

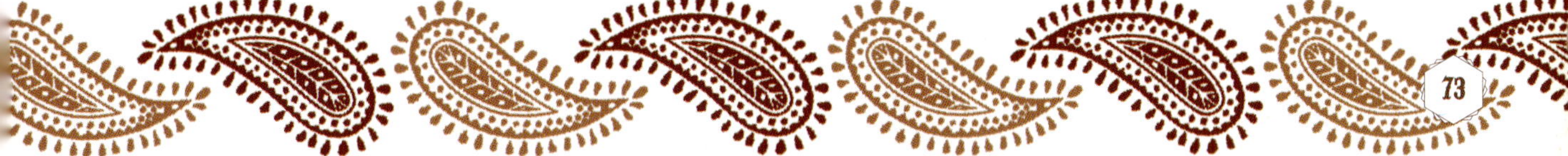

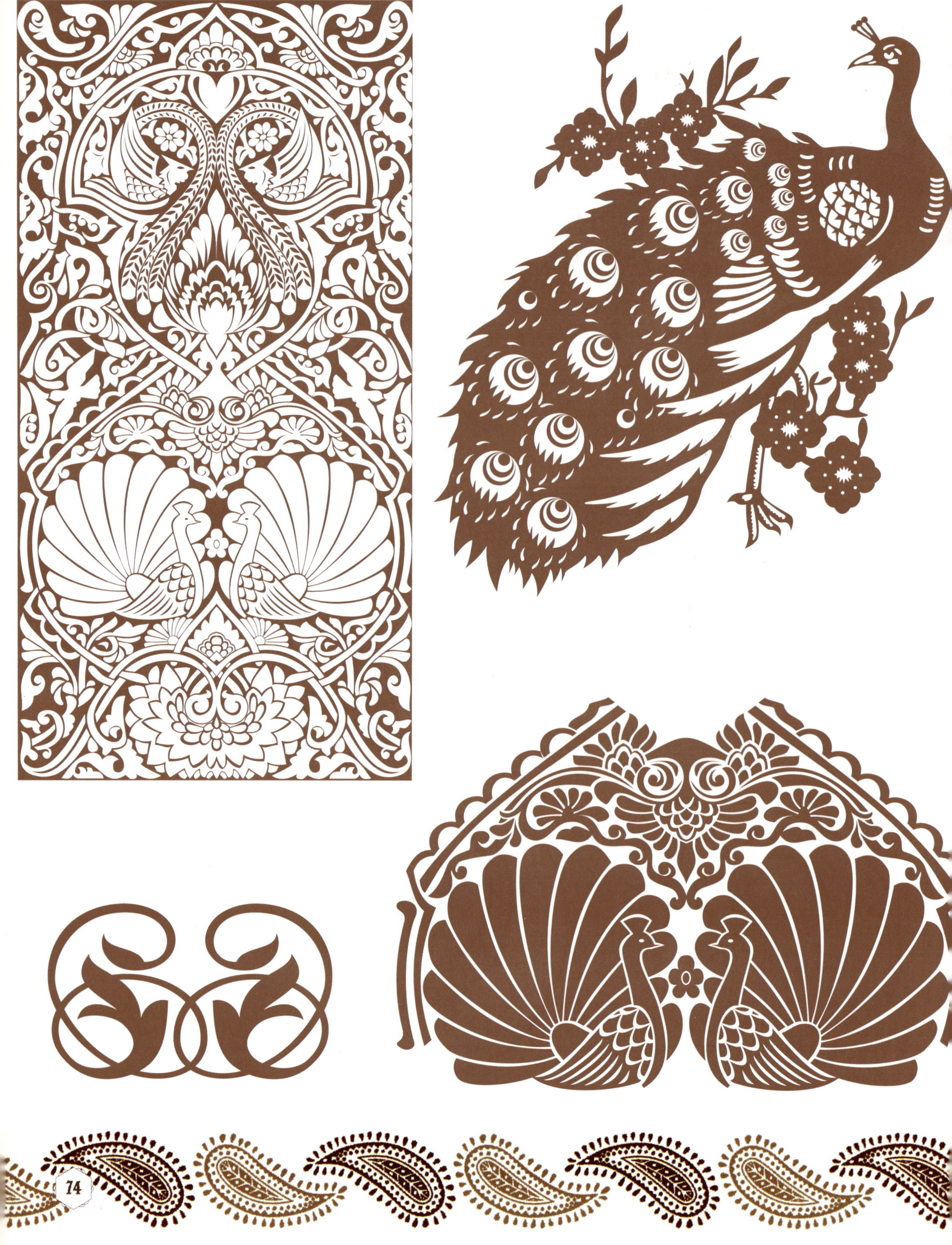

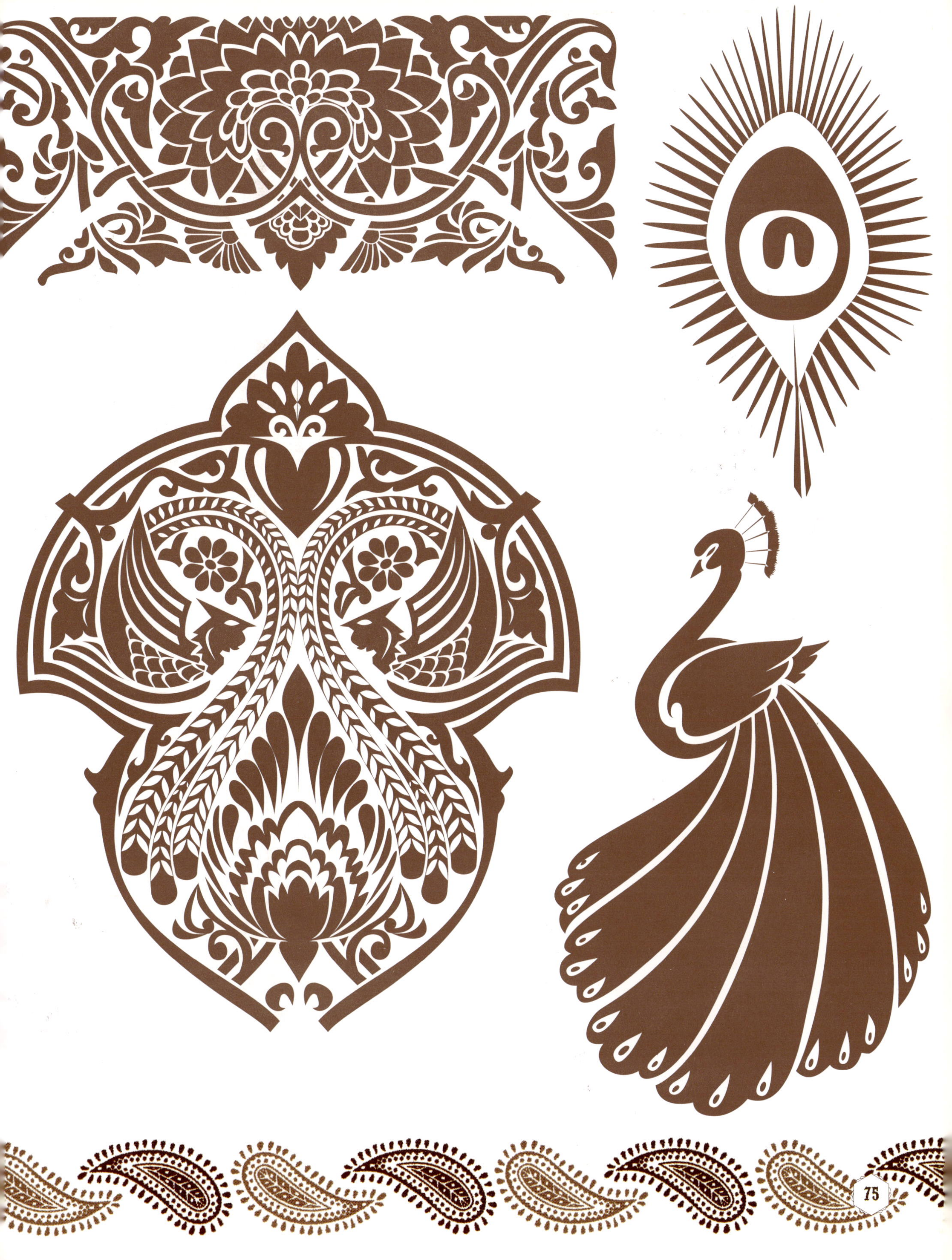

Other Bird Motifs

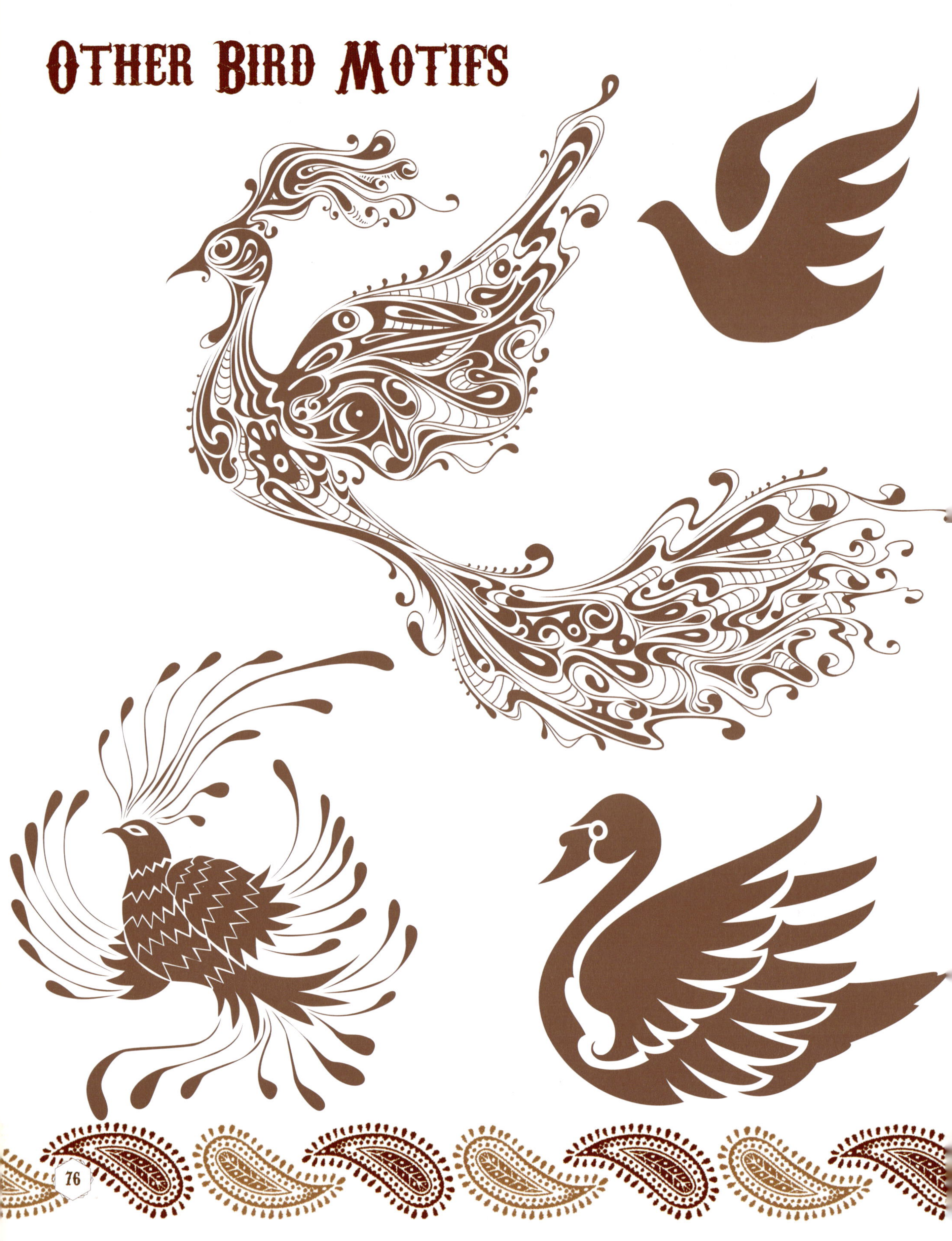

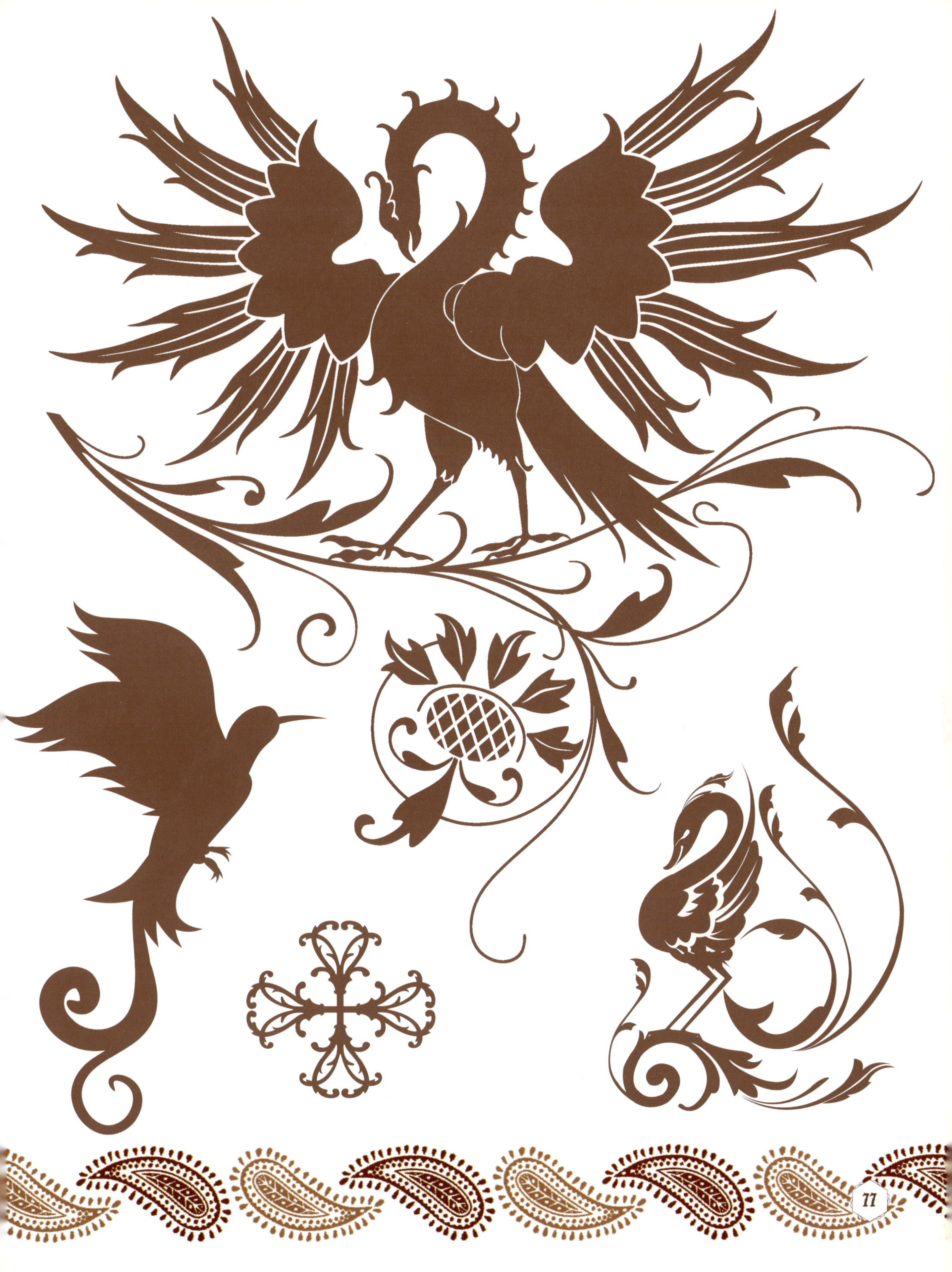

ANIMALS

Many henna designs include animals, such as the scorpion, a symbol of romantic love. The swan represents fidelity, while snakes represent wisdom and time. The symbol of the snake is a reminder to forget the past and live fully in the present.

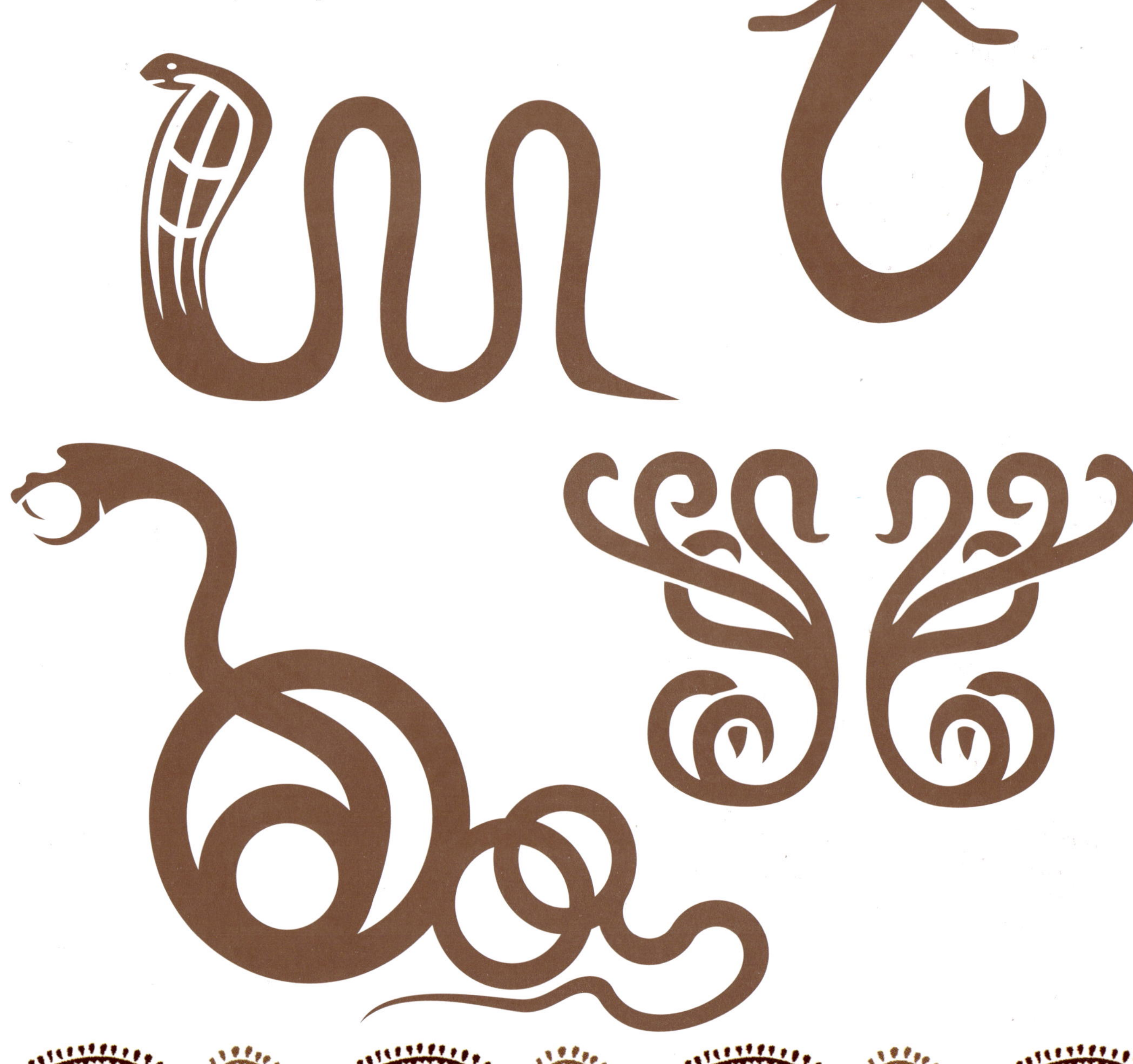

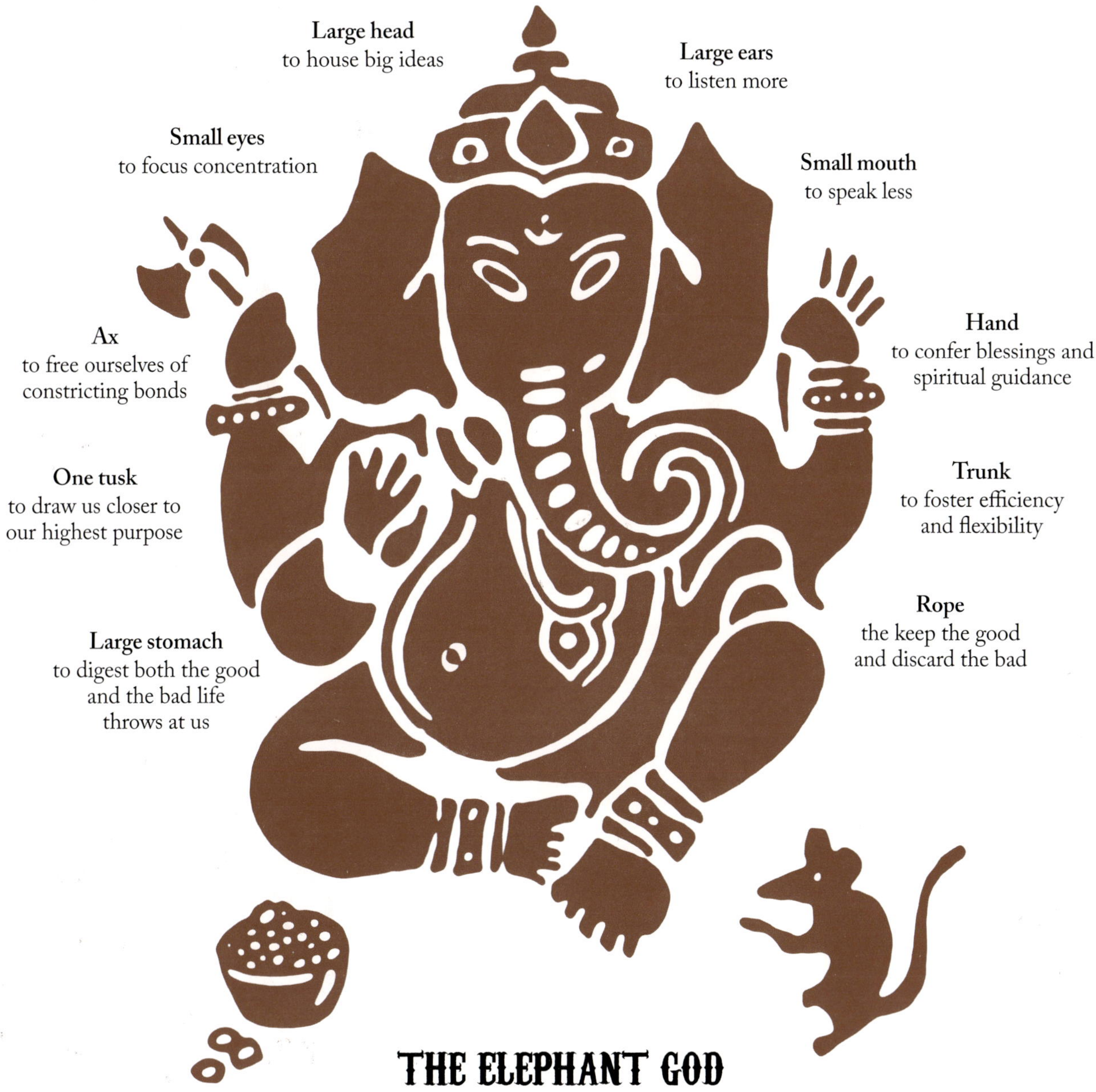

THE ELEPHANT GOD

In the Hindu religion, the elephant god Ganesh is the lord of success and remover of obstacles.

Religious Hindus begin every new undertaking with a prayer to Ganesh in the belief that he will remove all impediments to success and bestow his blessings of wisdom upon each new venture.

Geometric Patterns

The square is the Hindu symbol for honesty and stability. A triangle with its point facing skyward represents the male force, or Shiva, while a triangle pointed downward stands for female creativity, or Shakti. Superimposed upon each other they form a star, the symbol for the merging of male and female energy. The V-sign represents a fan, a symbol for tranquility. And the pentagram symbolizes the five elements: earth, wind, fire, water, and sky, and is often worn as a symbol of protection.

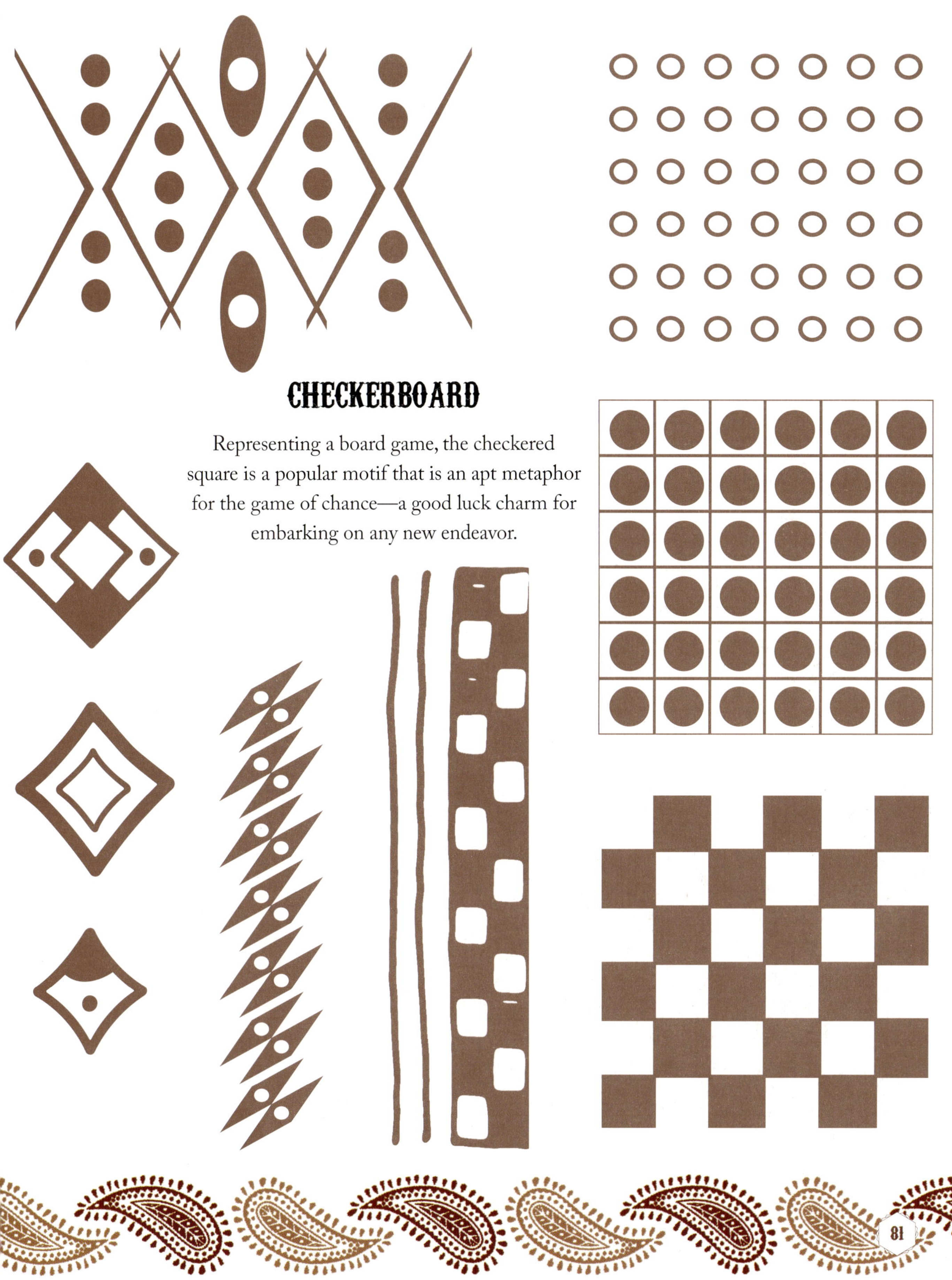

CHECKERBOARD

Representing a board game, the checkered square is a popular motif that is an apt metaphor for the game of chance—a good luck charm for embarking on any new endeavor.

CONNECTORS

A spiral, a curve, a meandering vine. While lending graceful cohesion to a henna design, connectors such as these are suggestive of the twists and turns of the soul's unpredictable path. Vines represent strength, perseverance, and devotion, while water ripples are the sustaining elements of life.

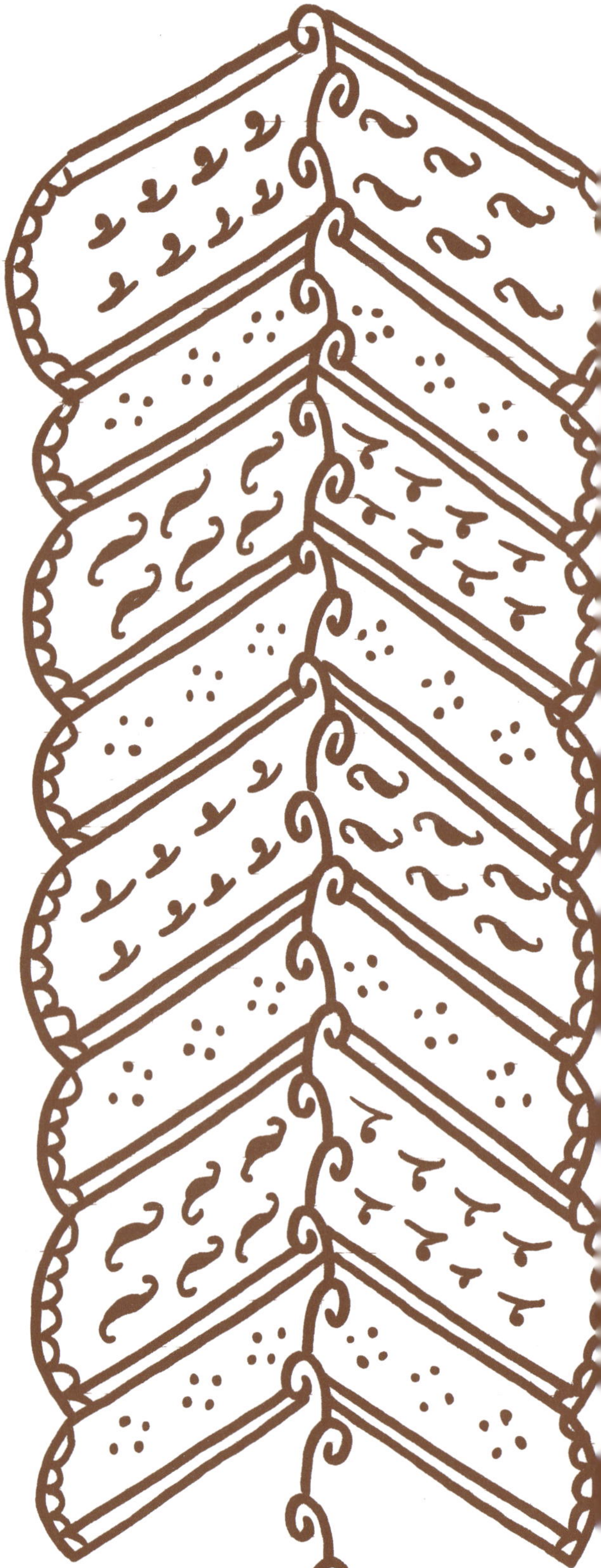

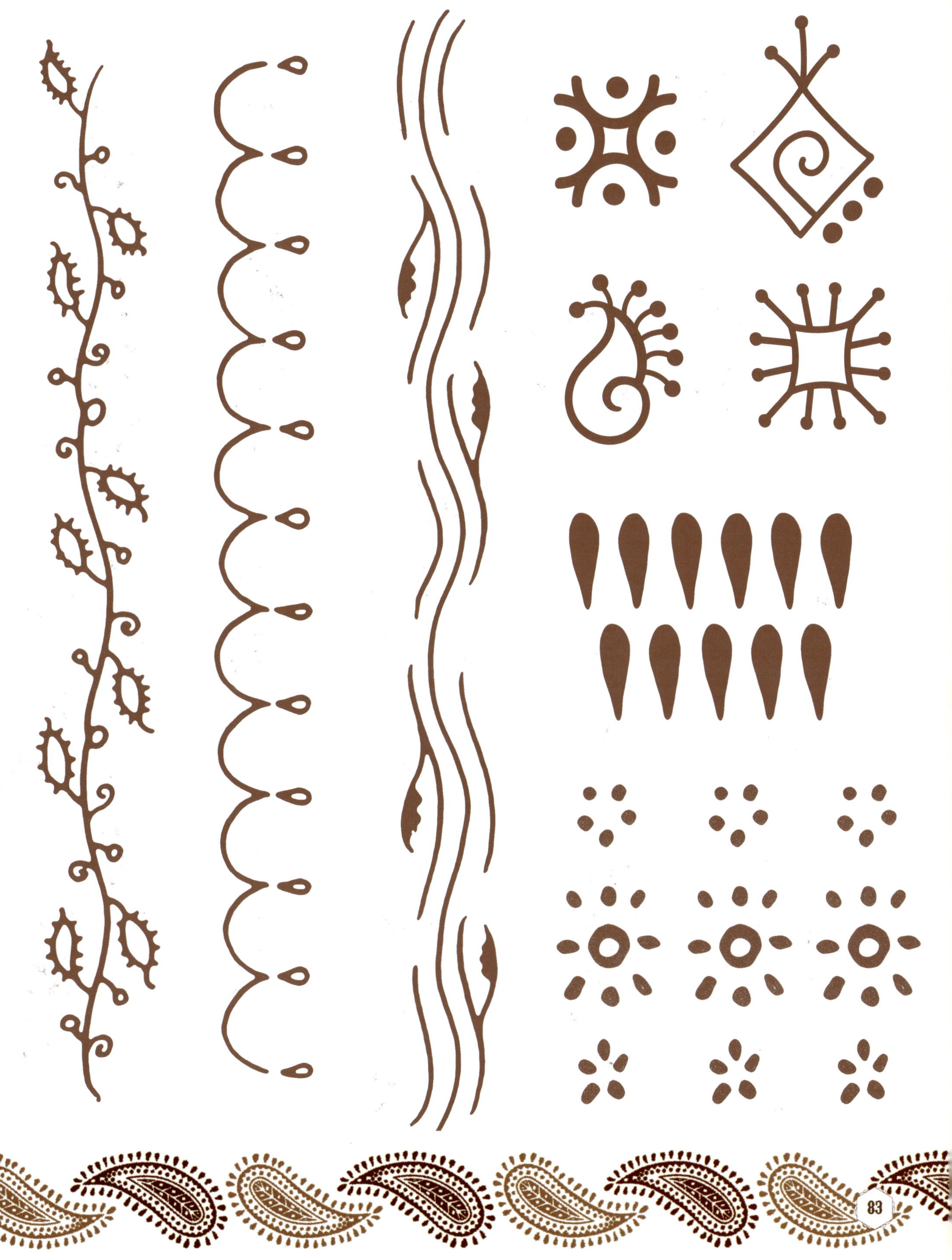

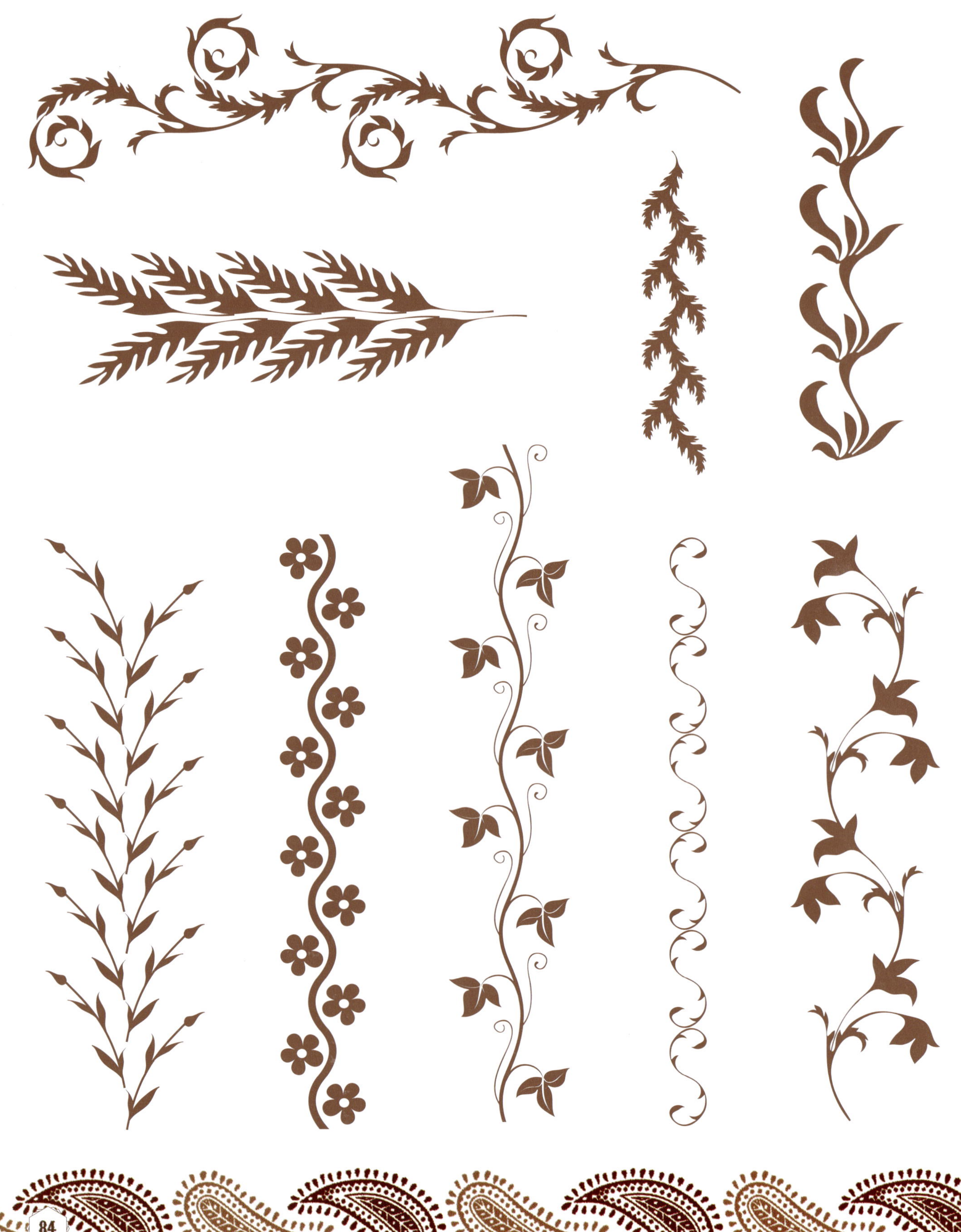

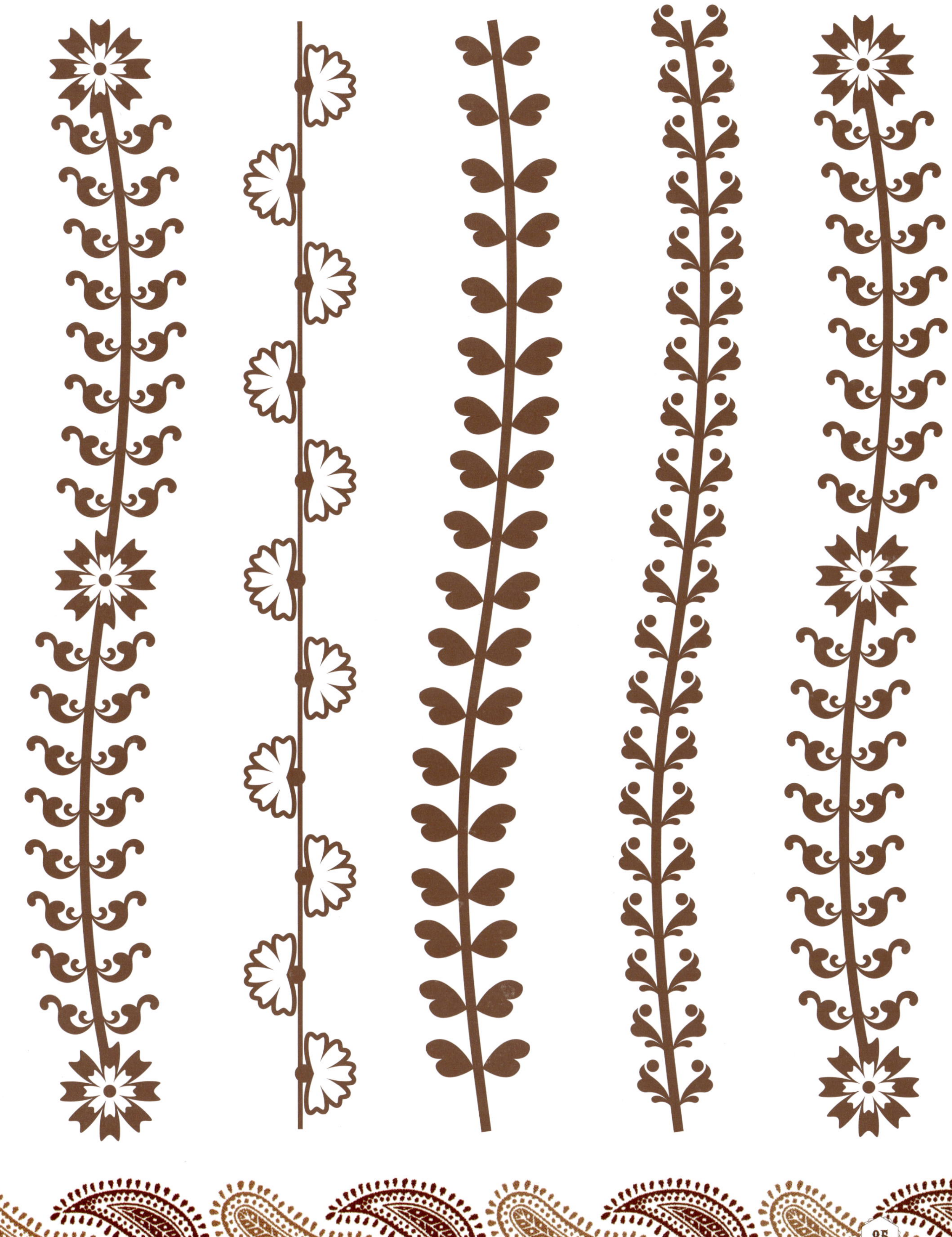

SANSKRIT SAYINGS

प्रतिकूलतायाः शक्तिः

Strength through adversity

शक्तिः दुर्दम्येच्छाशक्त्याः आगच्छति

Strength comes from an indomitable will

एकं जीवनम्, एकः अवसरः

One life, one chance

स्वात्मानं जानीहि

Know thyself

दिव्यः प्रकाशः

Divine light

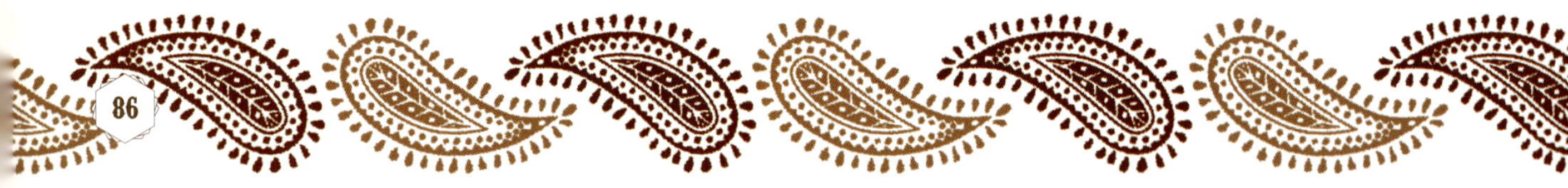

अस्माकं कार्याणि अस्मान्सावधीकरिष्यंति

Only action will define us

न कदापि खंडितः

Never broken

एतदपि गमिष्यति

This, too, will pass

तत्परिवर्तनं भव

Be the change

शक्त्याः धैर्यमायाति

From strength comes courage

मा कदापि त्यज

Never give up

मृत्युः न कदाप्यस्मान्पृथक्करिष्यति

Death will never separate us

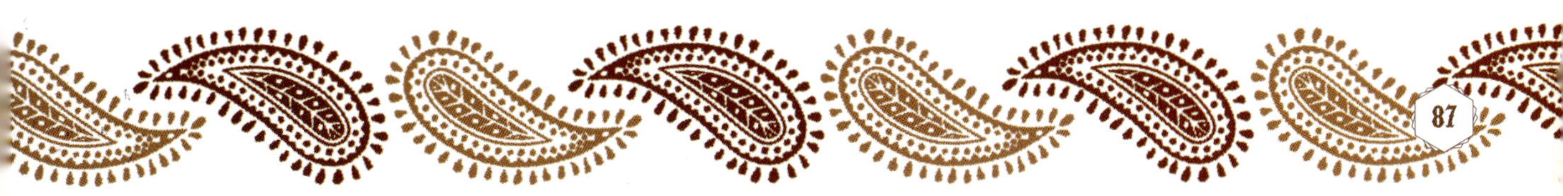

AFRICA

There is a rich tradition of henna use in Africa where the plant grows freely, especially along the Atlantic coast. The indigenous tribes of northern Africa in particular are known for a style of henna body art that is quite unique. They are a culturally diverse people who live in Algeria, Morocco, Libya, Tunisia, and Mauritania and who are linked by a common language. Commonly called Berber, a name originally given to them by the Greeks (it means "barbarian,"), the people in this region prefer to be called *Amazigh* (pronounced "ahma-zeer"; plural, *Imazighen*), which means "free" or "noble."

Africans from this region were first introduced to Islam in the seventh century, and today, most Amazigh peoples practice this religion and have adopted Arab/Islamic traditions. Because of the Islamic fear of committing the sin of idolatry, the depiction of human or animal forms is forbidden in a place of worship. As a result, their symbols are rendered in a highly abstract style, since historically, anyone wearing such a depiction would be prevented from entering a temple.

The word for henna body art in northern Africa is *hinna*. Hinna combines traditional patterns derived from textiles, pottery and metalwork with dense geometric motifs to create a body art of dazzling complexity. Many northern Africans believe that henna is invested with *baraka*, which means "blessing." It is this supernatural component that makes wearing henna much more than adornment. It is also a way to protect oneself from the forces of evil and to bring about blessings of fertility, good health, and financial security. Northern African symbols differ from region to region but all are laden with protective properties. Though bolder than designs from the Indian subcontinent, they are equally beautiful.

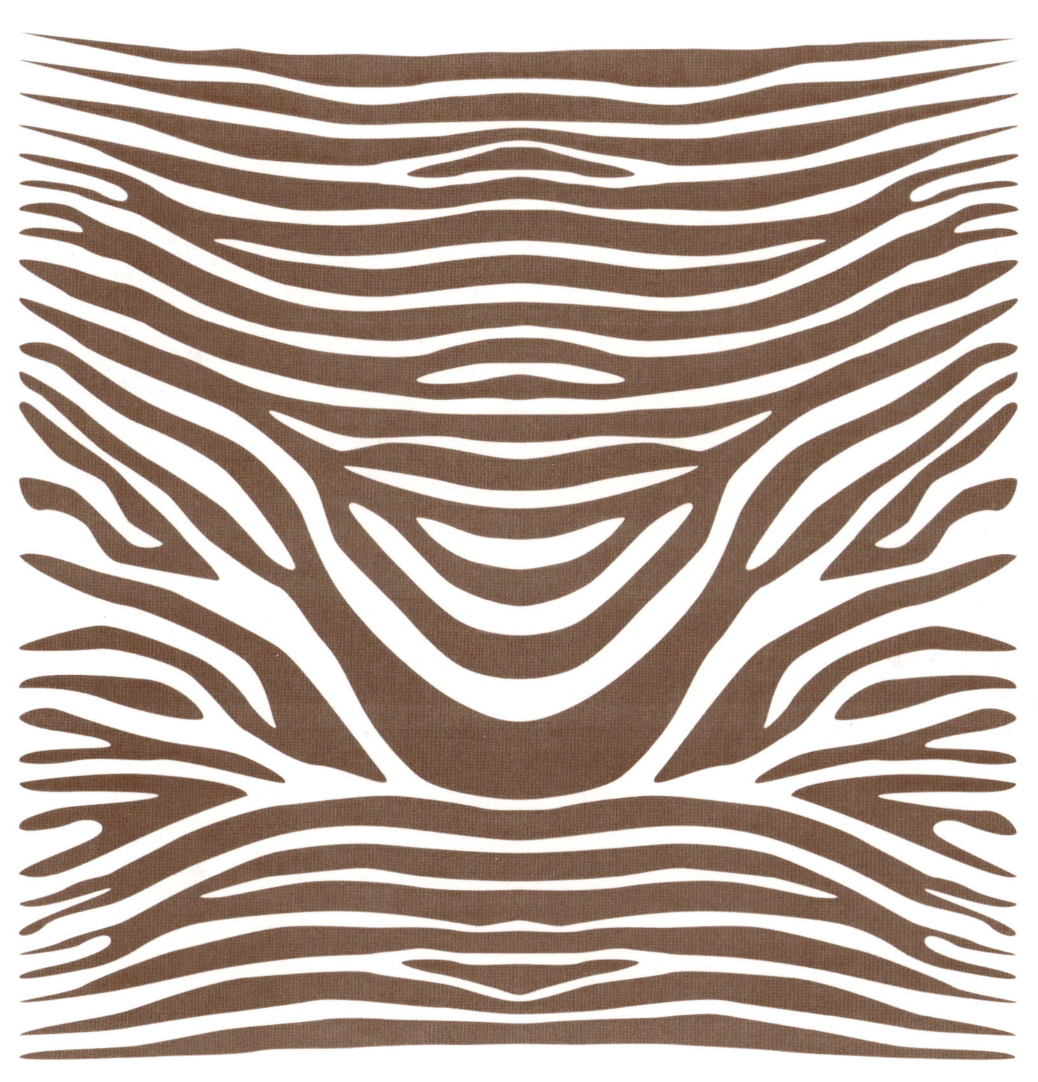

Shapes and Symbols of the Imazighen

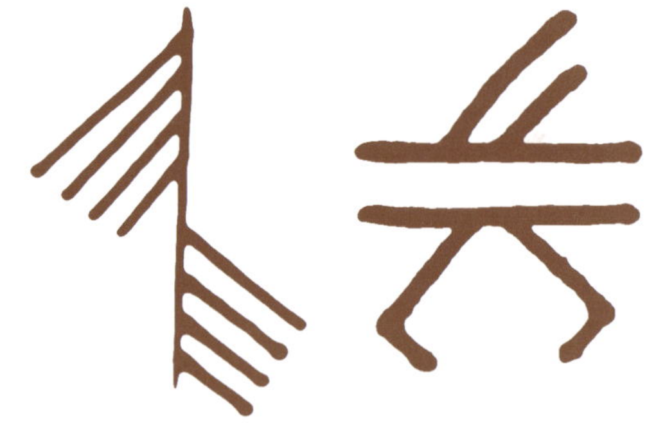

The visual vocabulary of the Amazigh people includes magical geometric shapes and spirals along with coded symbols for flowers, humans, eyes, plants, and everyday objects.

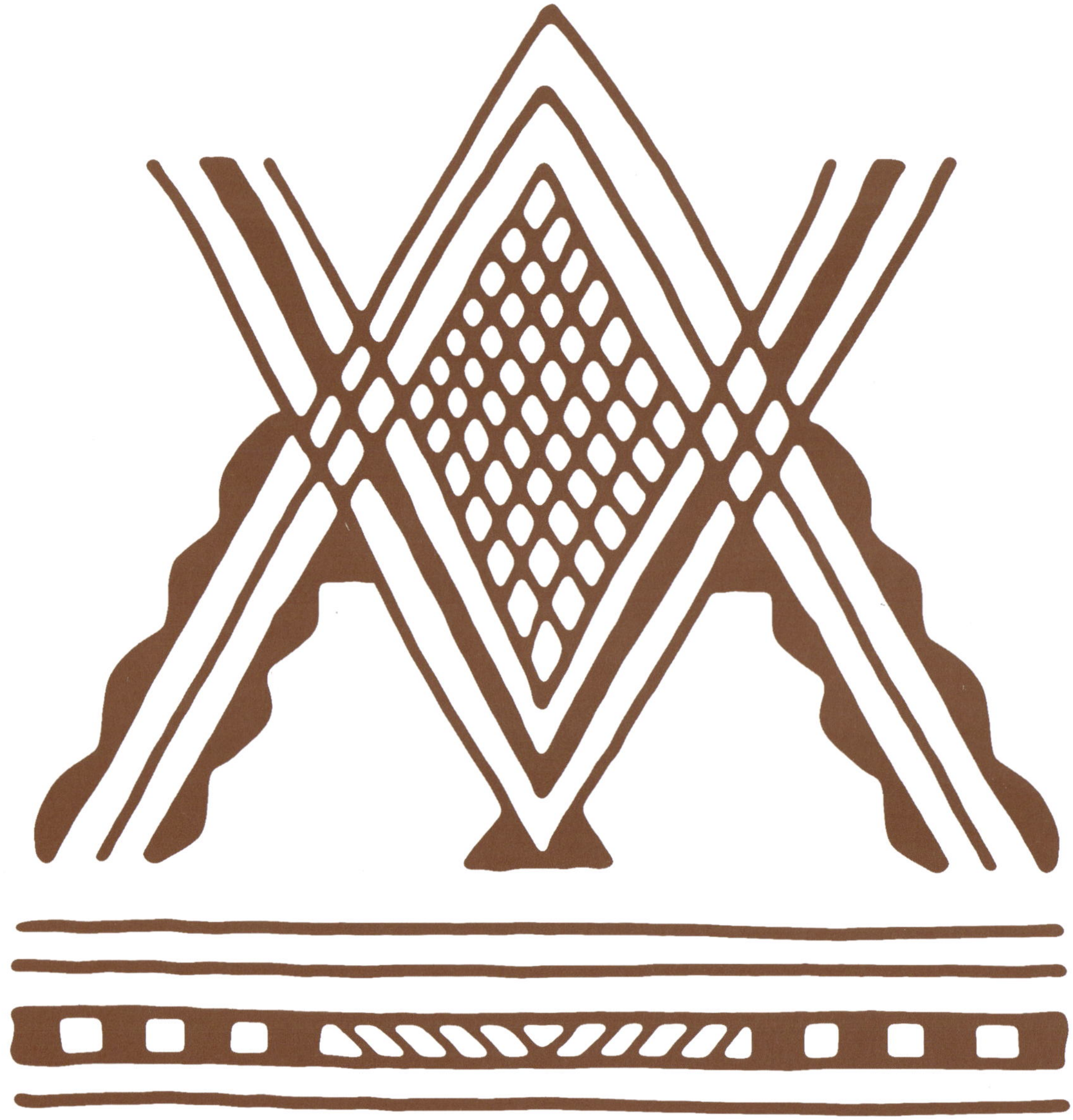

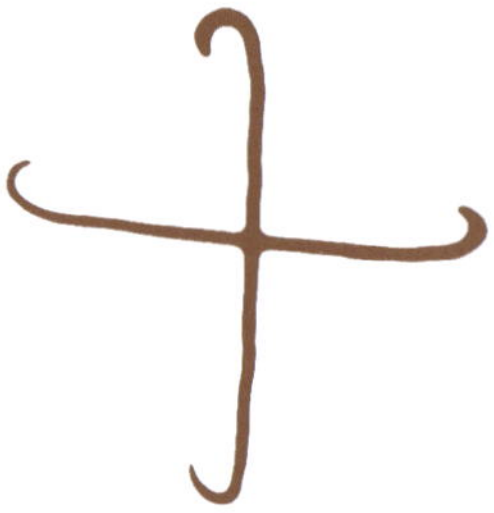

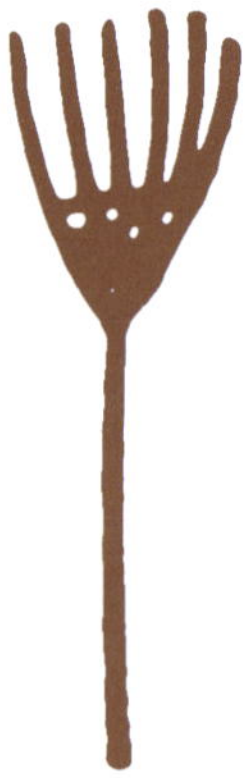

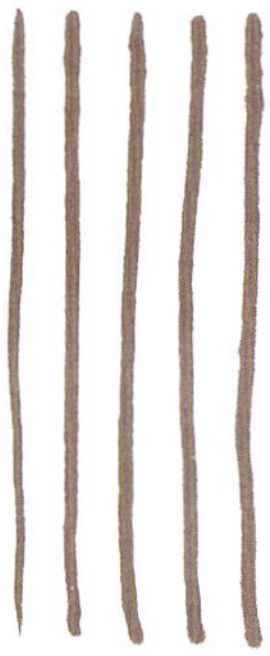

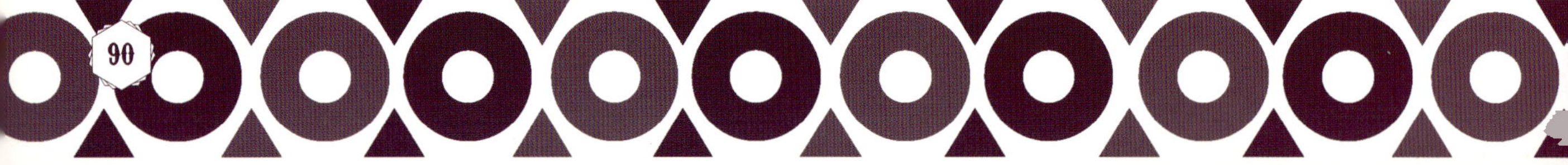

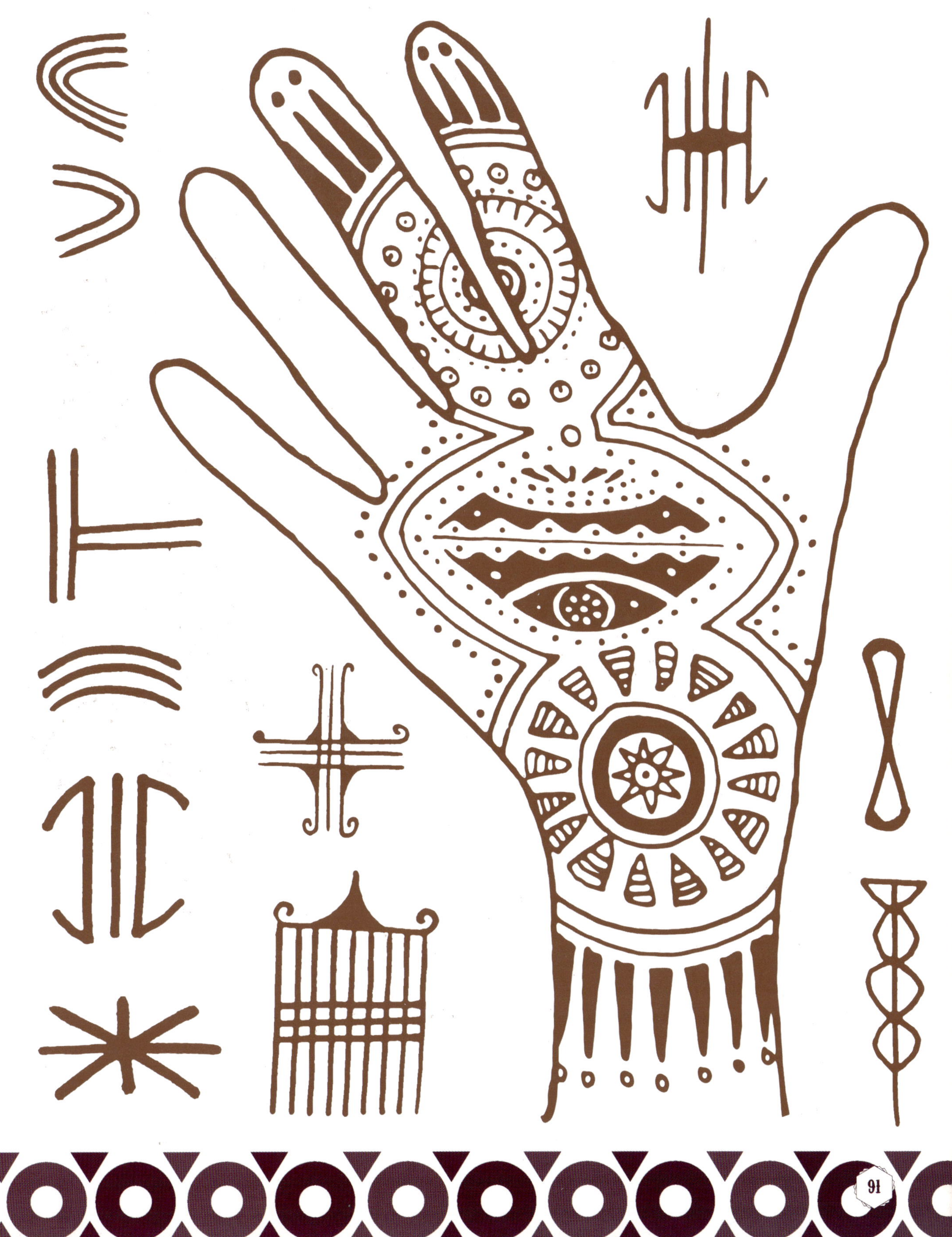

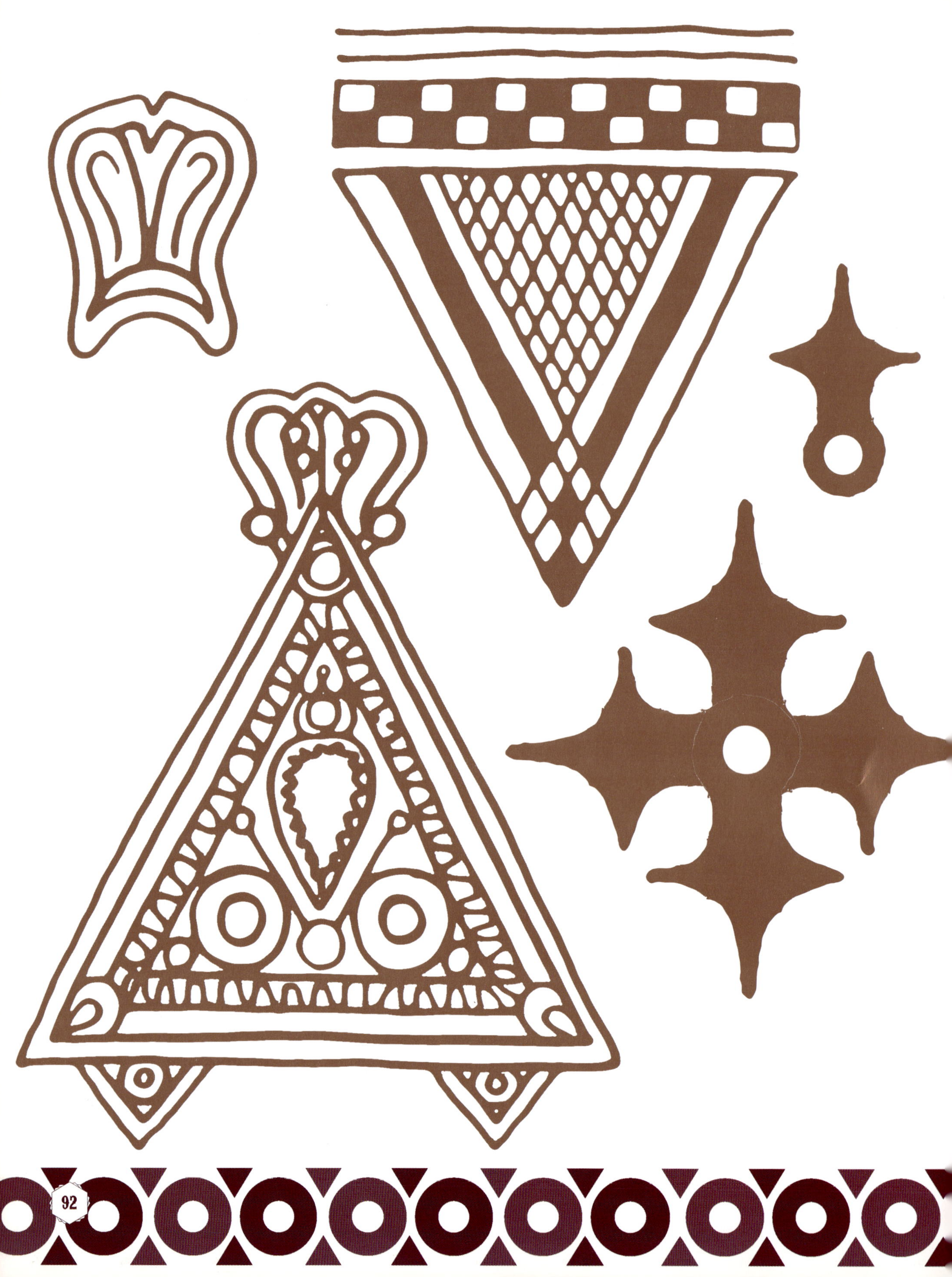

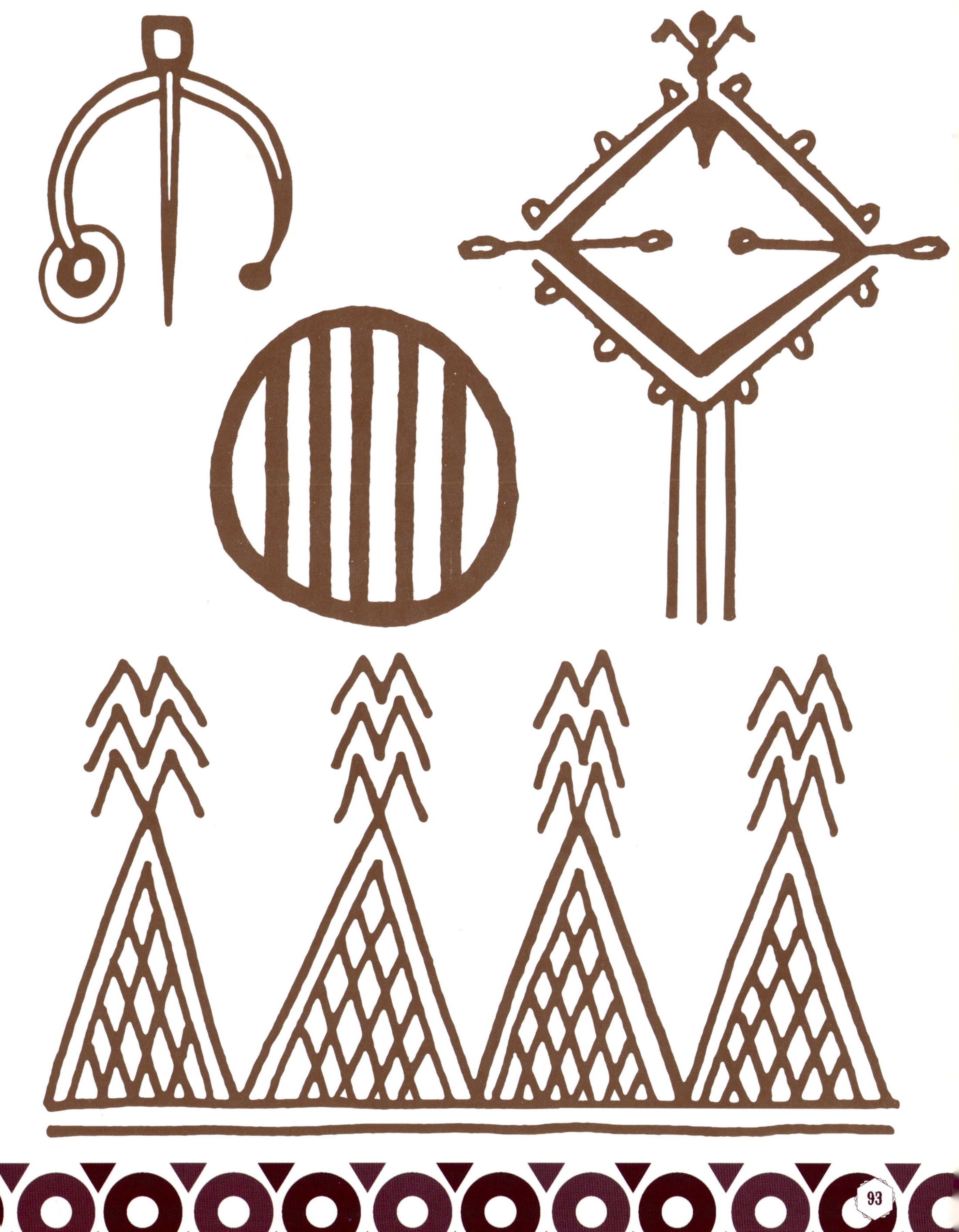

FAMILIAR OBJECTS

Images like these are abstract representations of objects like the moon, then sun, a tree, and more.

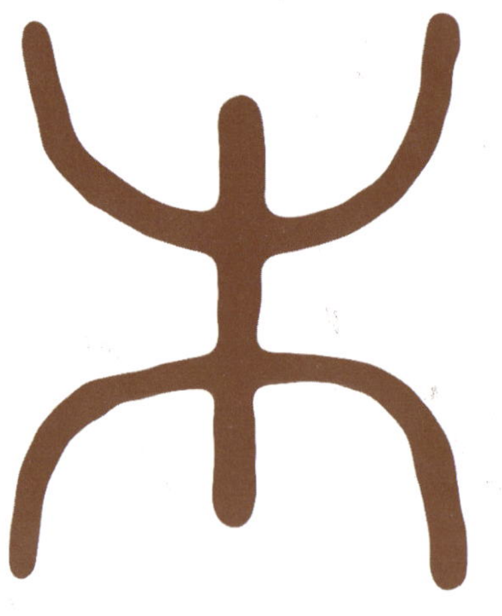

Man

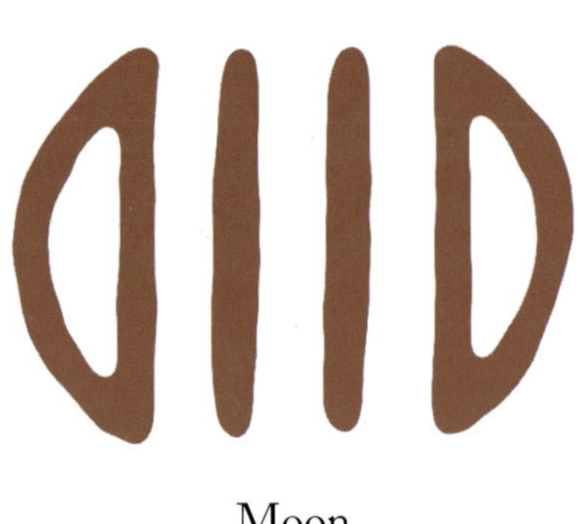

Moon

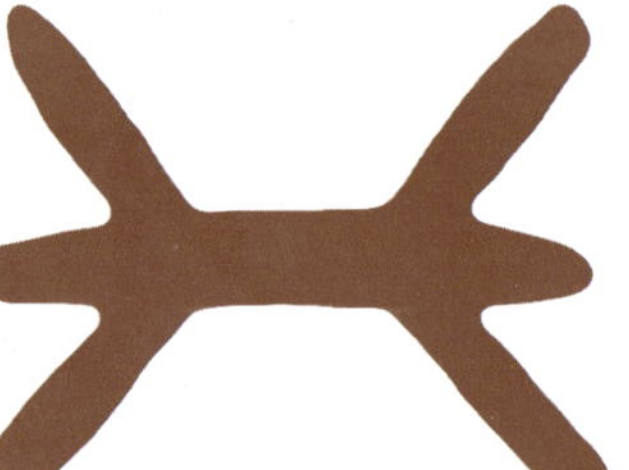

Swallow

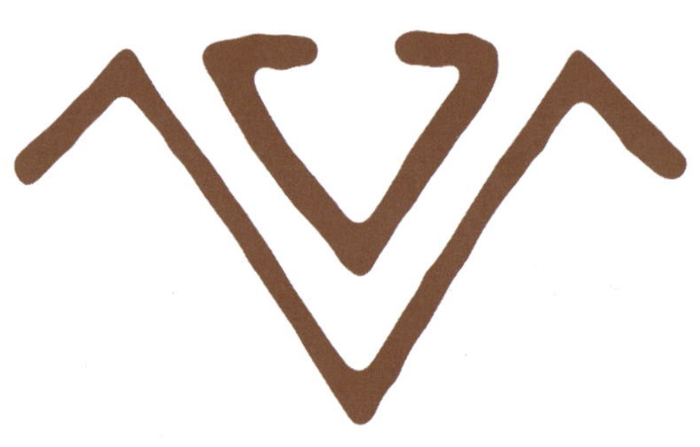

Taurus (Bull)

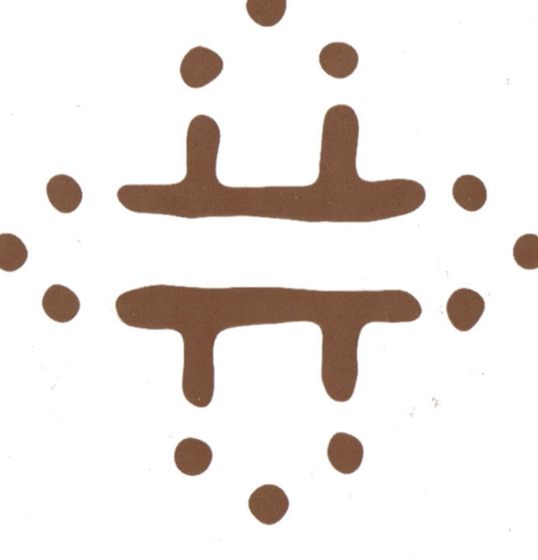

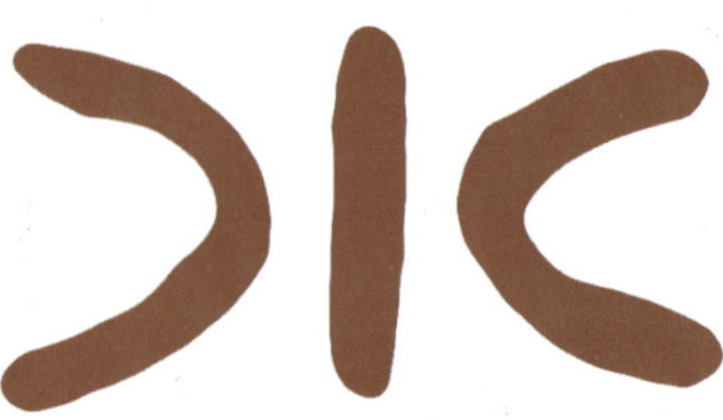

Salamander

Sun

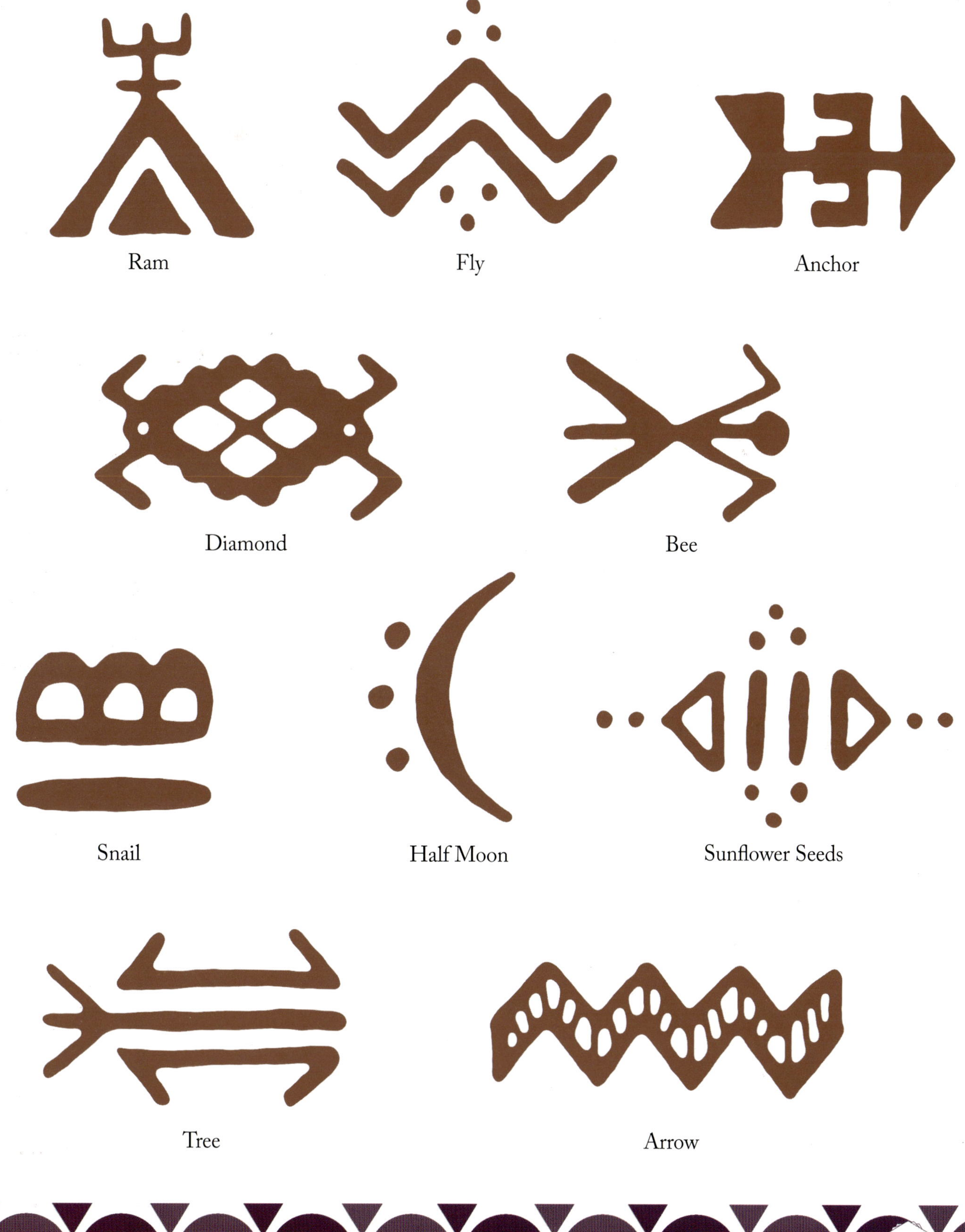
Ram
Fly
Anchor
Diamond
Bee
Snail
Half Moon
Sunflower Seeds
Tree
Arrow

Other North African Motifs

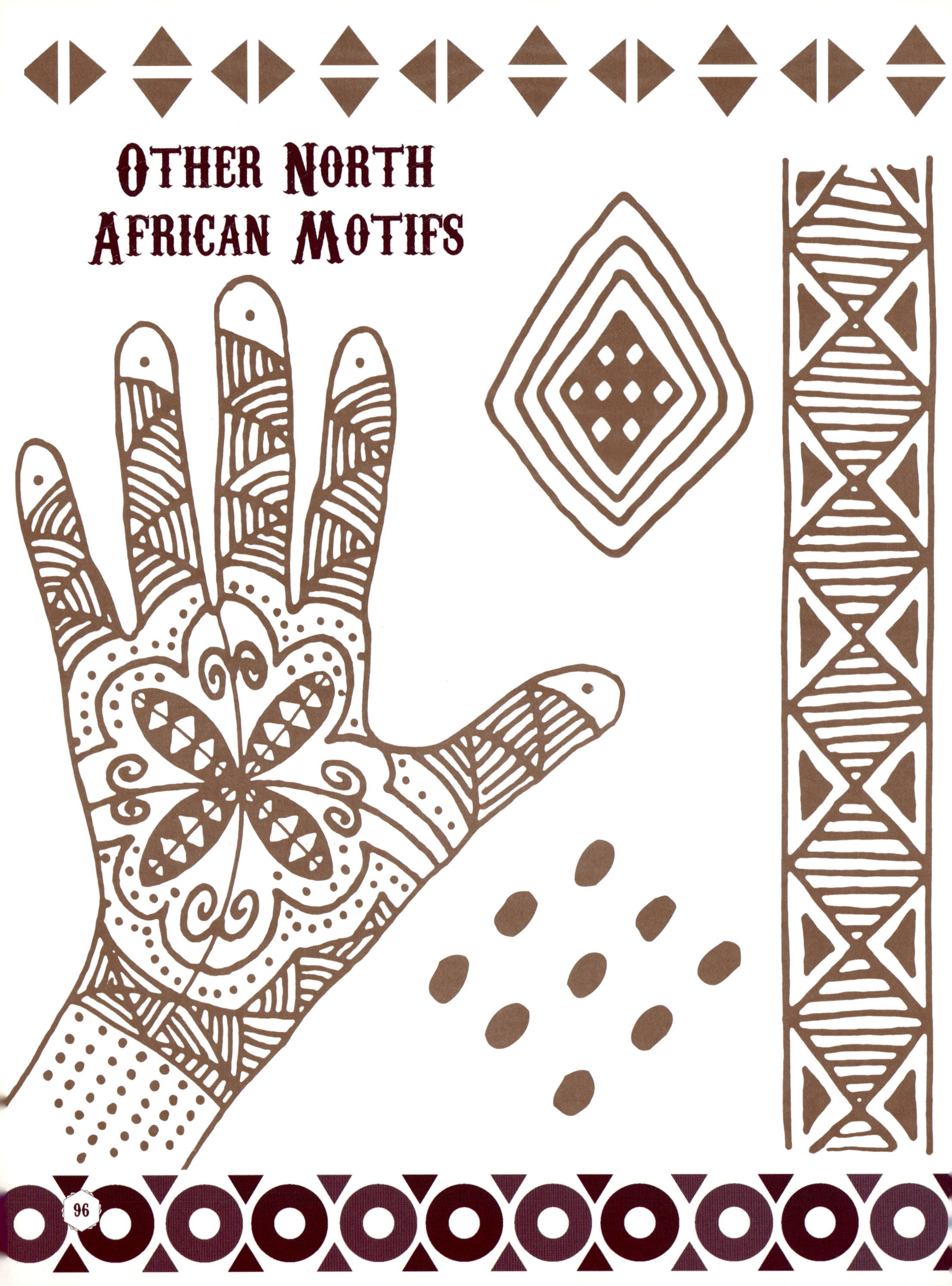

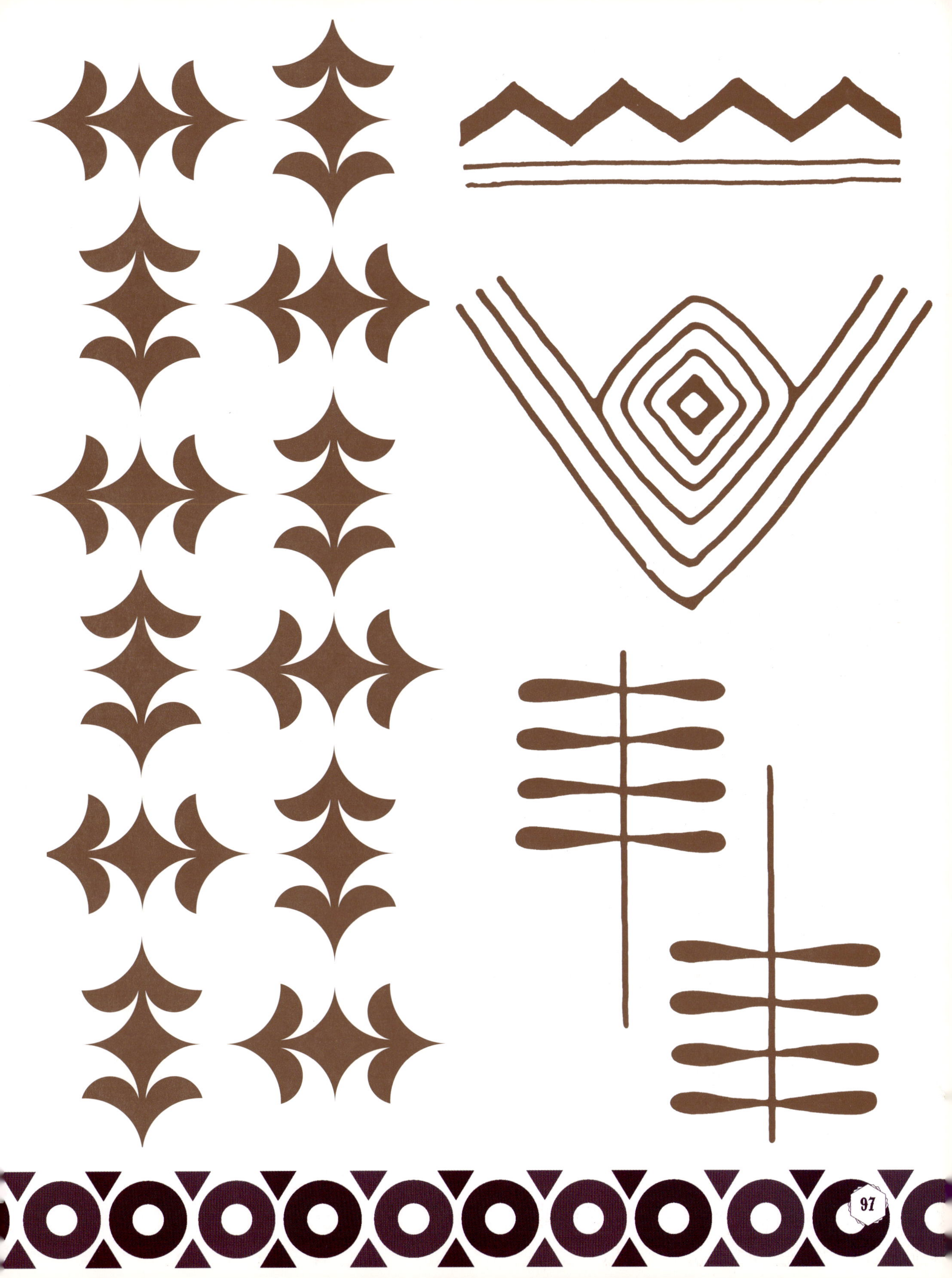

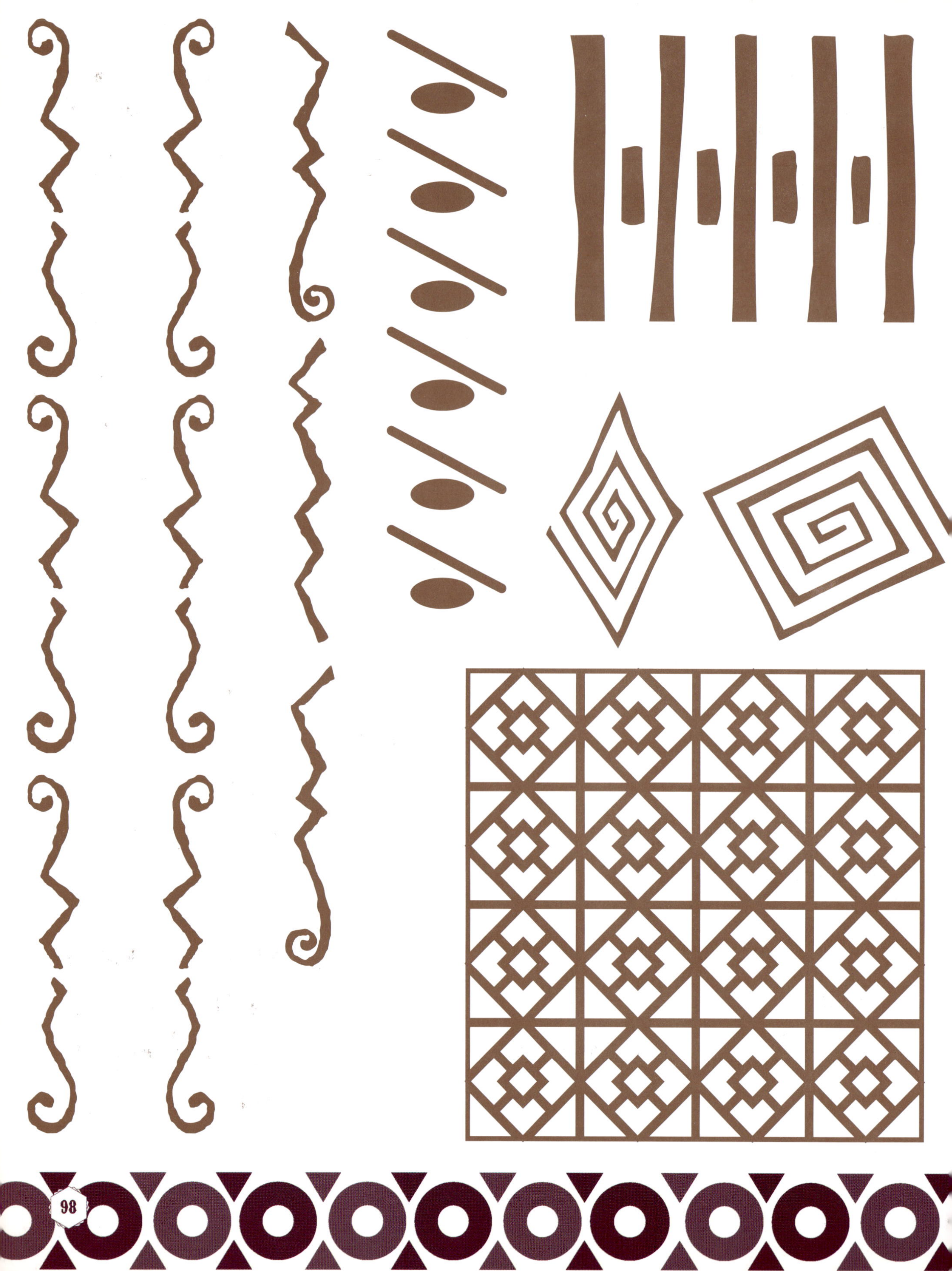

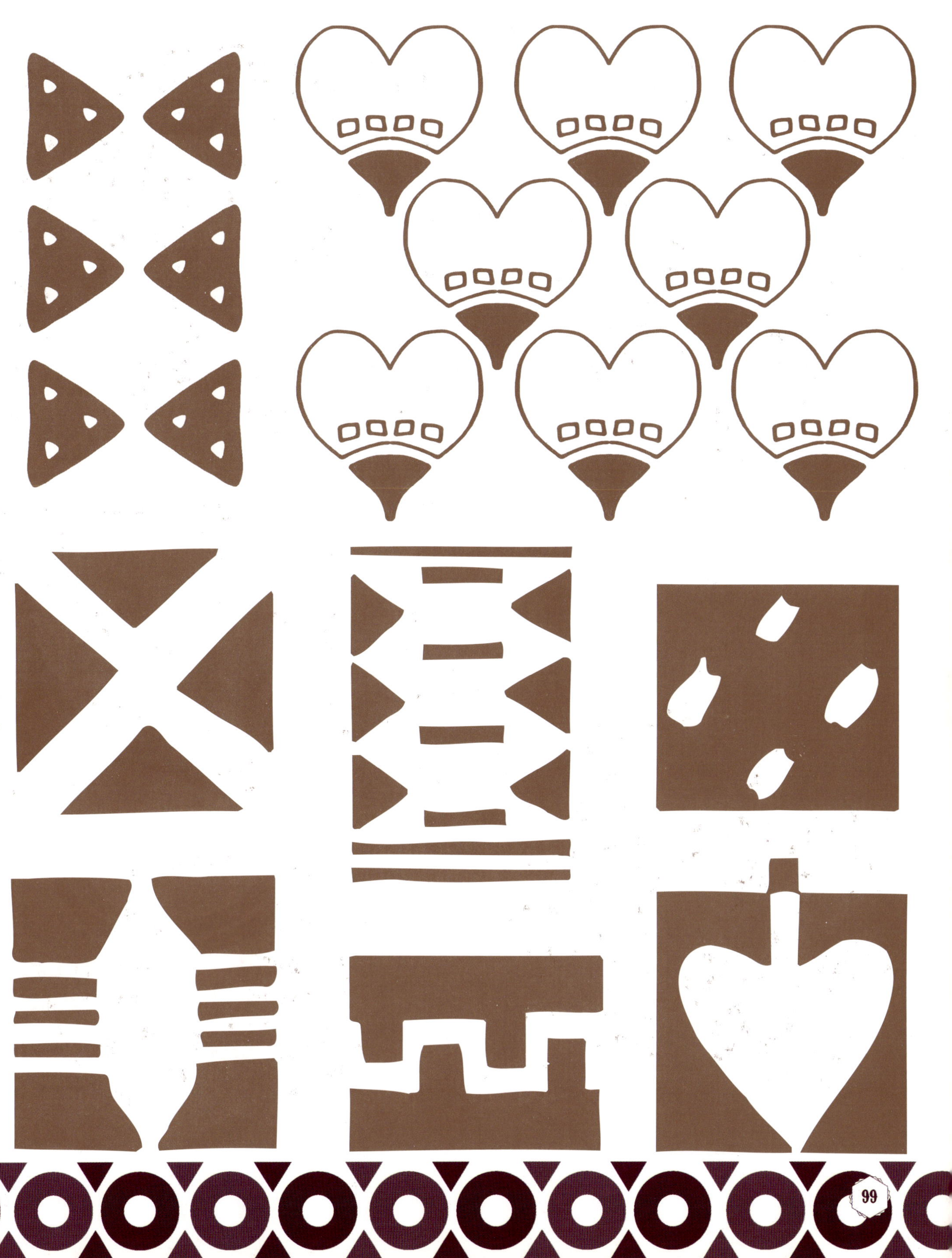

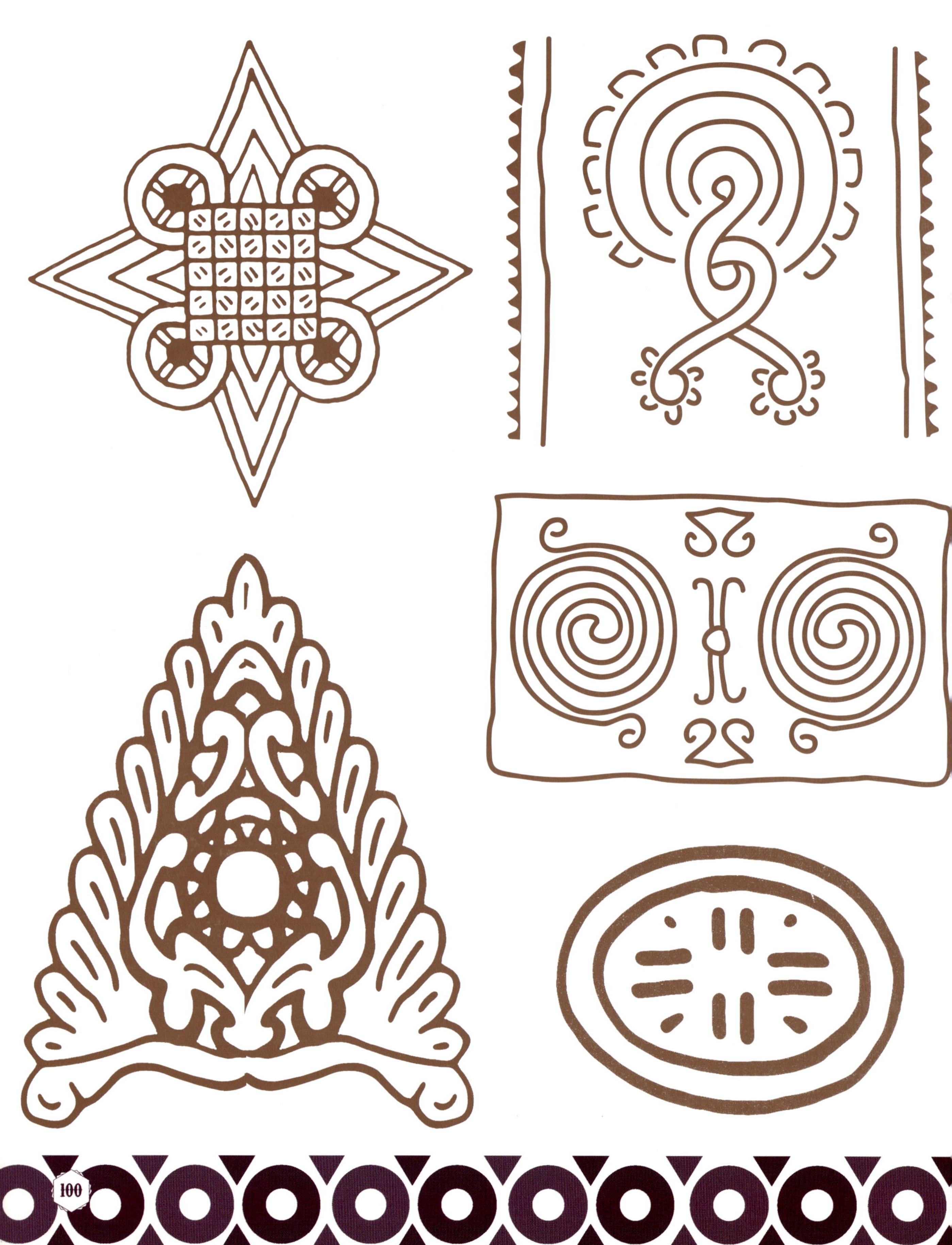

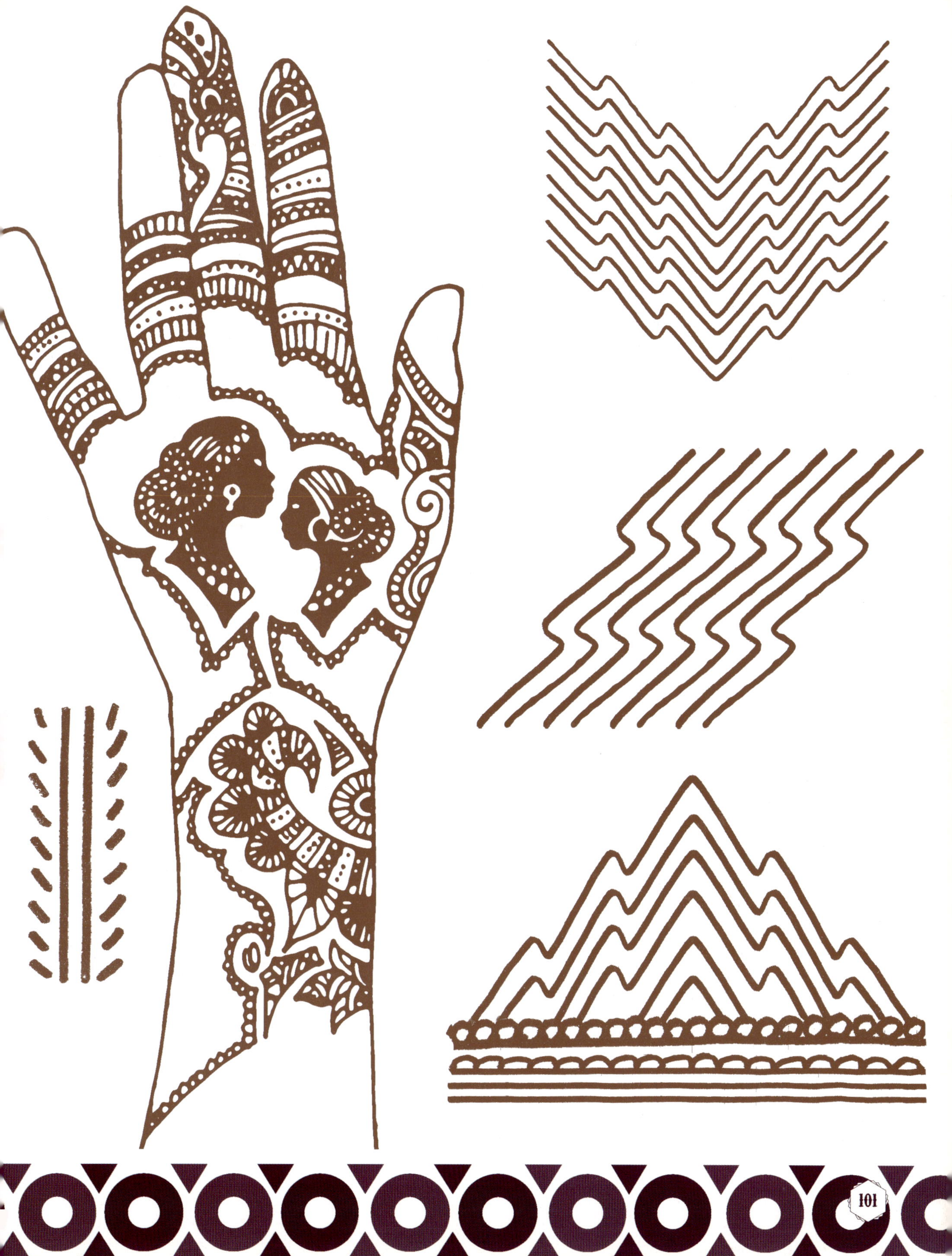

Animal Symbols

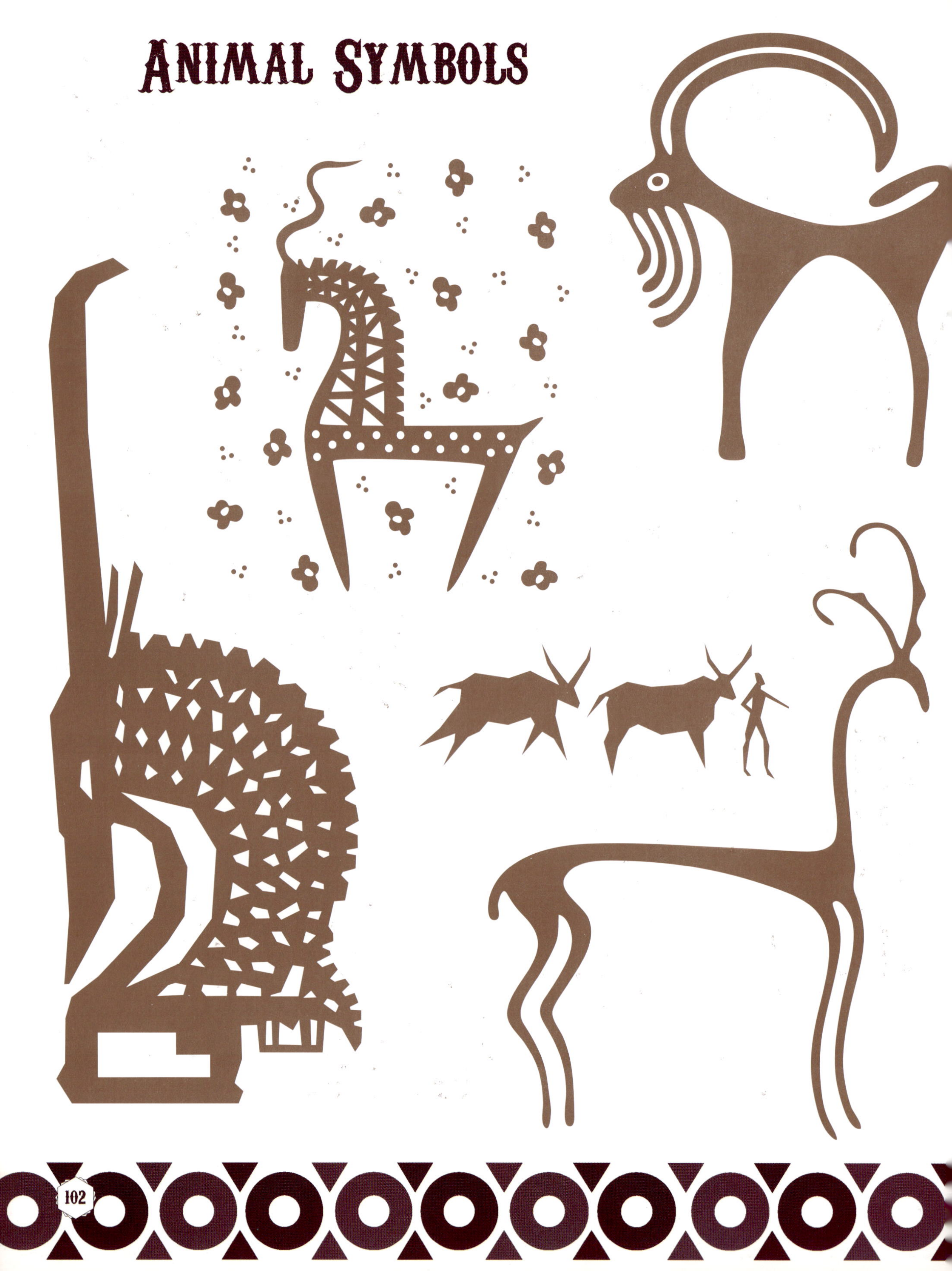

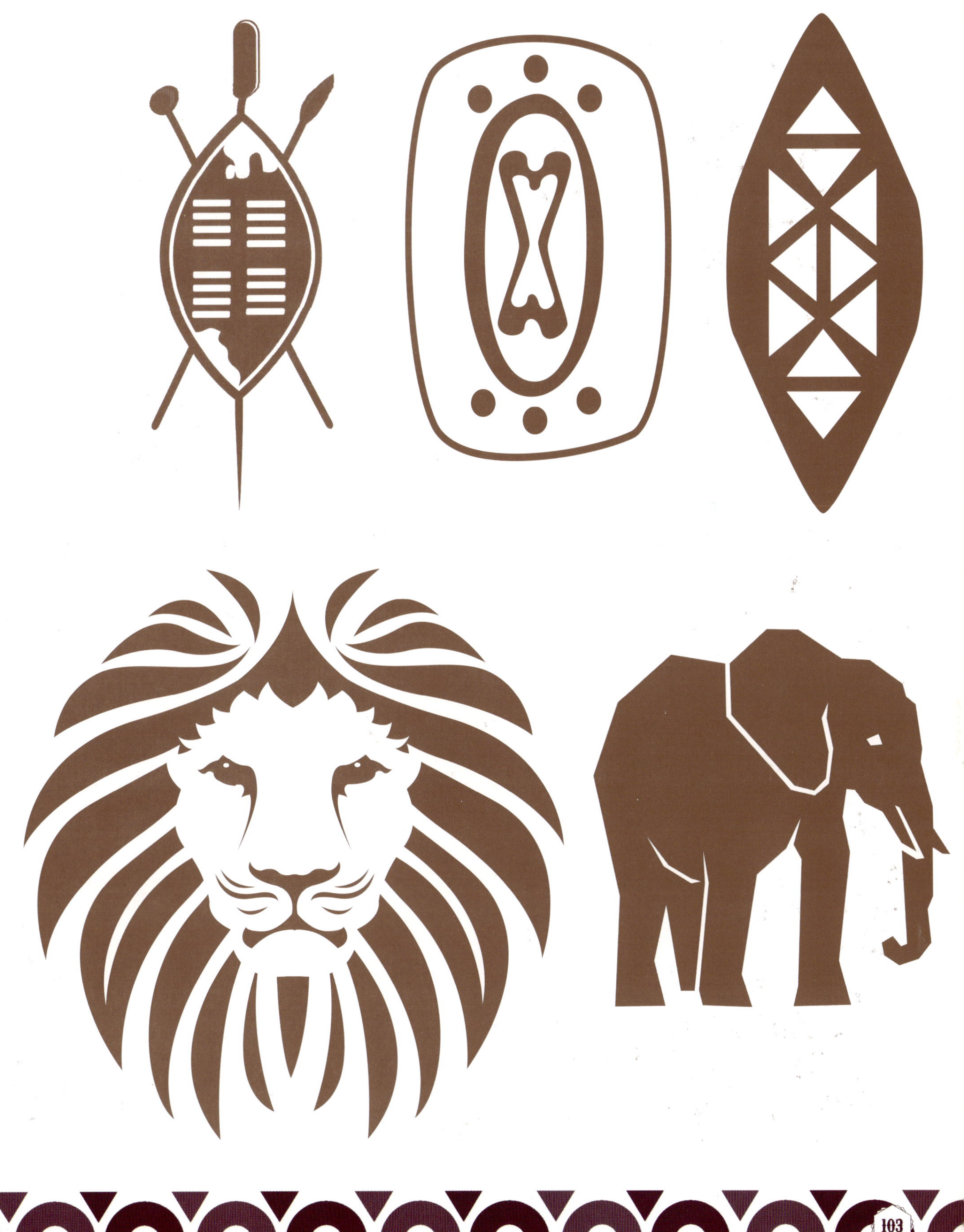

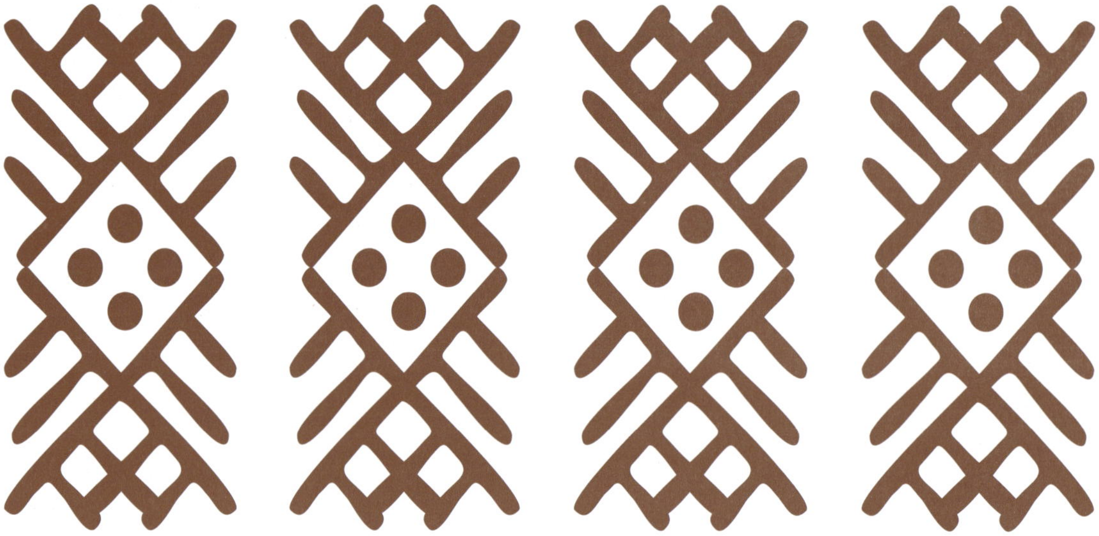

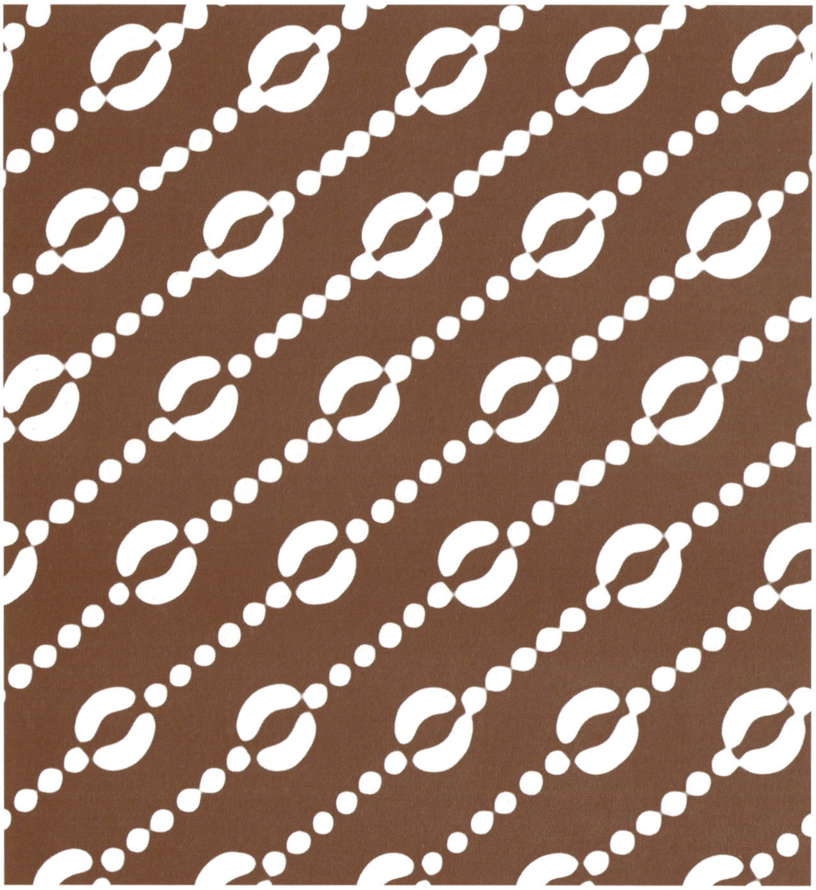

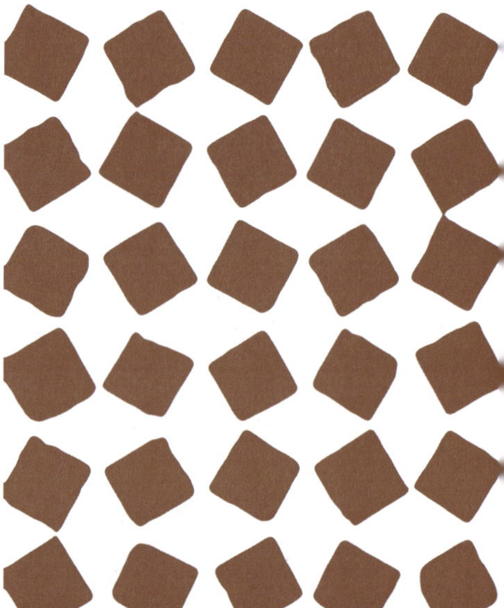

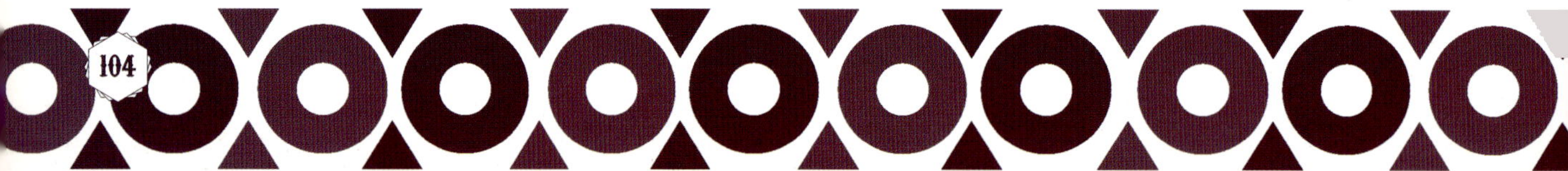

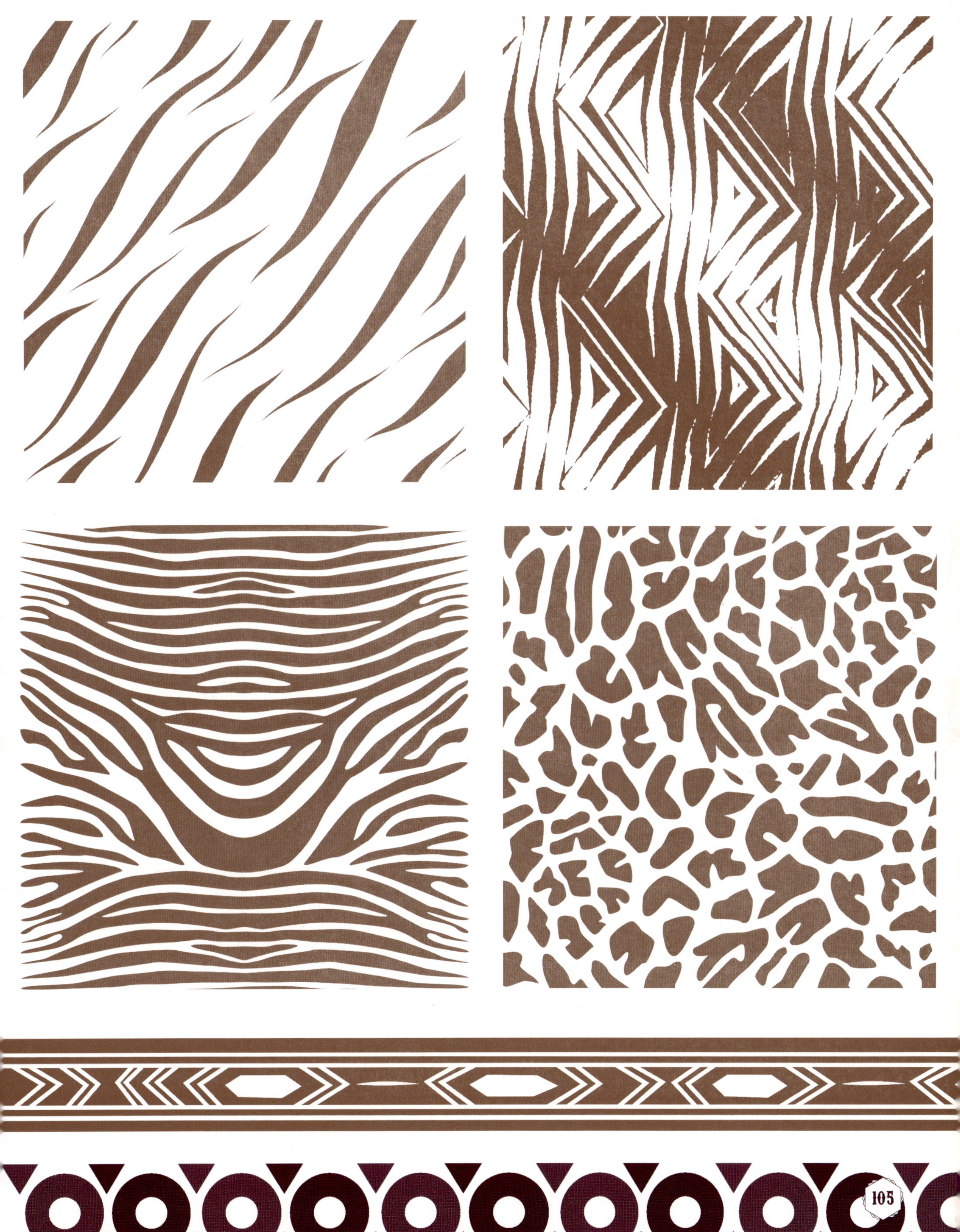

Geometric Patterns

Geometric patterns like these make beautiful body-art armbands. In Morocco, armbands are worn by both men and women.

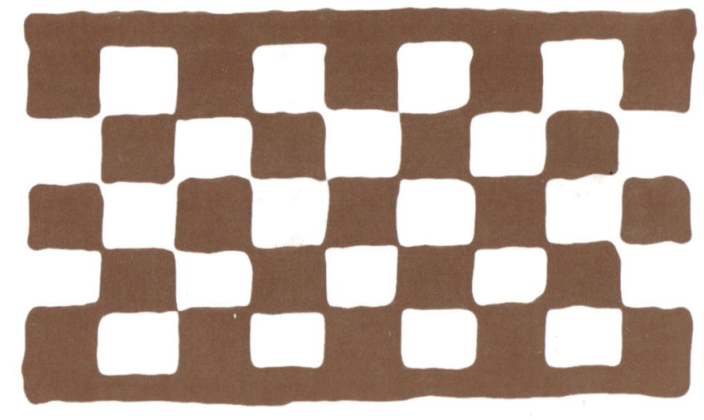

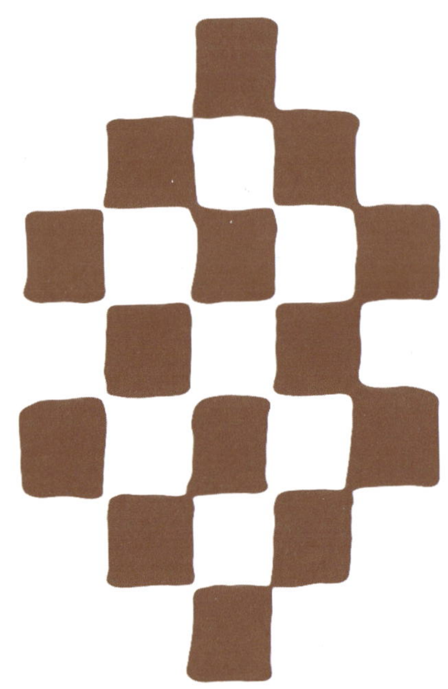

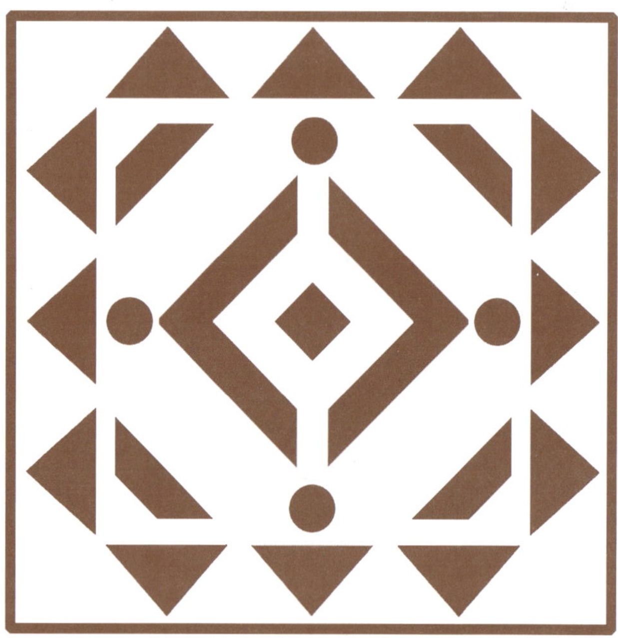

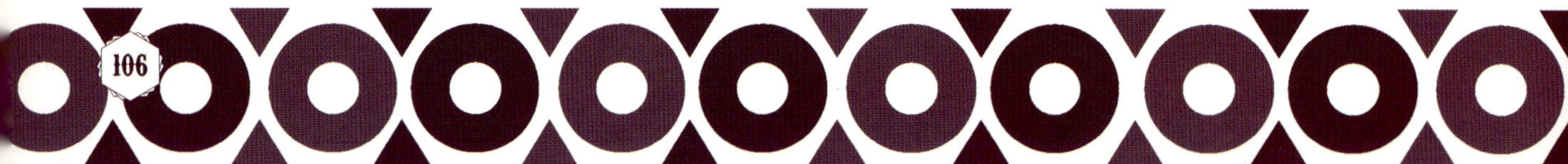

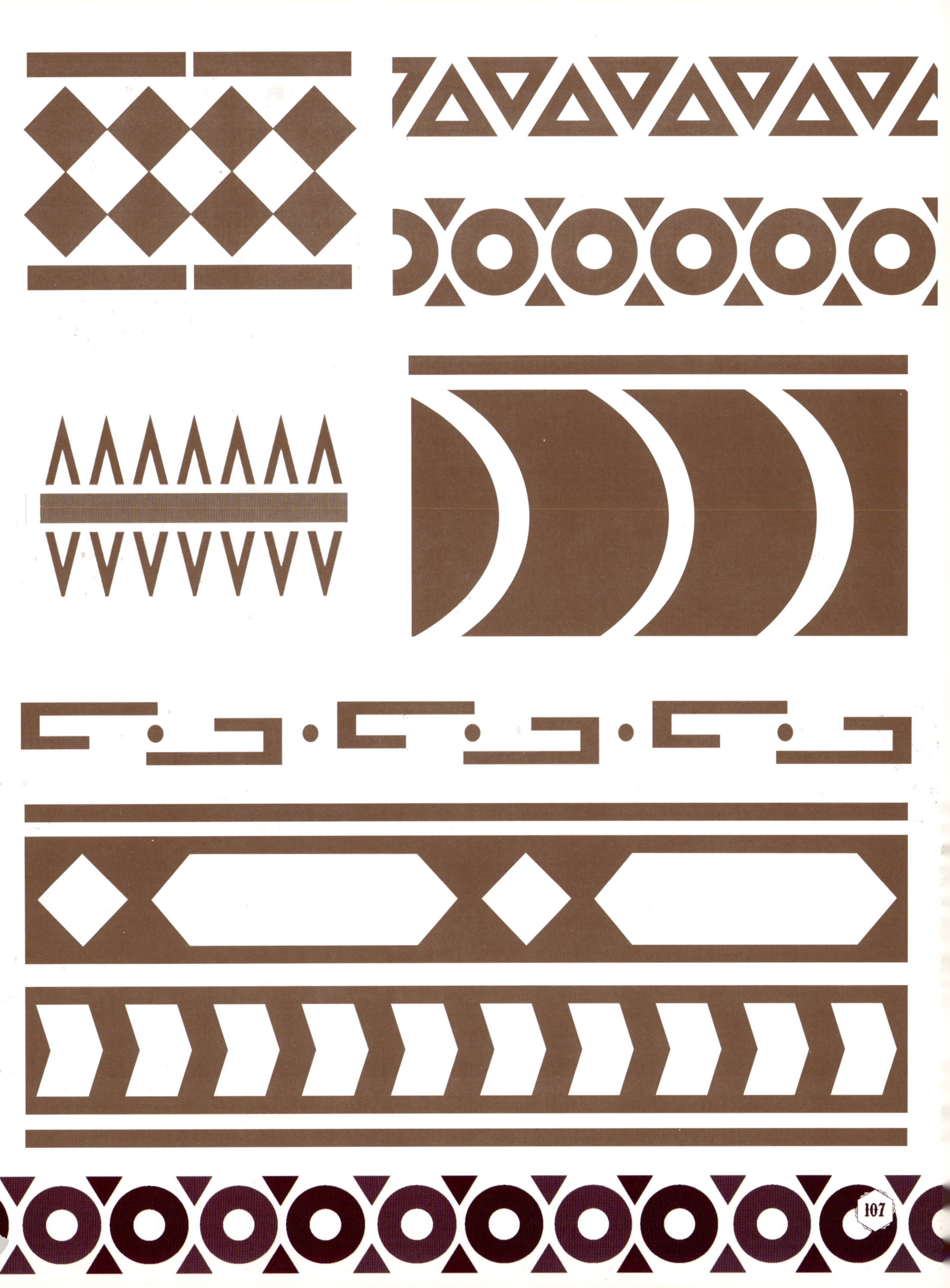

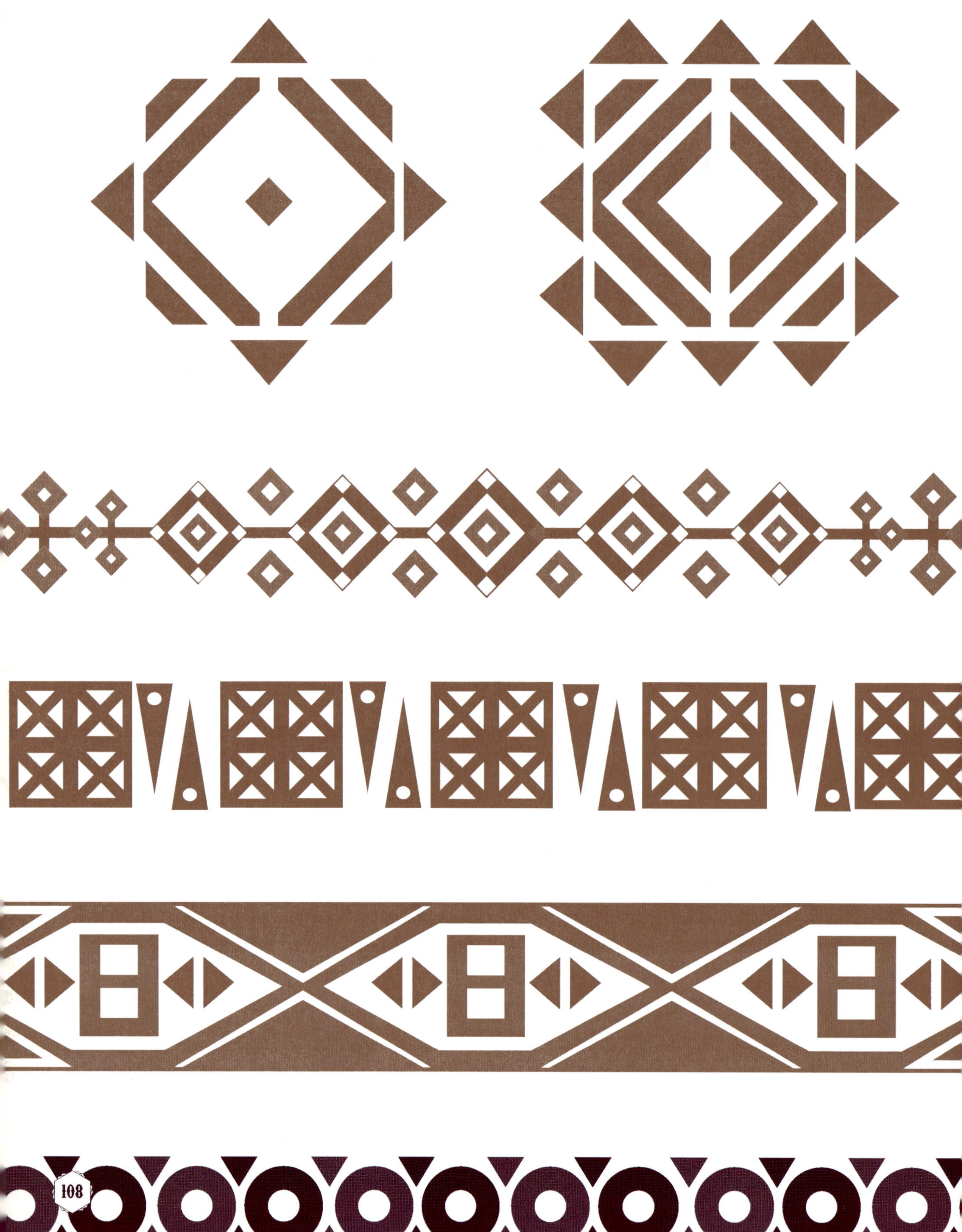

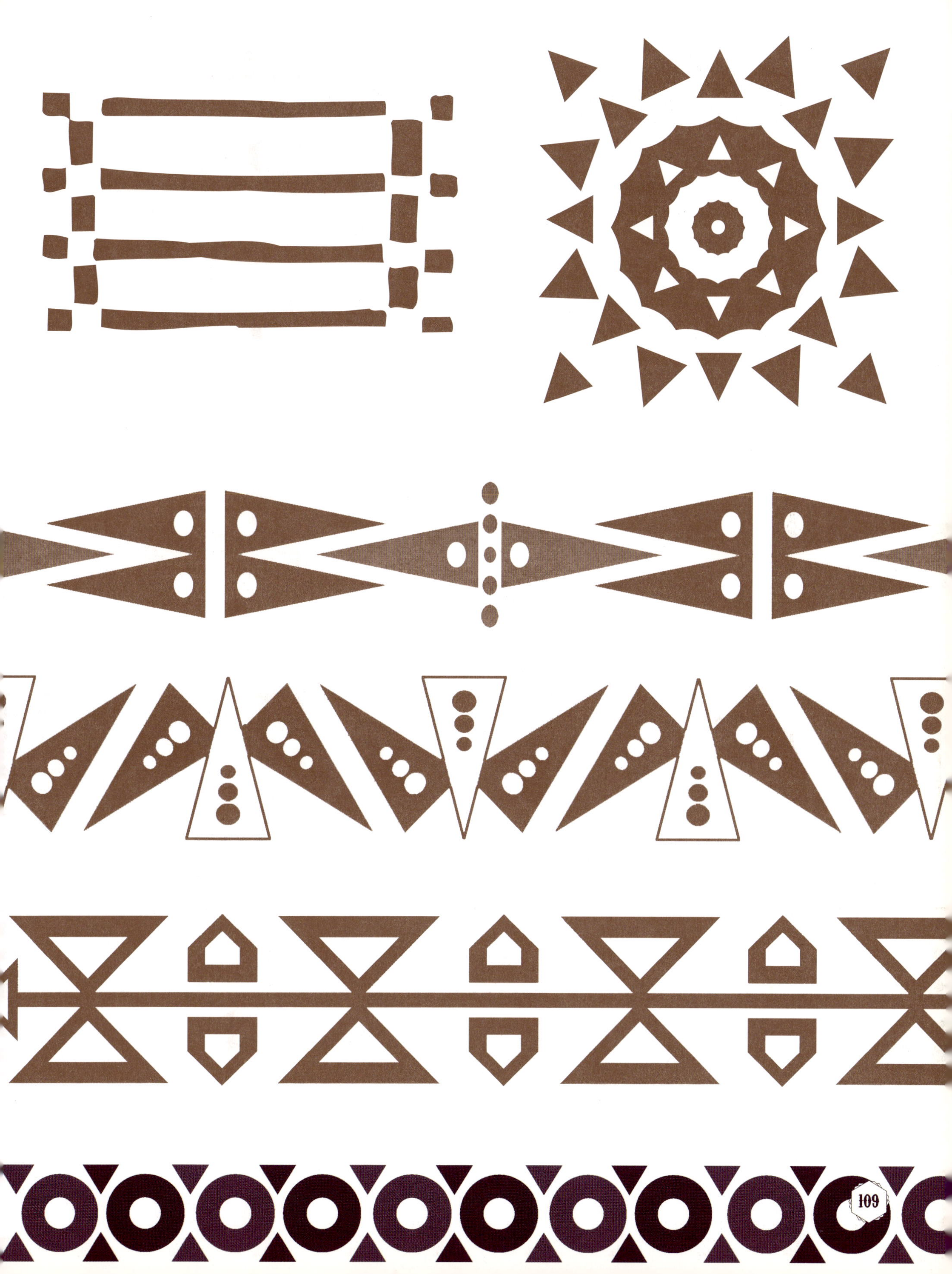

Motifs from Nature

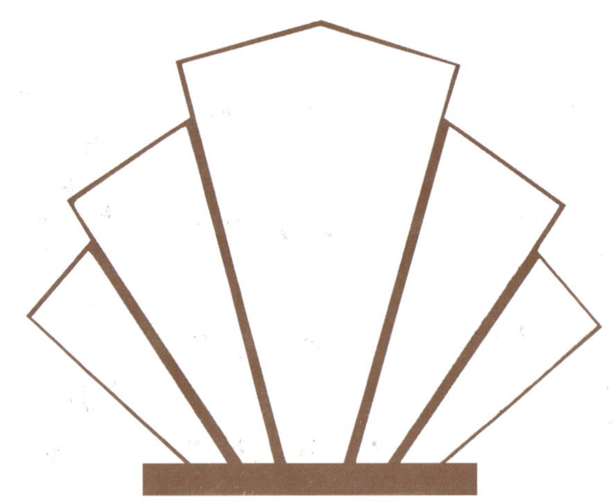

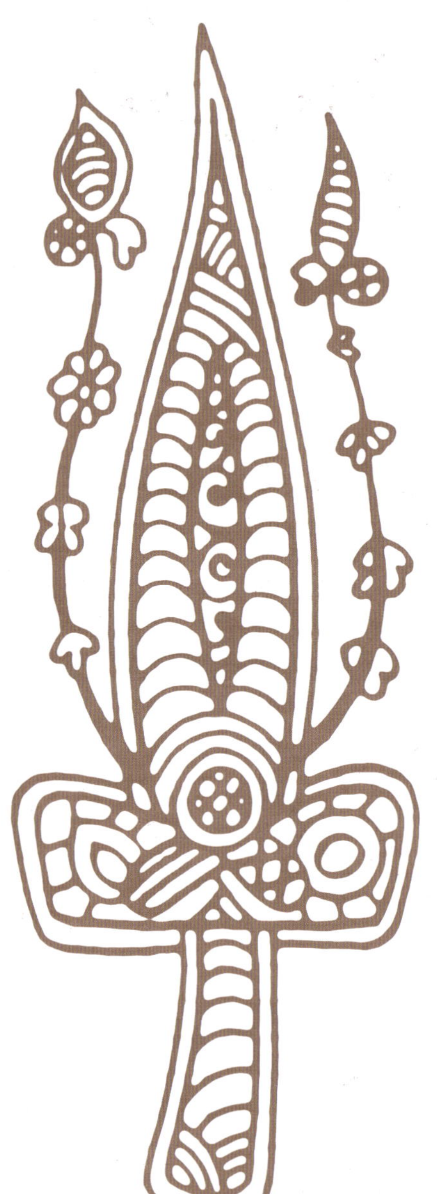

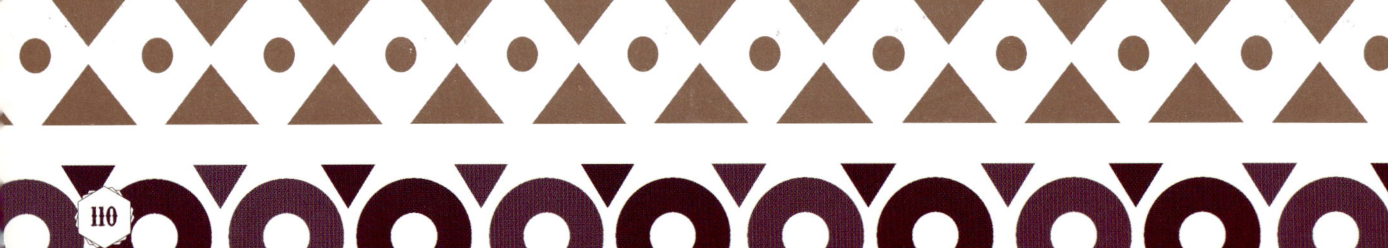

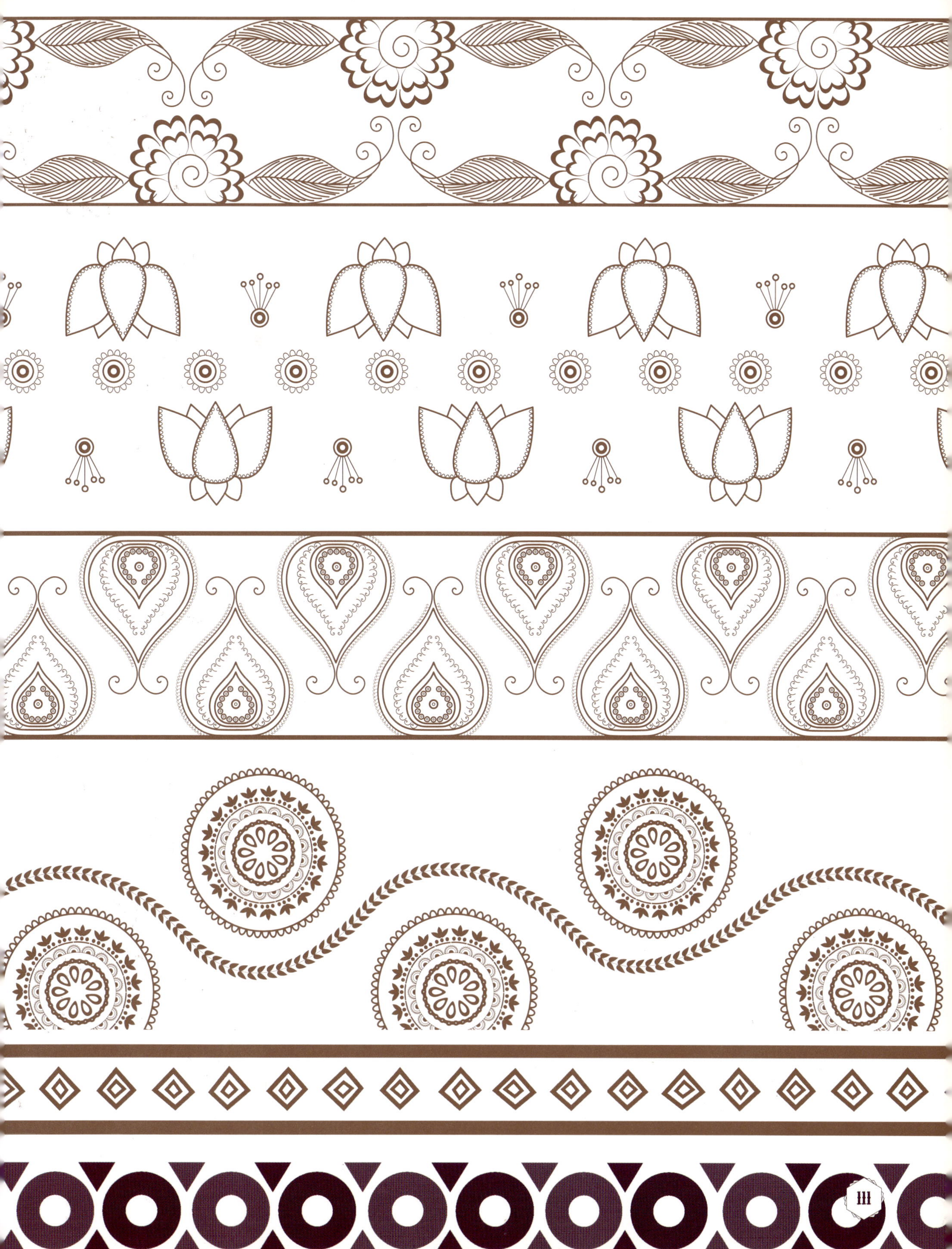

Heavenly Bodies

Imparting their cosmic powers to the wearer, representations of the full and crescent moon are feminine symbols of fertility. The sun symbol (the giver of life) and the cross (symbolizing the infinite space encompassed in all four directions) are ever present in northern African henna. Included in these pages are patterns for pregnant women and those who would like to be!

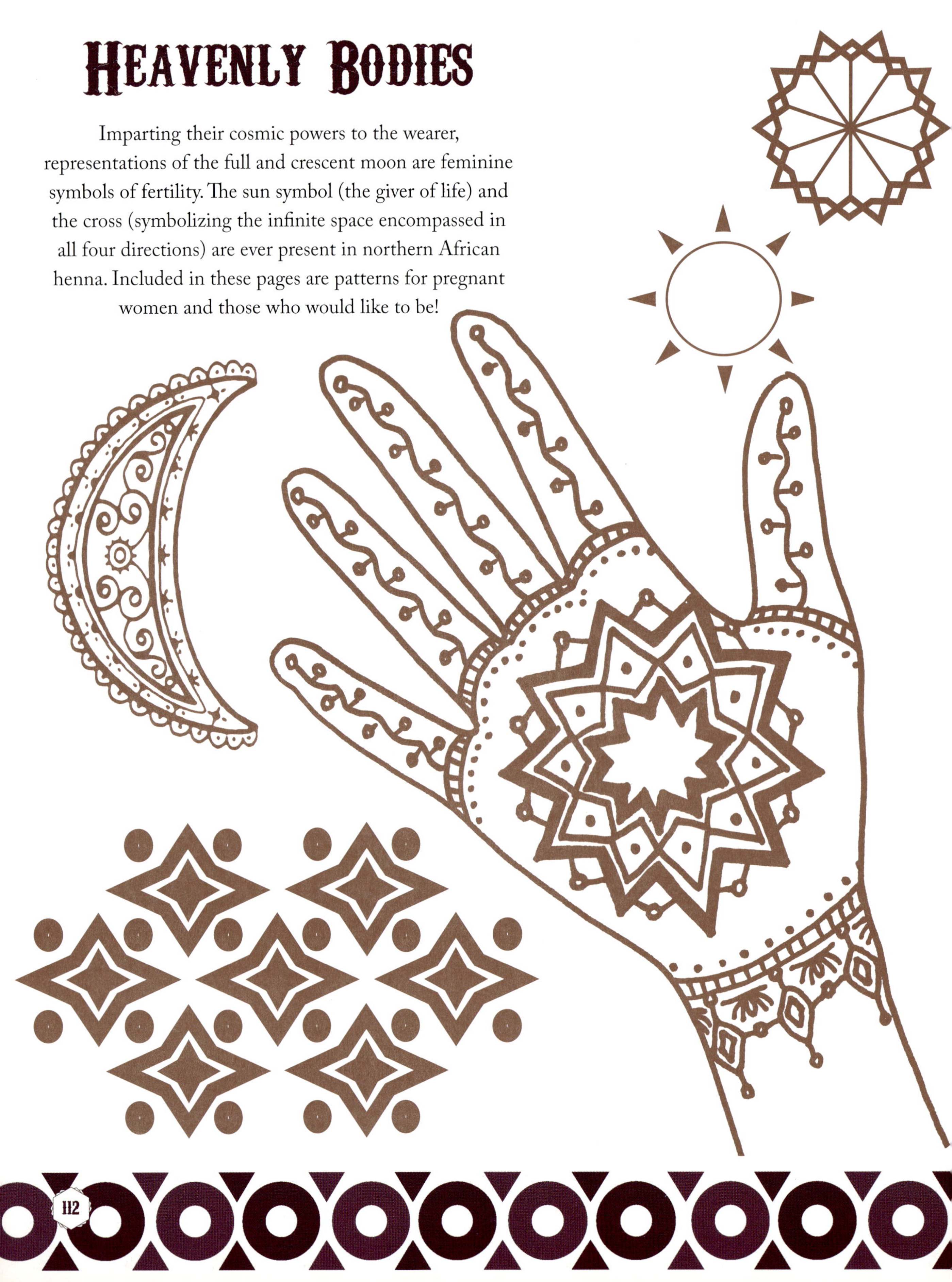

Adinkra Symbols

Inspired by the rich and varied flora and fauna of the African landscape, the Ashanti people of Ghana and Côte D'Ivoire created Adinkra, symbols that are meant to represent wise sayings or proverbs taken from their culture in addition to depicting familiar objects. Both decorative and meaningful, an Adinkra symbol is a worthy image for the personal expression of henna body art.

"Except for God"

Yellow flowered plant

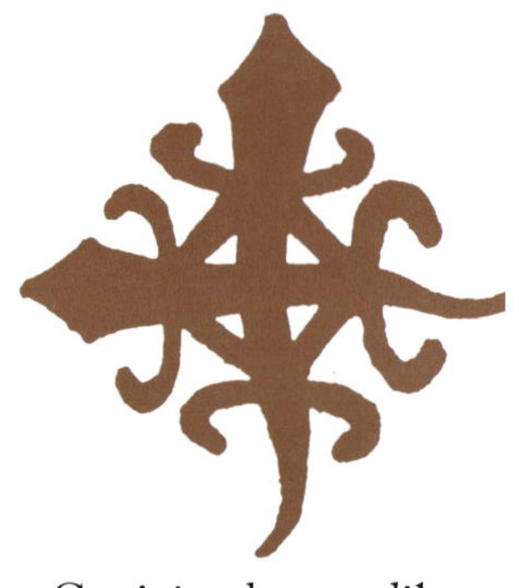

Conjoined crocodiles

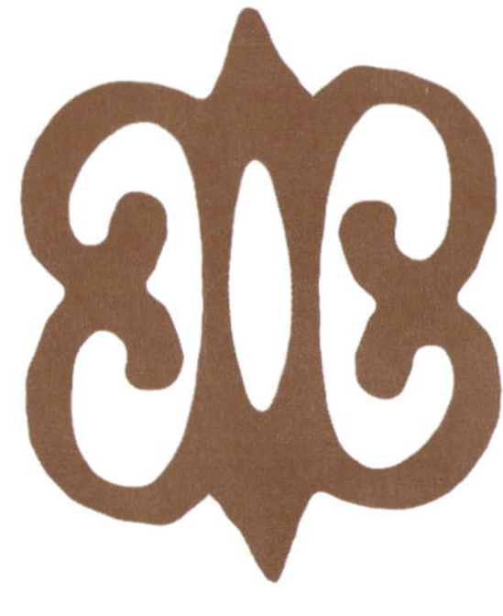

"That which does not burn"

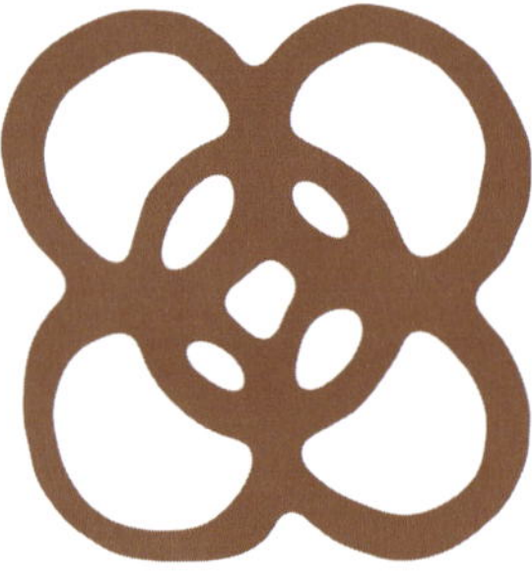

Puffed up extravagance

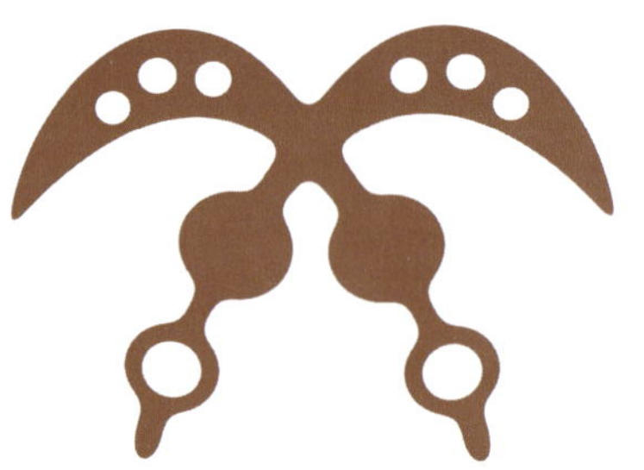

Sword of war

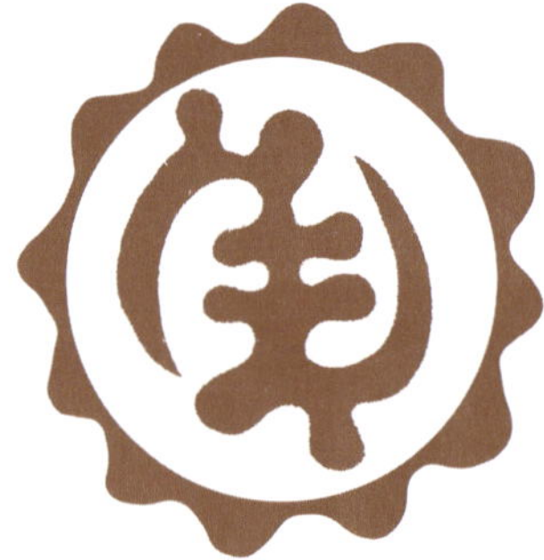

"God is king"

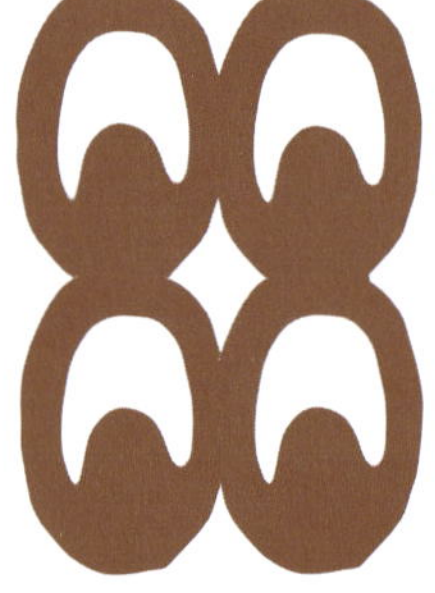

"What I hear I keep"

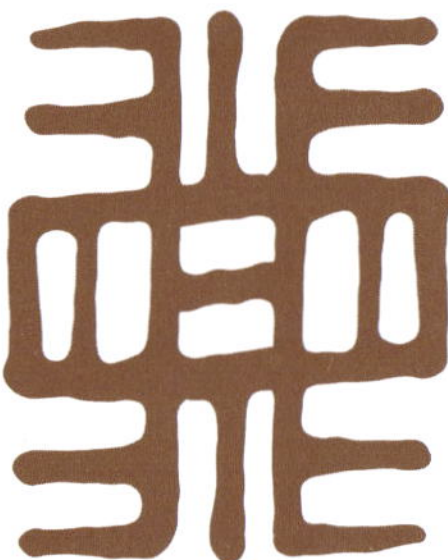

"He who does not know can know from learning"

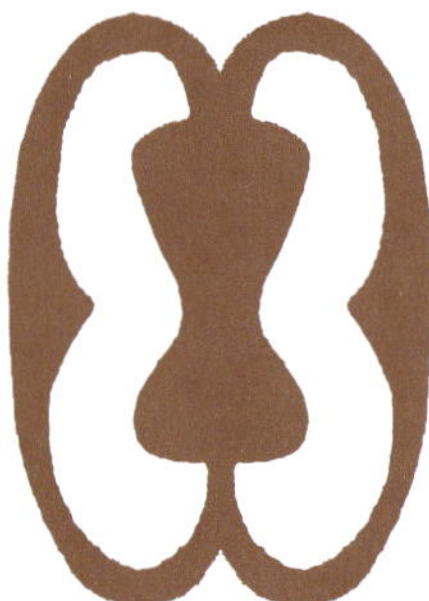

Chain link

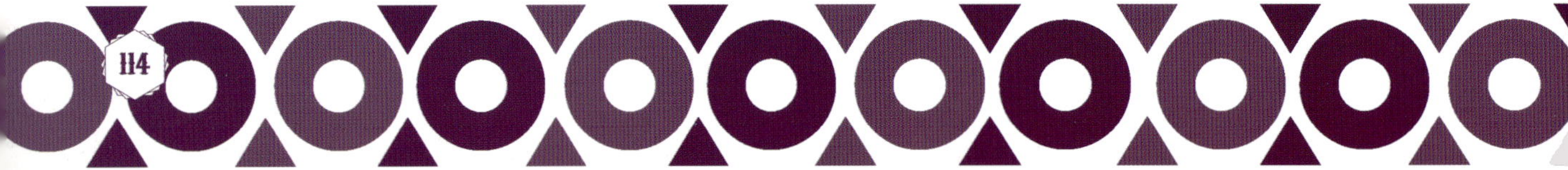

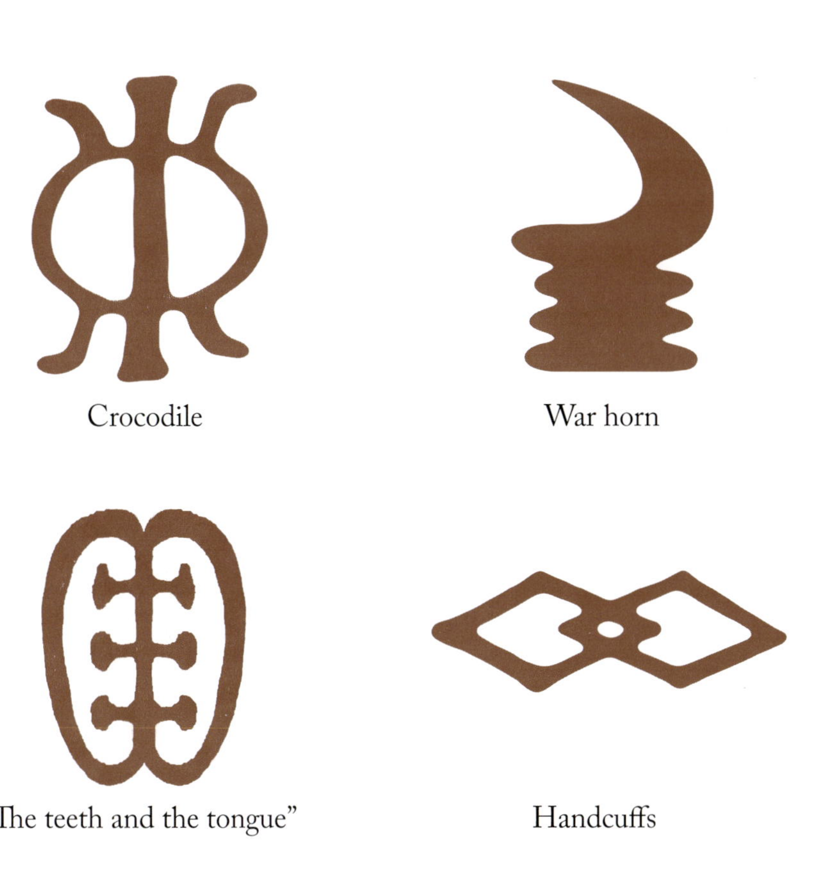

Crocodile

War horn

Independence

"The teeth and the tongue"

Handcuffs

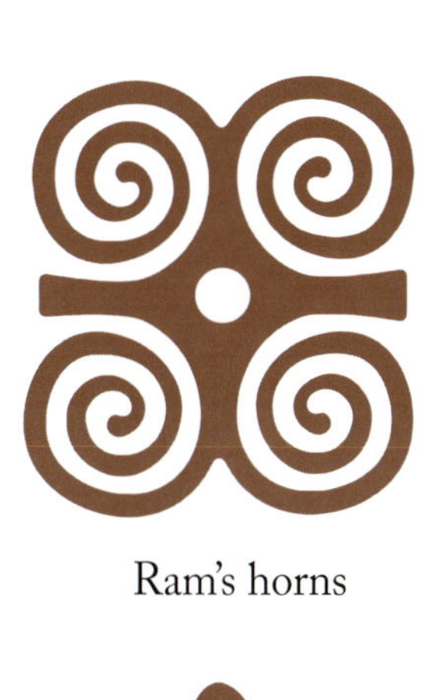

Ram's horns

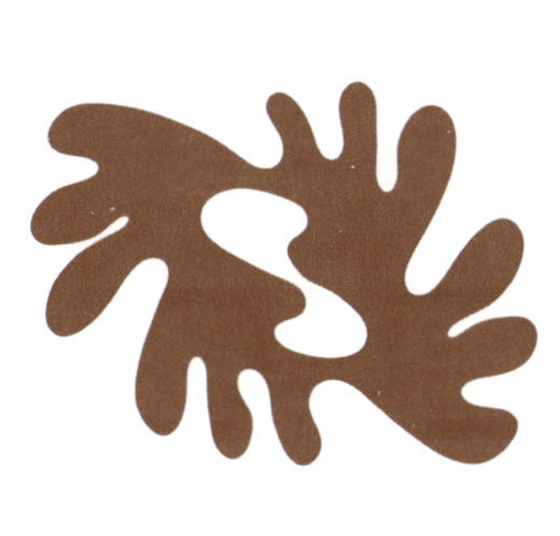

"No one should bite the other"

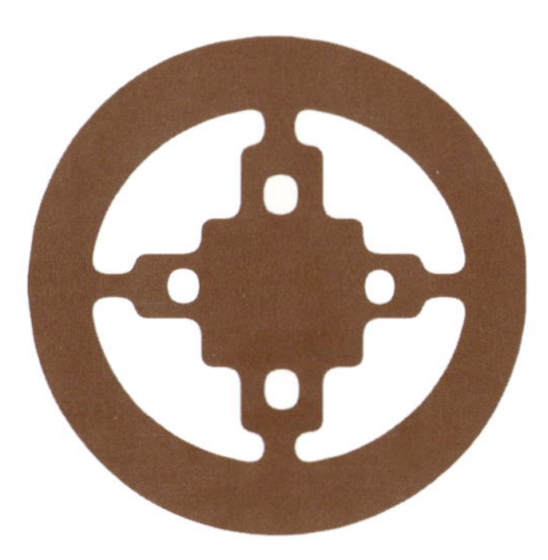

Dame-Dame game

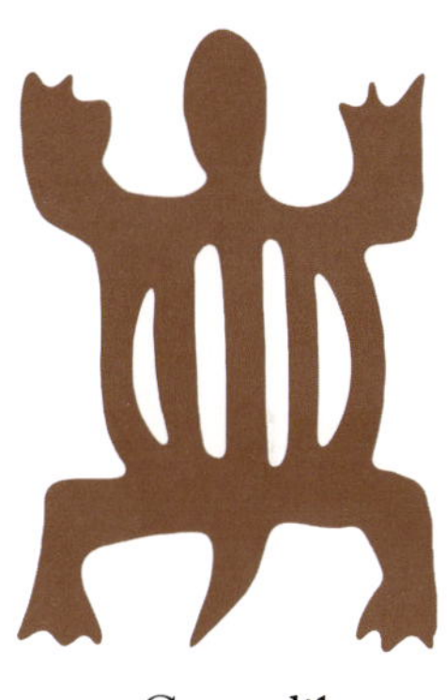

Crocodile

Sack of cola nuts

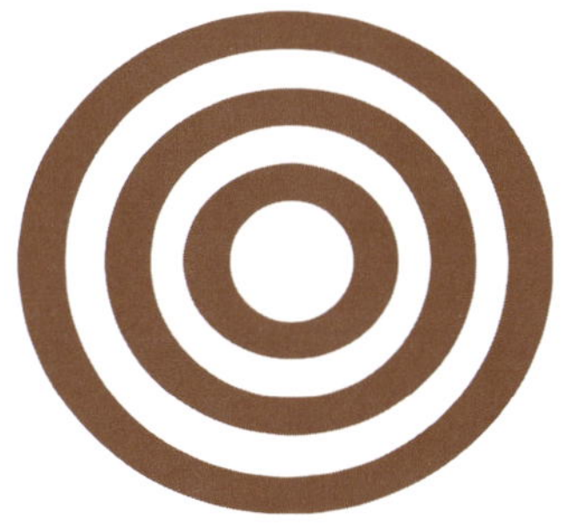

Chief of the Adinkra symbols

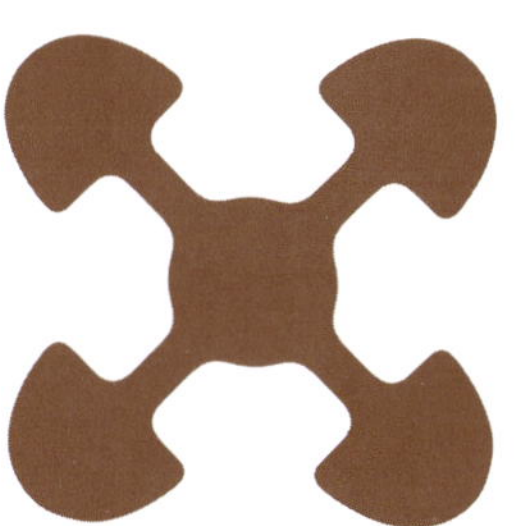

Linked hearts

Tree of God

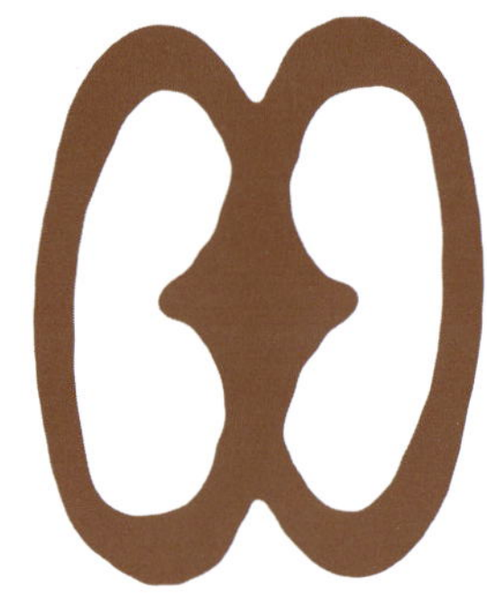

"God is in the heavens"

"God never dies, therefore I cannot die

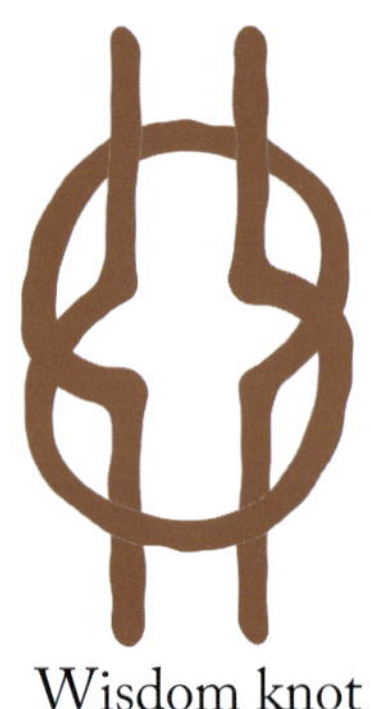

Wisdom knot

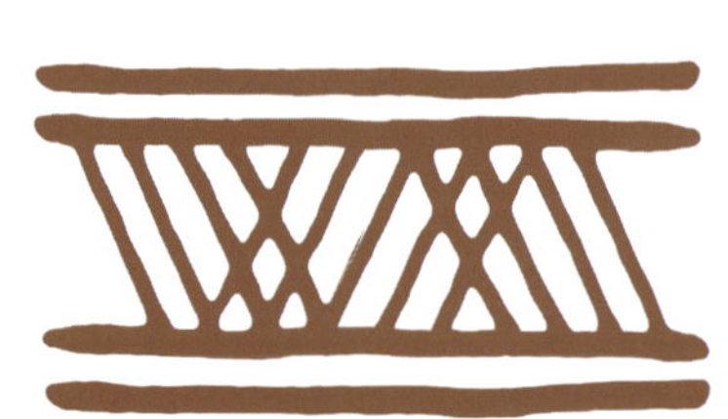

Snake climbing the raffia tree

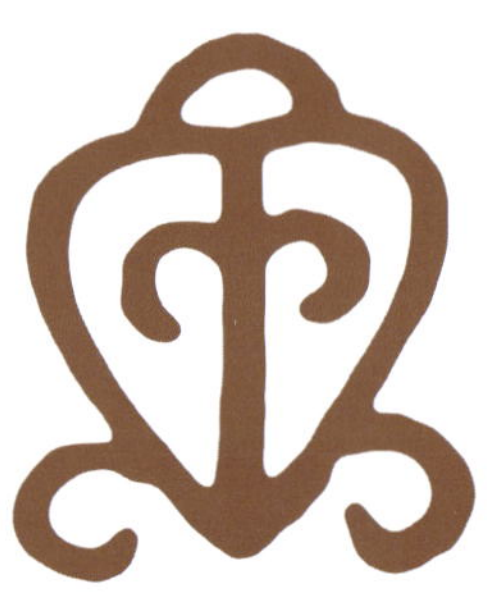

"Love never loses its way home"

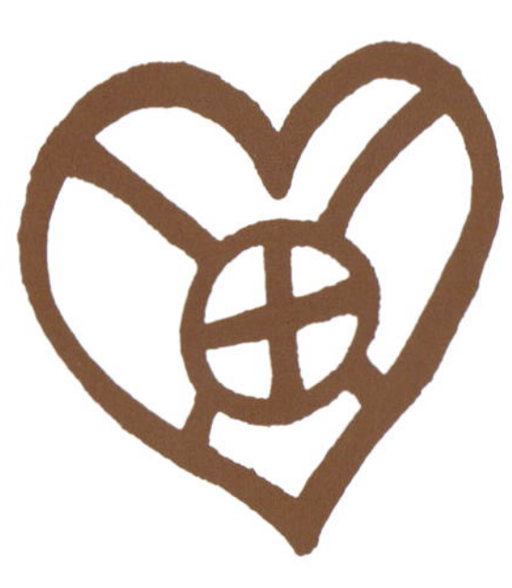

"By God's grace all will be well"

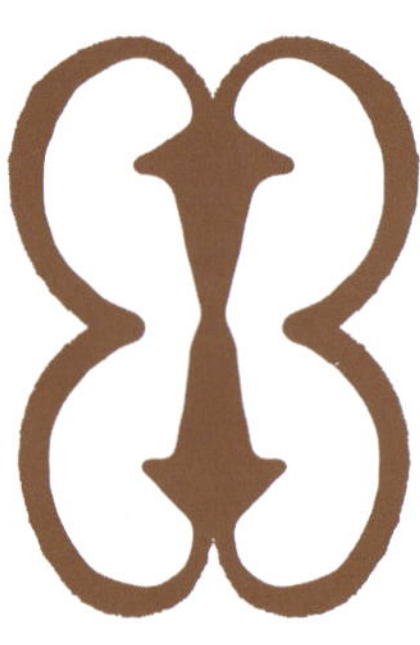

"Sew in readiness"

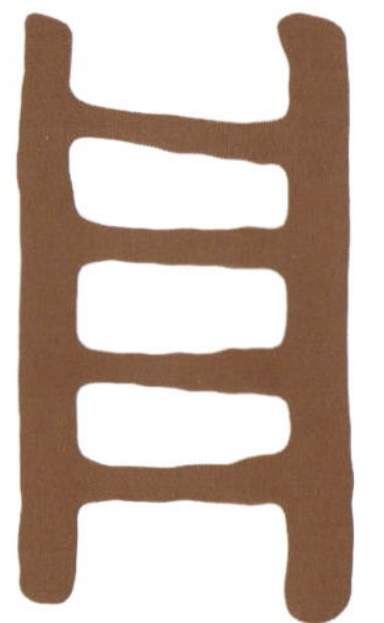

The ladder of death

The moon and the star

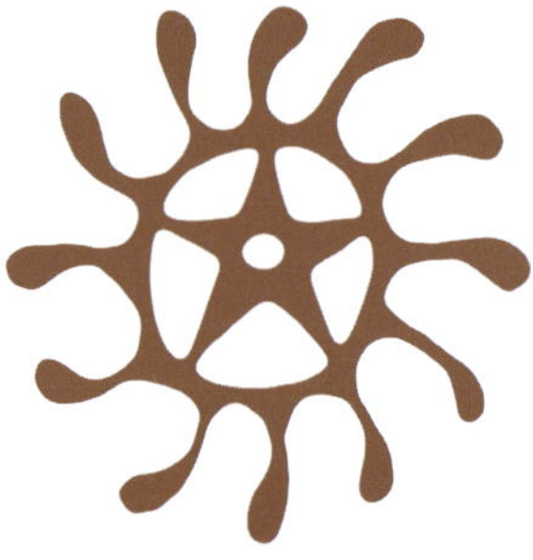

"Change or transform your character"

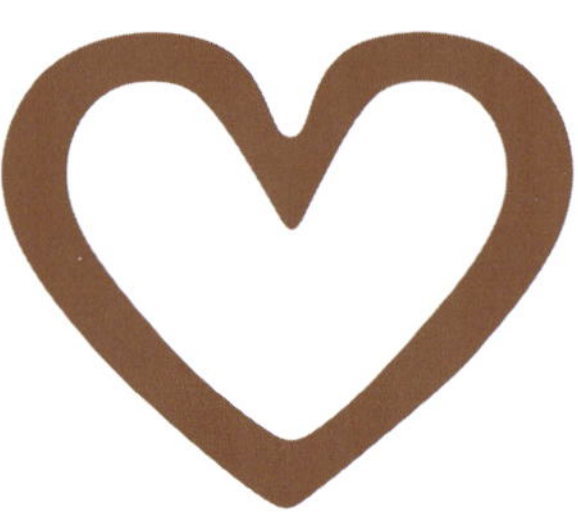

The heart

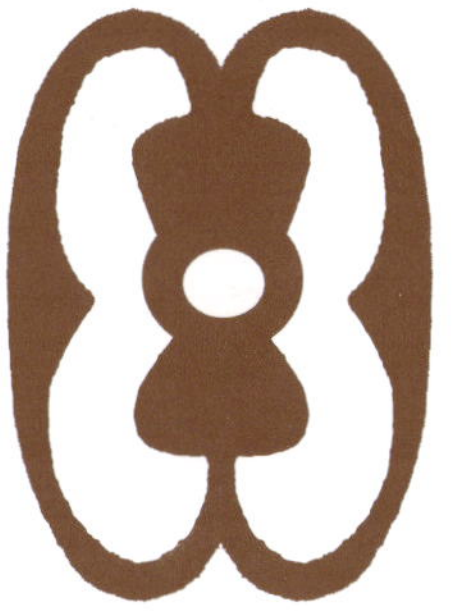

"If your hands are in the dish"

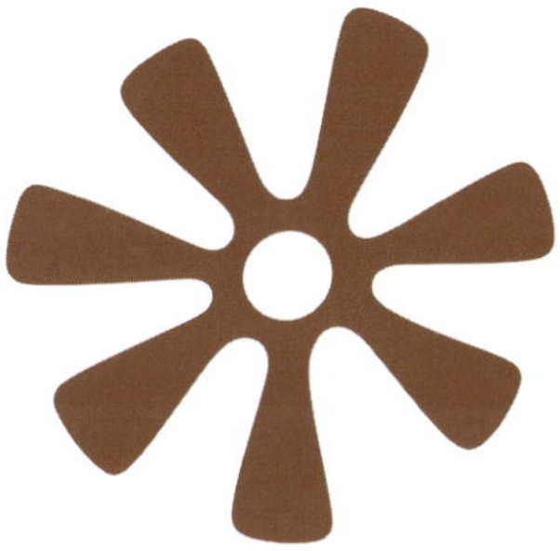

Spider's web

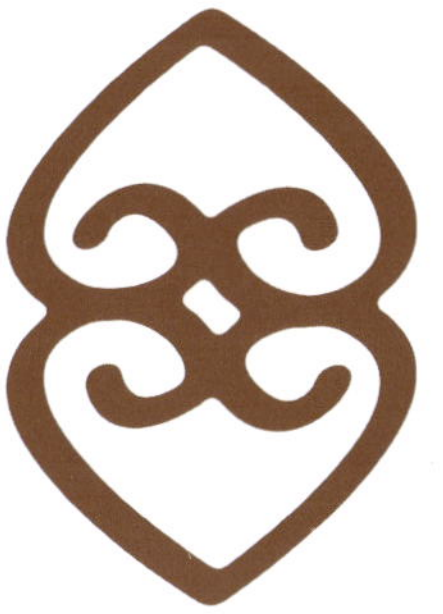

"The Earth has weight"

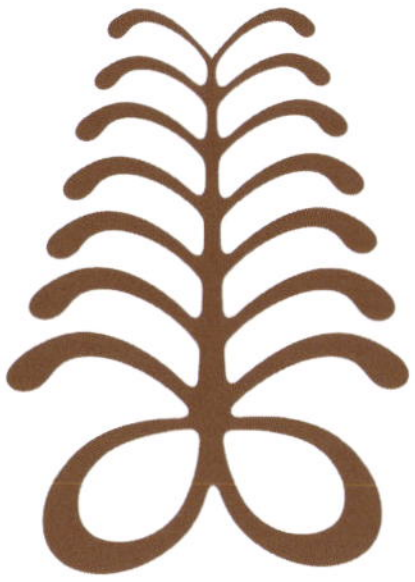

Fern

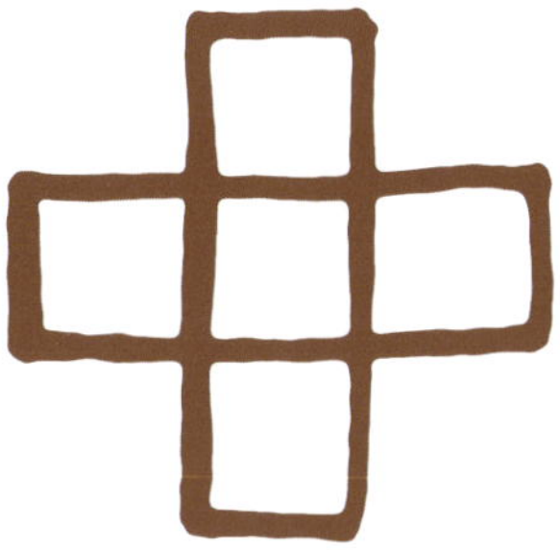

Bird

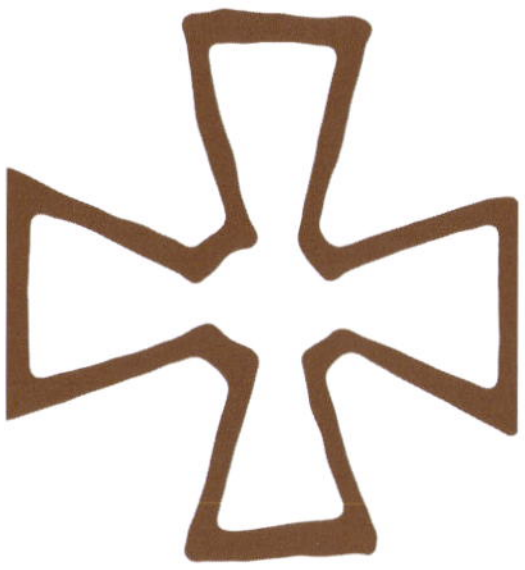

Cross

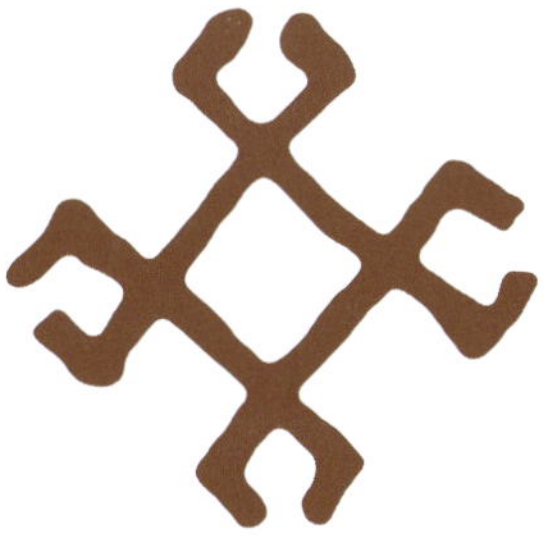

Spider

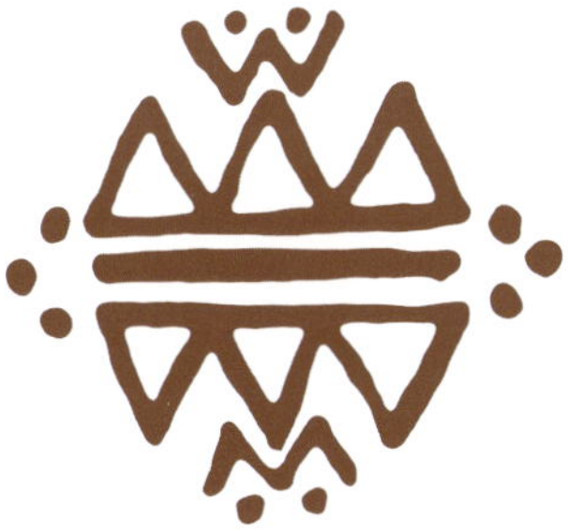

Ship

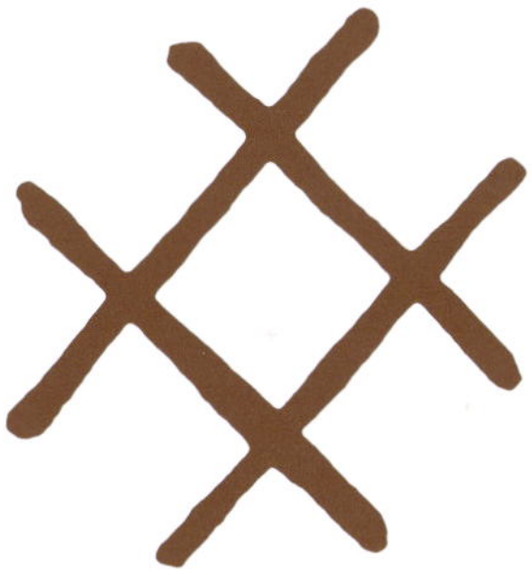

Finger

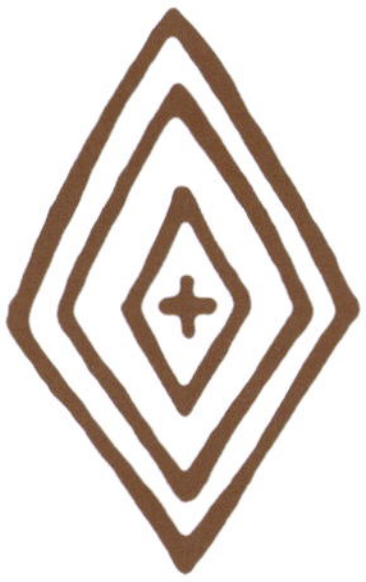

Eye

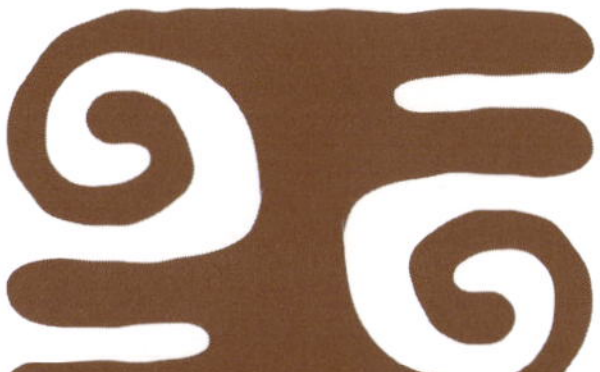

Hairstyle of an Ashanti war champion

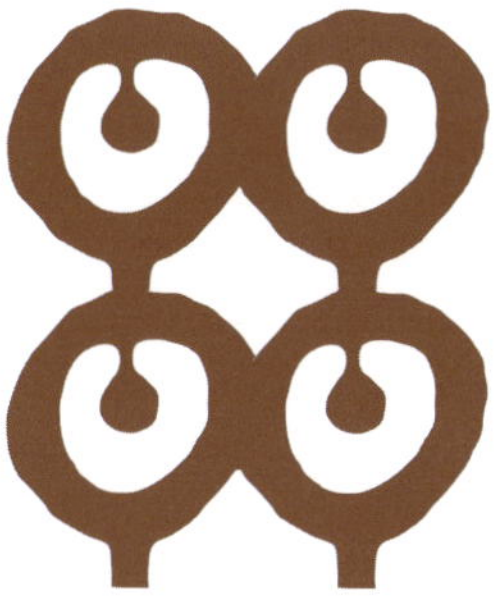

"I shall marry you"

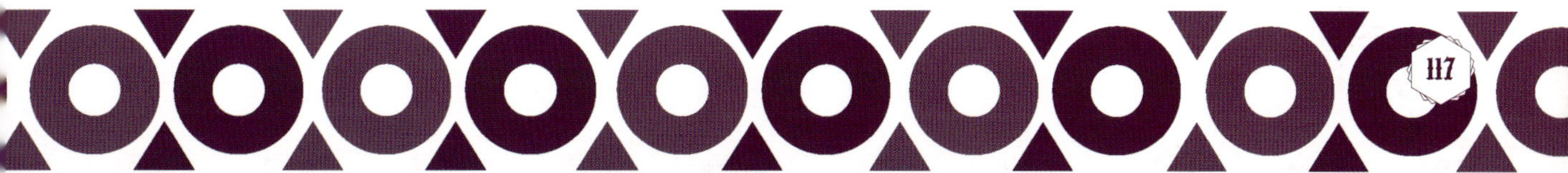

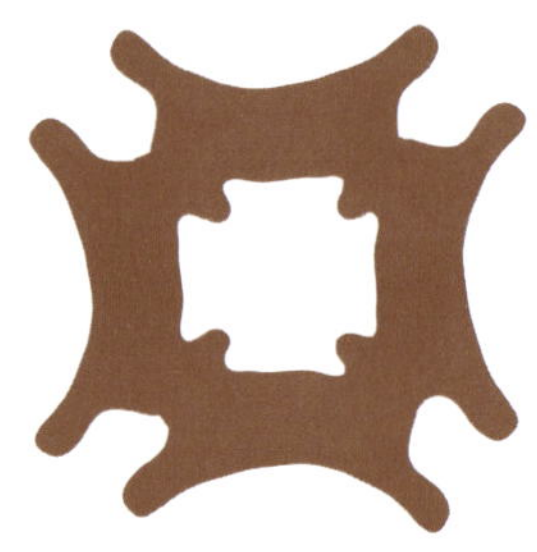

House

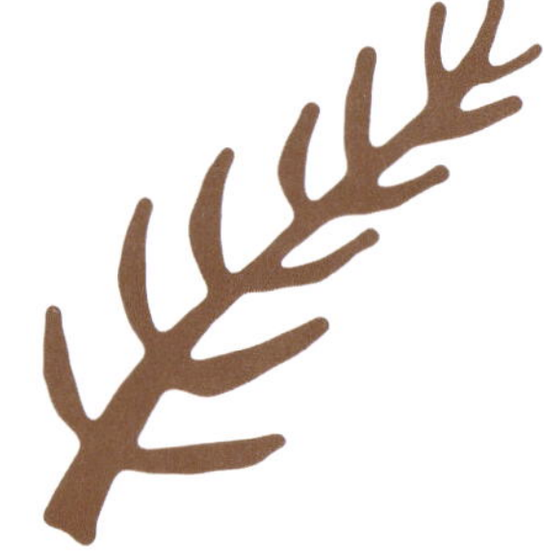

"By God's grace"

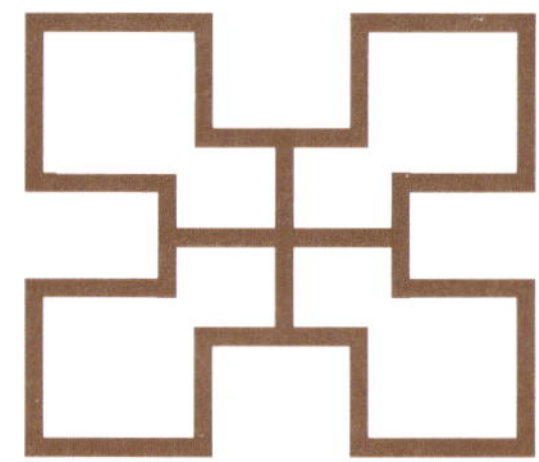

Nsaa fabric

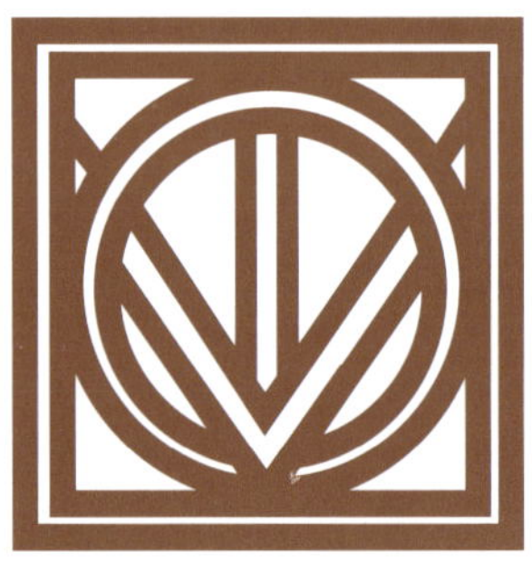

"He who wants to be king"

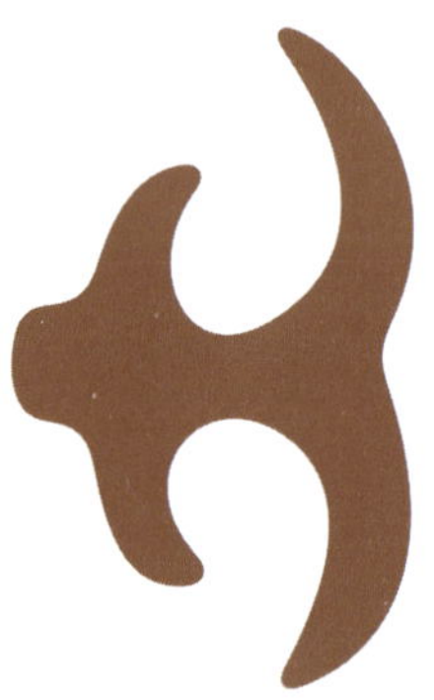

Leg of a hen

"The enemy will stew in his own juice"

"That which removes bad luck"

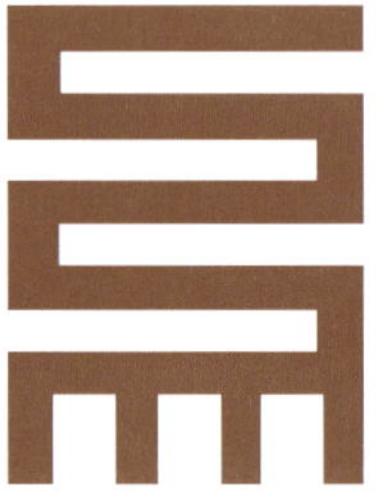

Twisting

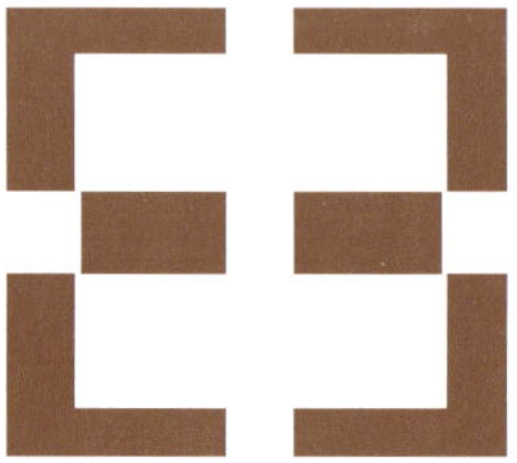

"When you climb a good tree"

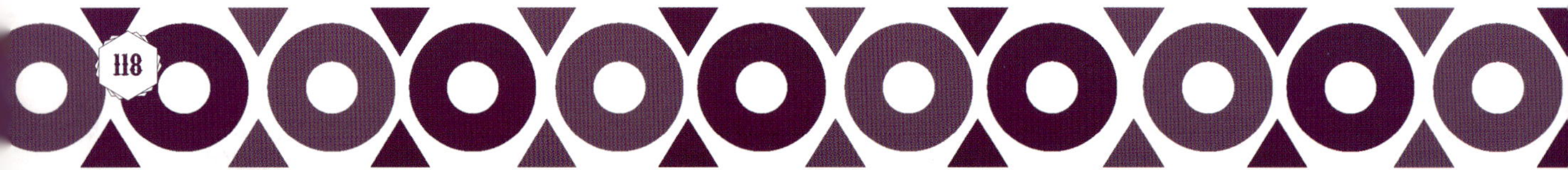

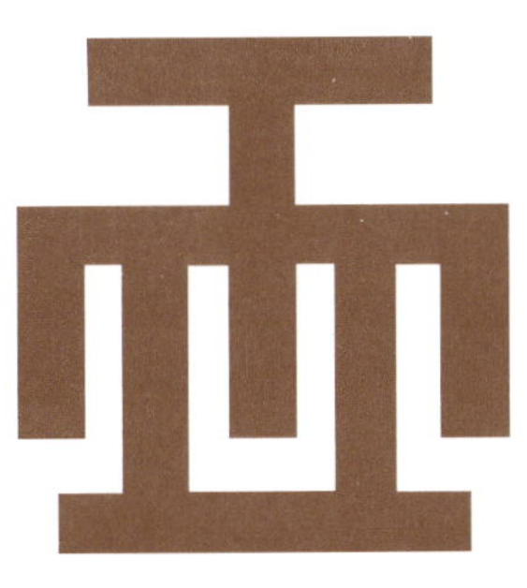

Measuring stick

"Return and get it"

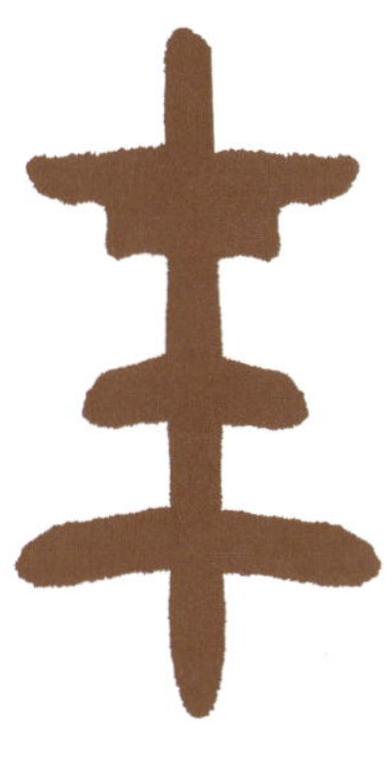

Eagle talons

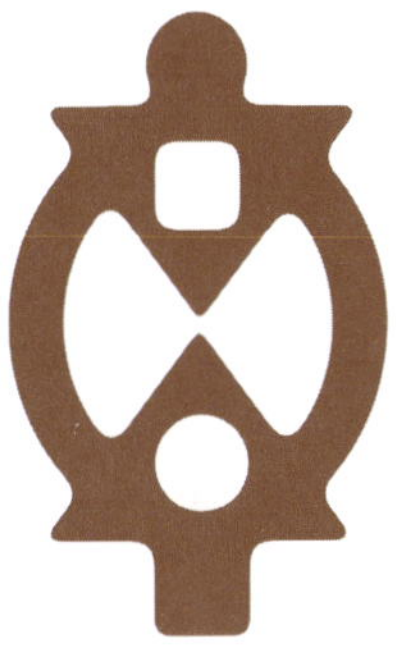

"Help each other"

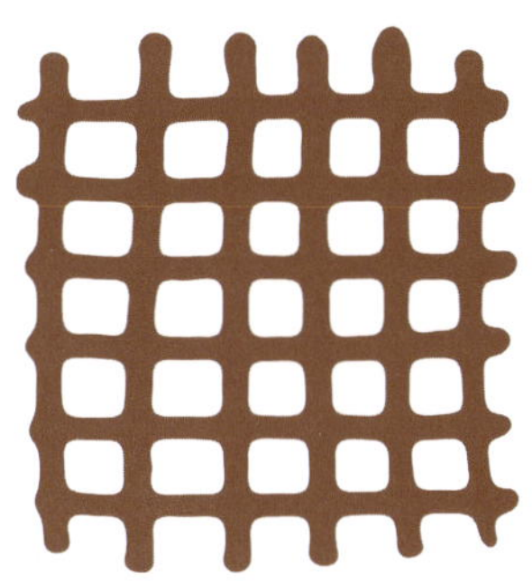

Good bed

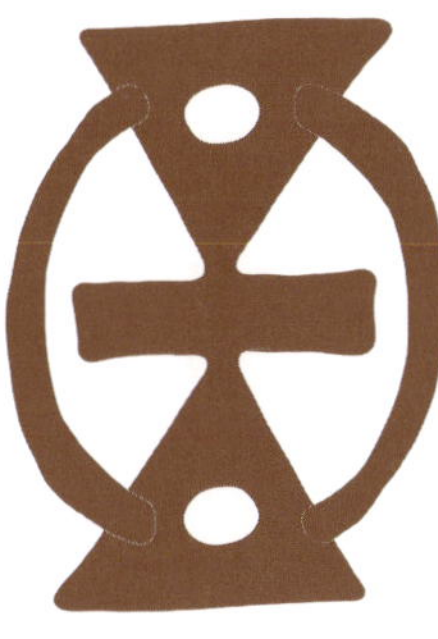

"Time changes"

Wooden comb

Star

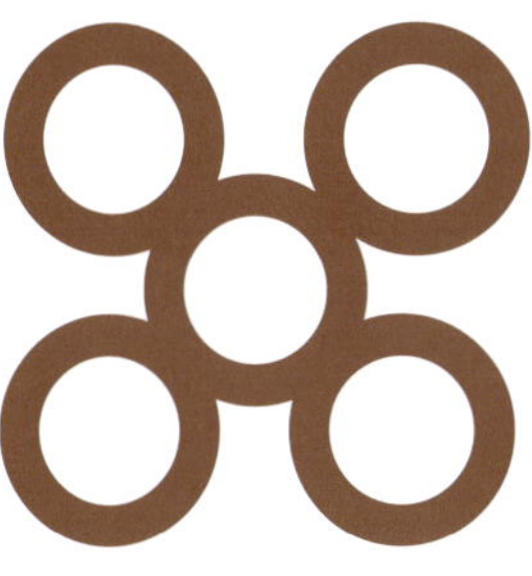

"Five tufts of hair"

Egyptian Symbols

Henna was used primarily as a hair dye in dynastic Egypt. Traces of henna were found on the mummified pharaohs buried in their ancient tombs. Buried with the bodies were magical charms and amulets to protect them in the afterlife. Egyptians assigned magical properties to hundreds of objects to protect them from every misfortune. From disease, to reptile and insect bites, to infertility and the evil eye, there was a specific protective amulet to counteract each threat.

Ancient Egyptian motifs are striking though nontraditional subjects for henna body art. The distinctive art gracing the pyramid walls—from the scarab to the Ankh, to the eye of Horus—provides henna artists with a wealth of evocative symbols.

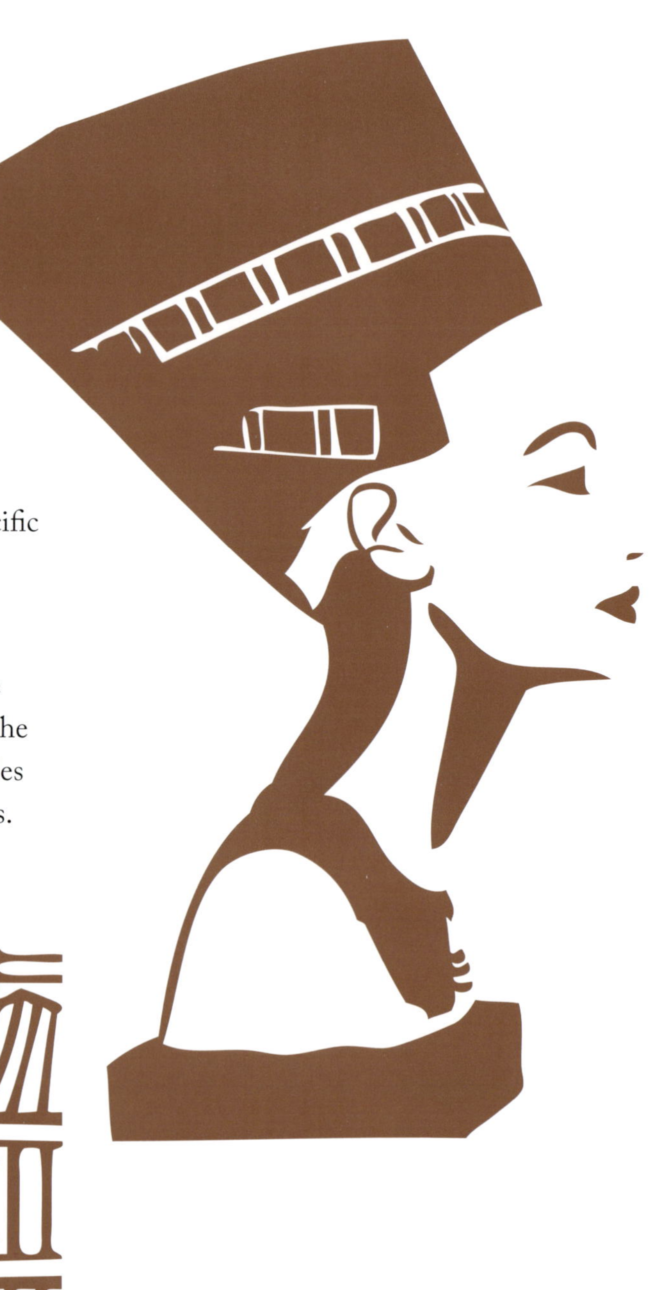

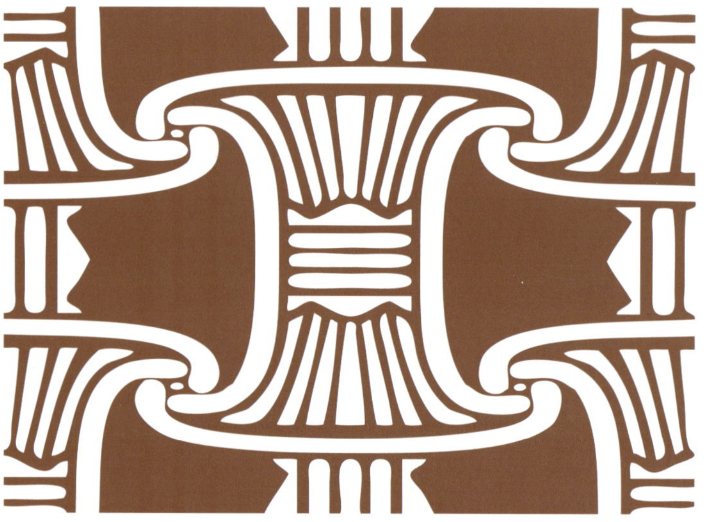

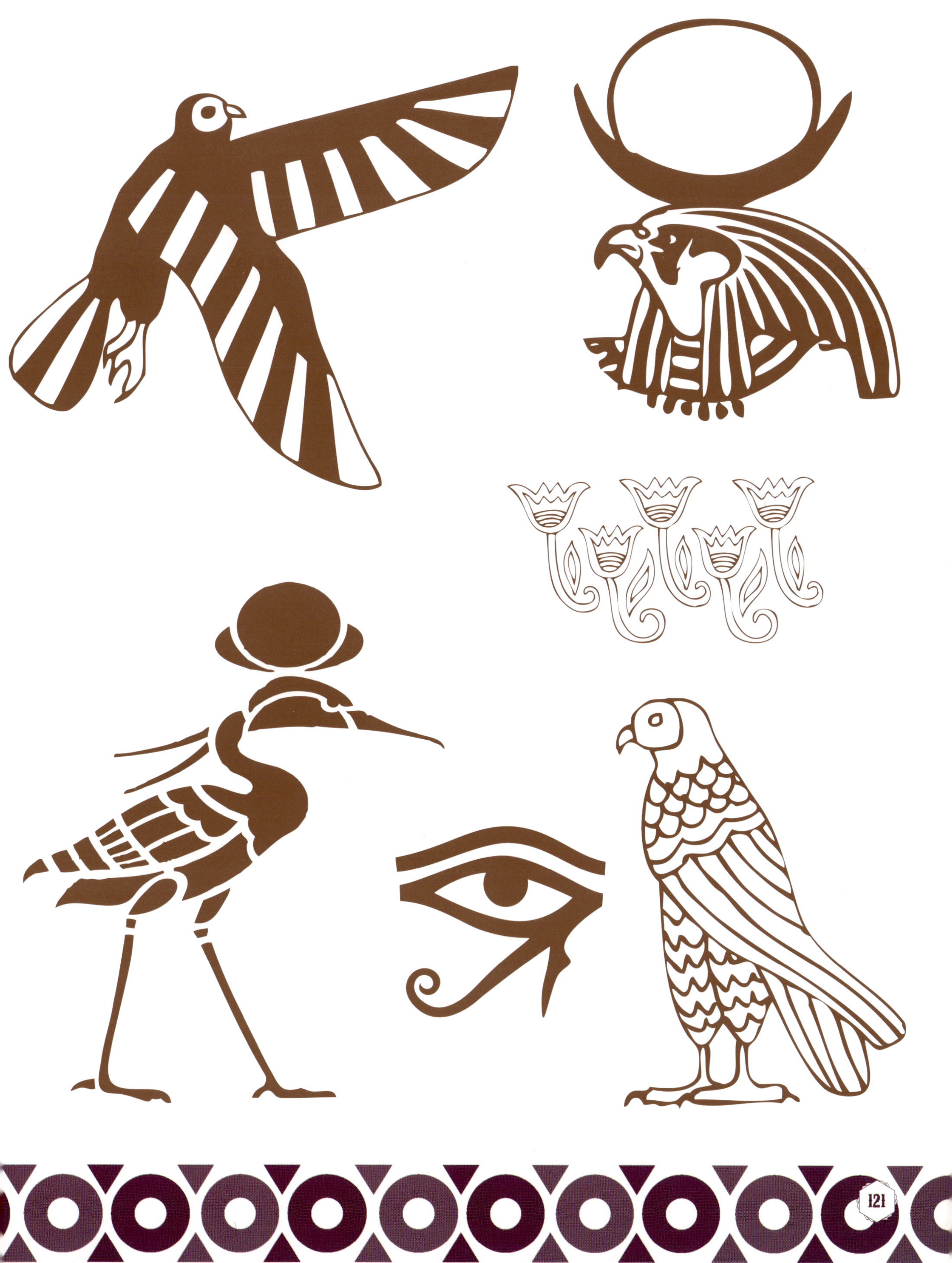

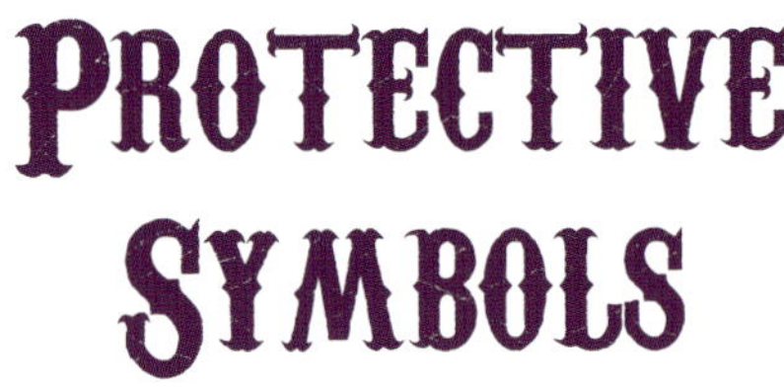

Protective Symbols

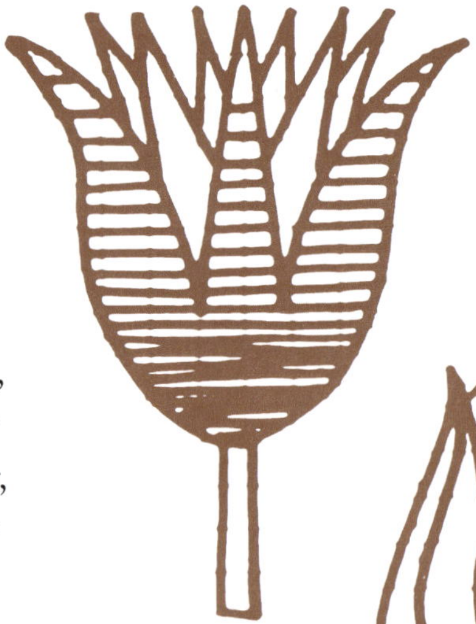

The ankh, one of the most powerful protective symbols, unites the female loop with the male to form the most sacred symbol representing eternal life. The lotus flower, the scarab, and the knot of Isis, are also sacred symbols that figure prominently in Egyptian art.

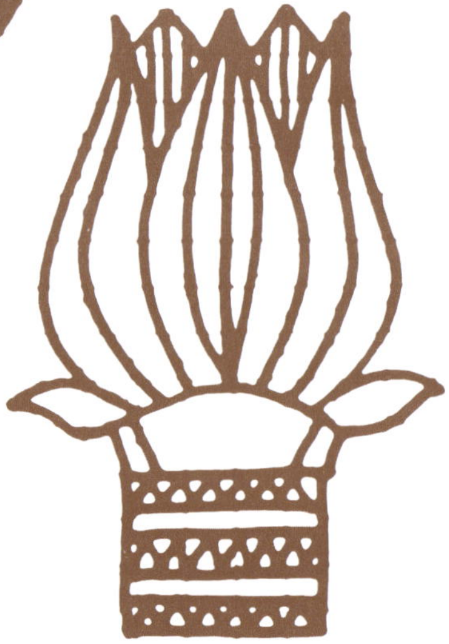

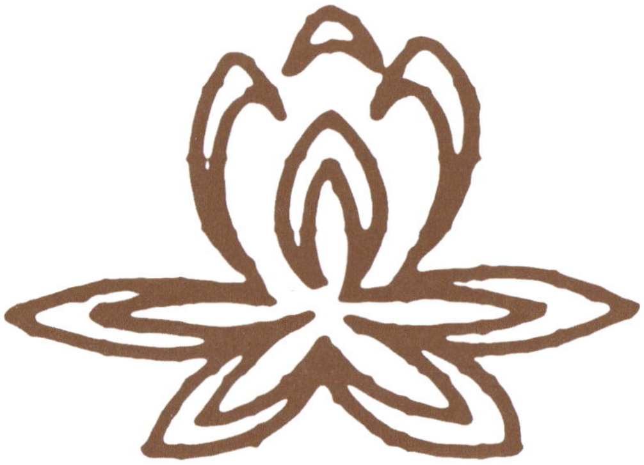

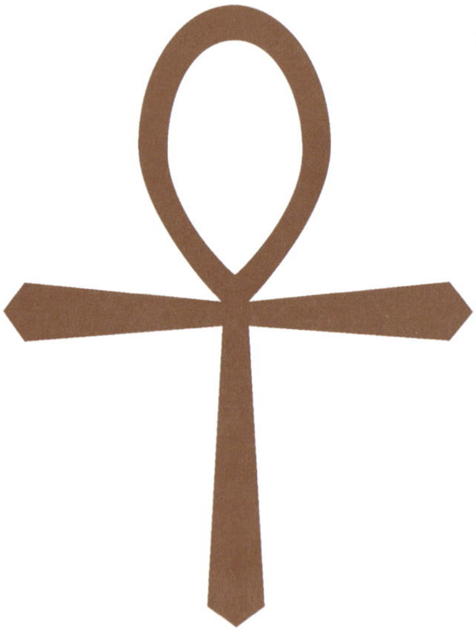

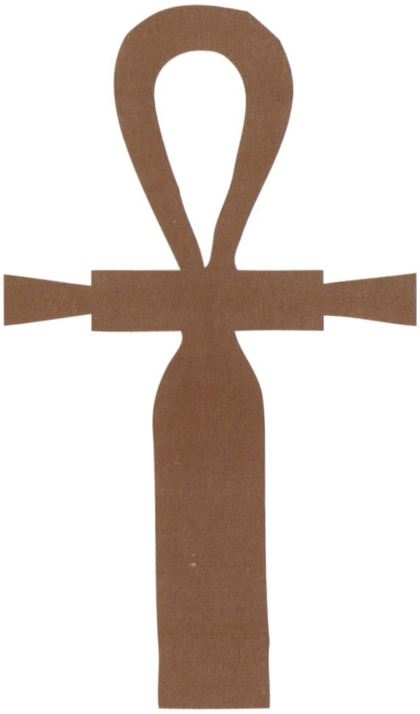

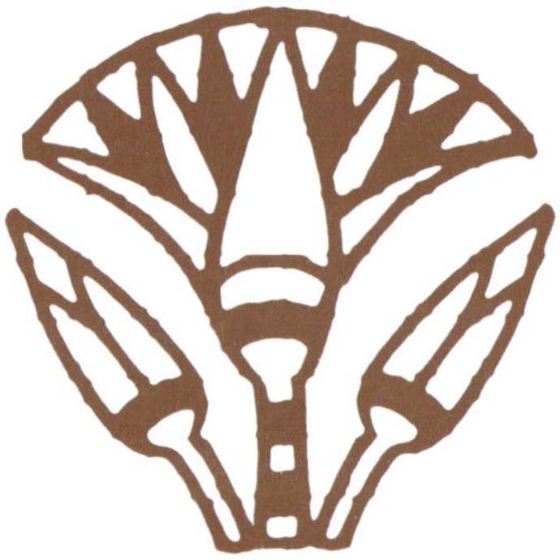

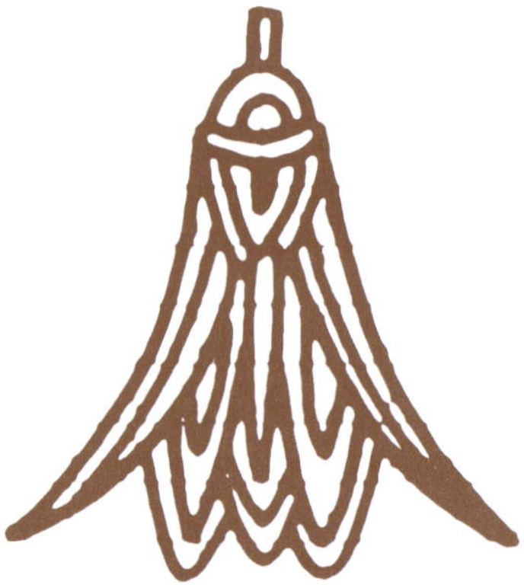

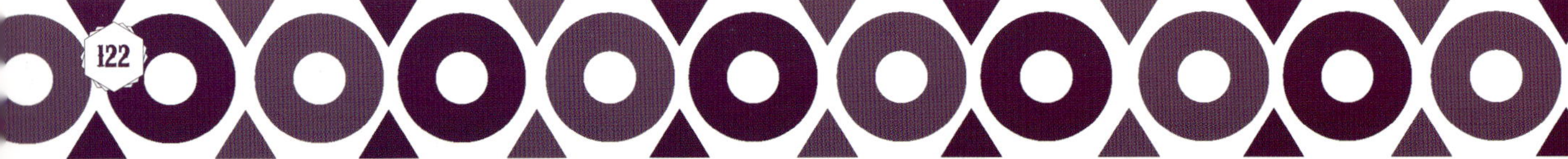

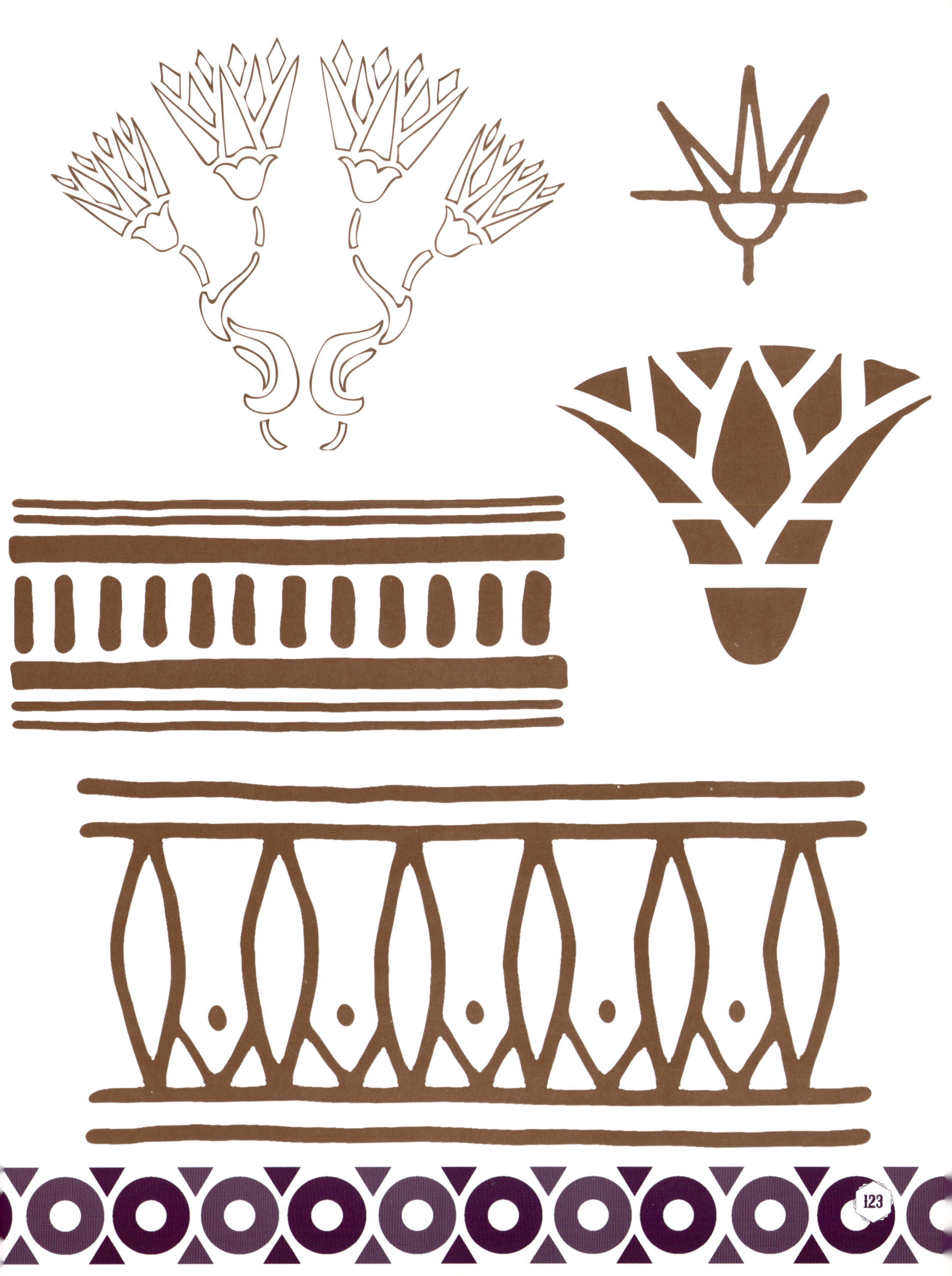

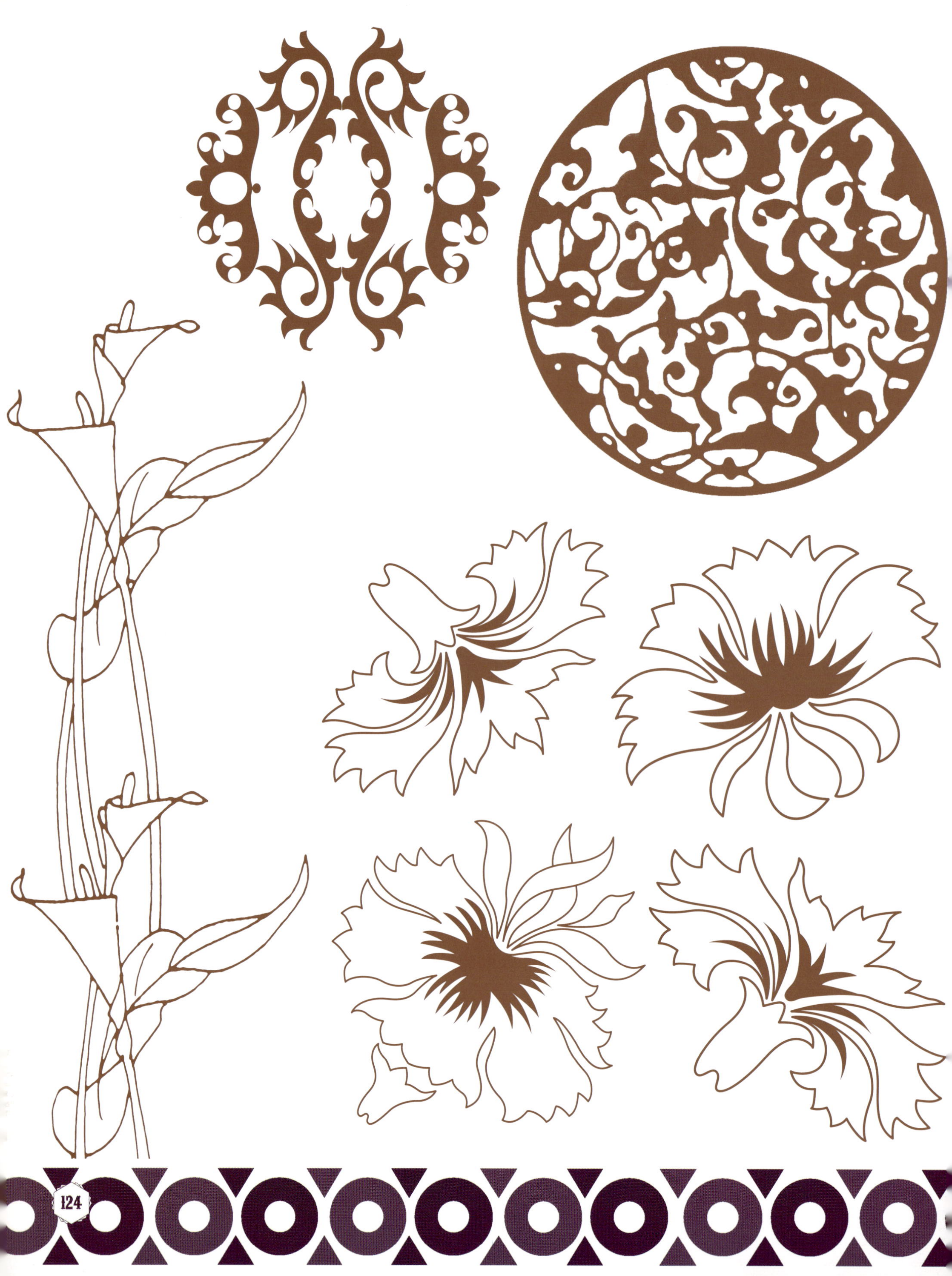

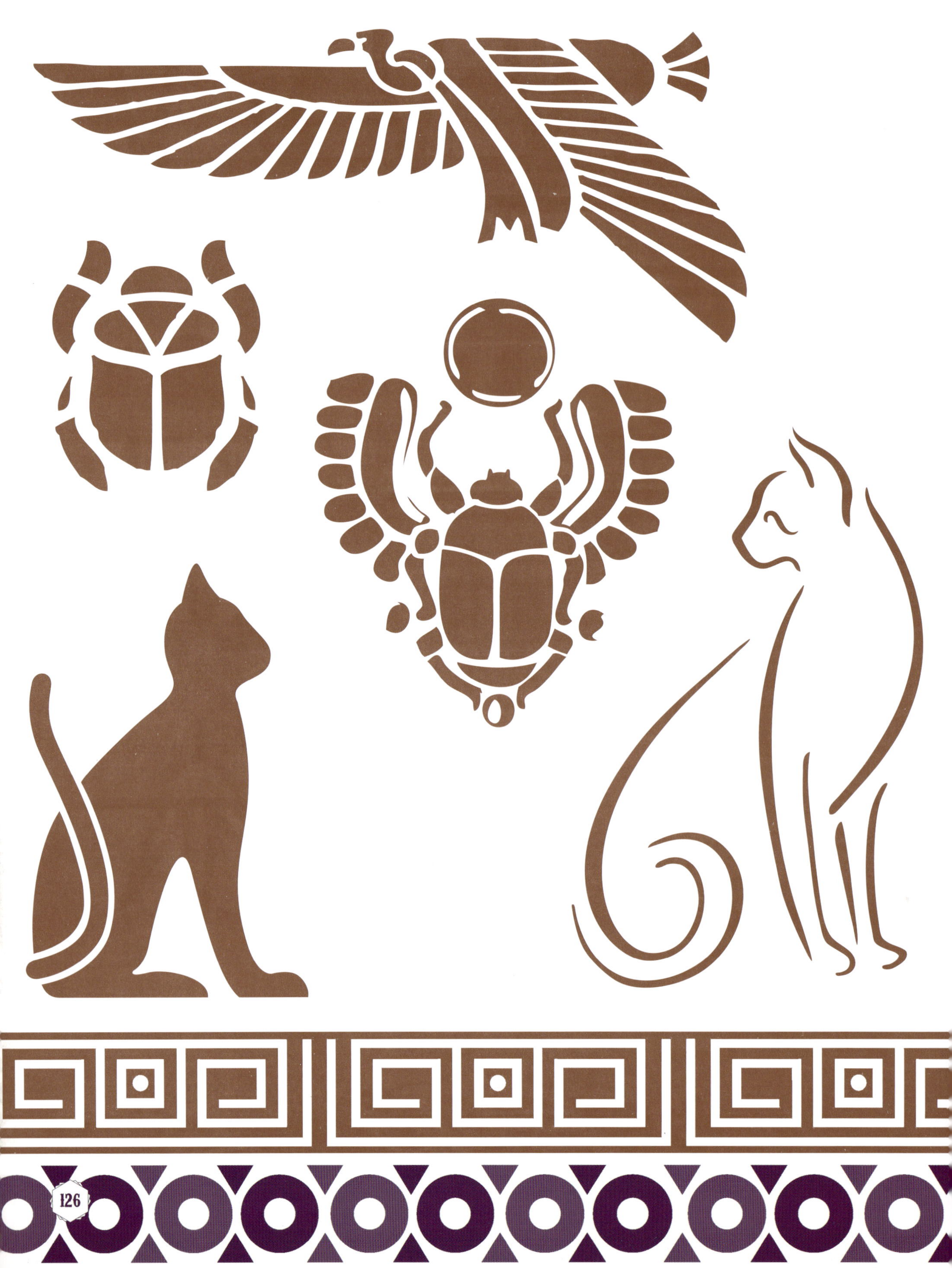

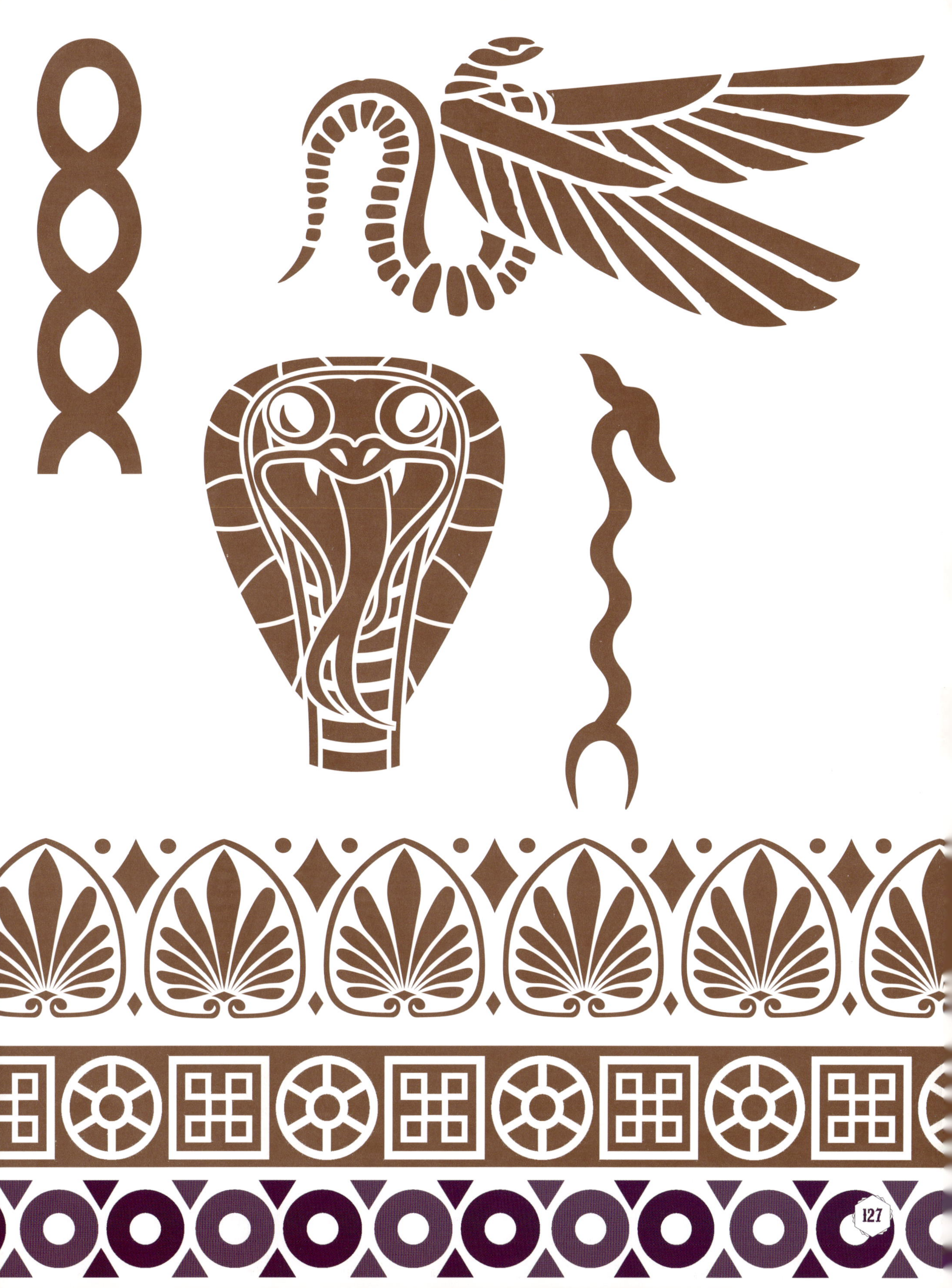

THE MIDDLE EAST

A multitude of rich and varied patterns has emerged from the ethnic and religious mosaic that is the Middle East. Henna designs from this region incorporate Arab, Persian, Syrian, and Turkish elements with threads of Indian and Pakistani motifs mixed in.

Overall, patterns from the Middle East include flowers, leaves, and geometric shapes. These elements tend to be larger, with more space between decorative elements than Hindi designs. Individual motifs are often symbolic of the universally desired blessings of good health, fertility, wisdom and enlightenment with differing connotations from culture to culture.

Because equal attention has been given to the concepts of unity and harmony, the mingling of all these cultural influences has resulted in stunningly beautiful and meaningful henna designs. A common practice among henna artists of the Middle East is to complete hand decoration by dying the fingernails with henna.

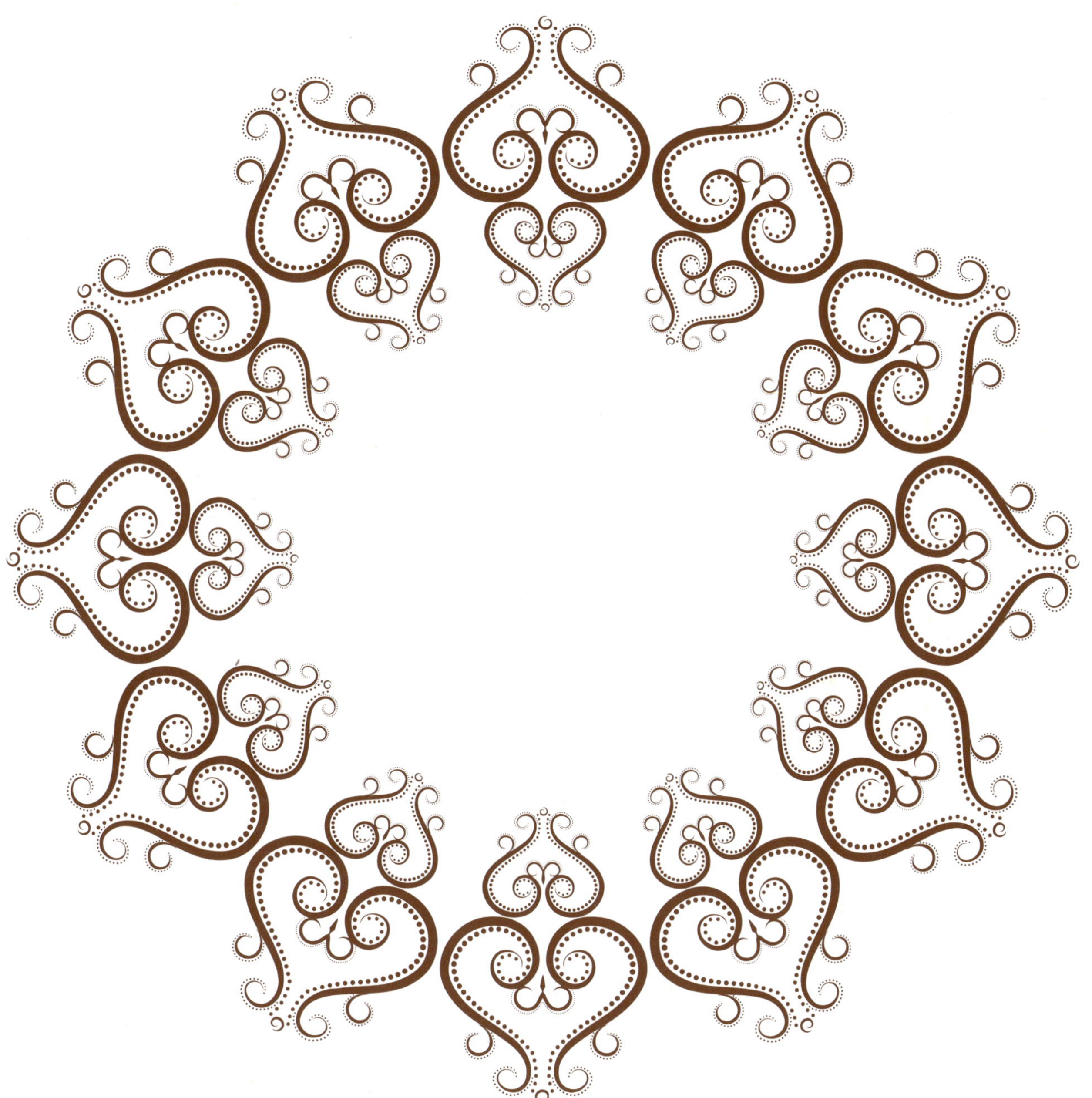

Early Islamic Motifs

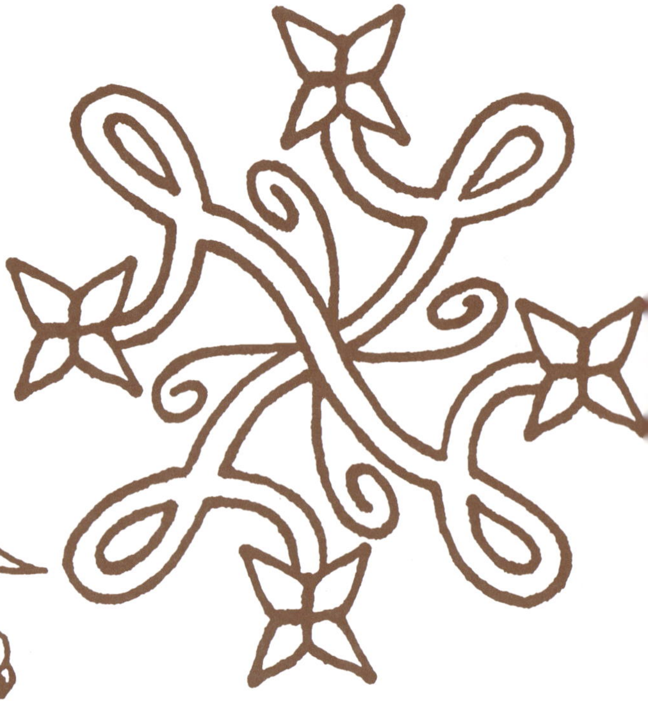

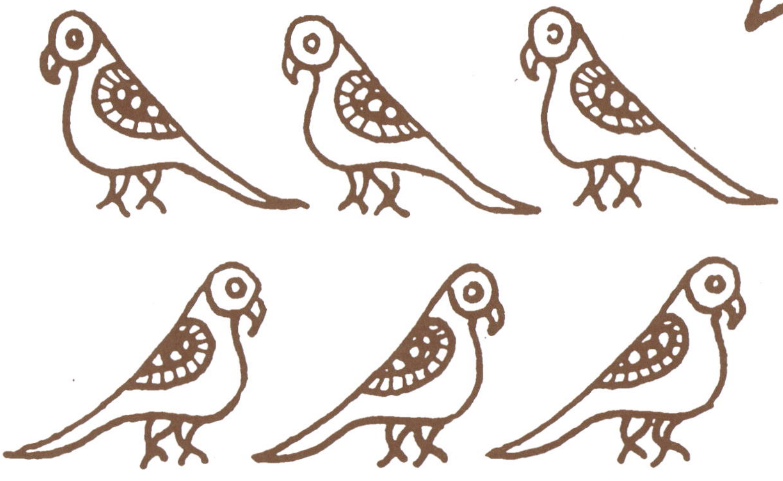

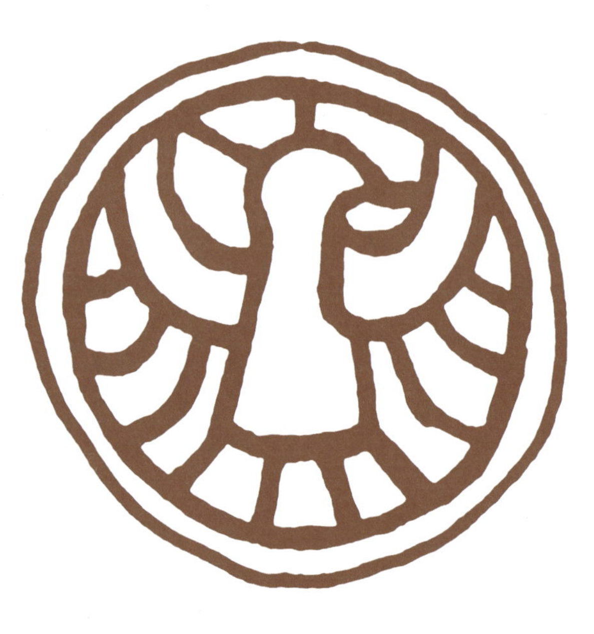

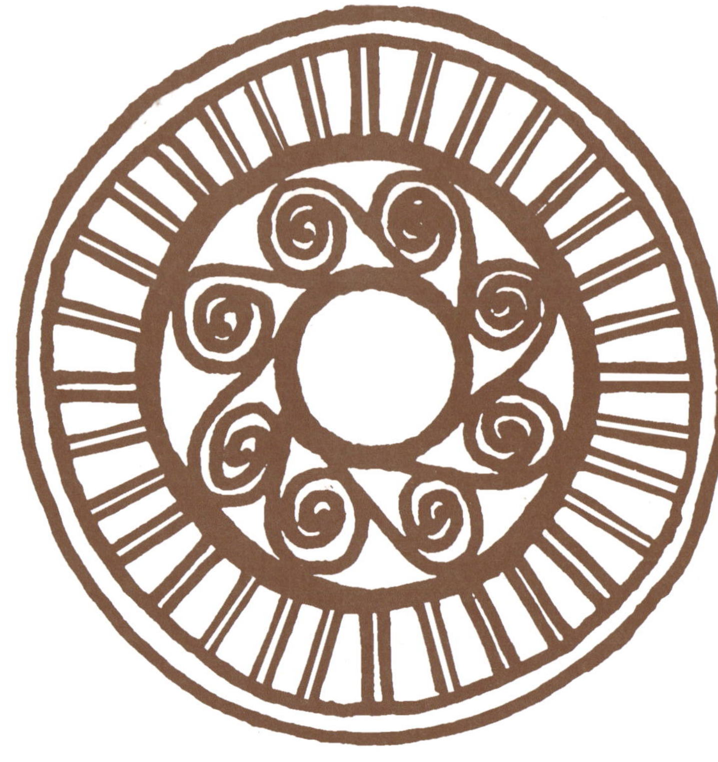

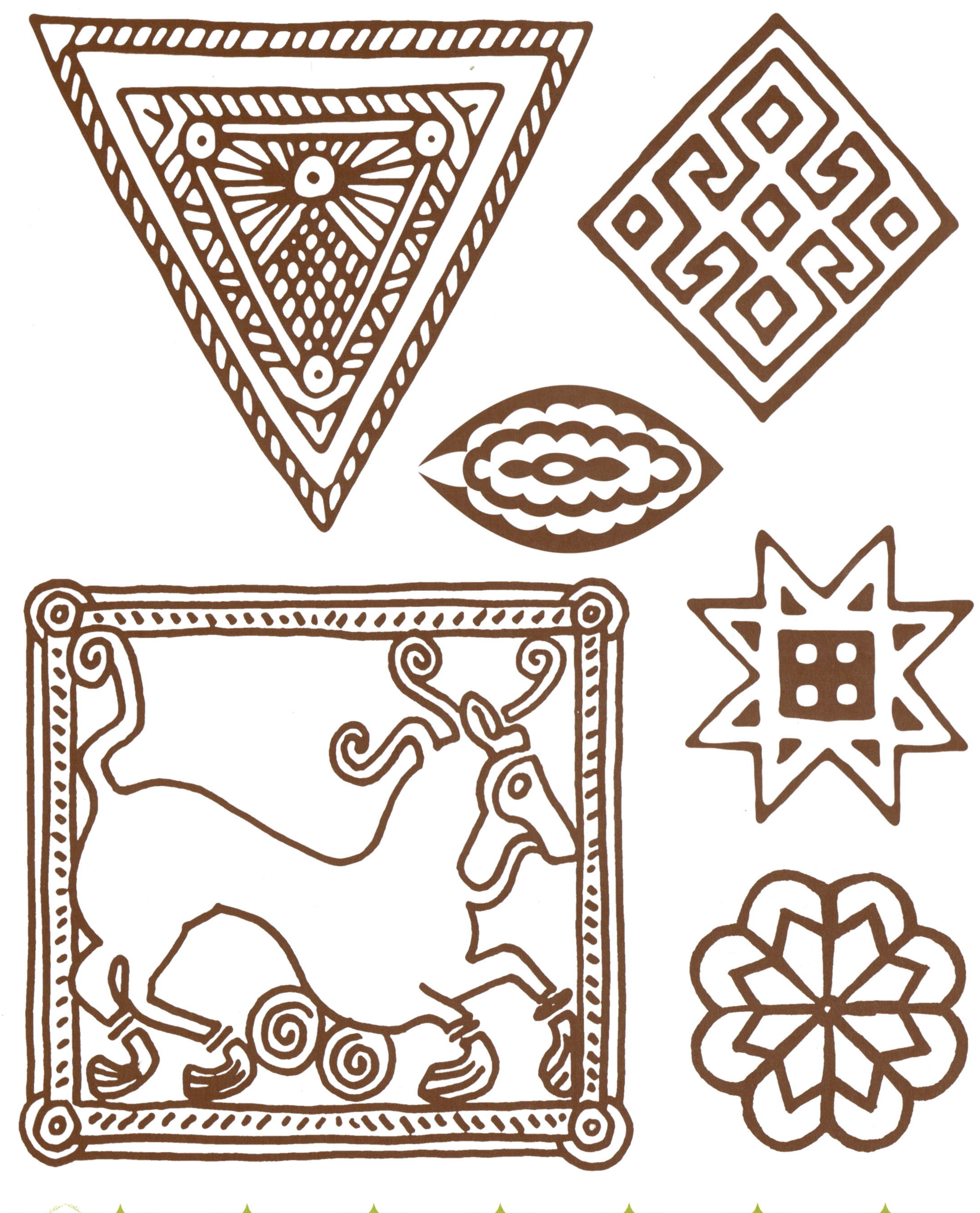

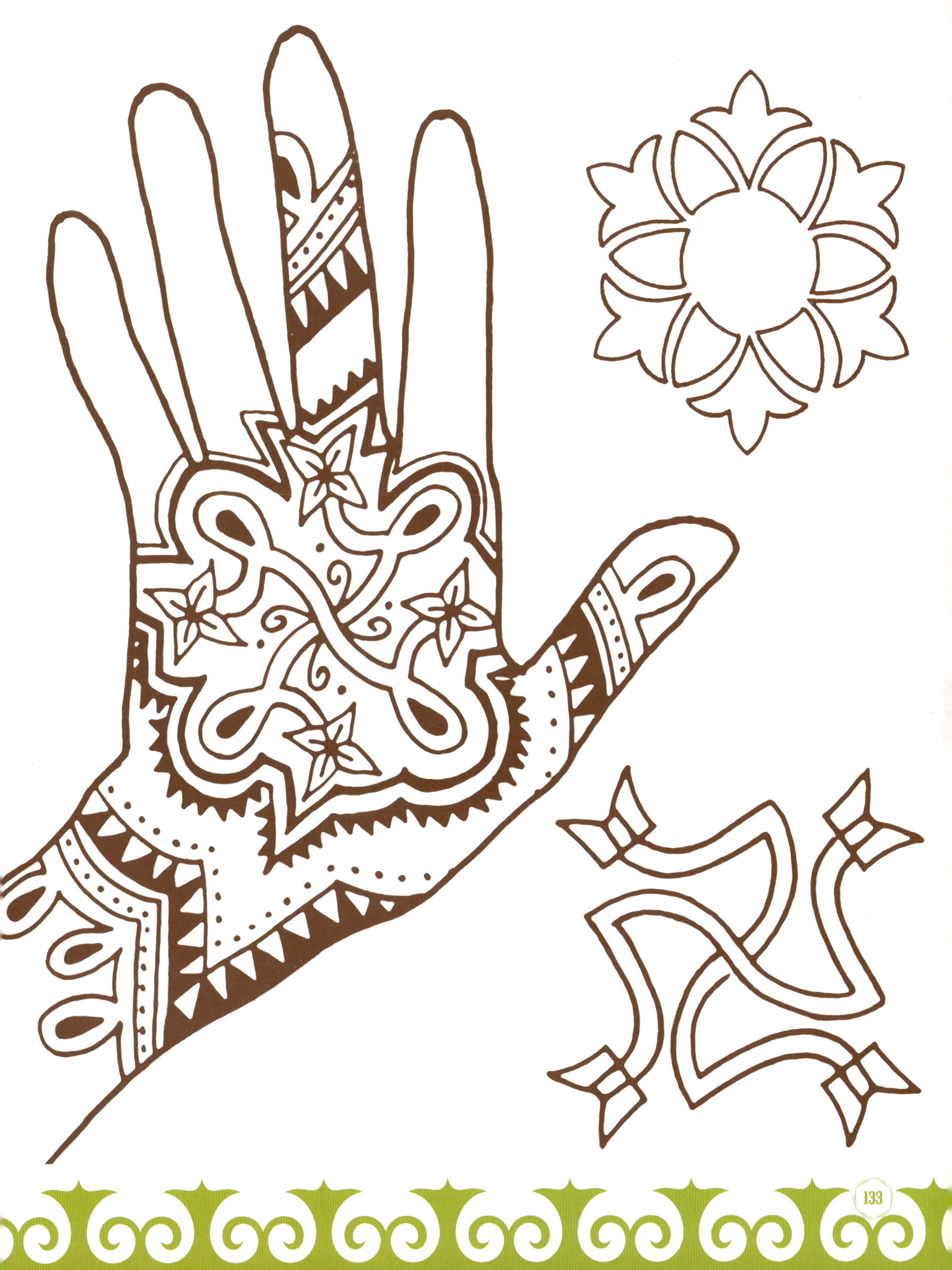

Arabian Mathematical/ Geometric Motifs

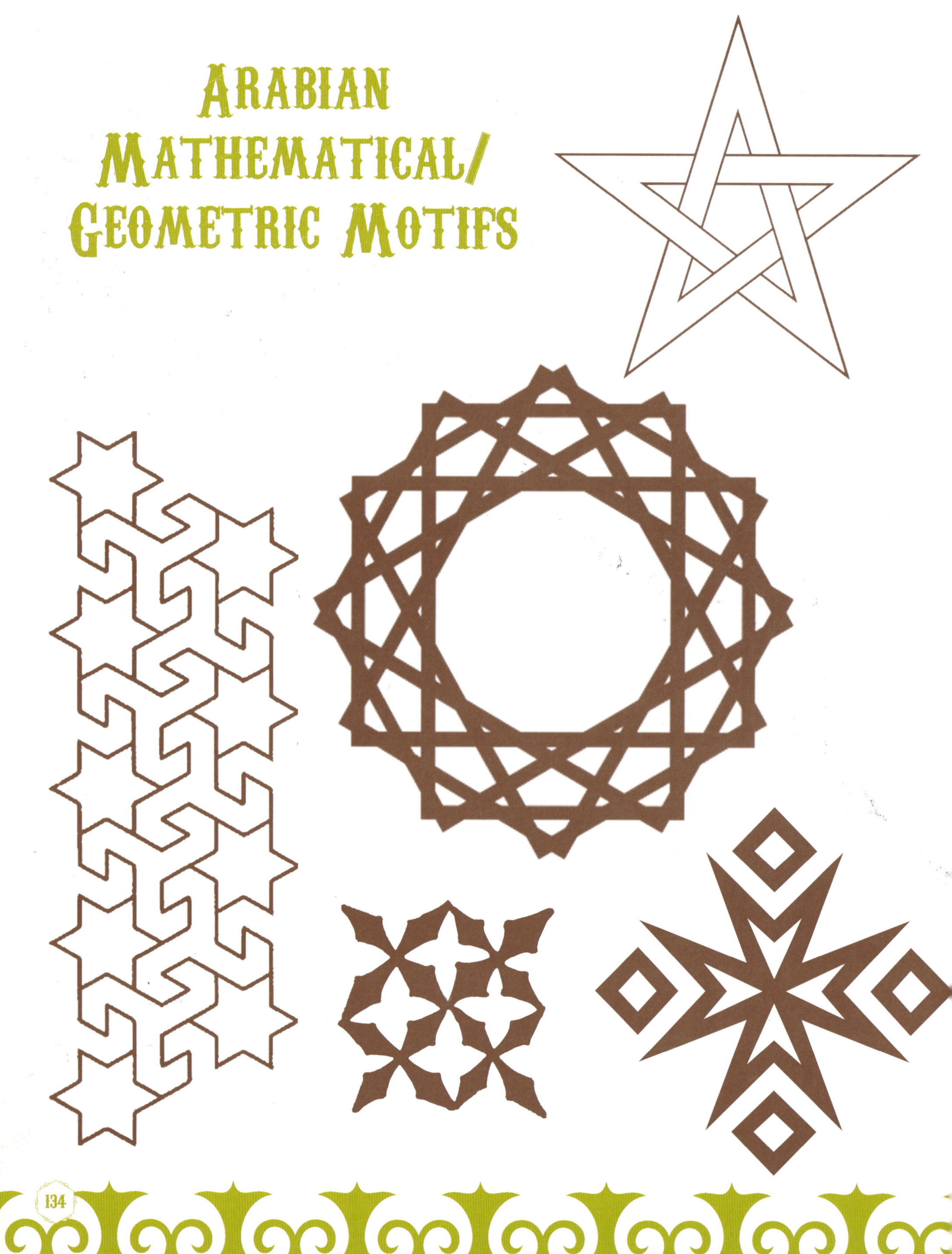

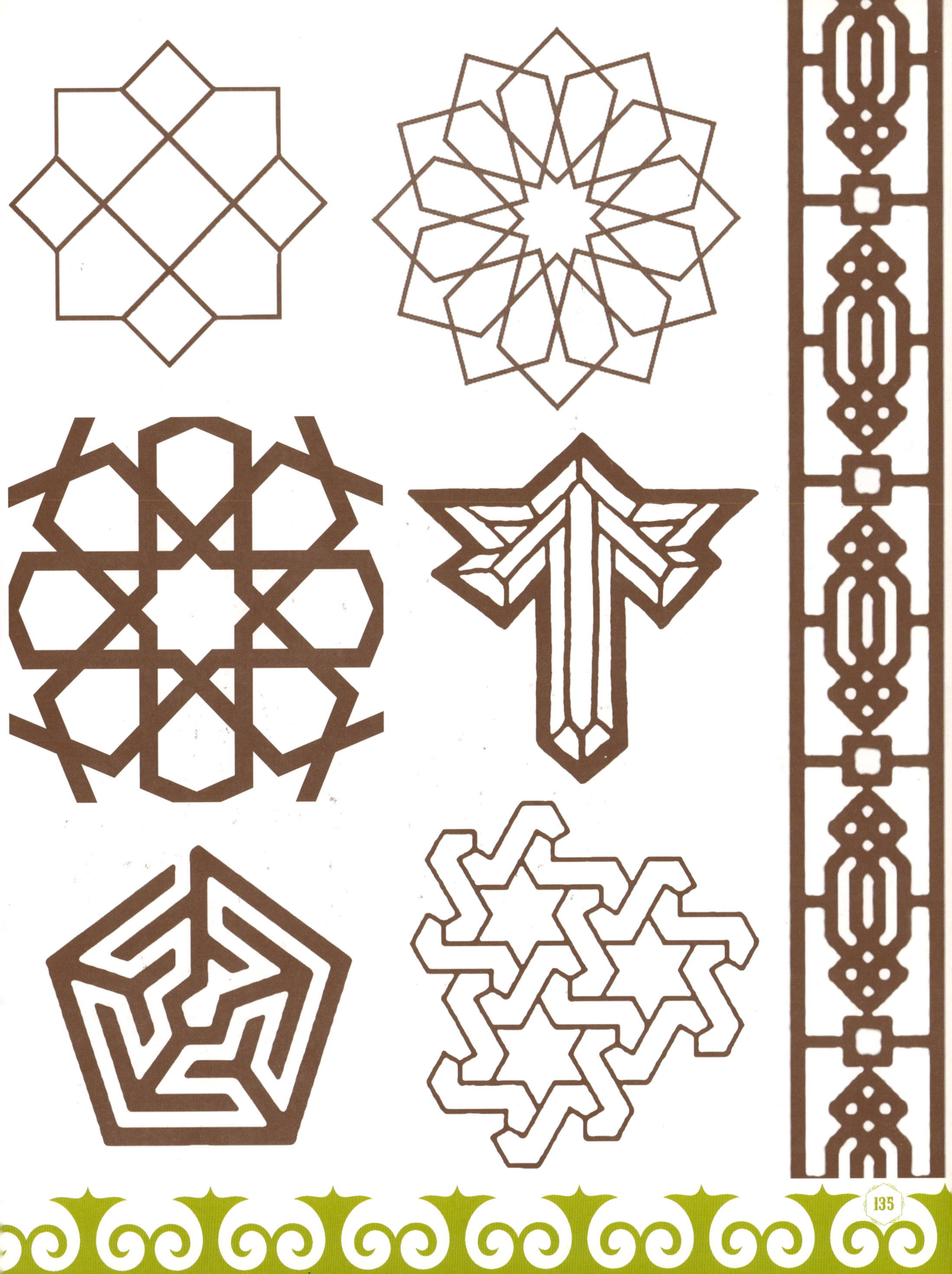

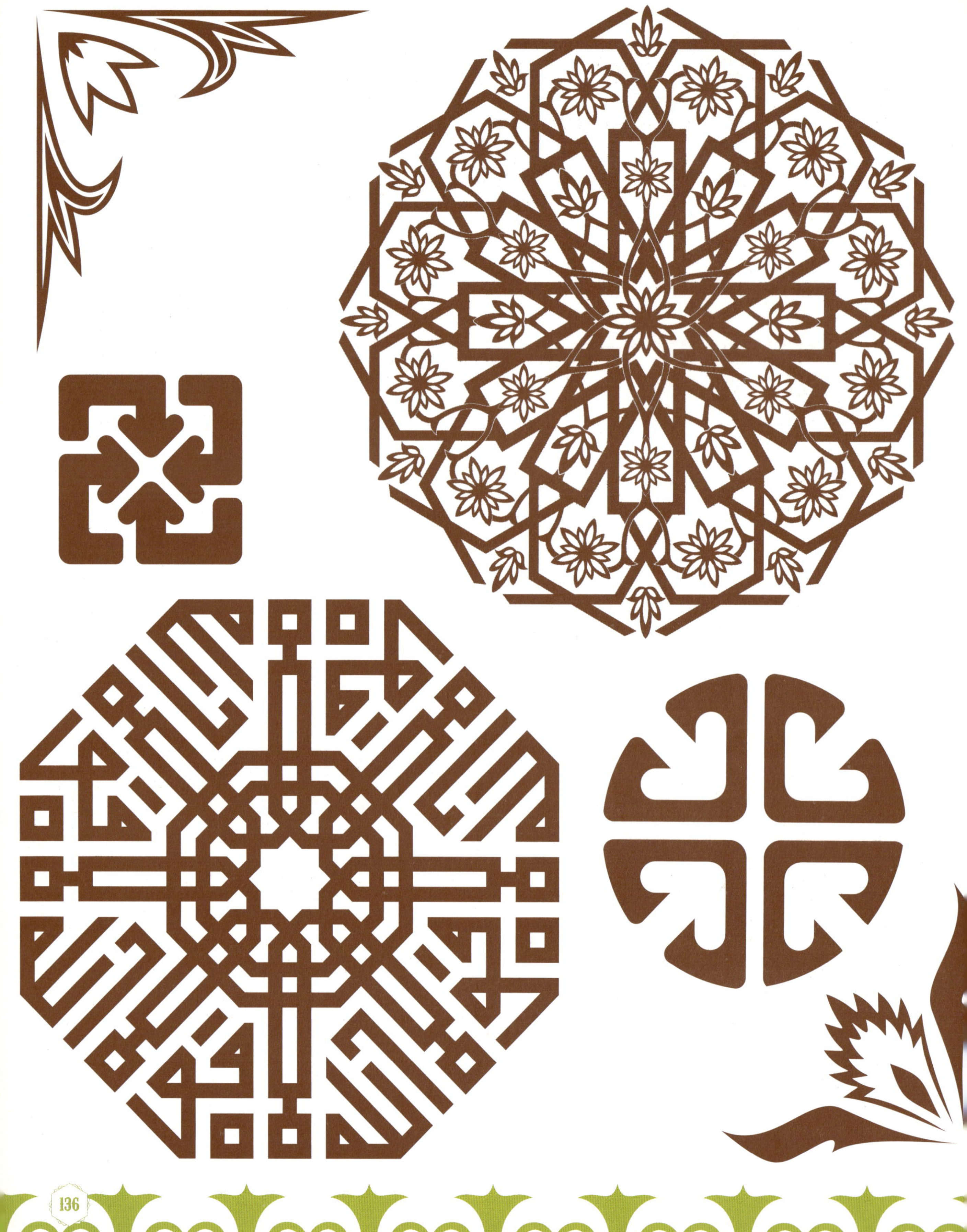

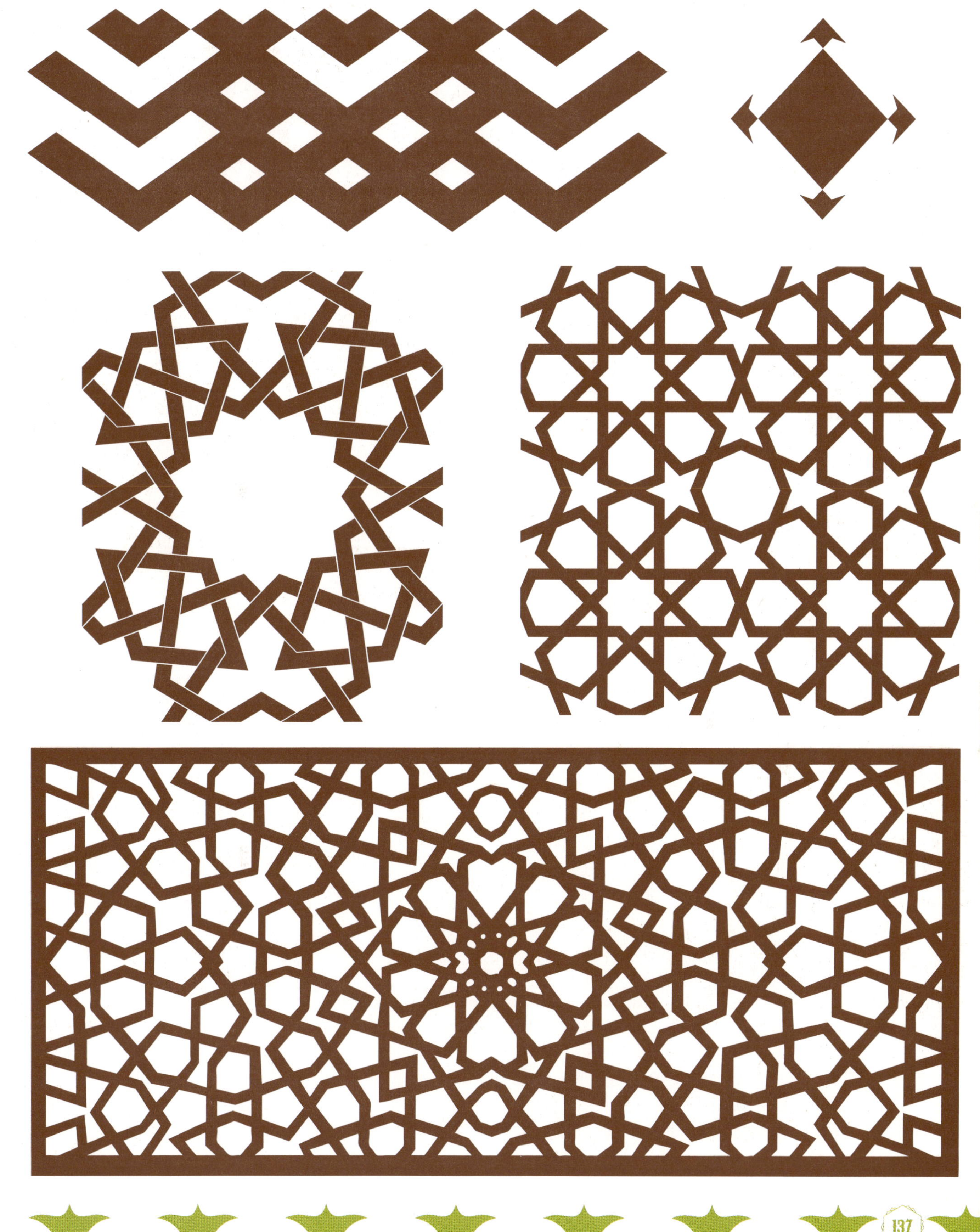

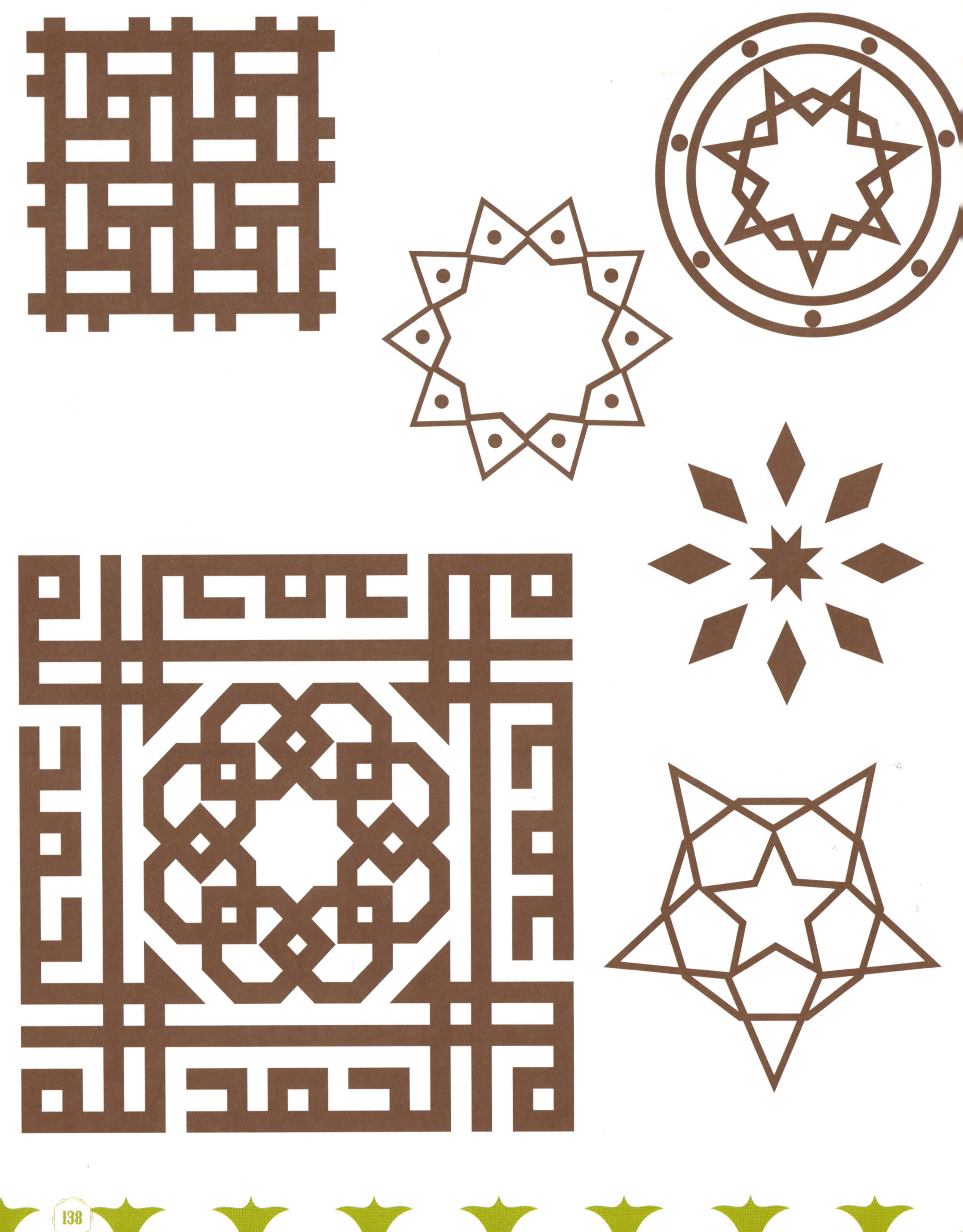

THE HAND AND THE EYE

A great many symbols are meant to protect against the "evil eye" and the negative energy generated by dislike and envy. The *khmasa*, also known as "the five," is one such symbol. The khamsa represents the five fingers of the hand of Fatima, the Prophet Muhammad's daughter. She is believed to be the first woman who ever used henna to decorate her hands. The eye is represented by a number of abstract forms including the lozenge shape and triangles. A symbol meant to ward off the "Evil Eye," it sometimes appears as eyebrows, represented by upside-down triangles.

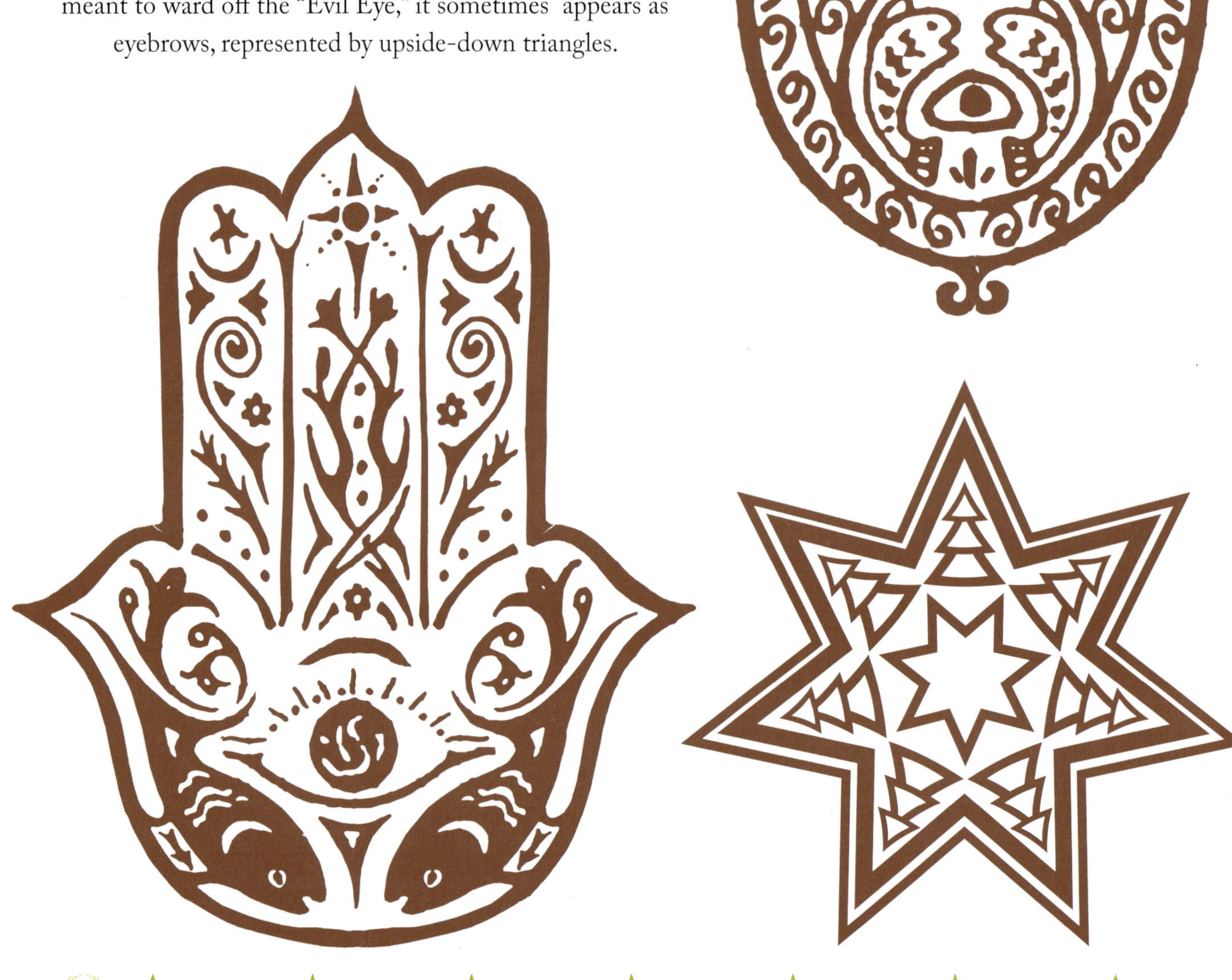

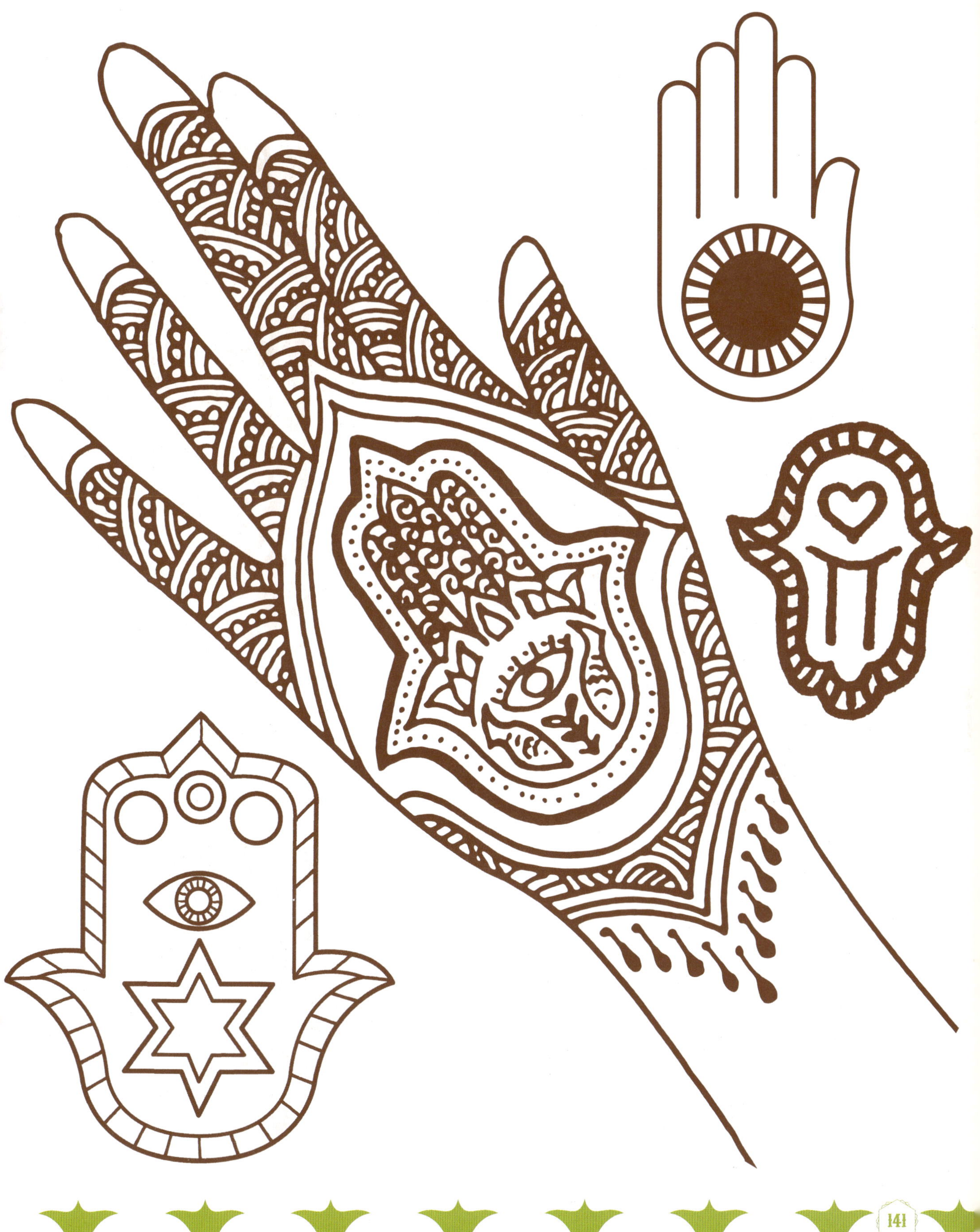

PERSIAN SYMBOLS

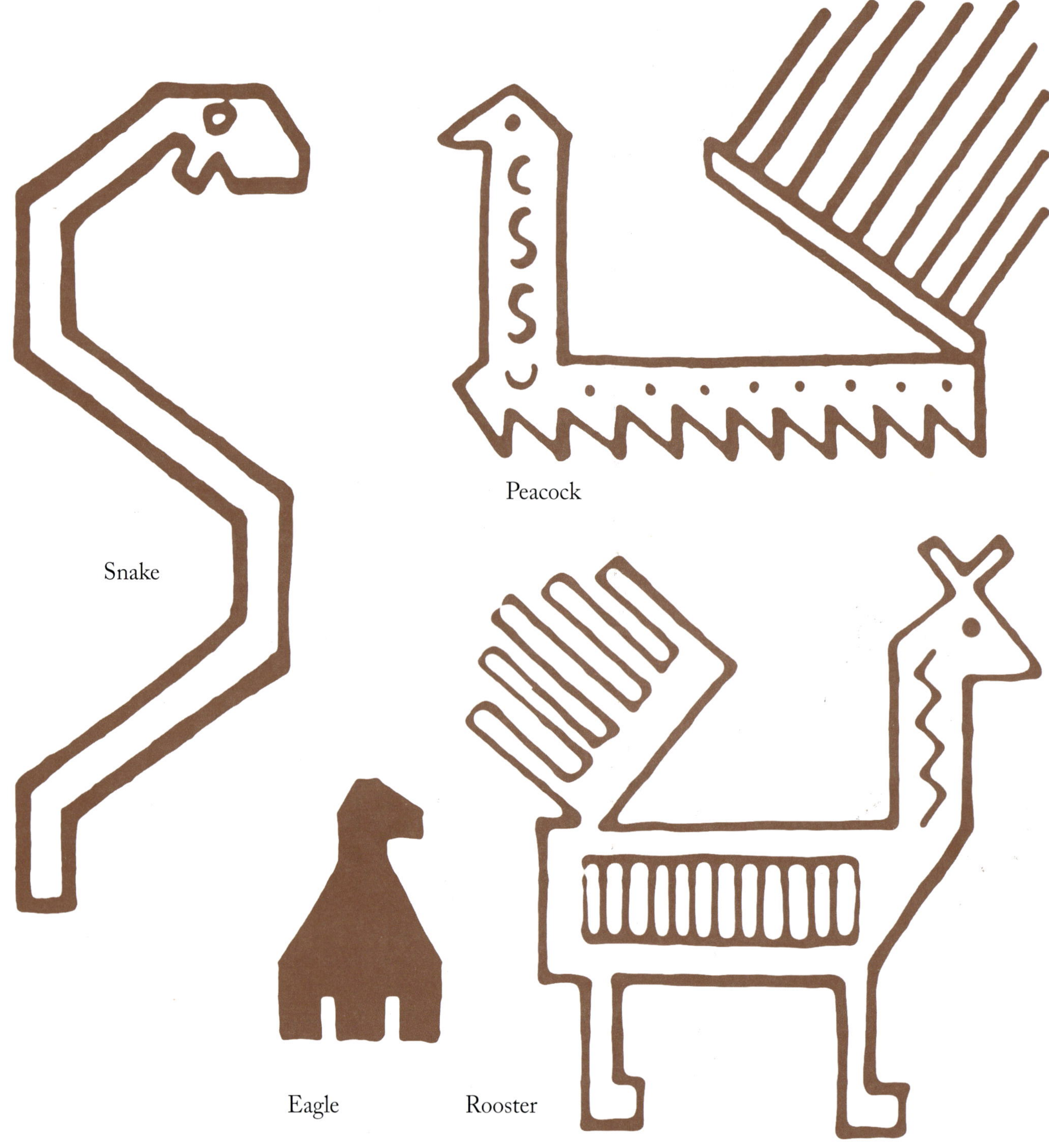

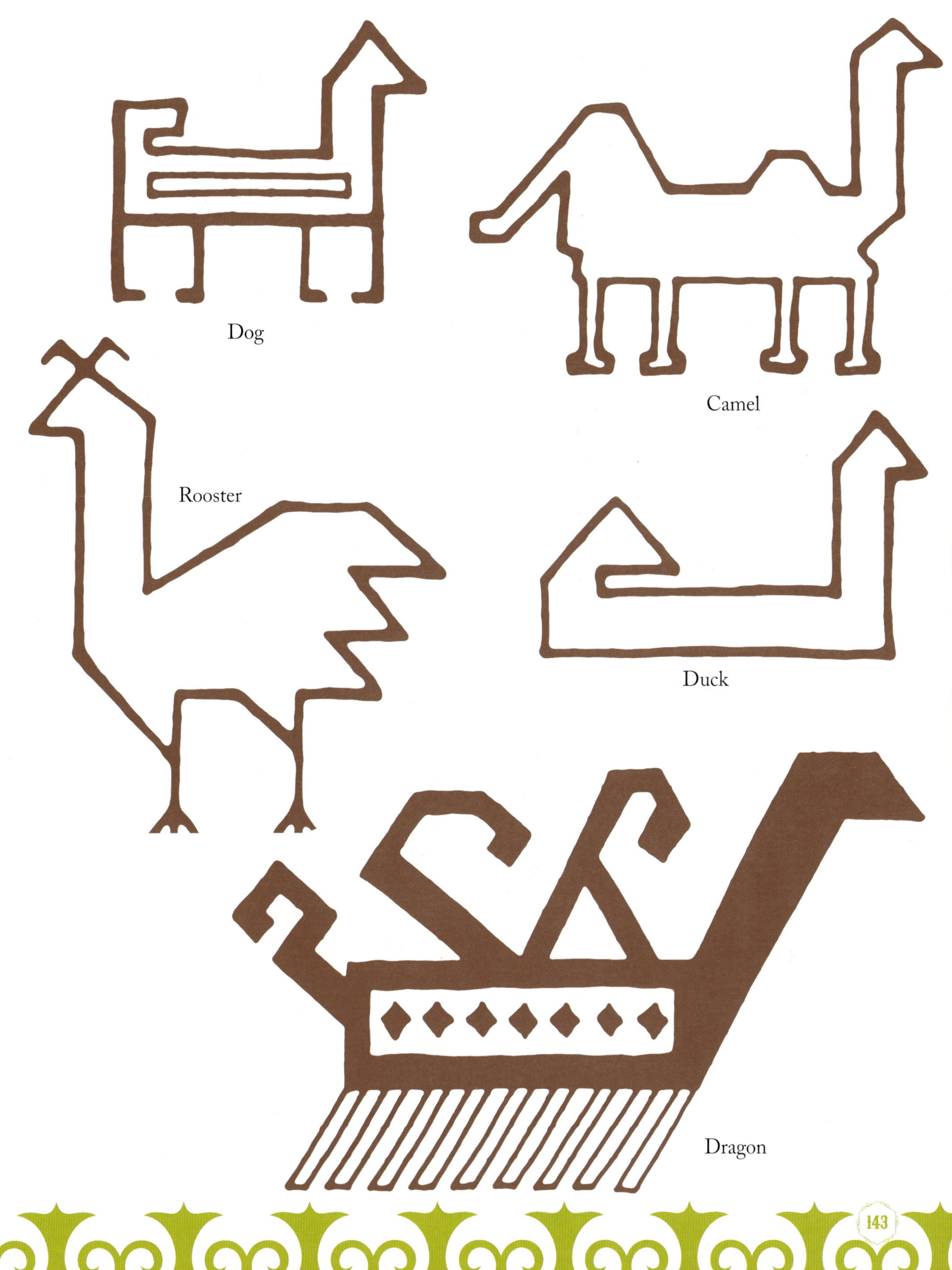
Dog
Camel
Rooster
Duck
Dragon

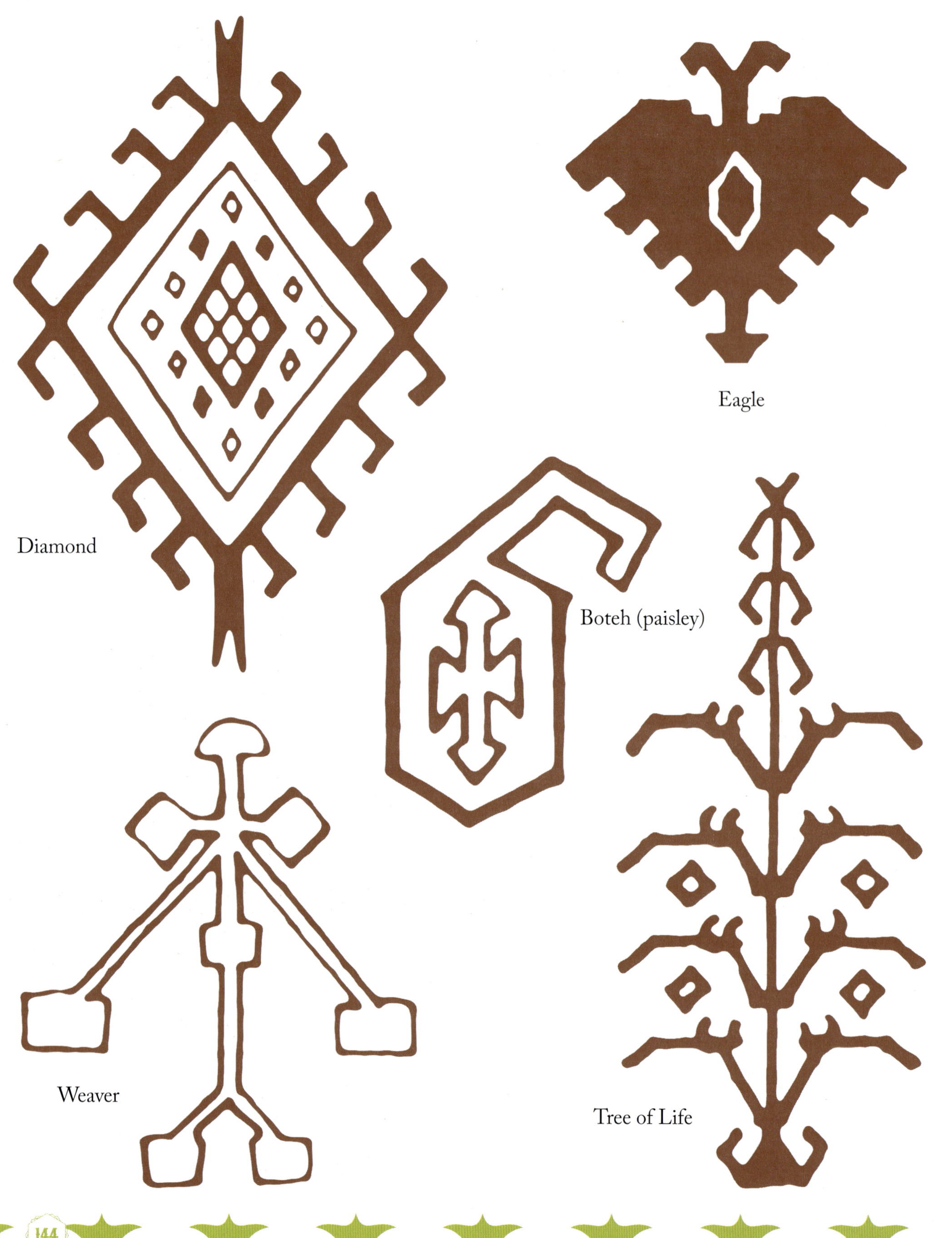

Diamond
Eagle
Boteh (paisley)
Weaver
Tree of Life

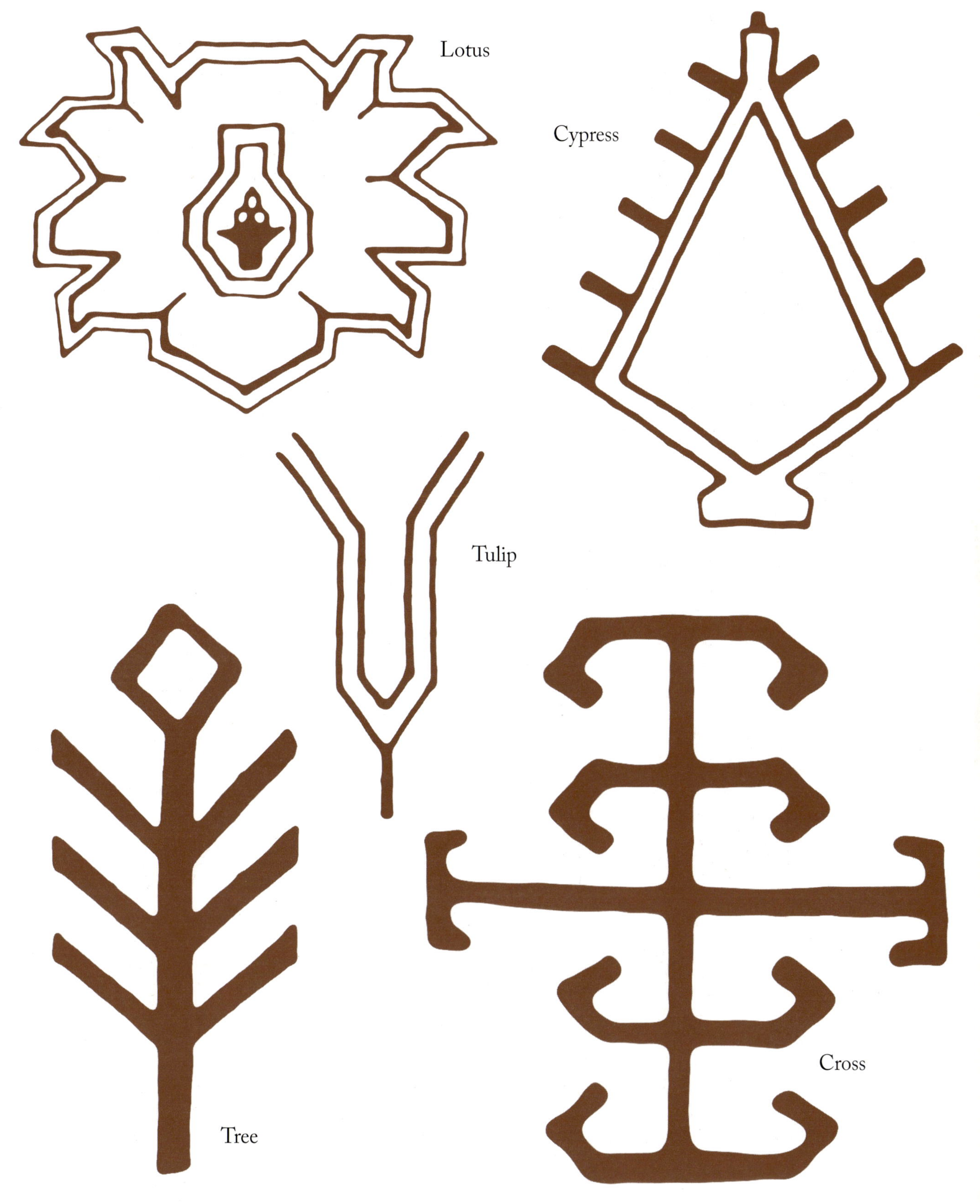
Lotus
Cypress
Tulip
Tree
Cross

Arabesque Patterns

Based on the elaborate, scrolling forms of leafy plants, arabesque patterns are an important element in Islamic art. The word comes from the Latin, meaning "of Arabic design."

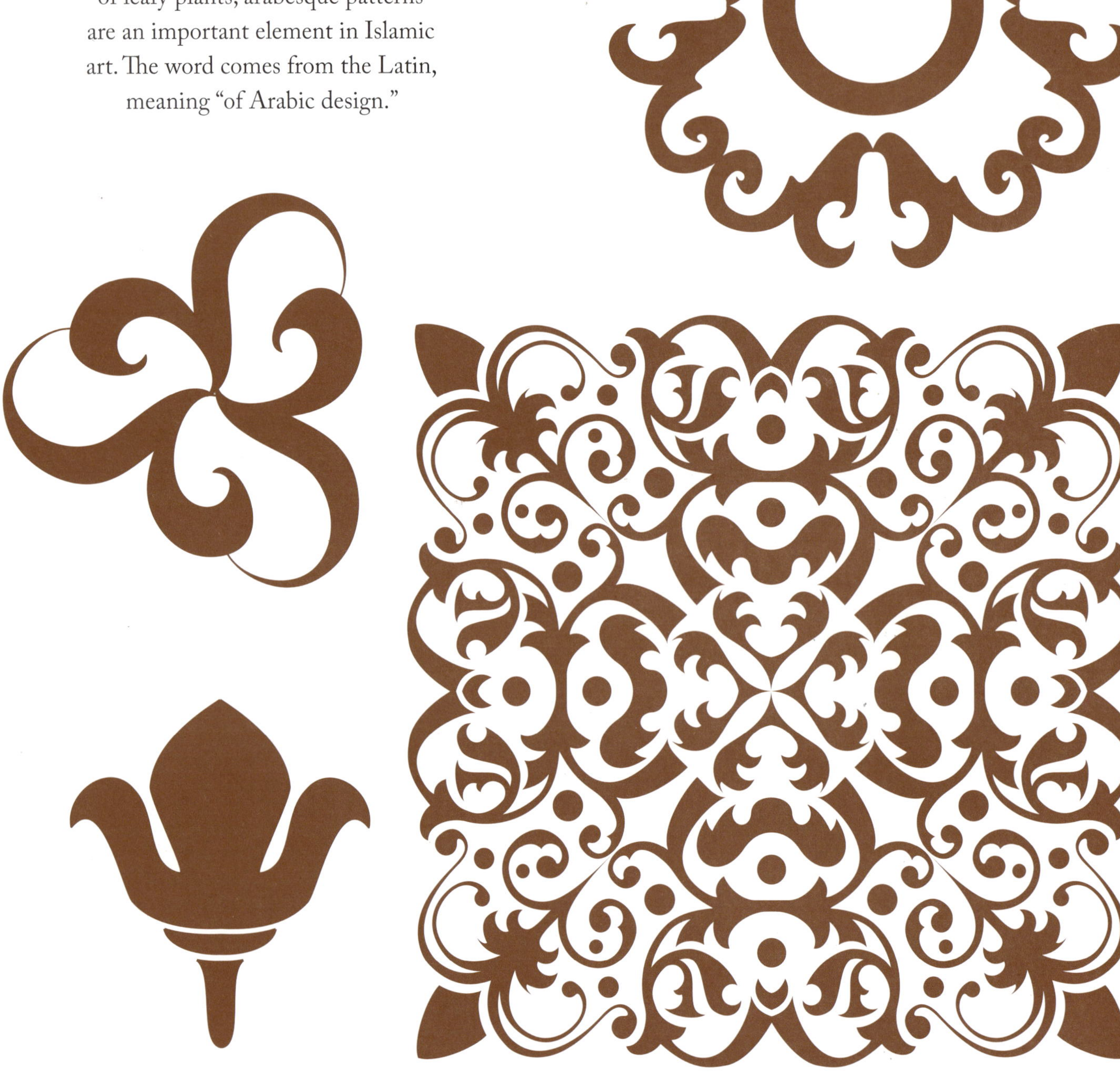

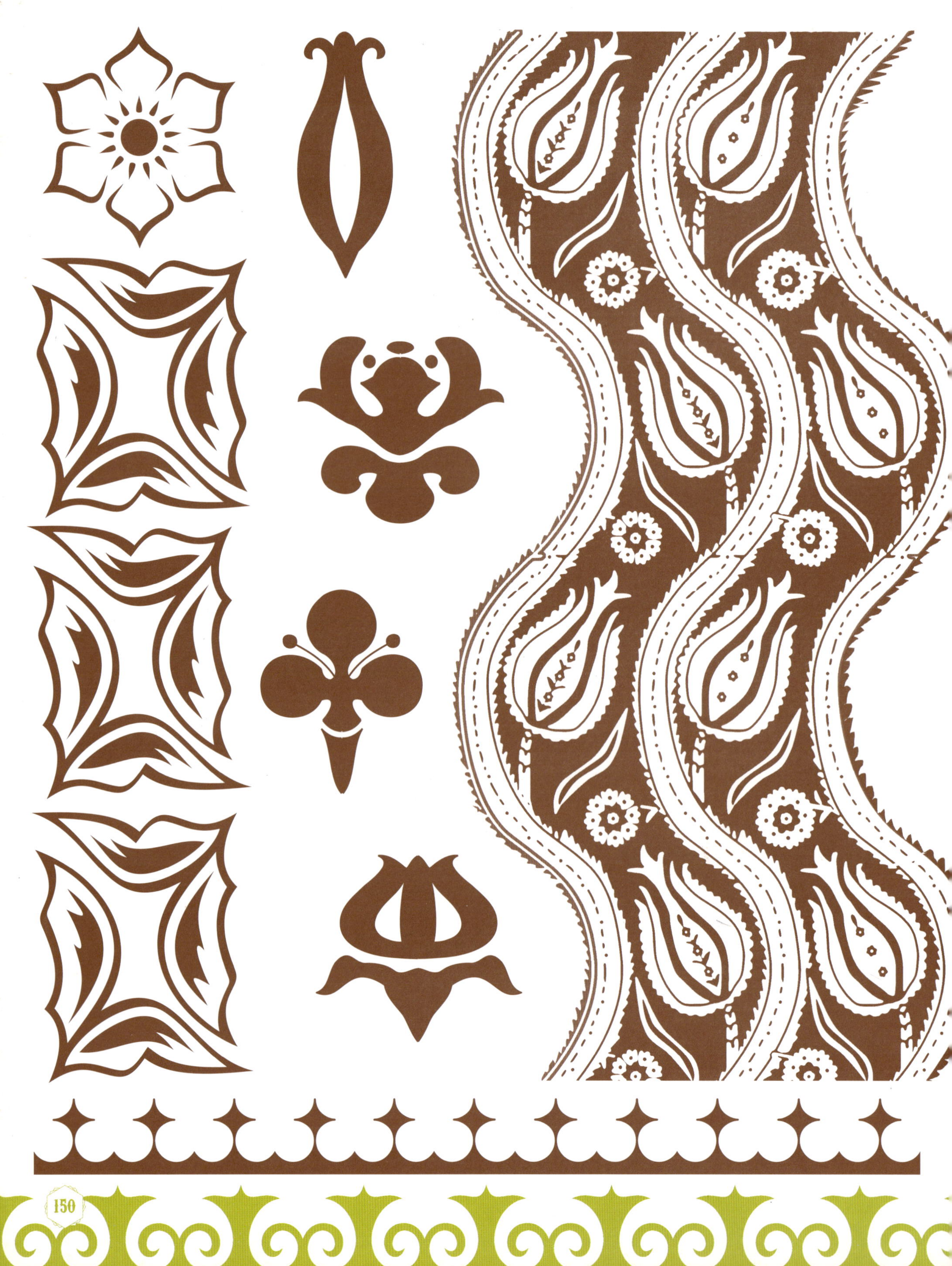

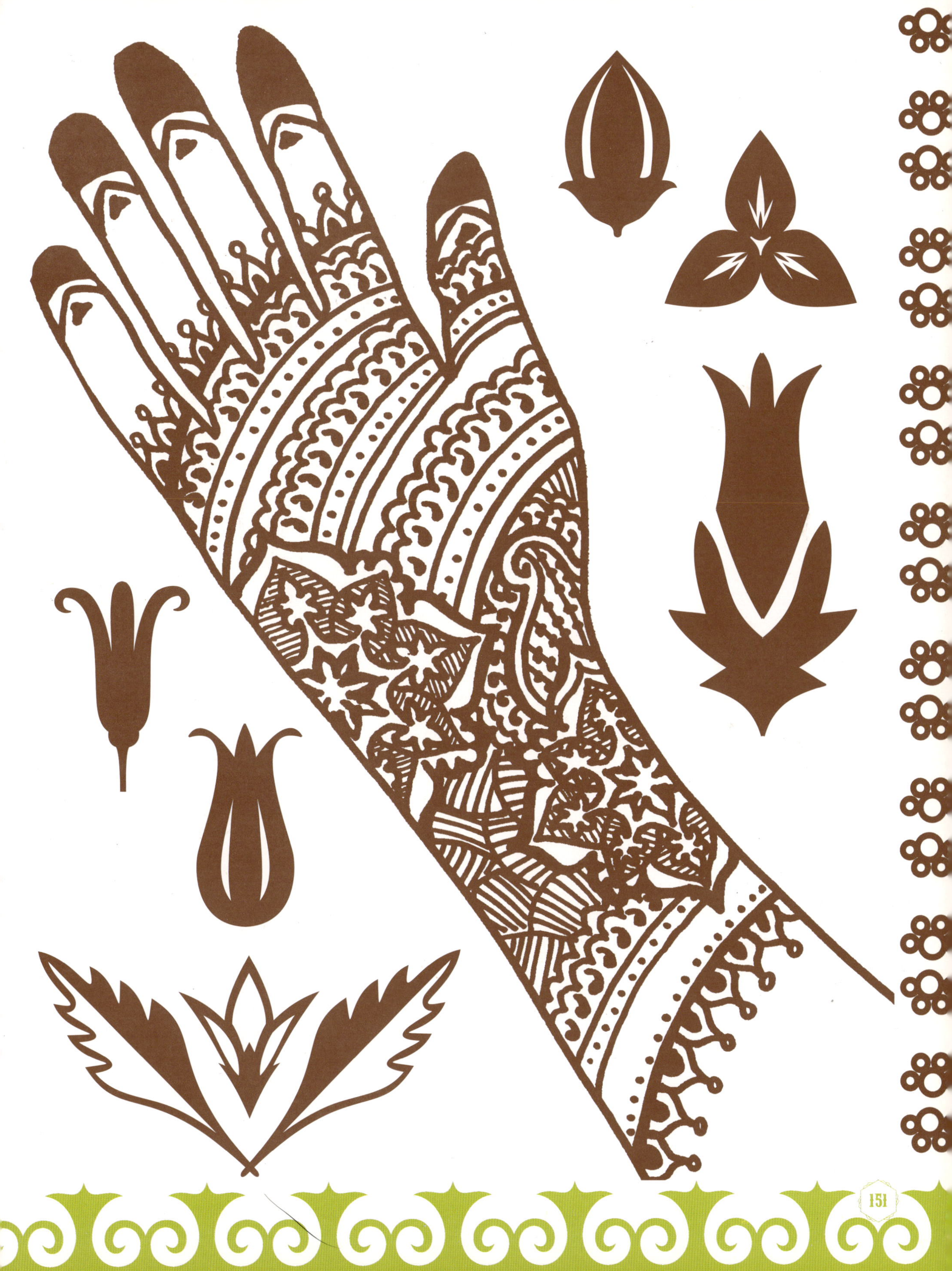

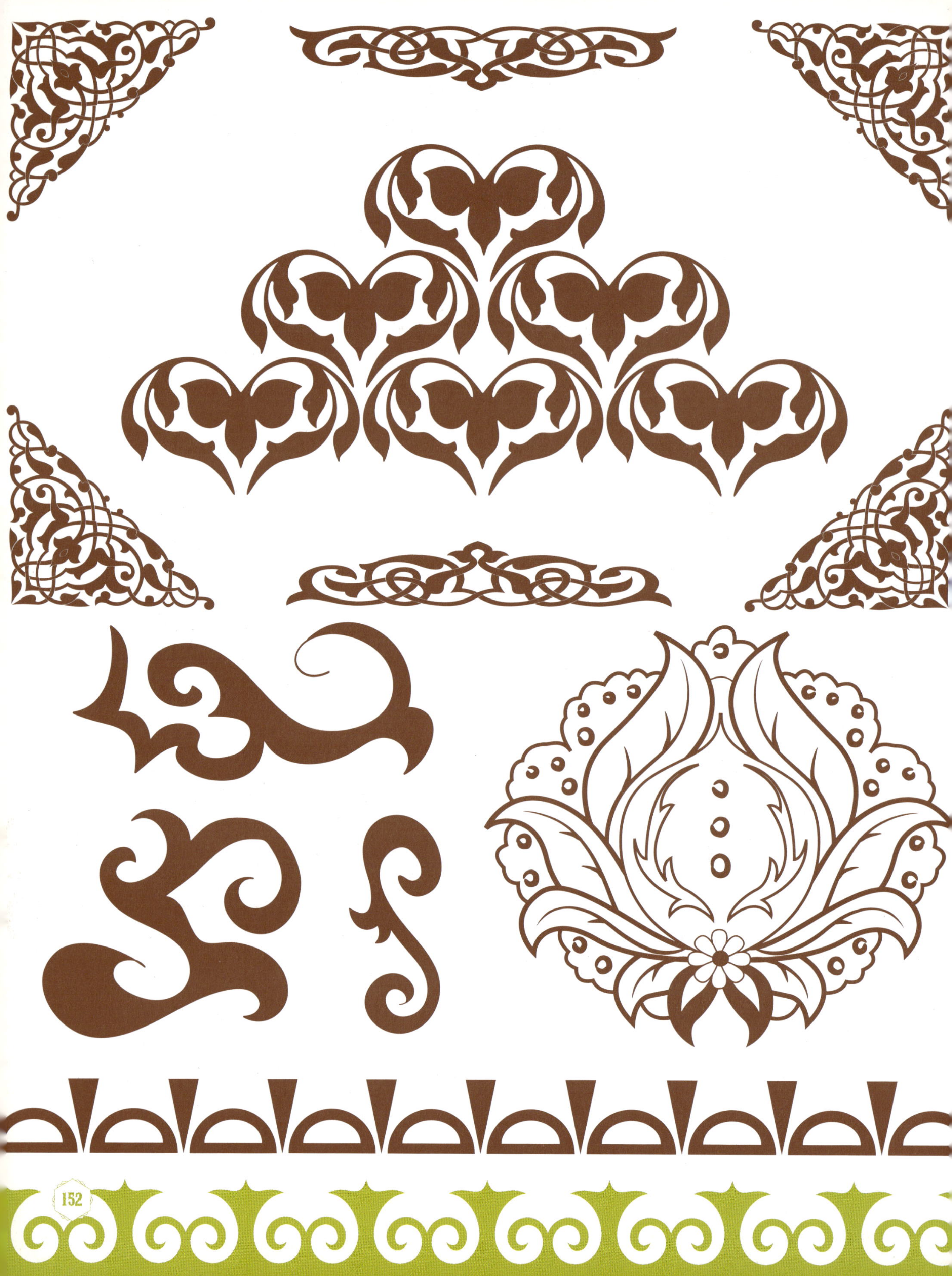

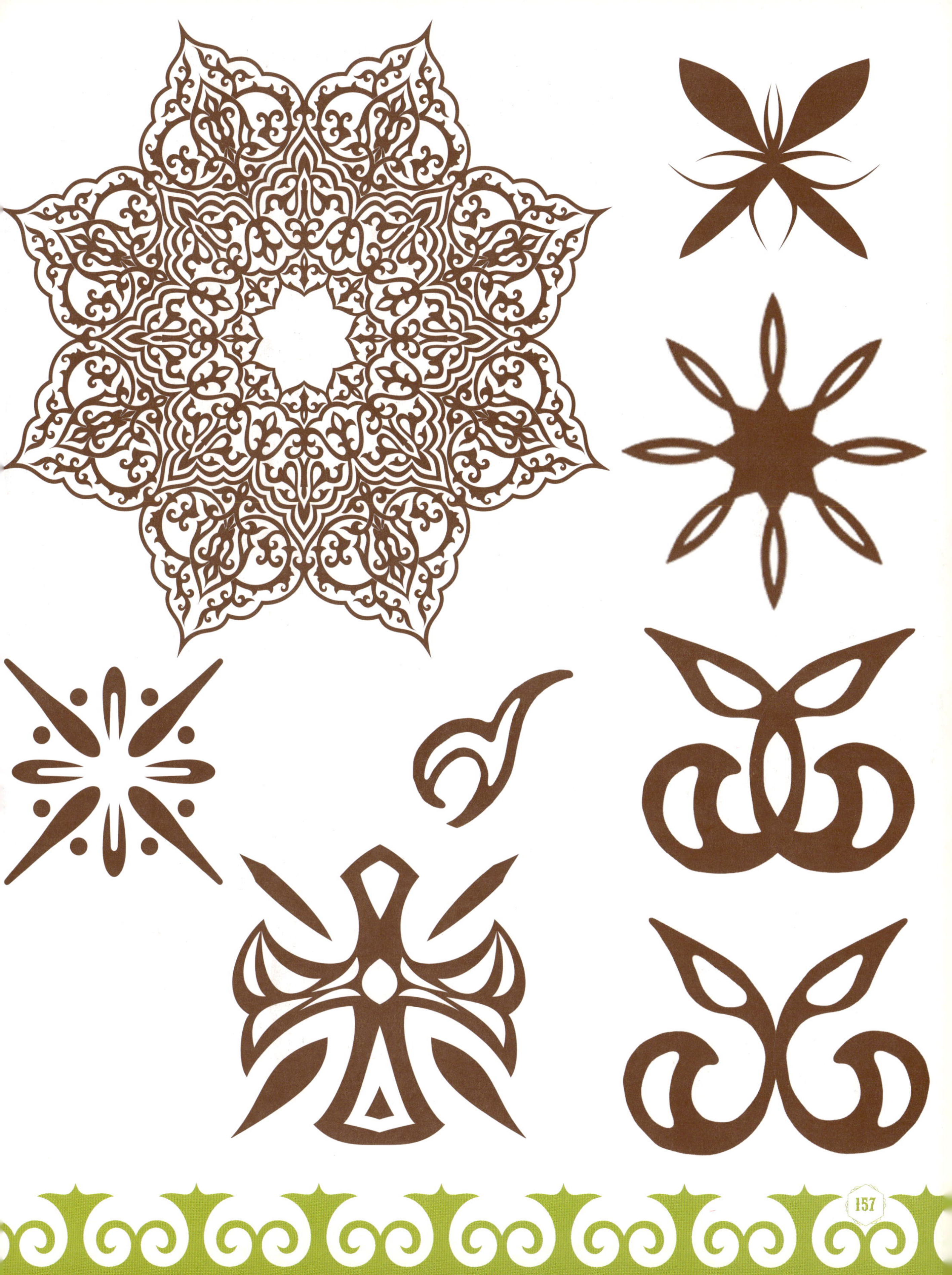

Floral and Vegetable Motifs

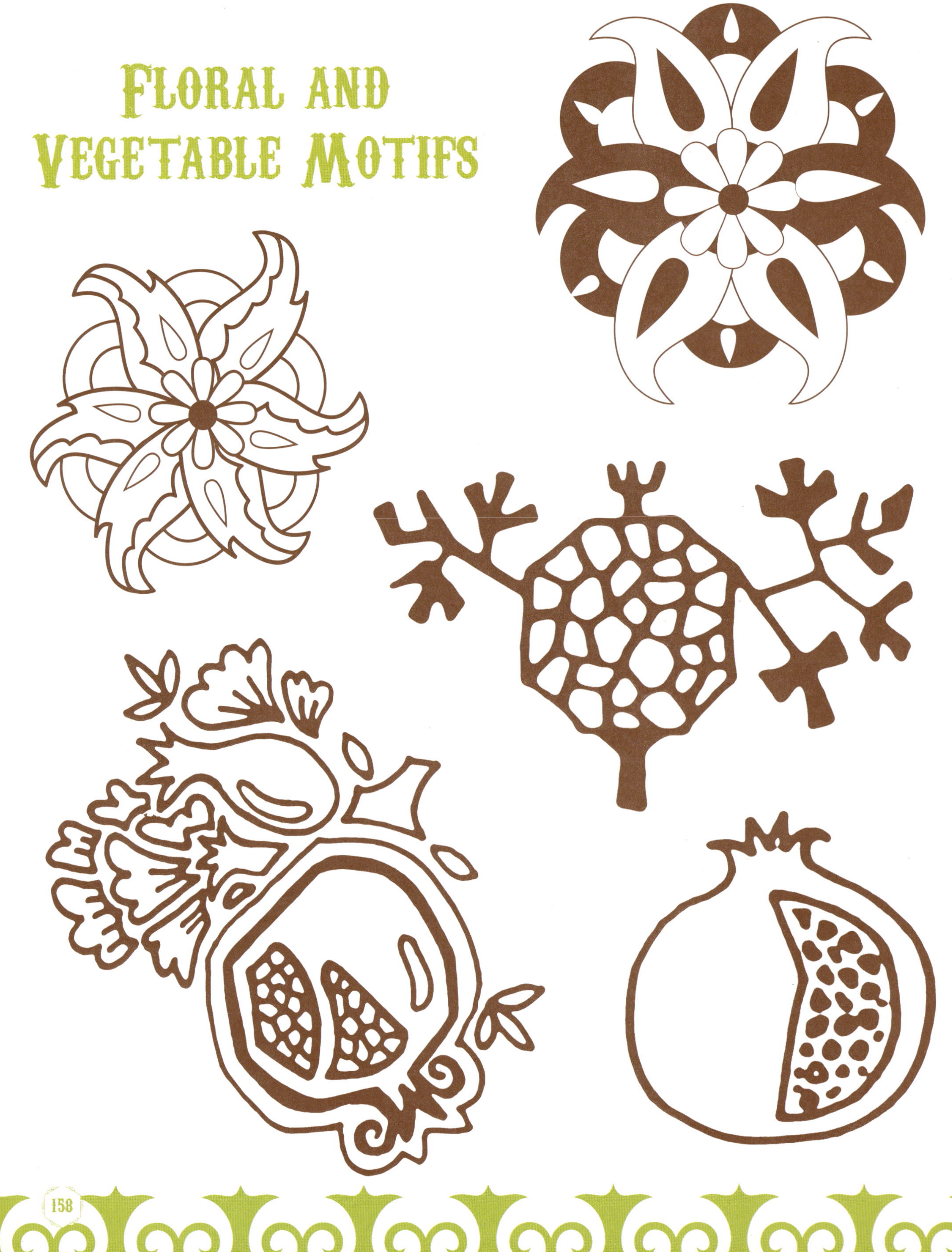

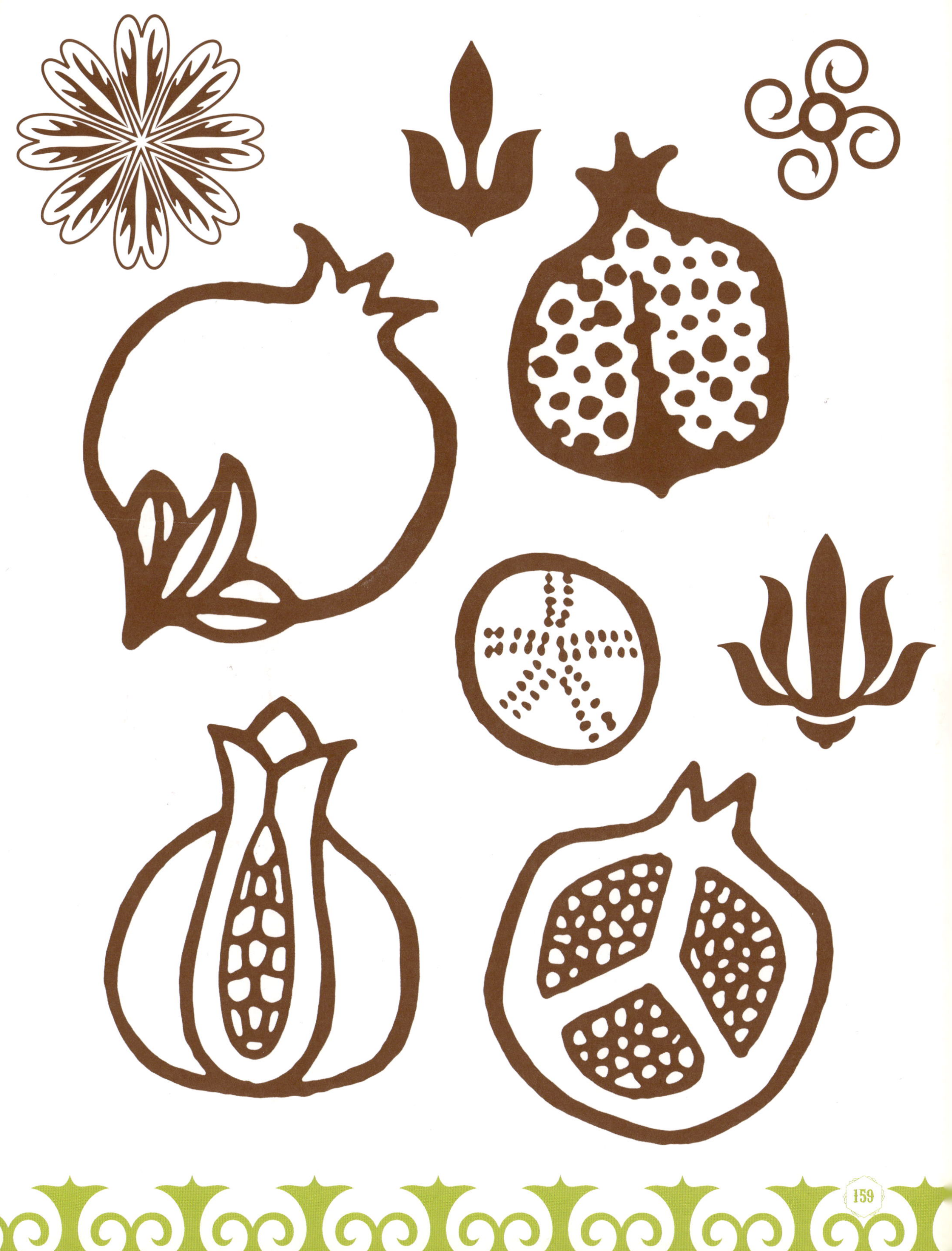

Turkish Floral Motifs

Tulips and carnations, viewed as tokens of commitment and luck, are popular motifs in Turkey.

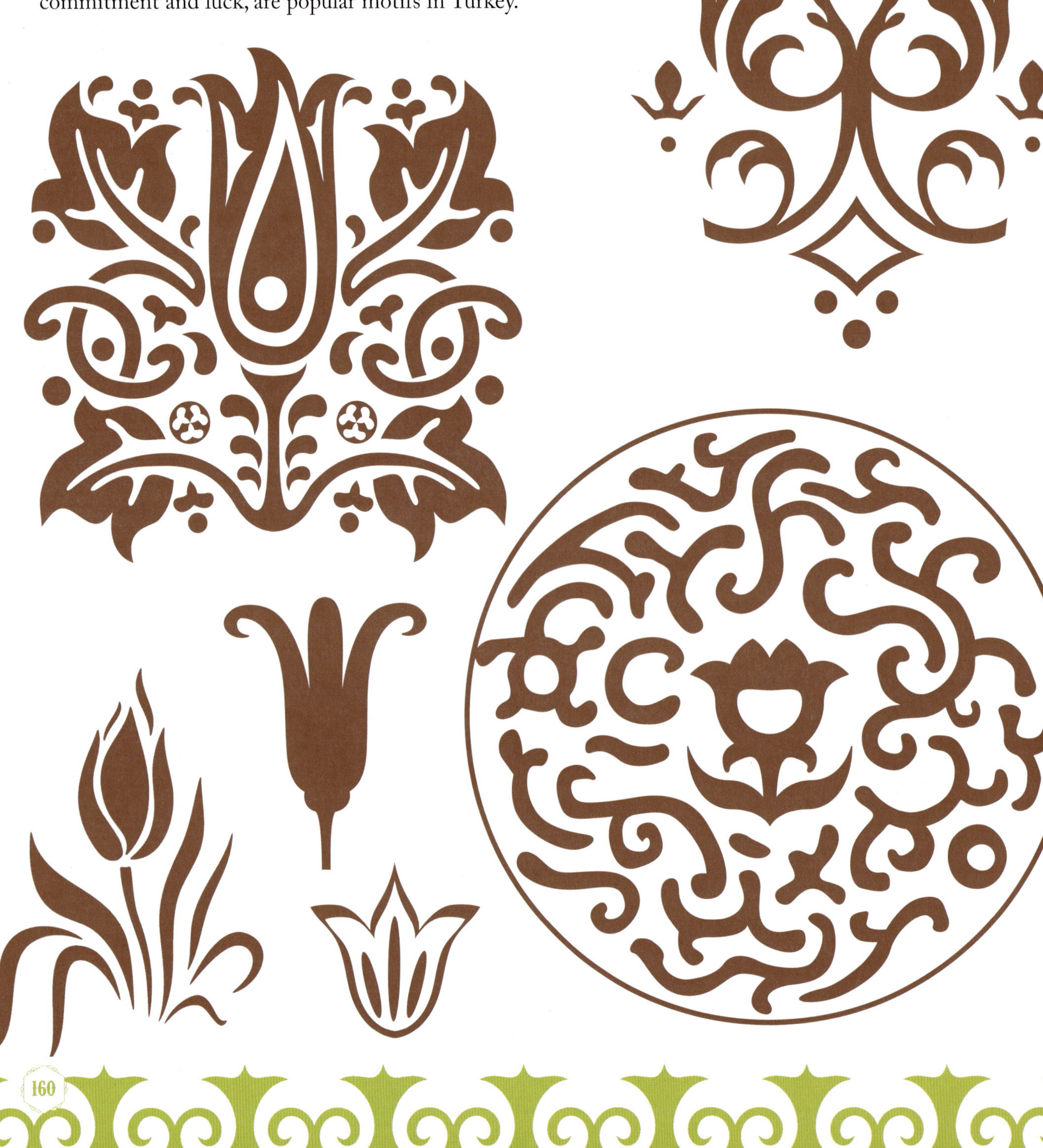

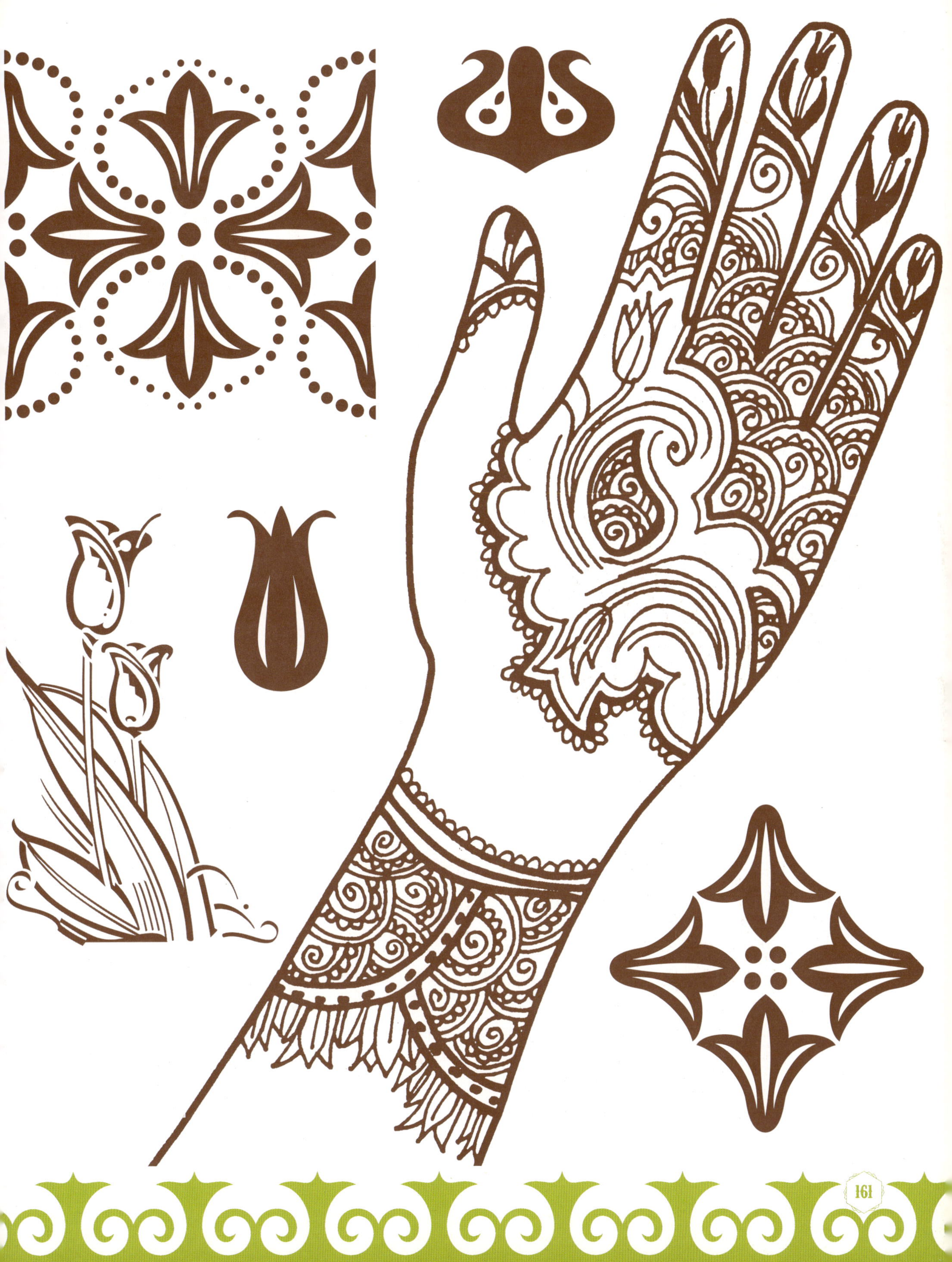

PATTERNS FROM OTHER LANDS

Although henna as body art began in India, North Africa and the Middle East, the use of henna is now an ever-growing trend all over the world, thanks to the globalization of commerce. And for good reason. Anything that can be tattooed can also be hennaed. Henna patterns can be renewed and refreshed, but without attention they will eventually fade. This means that you'll never be stuck wearing a design that your taste has outgrown. With henna, you can experiment to your heart's content, trying out one design after another.

Every society—from China to tribal North America—has its own beautifully conceived and executed designs to delight the eye and inspire the soul. Choose from among them to find the ones that best express your own esthetics and personal values.

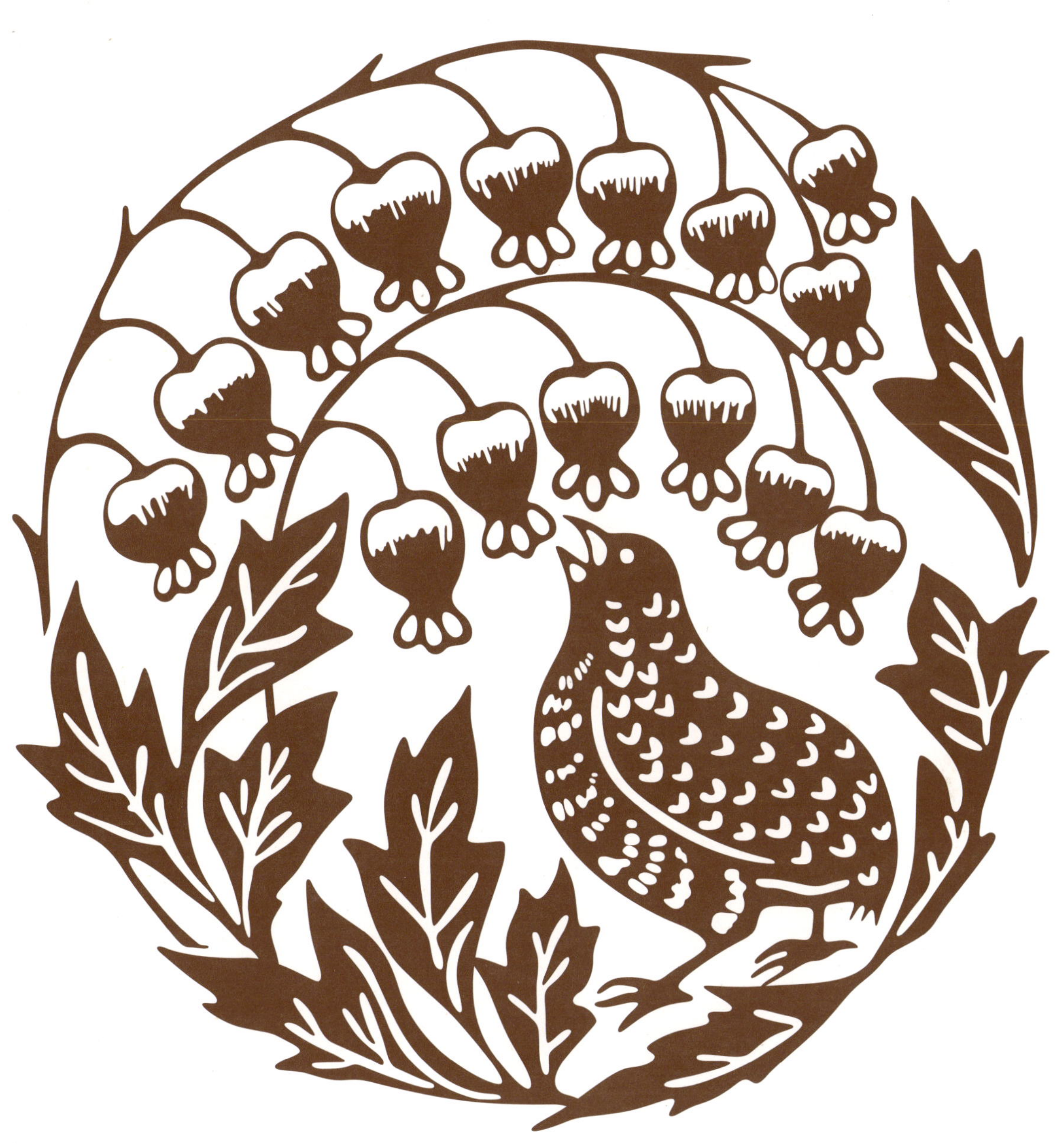

CHINESE ART

When is a dragon not a dragon? When it inhabits a Chinese painting; then it is a stand-in for the Emperor. A dragon in Chinese art is a divine, all-knowing being and bringer of prosperity. Signs and symbols can be powerful expressions of ethnic identity.

Chinese art is filled with images borrowed from the natural world: flowers, animals, insects, and trees abound.

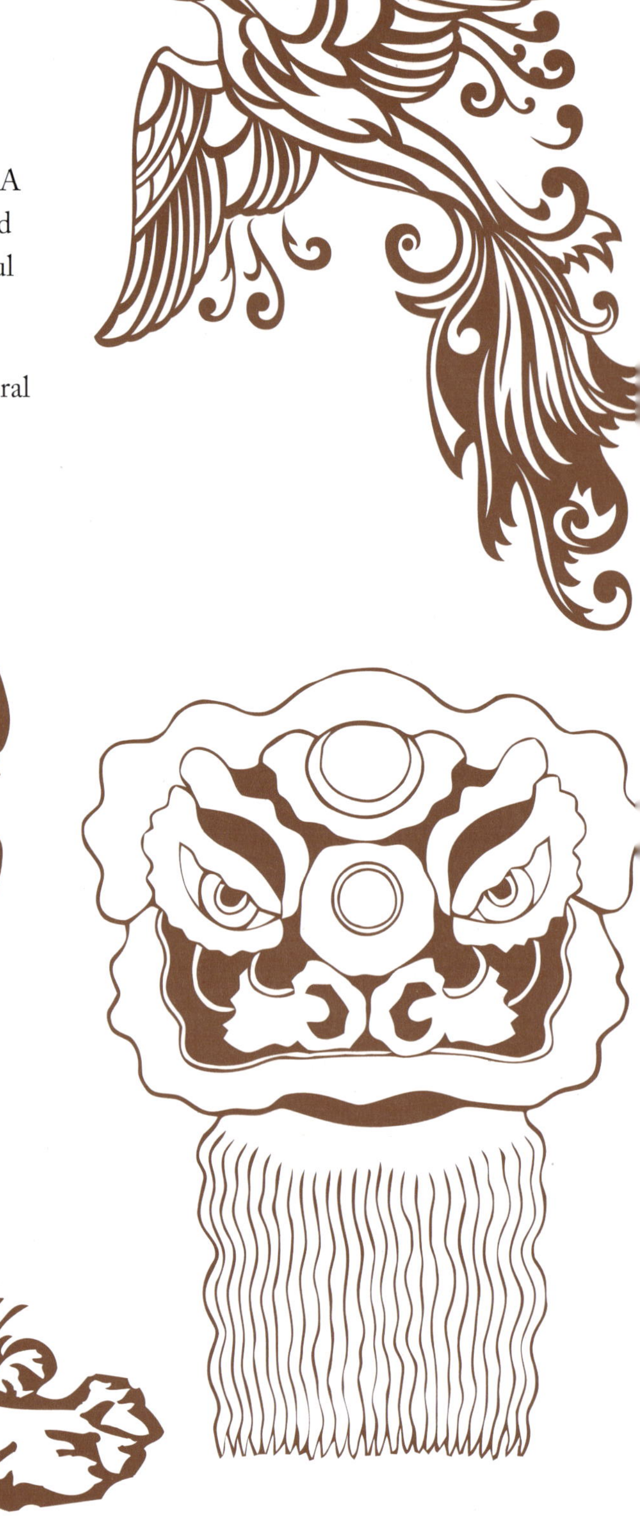

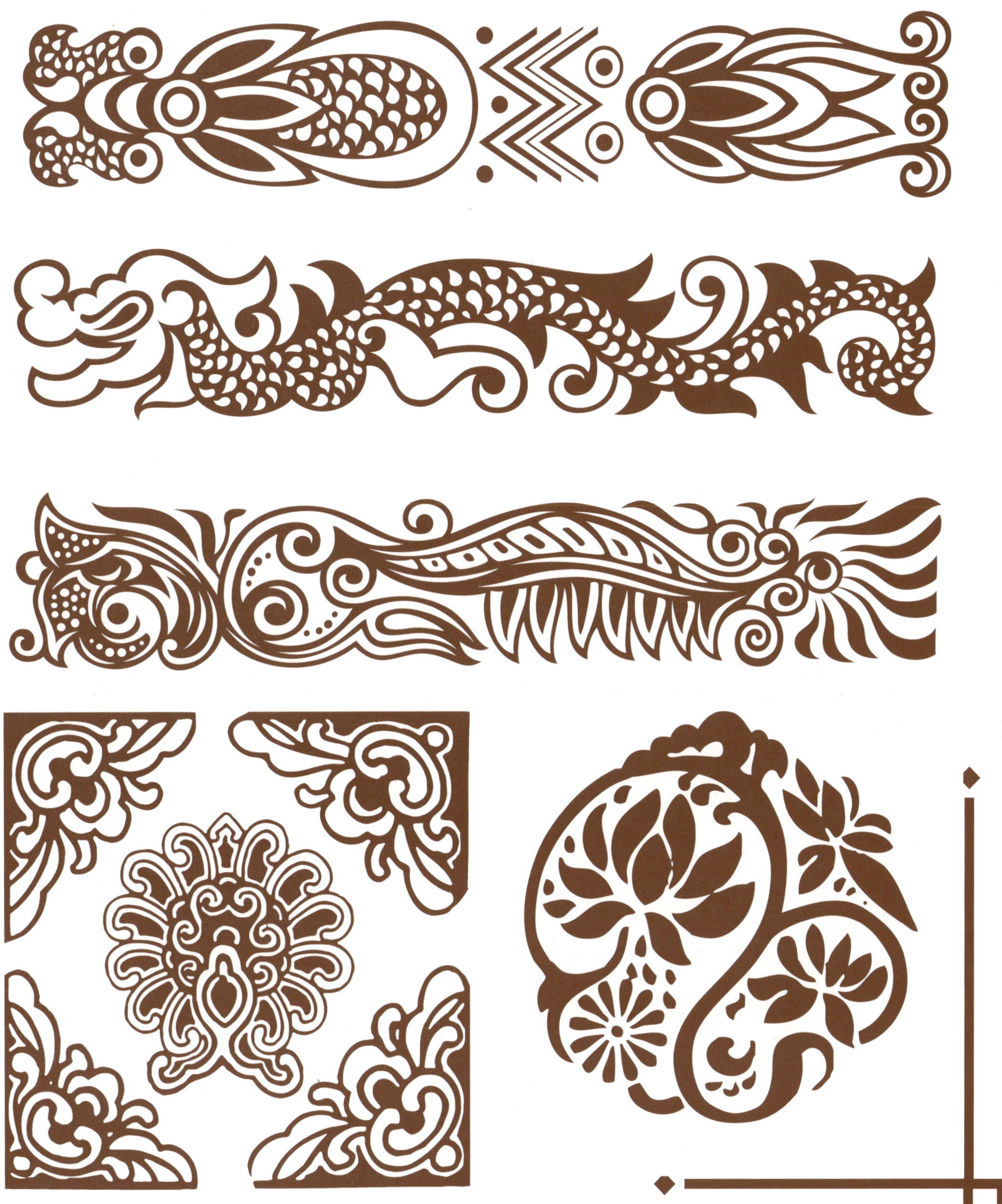

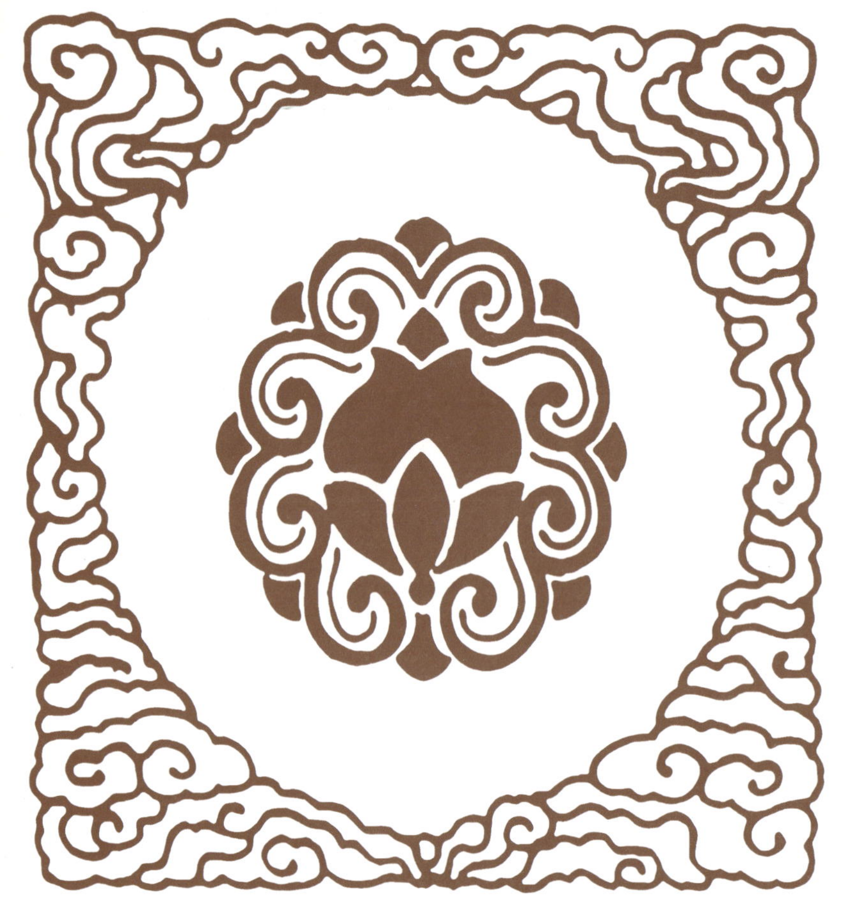

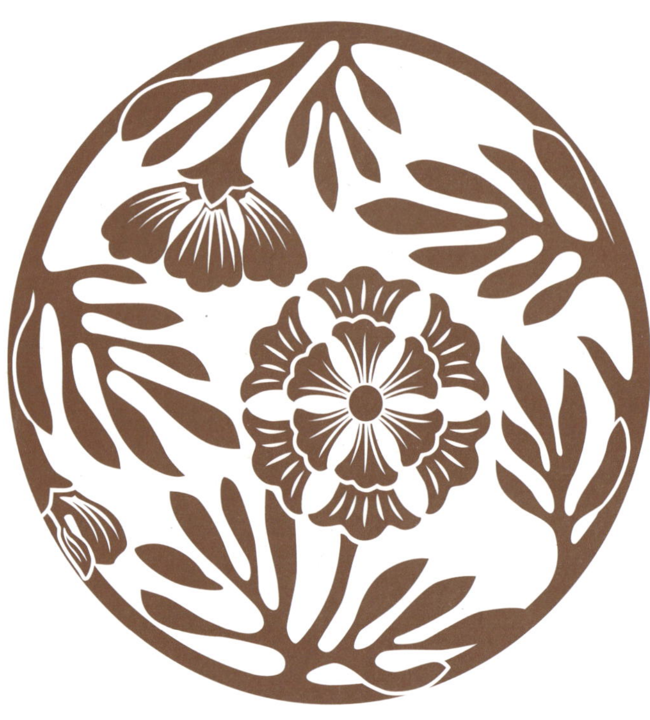

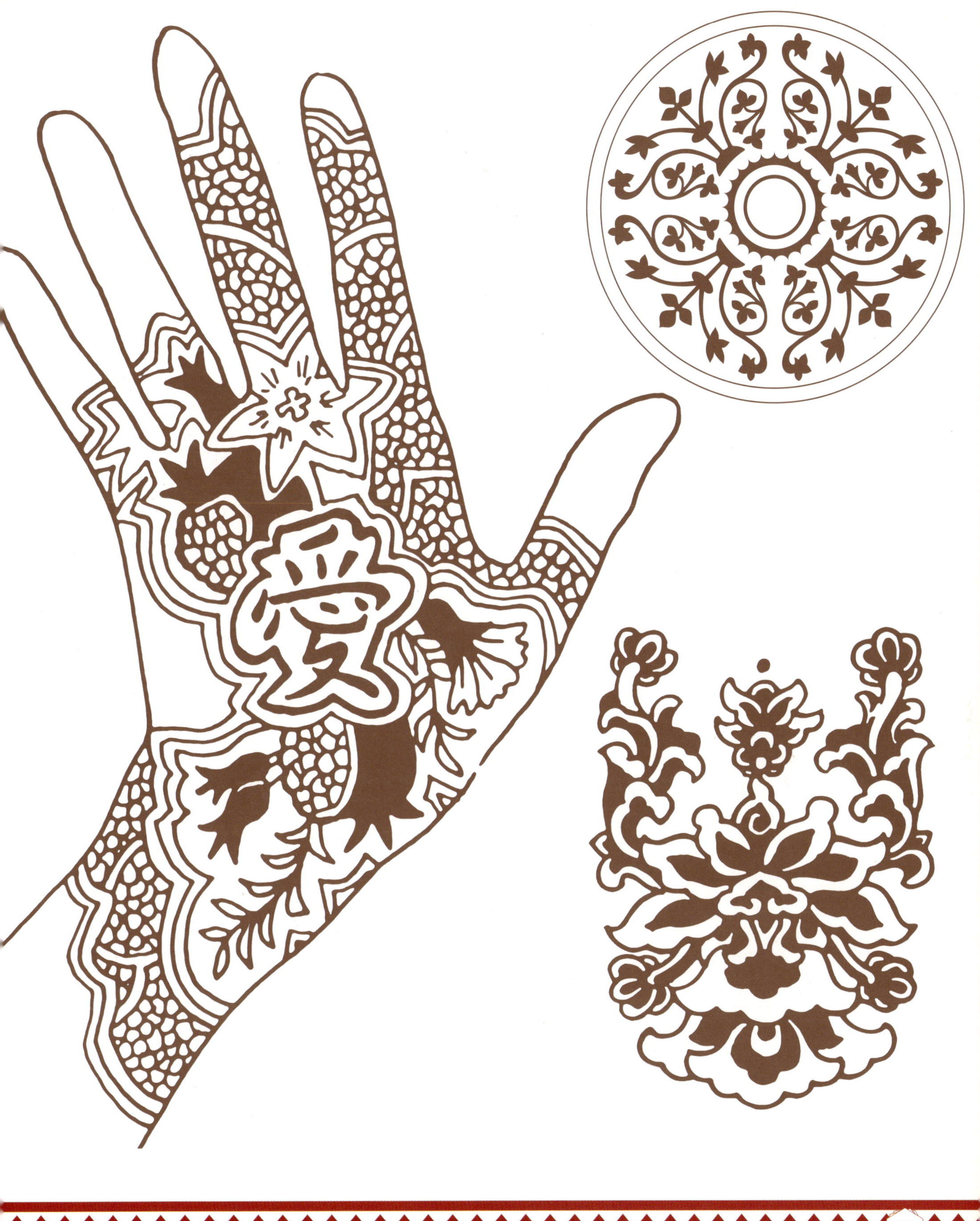
爱

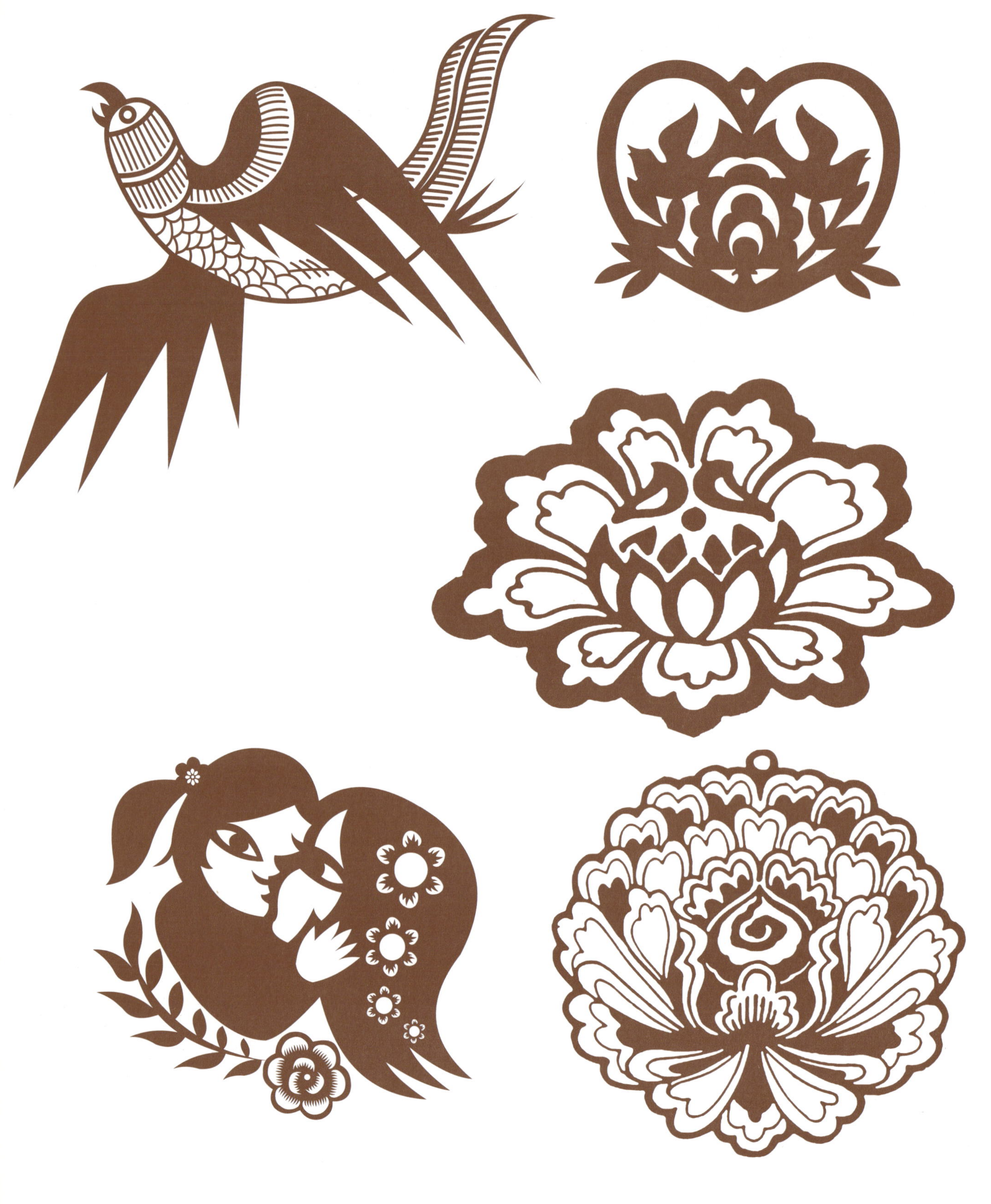

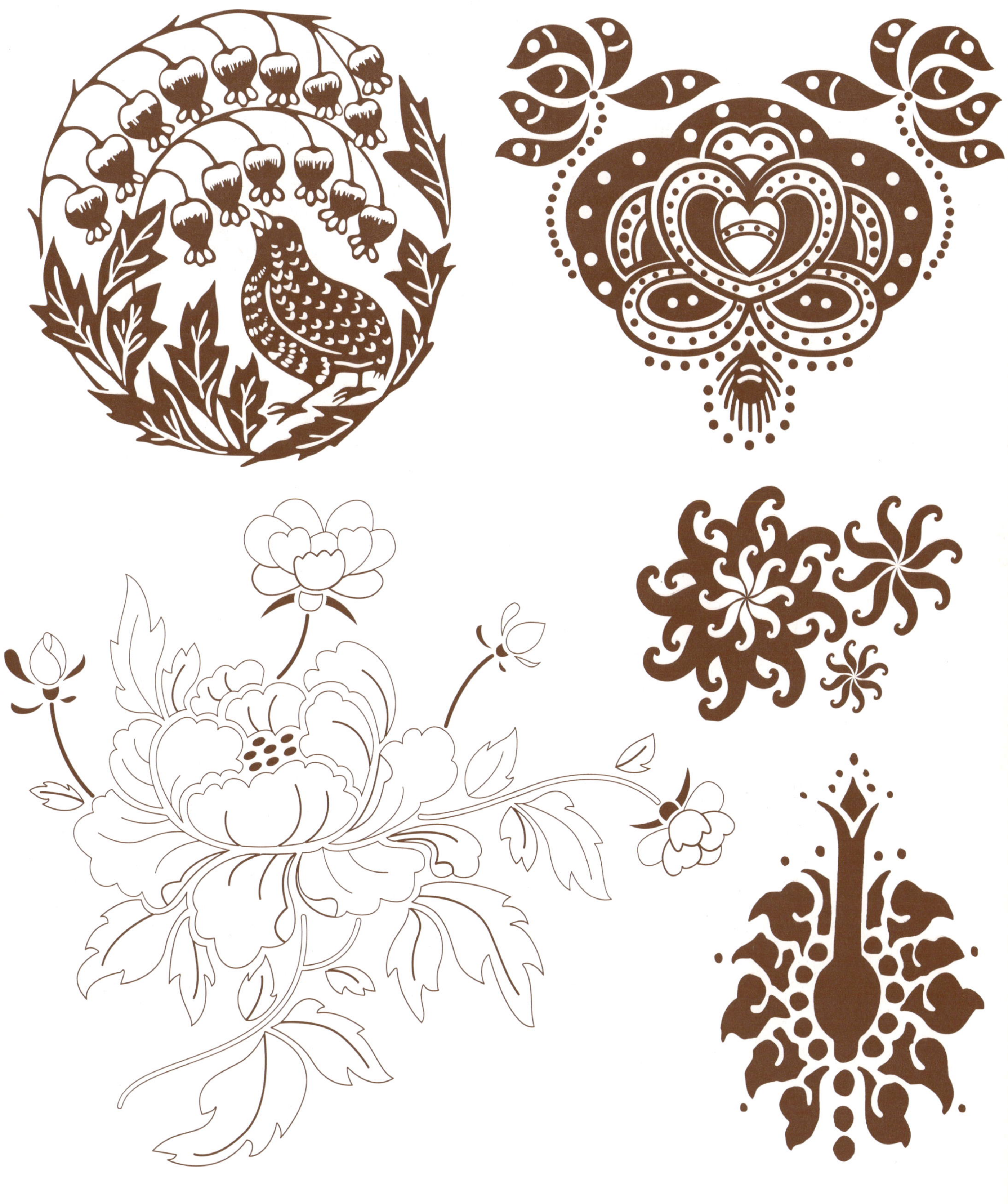

ANIMALS OF THE CHINESE ZODIAC

Locate your birth year to identify your sign.

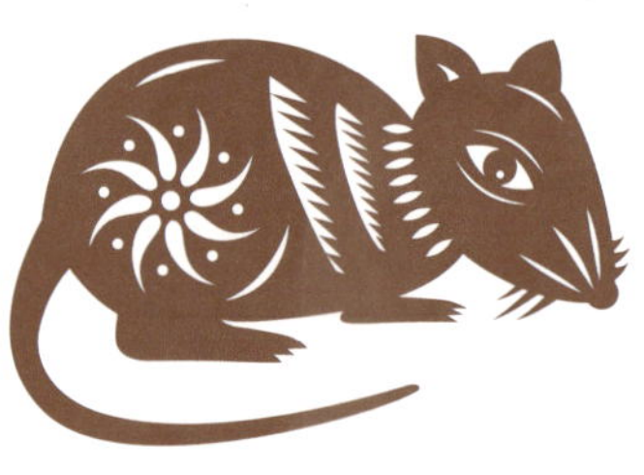

鼠

RAT

Traits: forthright, tenacious, shrewd

1936
1948
1960
1972
1984
1996
2008

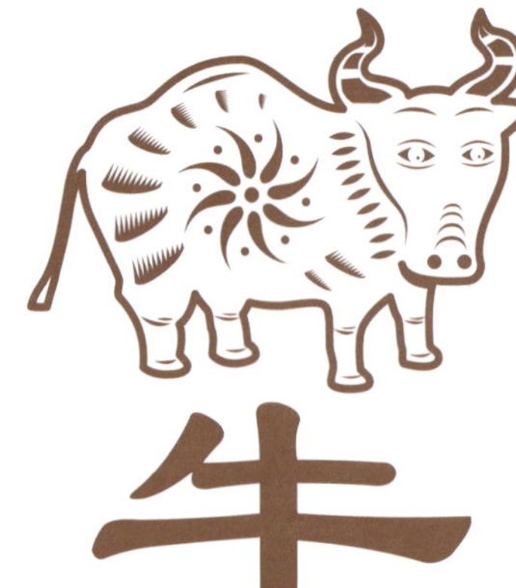

牛

OX

Traits: dependable, calm, steady

1937
1949
1961
1973
1985
1997
2009

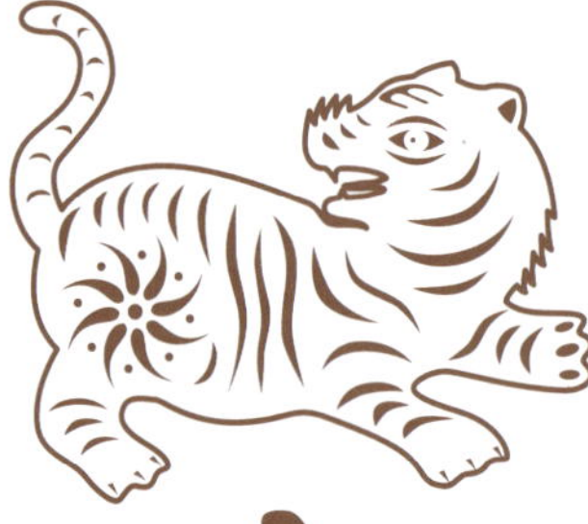

虎

TIGER

Traits: powerful, passionate, daring

1938
1950
1962
1974
1986
1998
2010

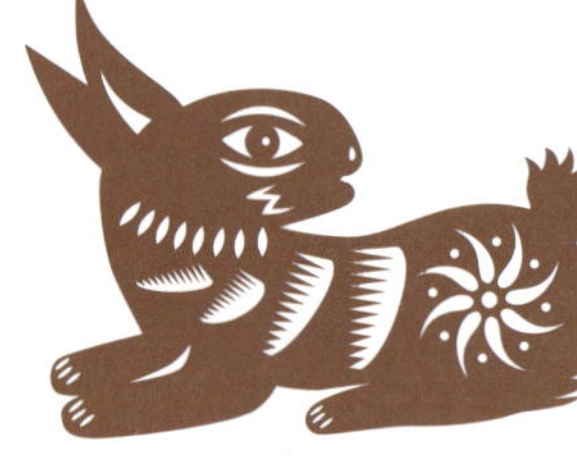

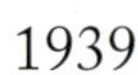

兔

RABBIT

Traits: good friend, sensitive, elegant

1939
1951
1963
1975
1987
1999
2011

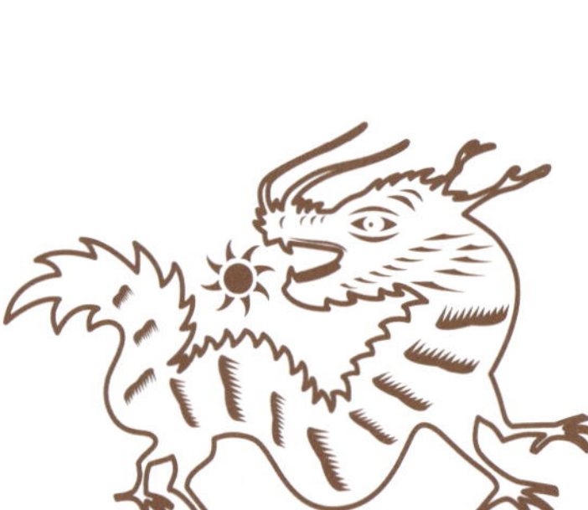

龍

DRAGON

Traits: strong, proud, noble

1940
1952
1964
1976
1988
2000
2012

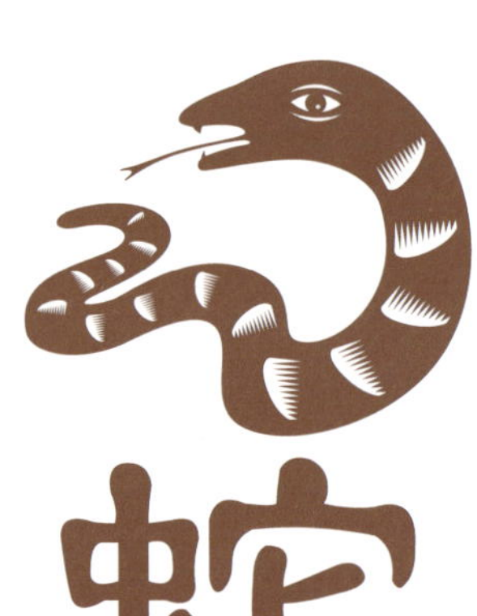

蛇

SNAKE

Traits: wise, sensual, graceful

1941
1953
1965
1977
1989
2001
2013

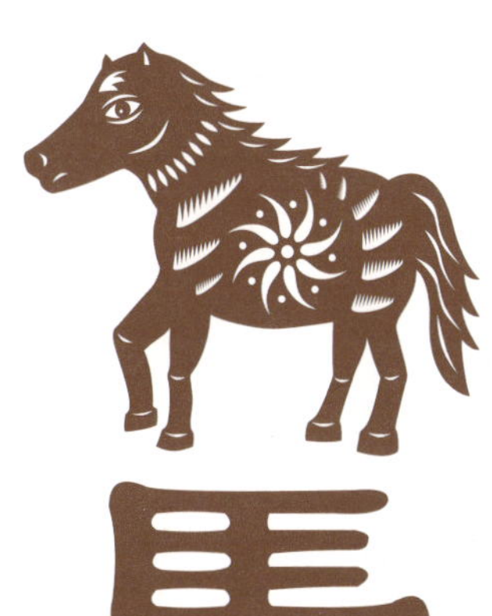

馬

HORSE

Traits: cheerful, popular, perceptive

1930
1942
1954
1966
1978
1990
2002

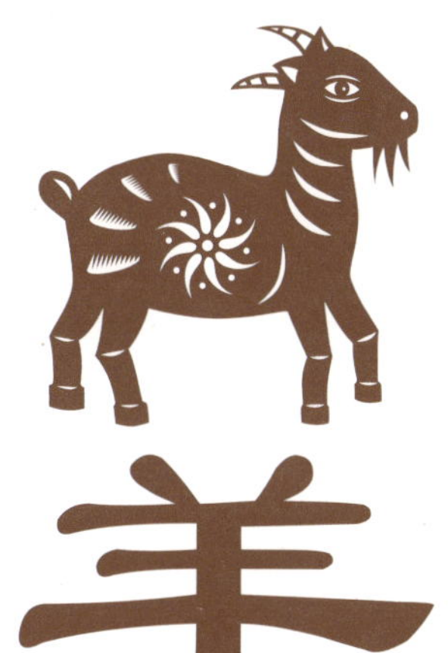

羊

GOAT

Traits: righteous, observant, artistic

1931
1943
1955
1967
1979
1991
2003

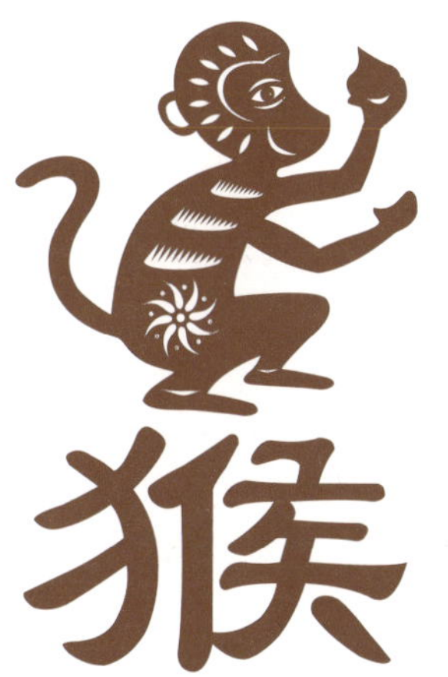

猴

MONKEY

Traits: innovative, quick-witted, inquisitive

1932
1944
1956
1968
1980
1992
2004

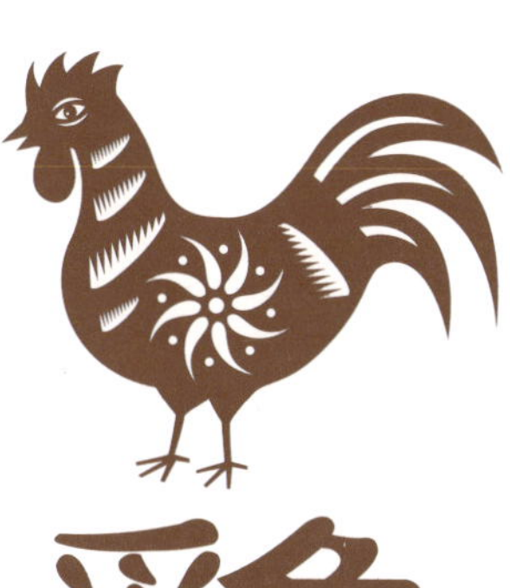

雞

ROOSTER

Traits: organized, self-assured

1933
1945
1957
1969
1981
1993
2005

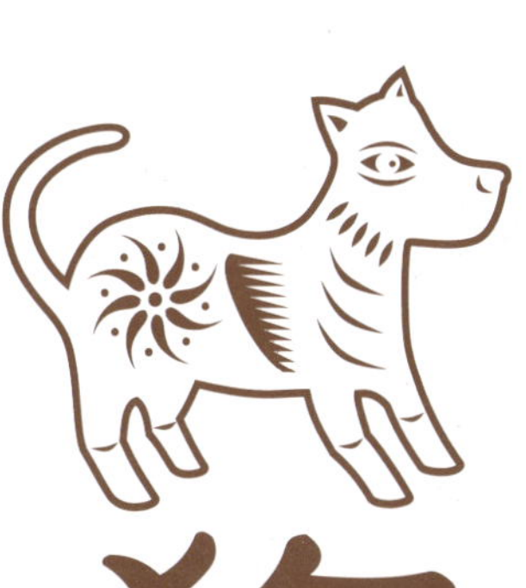

狗

DOG

Traits: honest, intelligent, loyal

1934
1946
1958
1970
1982
1994
2006

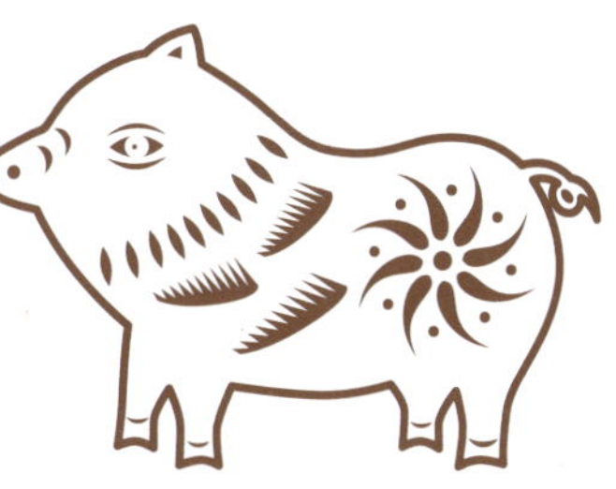

豬

PIG

Traits: sociable, patient

1935
1947
1959
1971
1983
1995
2007

Eight Symbols of Buddhism

Eight auspicious symbols of Buddhism appear often in Chinese art and are thought to bring peace, blessings and abundant virtues. They can also be combined, incorporating two or more symbols together, as shown on the facing page.

Conch Shell—the sound it makes banishes evil spirits

Lotus—spiritual perfection

The Wheel—the spokes represent the end of all suffering

The Parasol—shelters and protects from harmful forces

Pair of Fishes—fidelity

The Banner of Victory—Buddha's victory over four vices: impurity, unbridled passion, pride/lust, and death

Vase of Sacred Water—satisfaction of material desires

Knot of Eternity—connection of all things; infinite wisdom

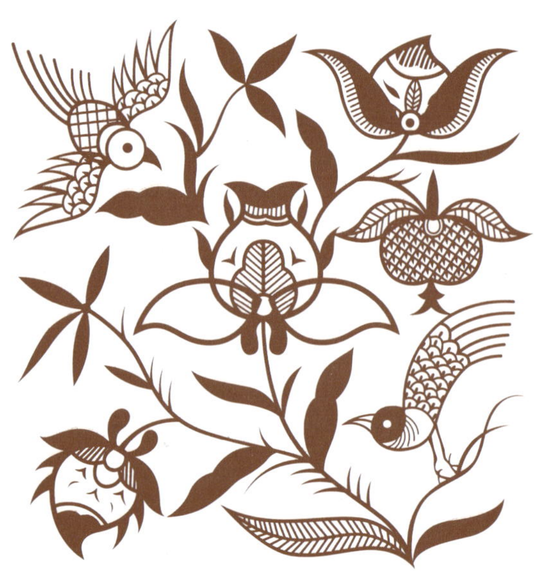

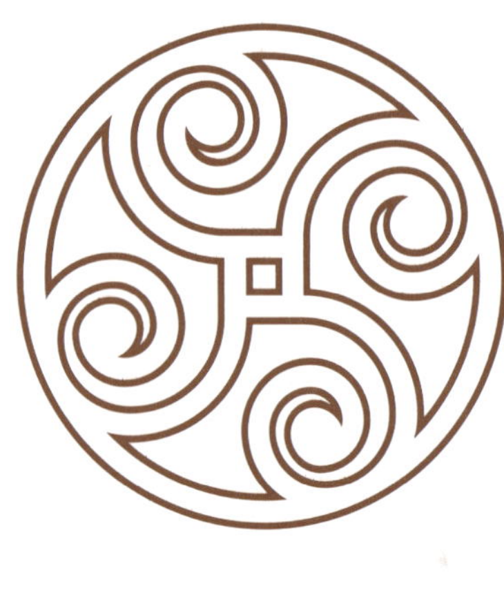

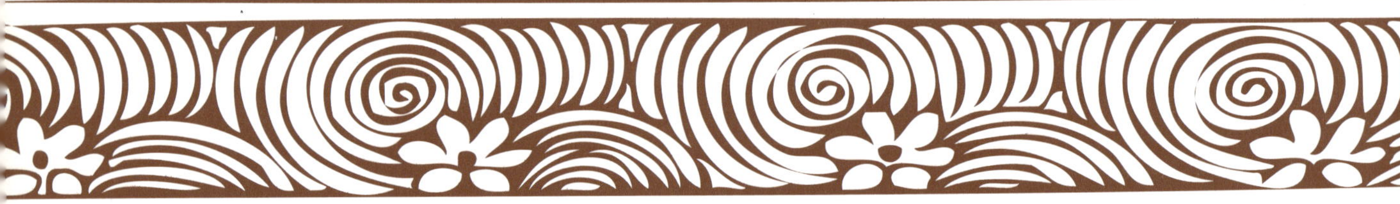

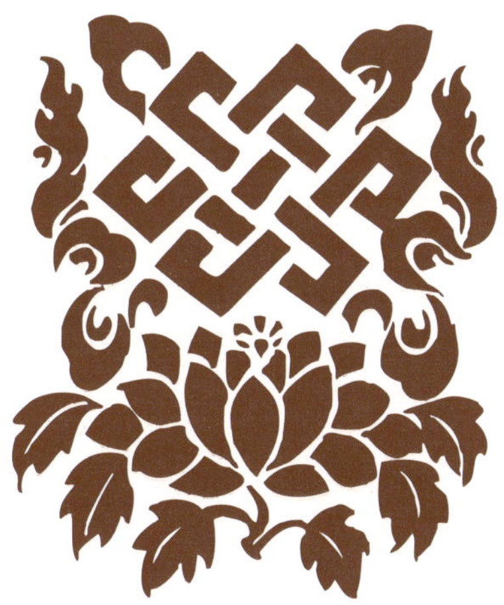

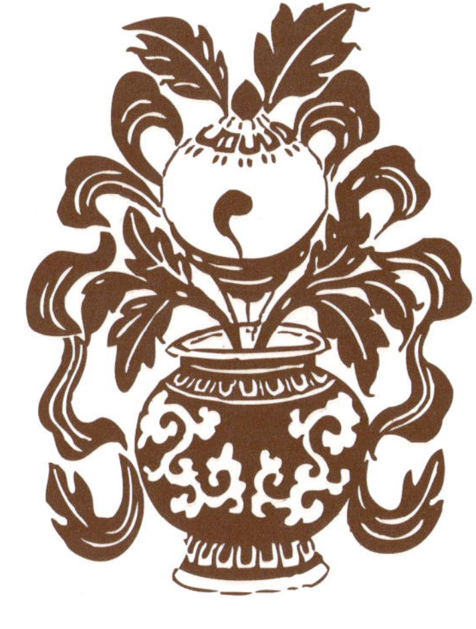

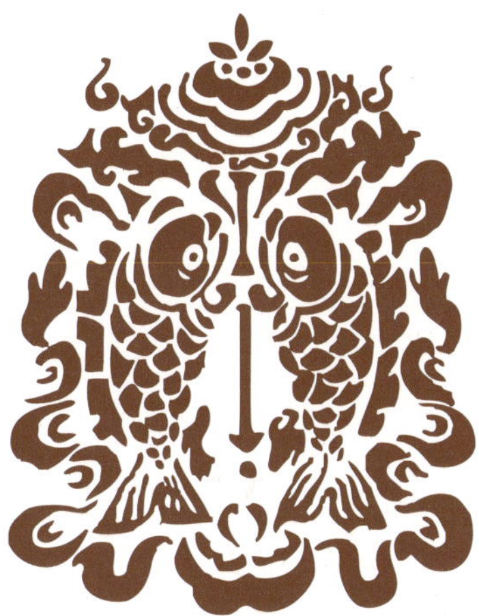

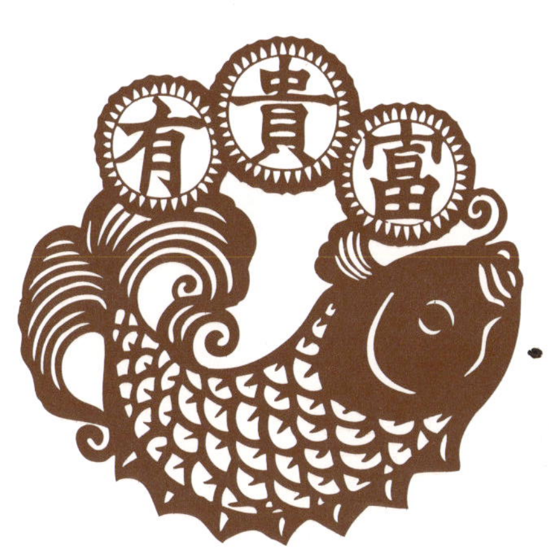
有
貴
富

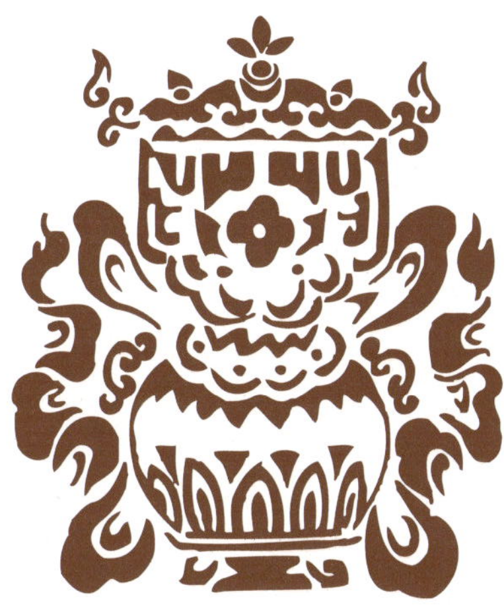

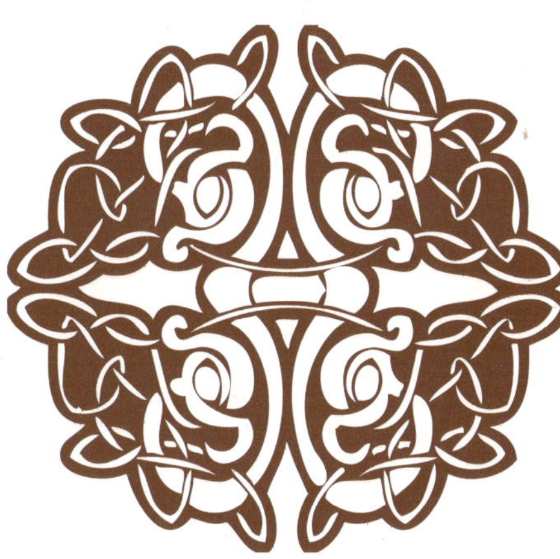

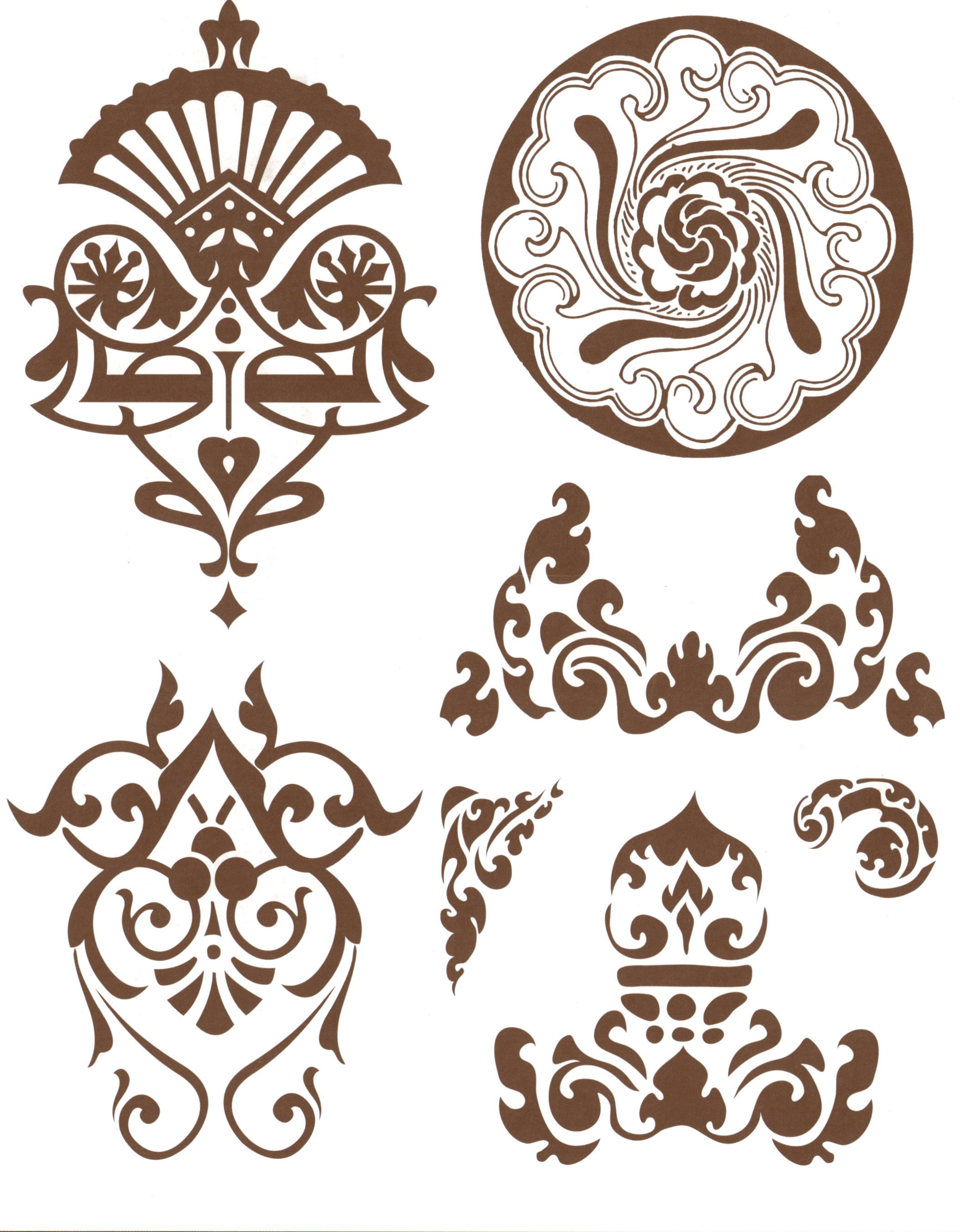

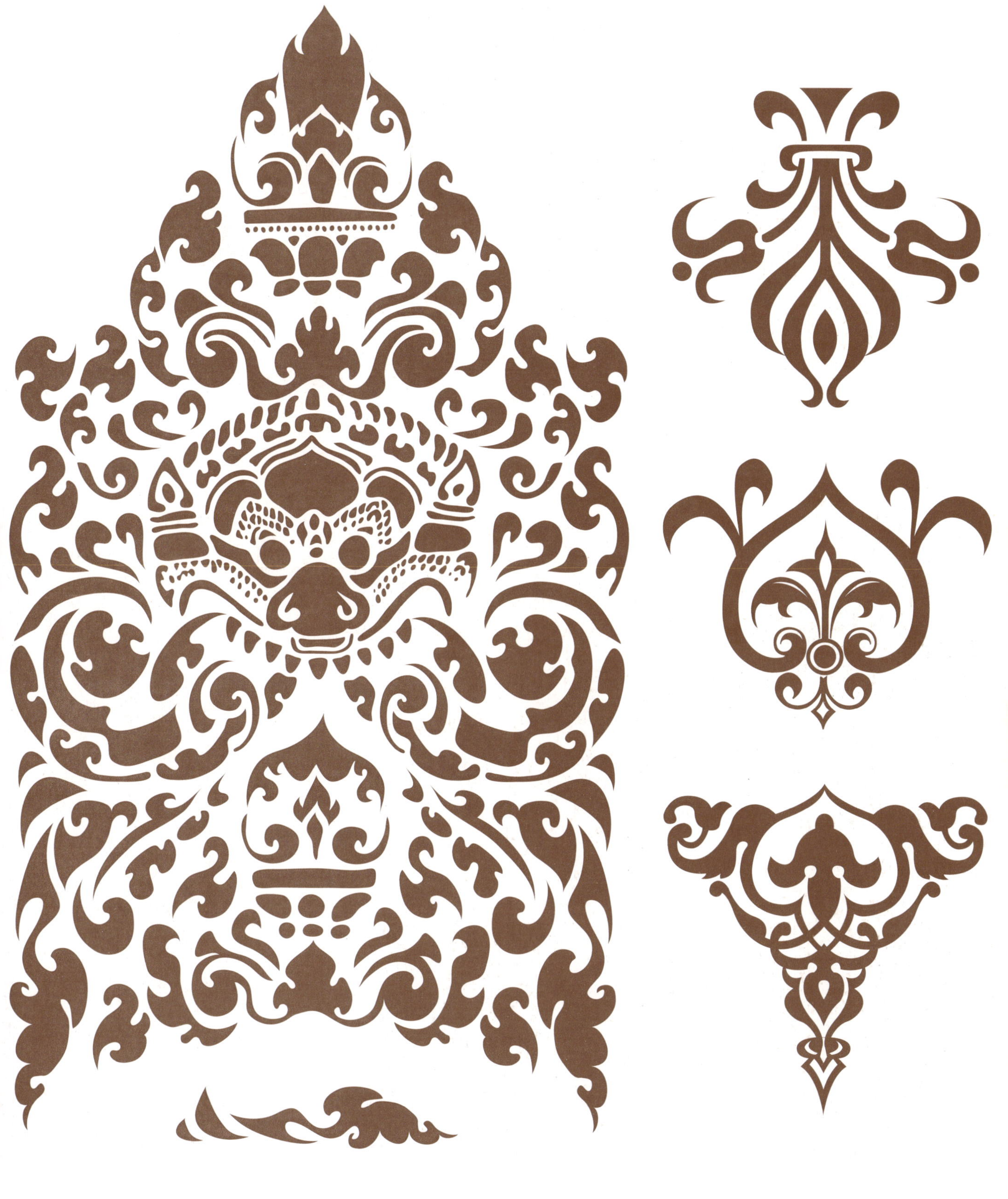

HANSI OR KANJI?

The Chinese language is written with such graceful brushstrokes that a single word might serve as its own artistic expression—and an attractive design for a henna tattoo. In the fifth century CE, the Japanese adopted these symbols, which the Chinese called Hansi, and tweaked them to conform to their own pronunciation and language structure. Combining beauty of form with inspirational concepts, the following Japanese characters, called Kanji, have become popular tattoo motifs in Japan.

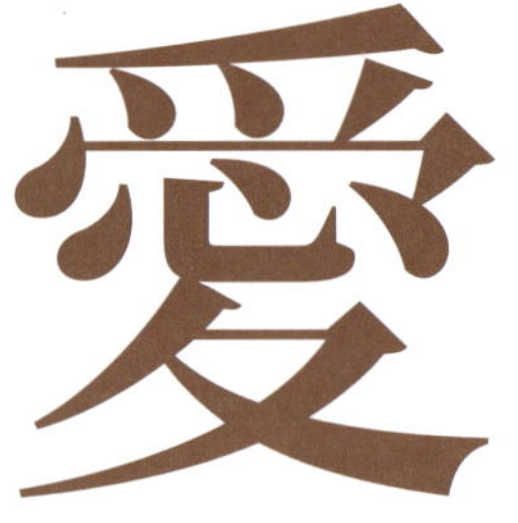

Love

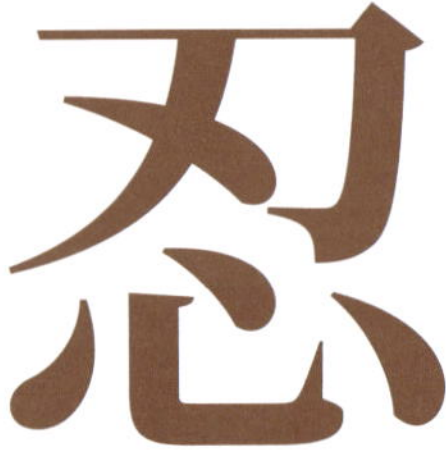

Perseverance

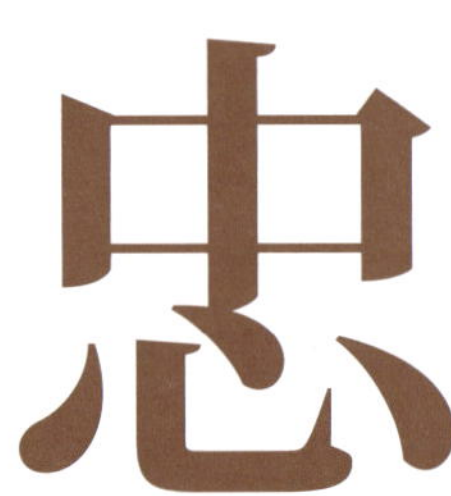

Loyalty

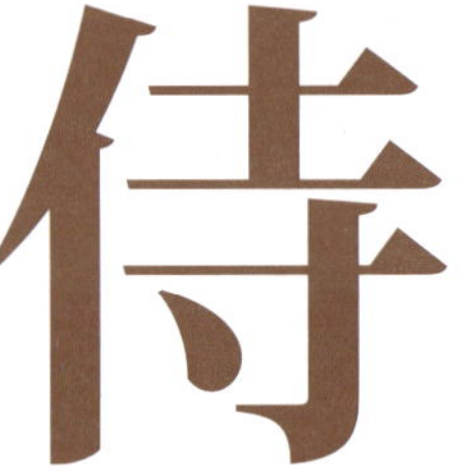

Samurai

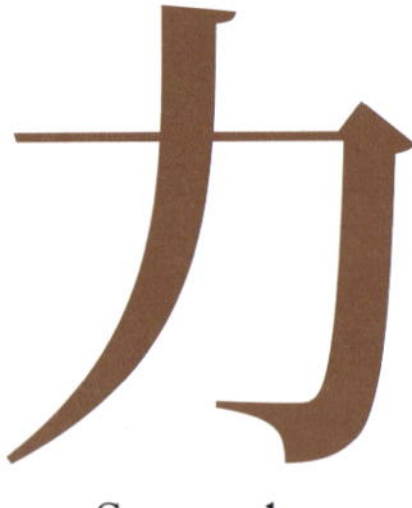

Strength

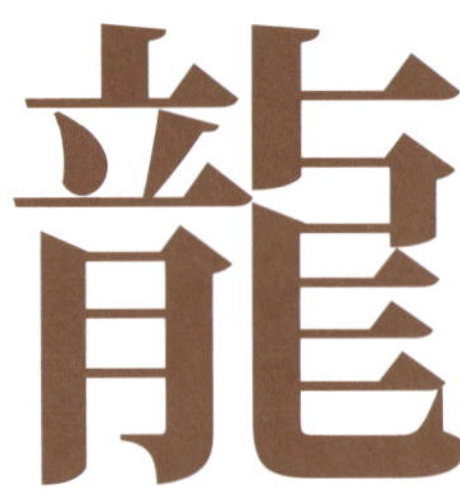

Dragon

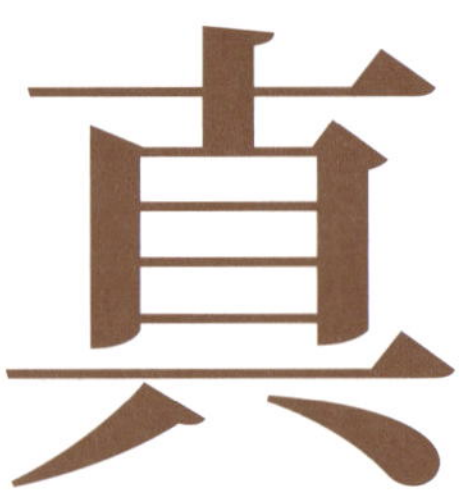

Truth

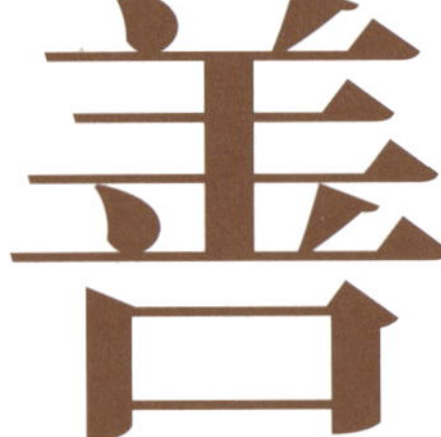

Kindness

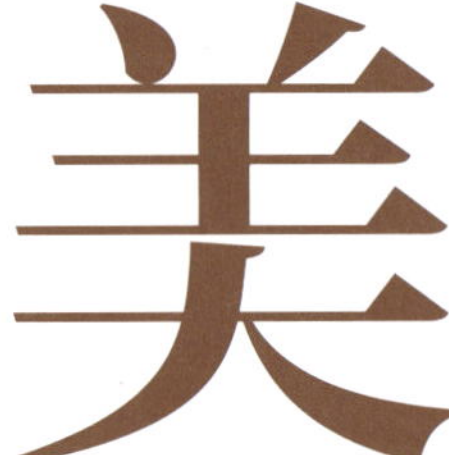

Beauty

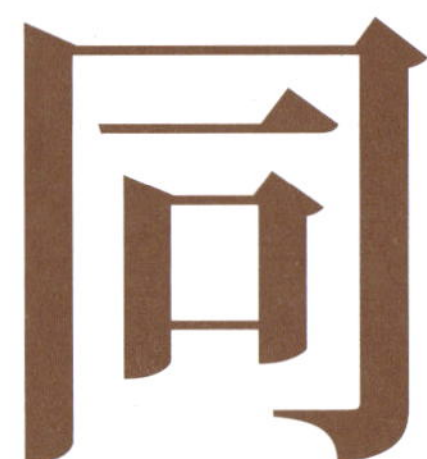

Togetherness

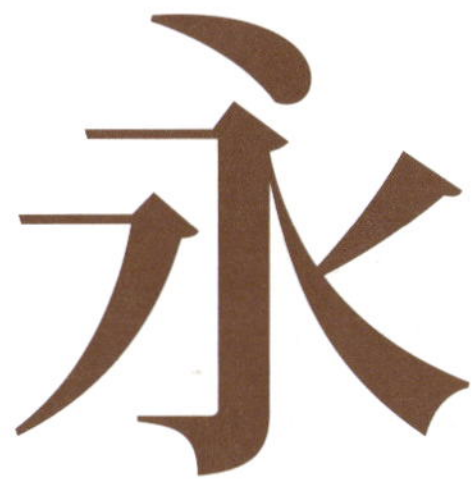

Forever

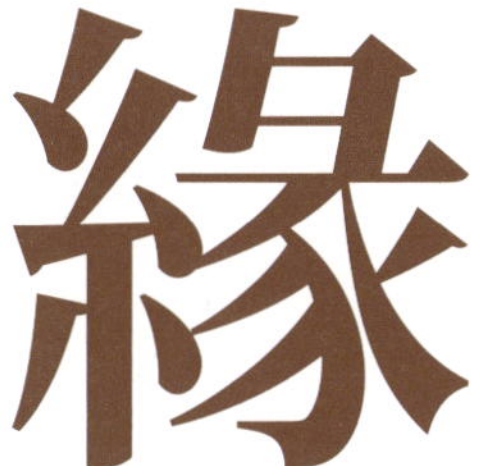

Chance

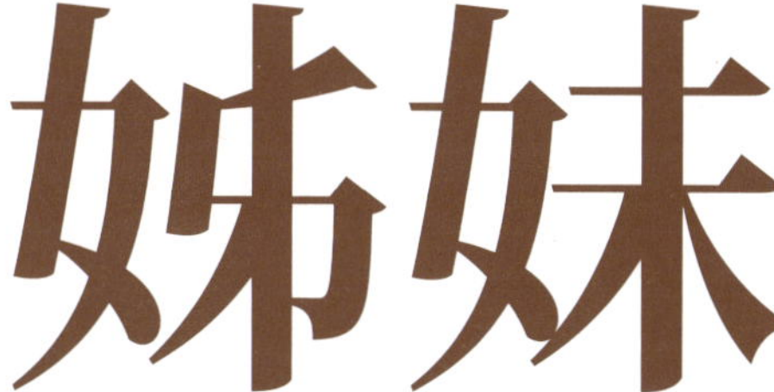

Sisterhood

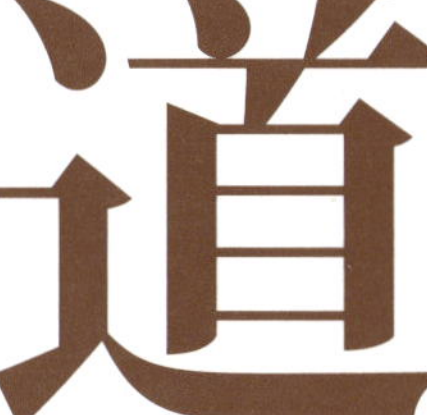

Tao (the Way)

兄弟

Brotherhood

親友

Best friend

勇

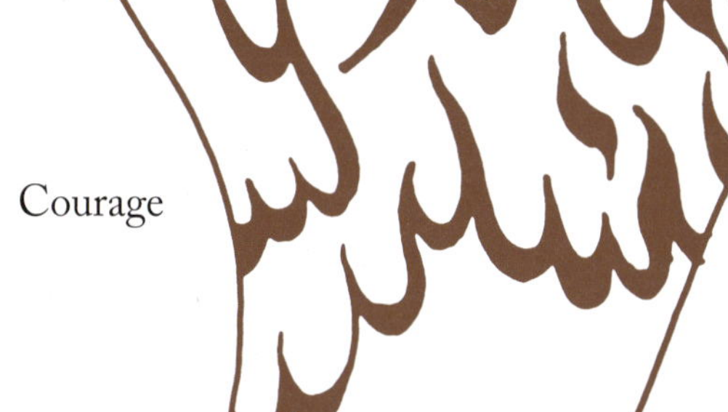

Courage

努力

Hard work

IMAGES FROM JAPAN

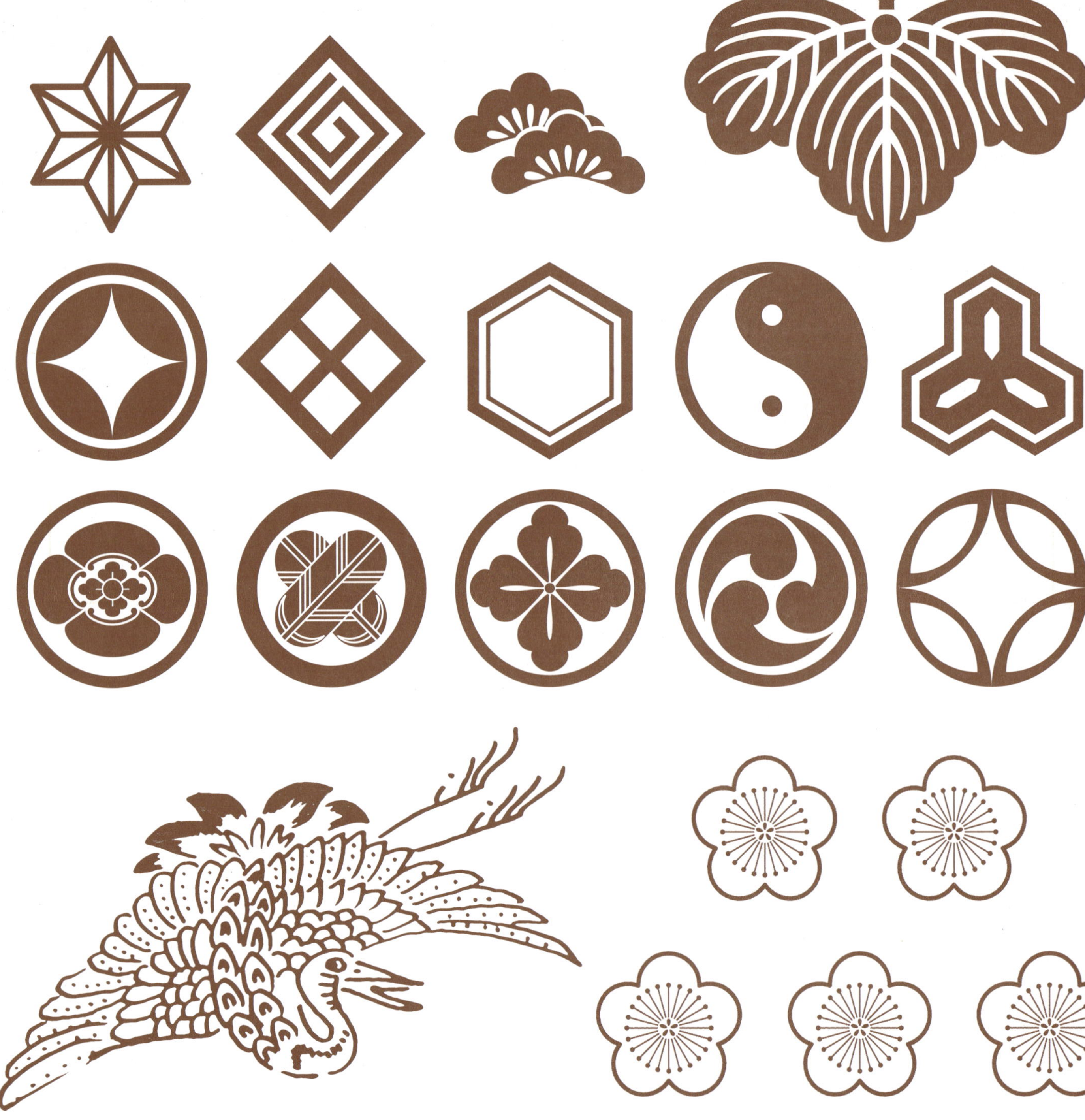

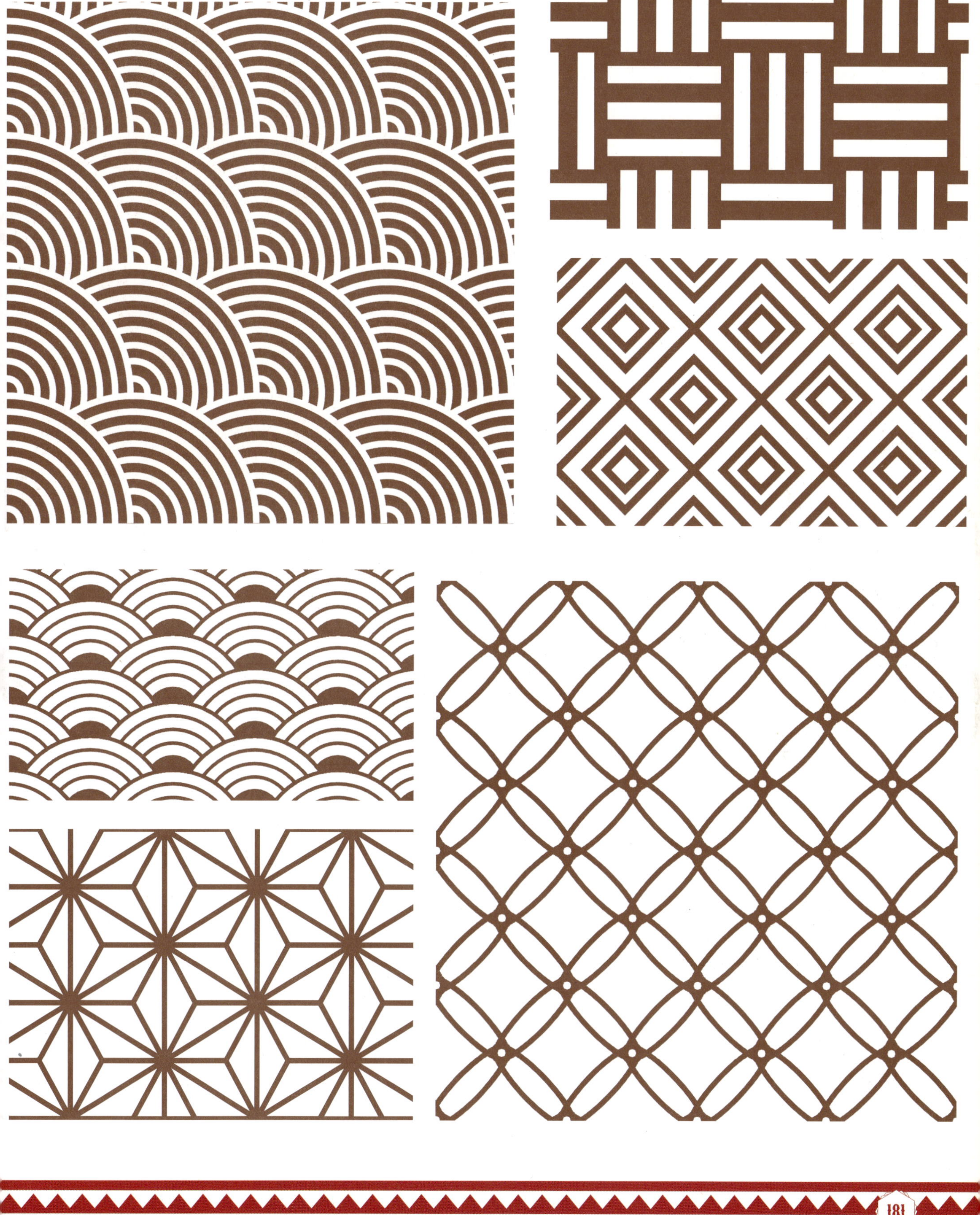

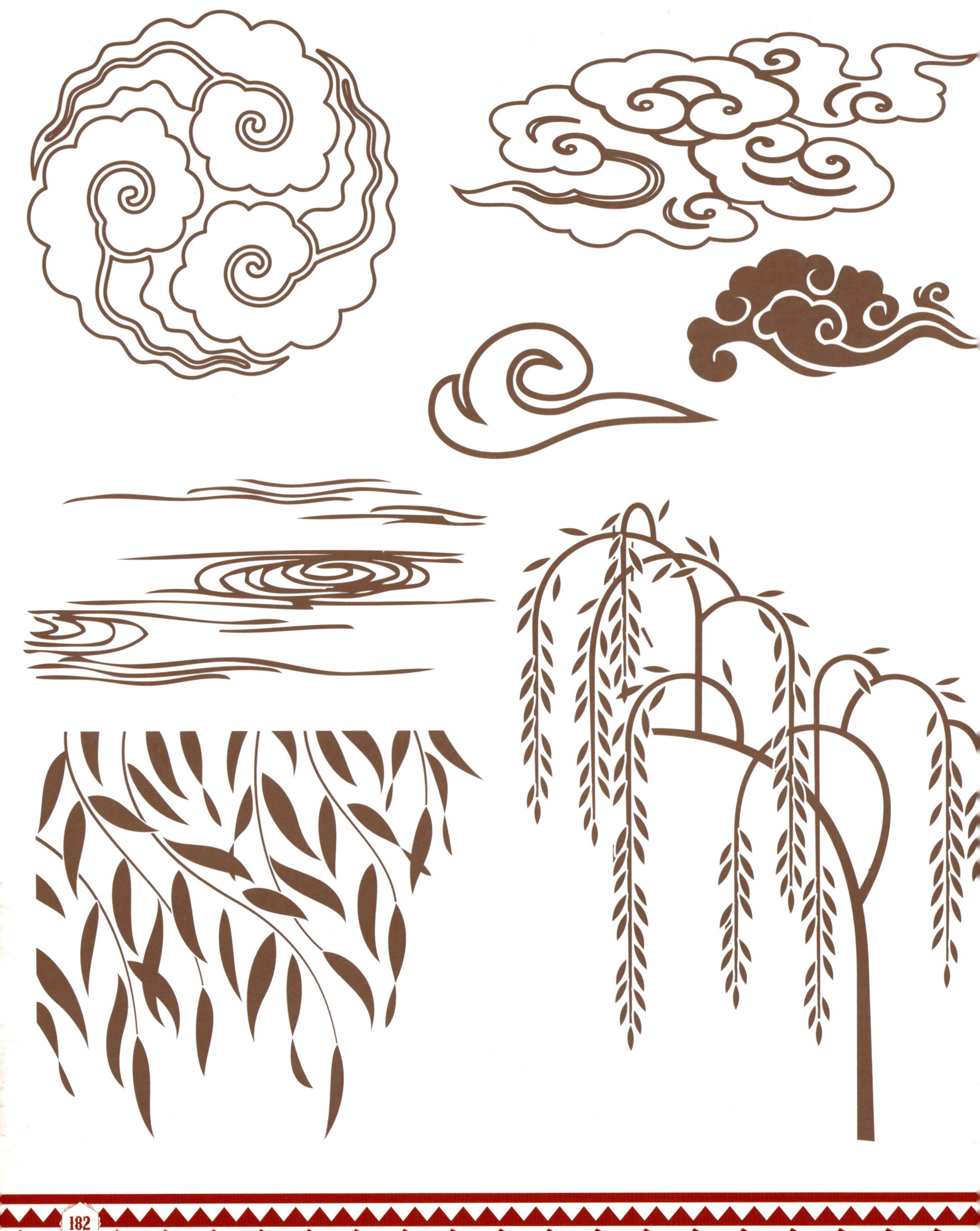

Indonesian Batik Motifs

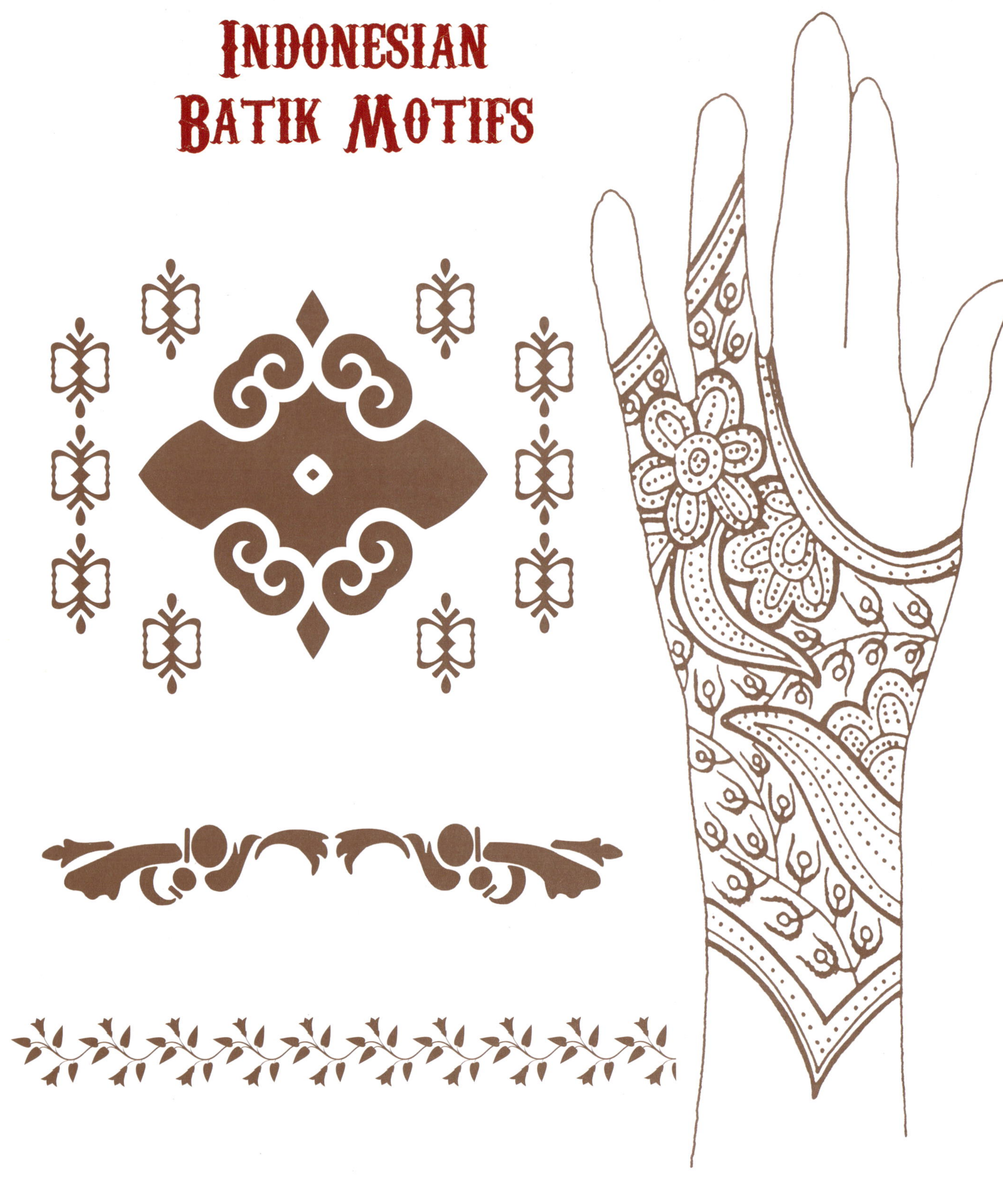

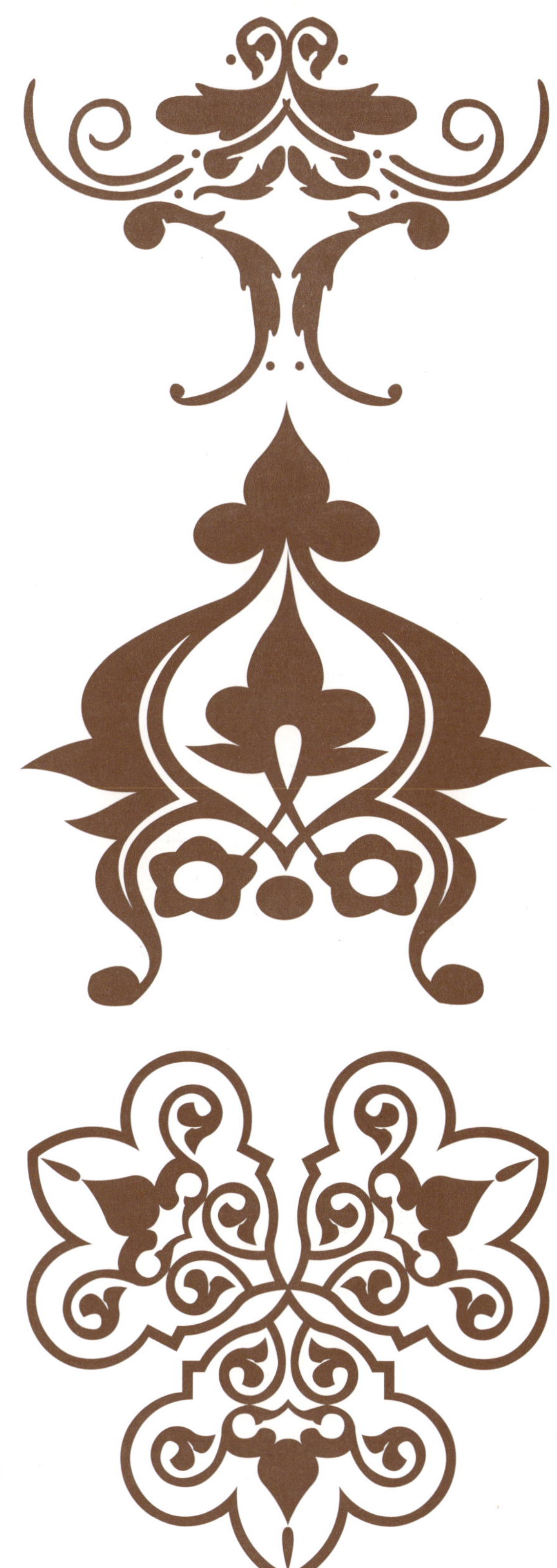

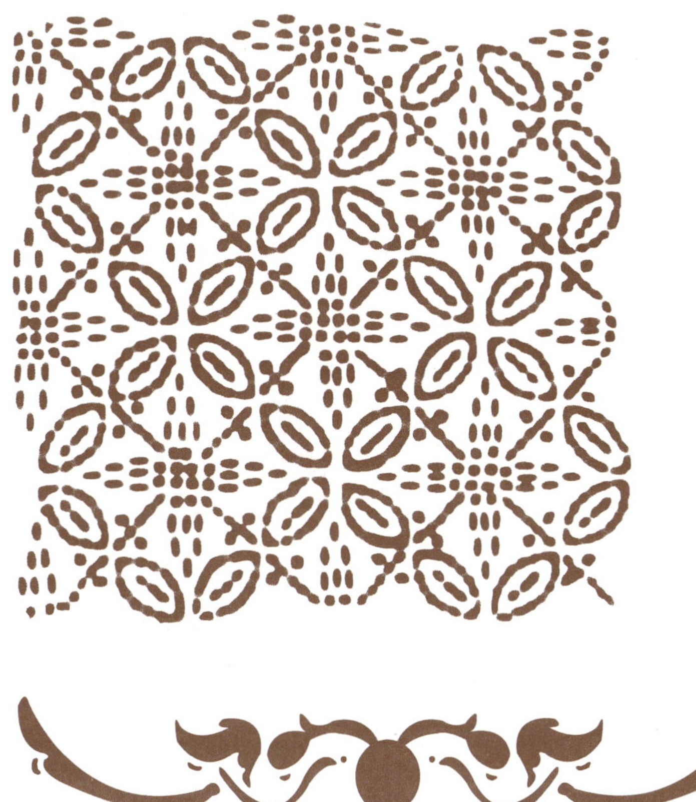

ART FROM EASTERN EUROPE

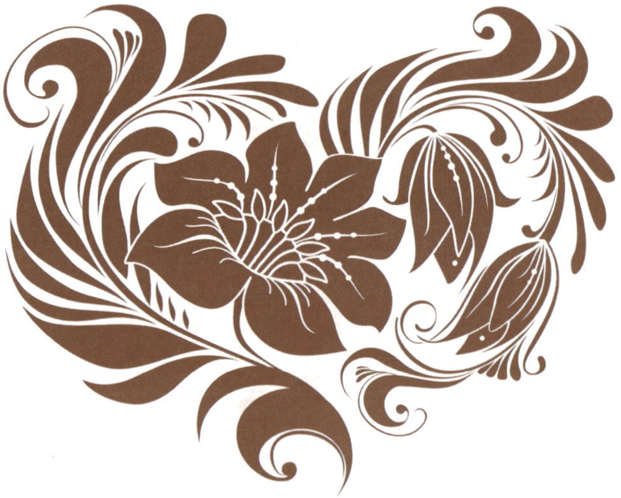

Although the decorated egg known as *pysanka* has become widely associated with Easter, it originated 5,000 to 3,000 years BCE. As a pagan amulet, it was a symbol of nature's rebirth and used as a ceremonial object in sun worshipping rites. Today the eggs have come to symbolize good luck and as such are thought to ward off evil.

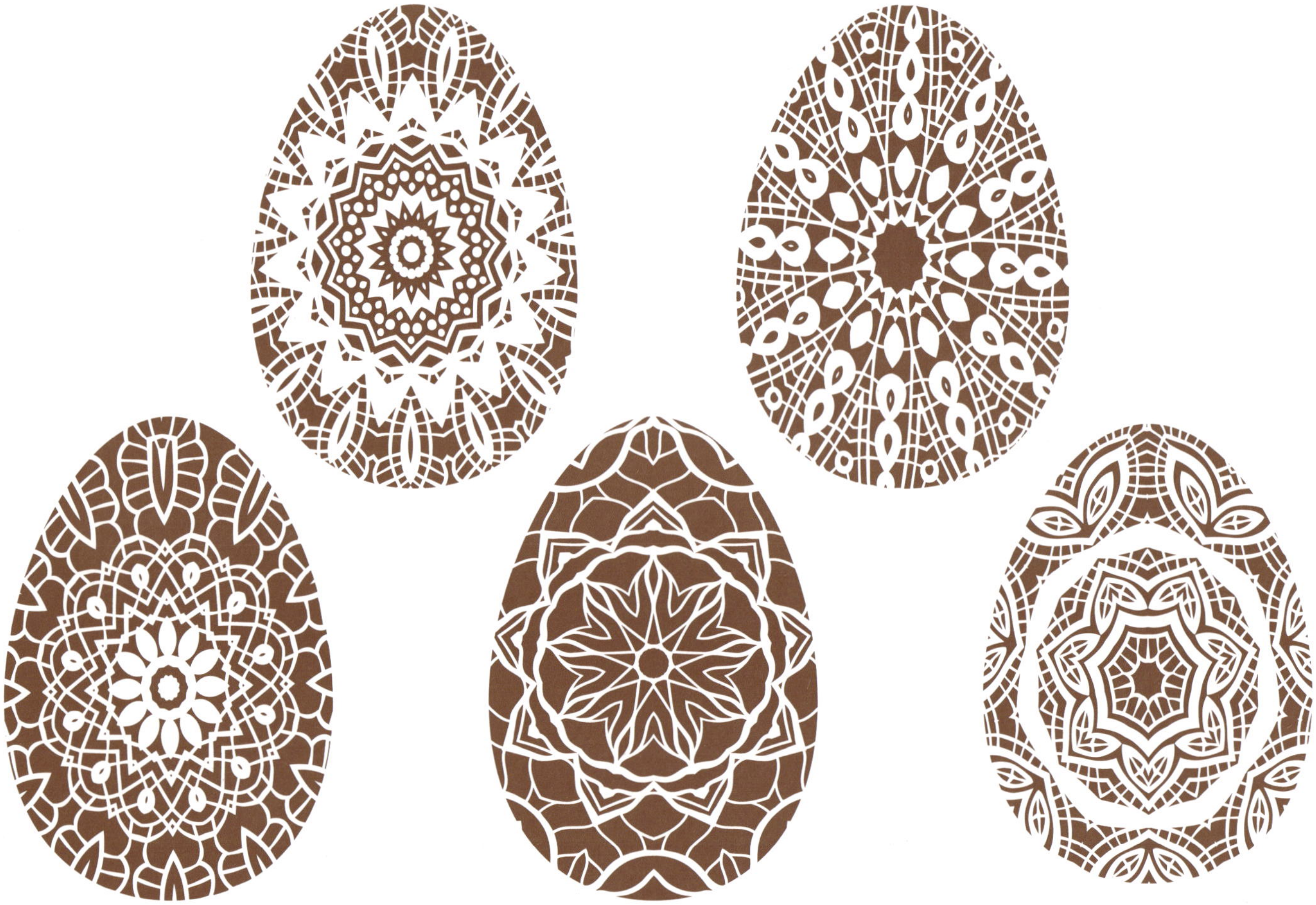

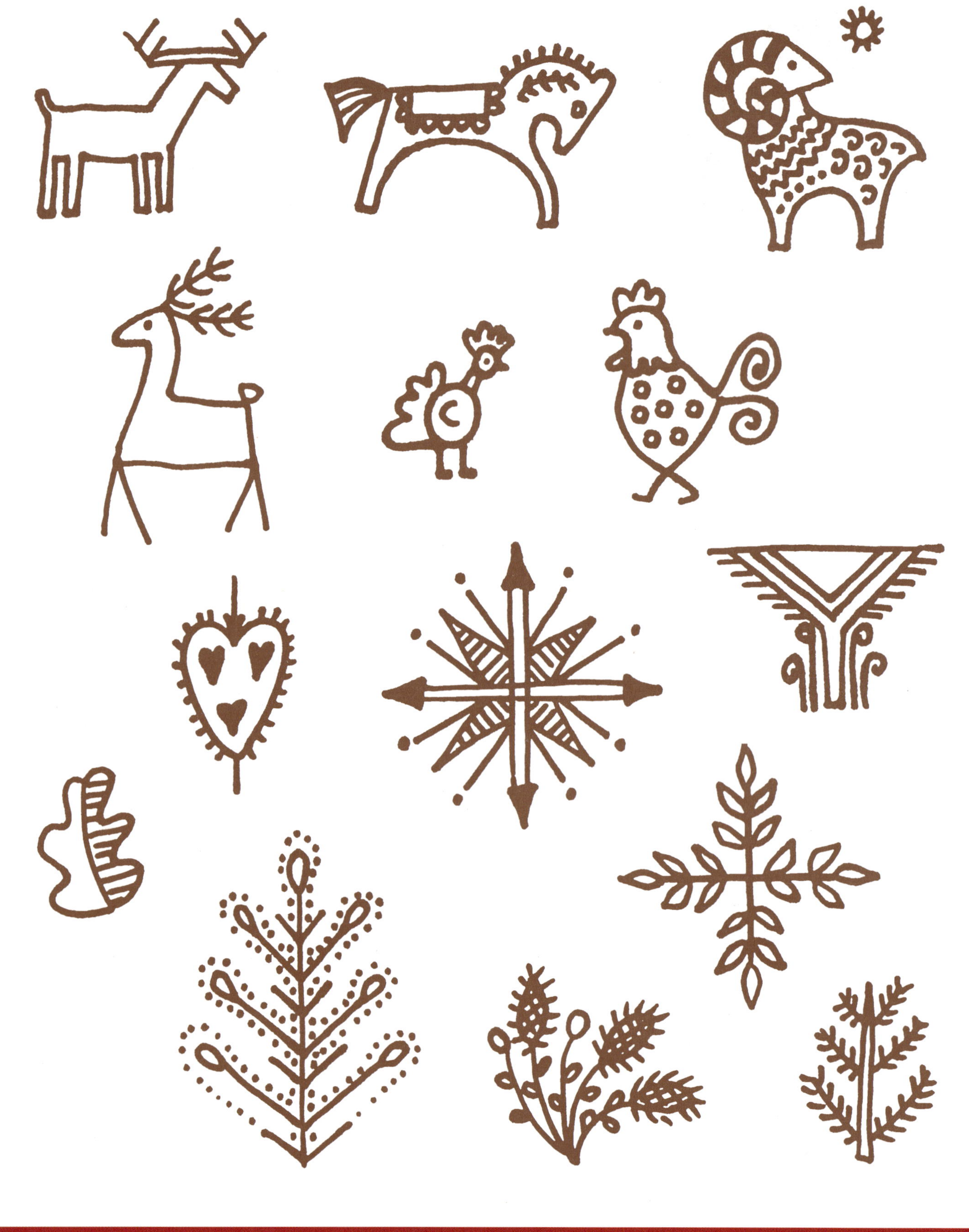

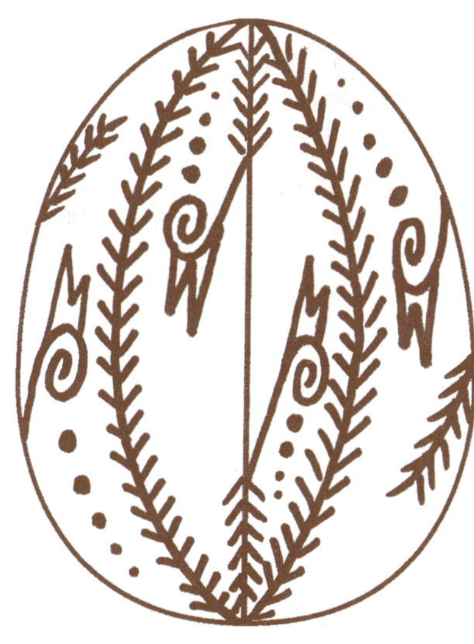

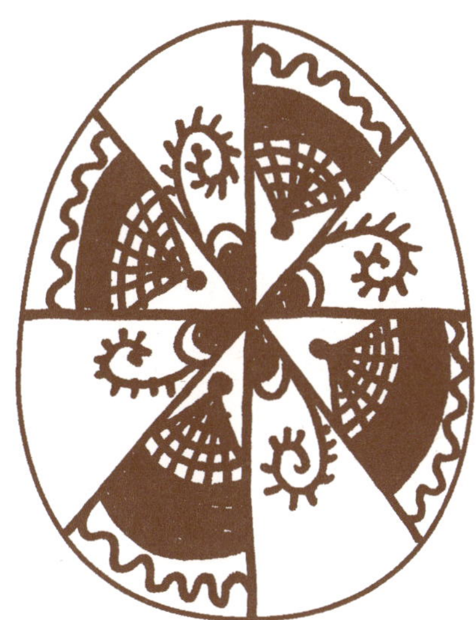

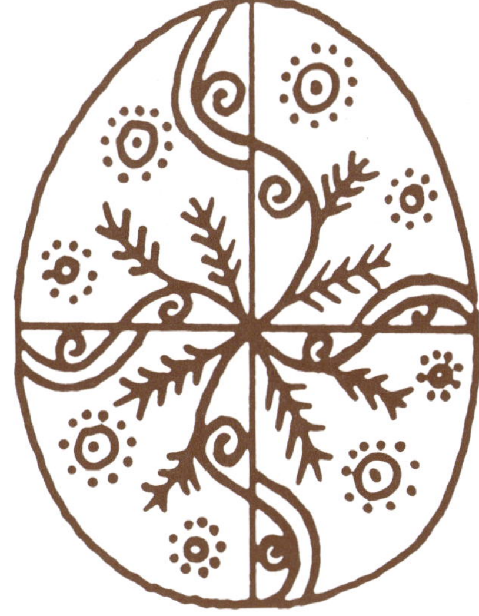

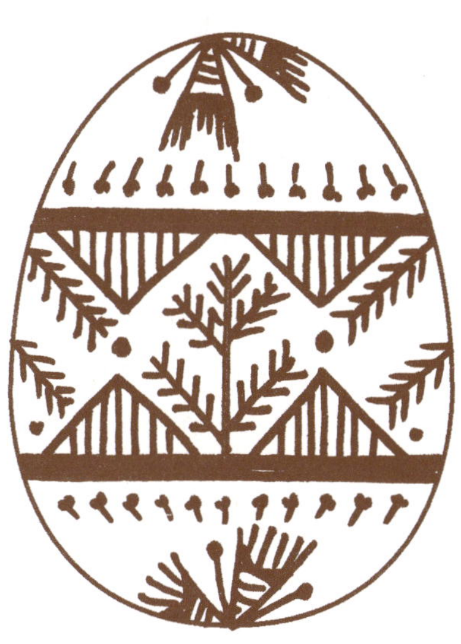

THE GREEK ZODIAC

Aries
March 21–April 19

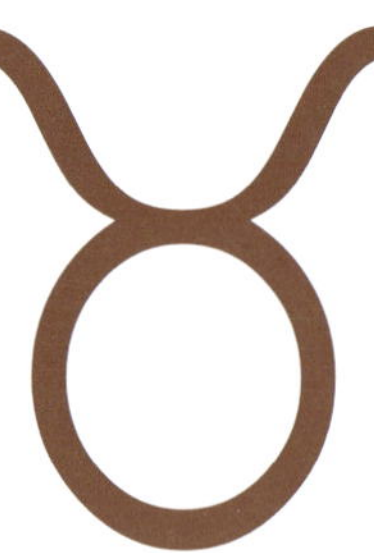

Taurus
April 20–May 20

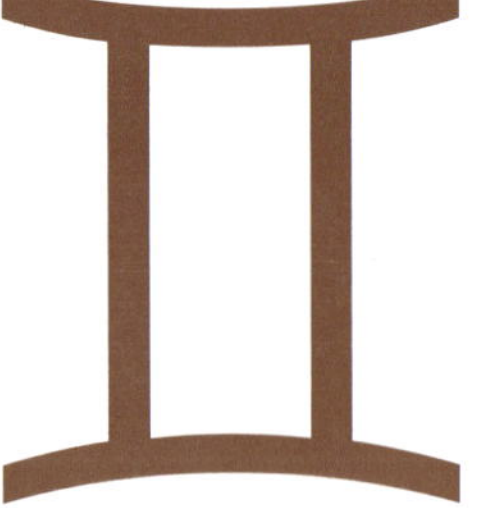

Gemini
May 21–June 20

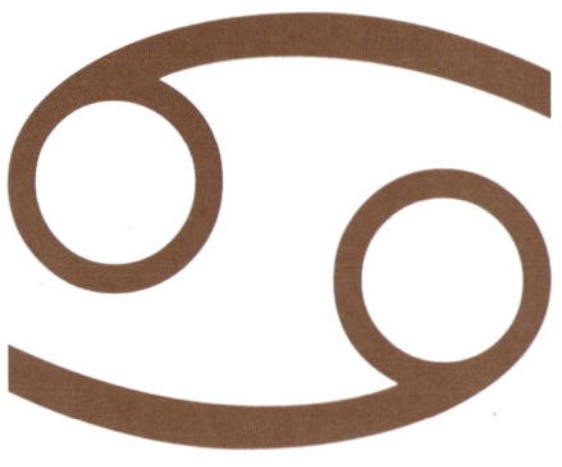

Cancer
June 21–July 22

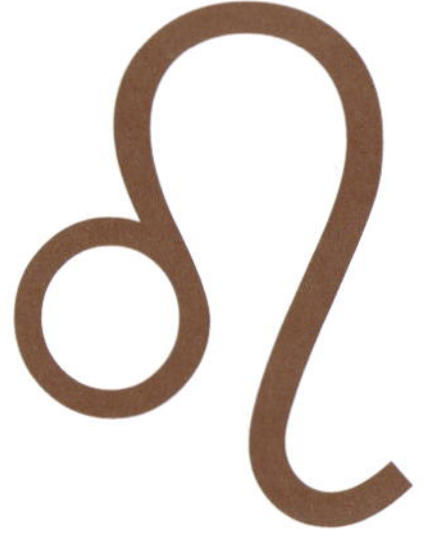

Leo
July 23–August 22

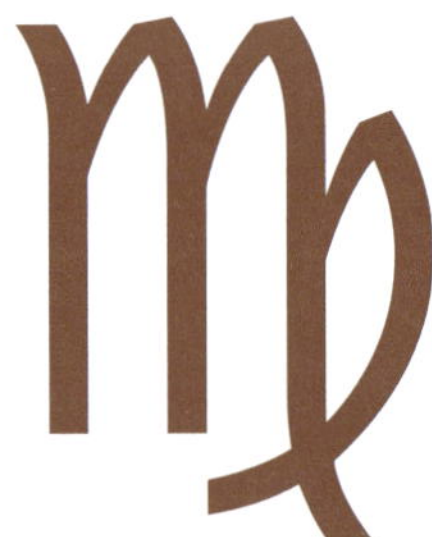

Virgo
August 23–September 22

Libra
September 23–October 23

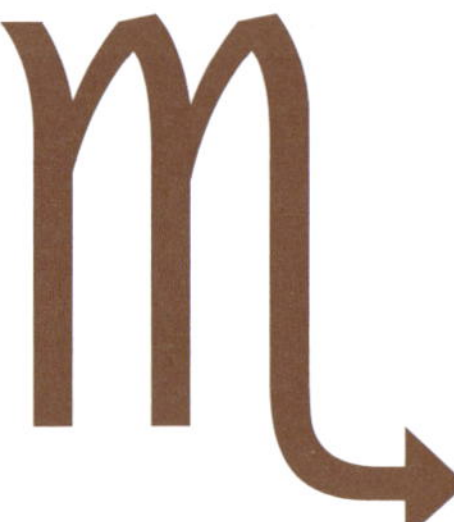

Scorpio
October 23–November 21

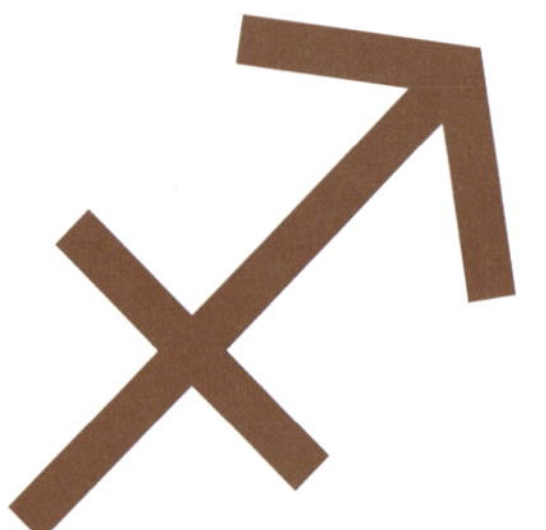

Sagittarius
November 22–December 21

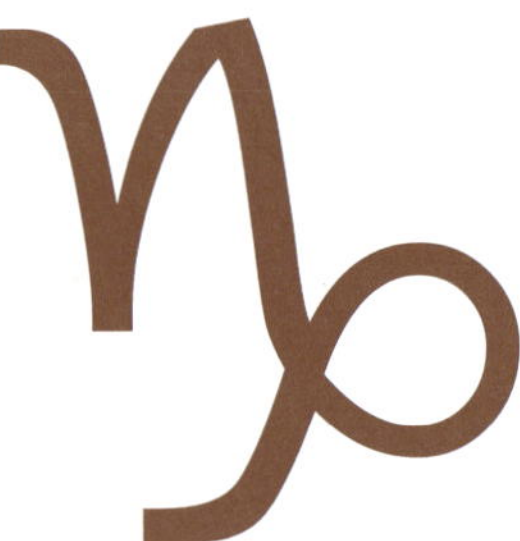

Capricorn
December 22–January 20

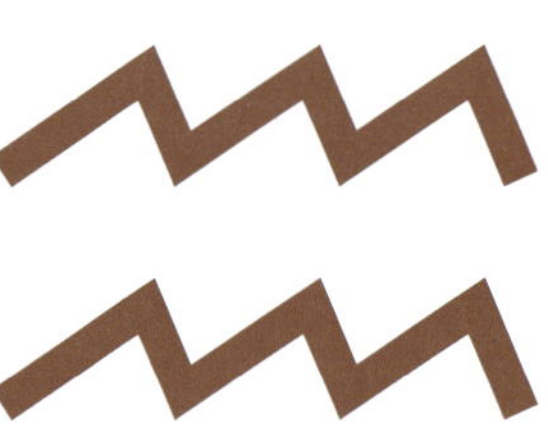

Aquarius
January 21–February 19

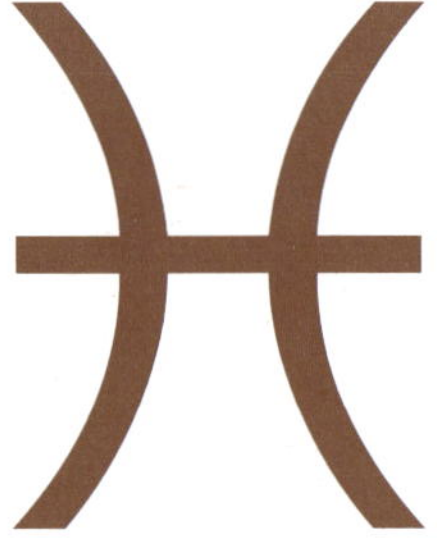

Pisces
February 20–March 20

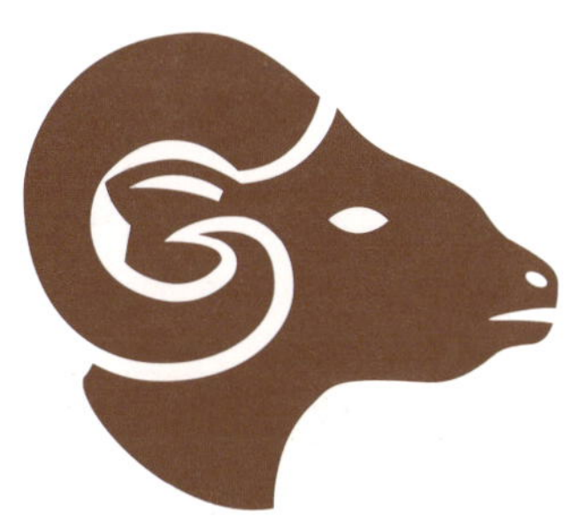
Aries the Ram

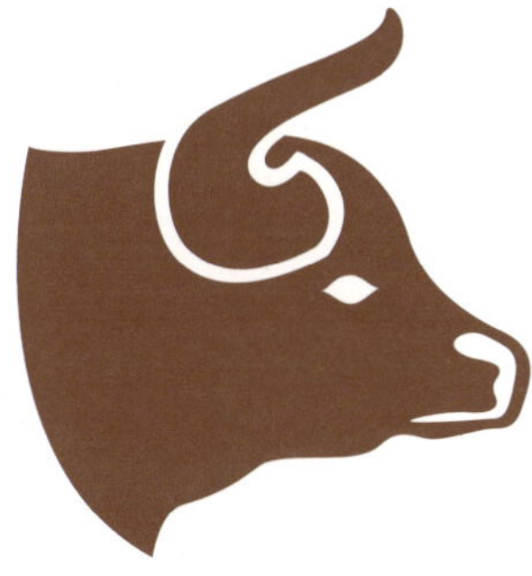
Taurus the Bull

Gemini the Twins

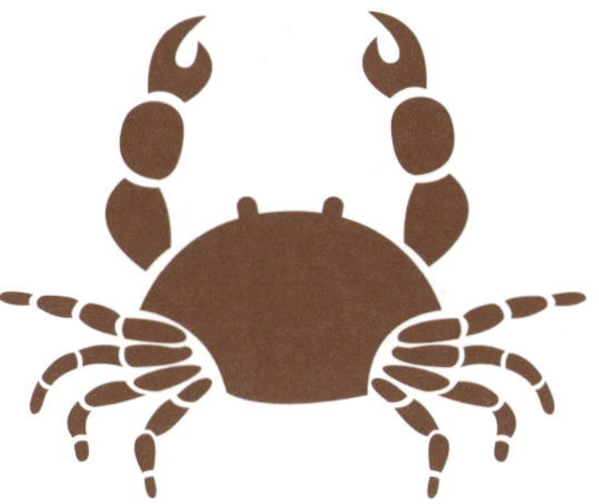
Cancer the Crab

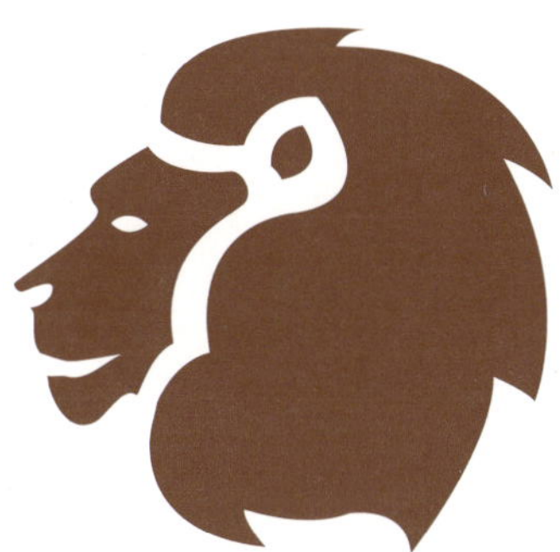
Leo the Lion

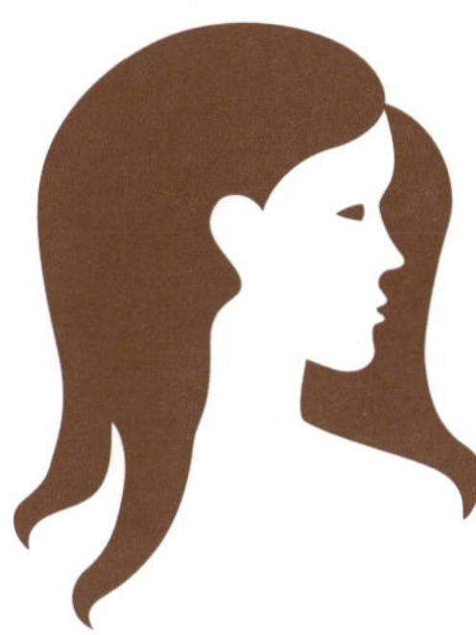
Virgo the Virgin

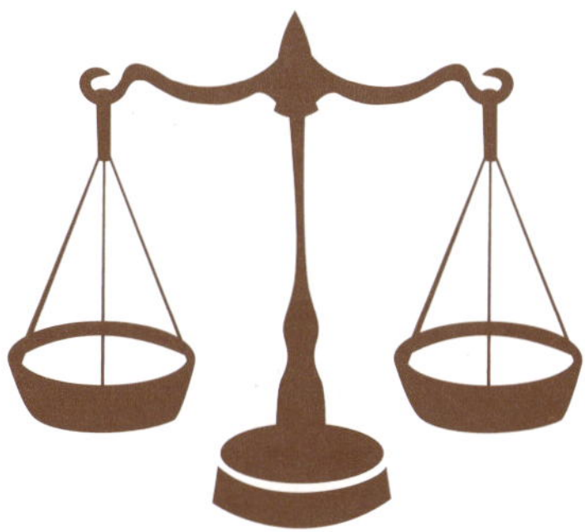
Libra the Scale

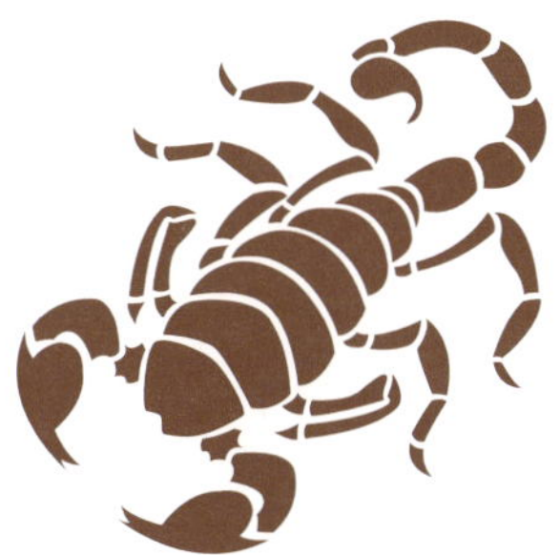
Scorpio the Scorpion

Sagittarius the Archer

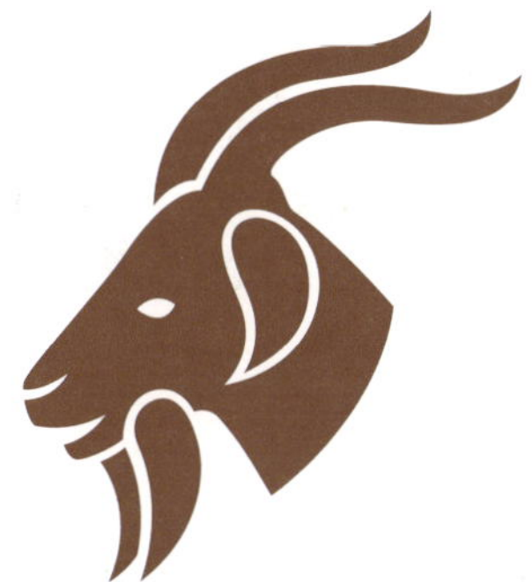
Capricorn the Goat

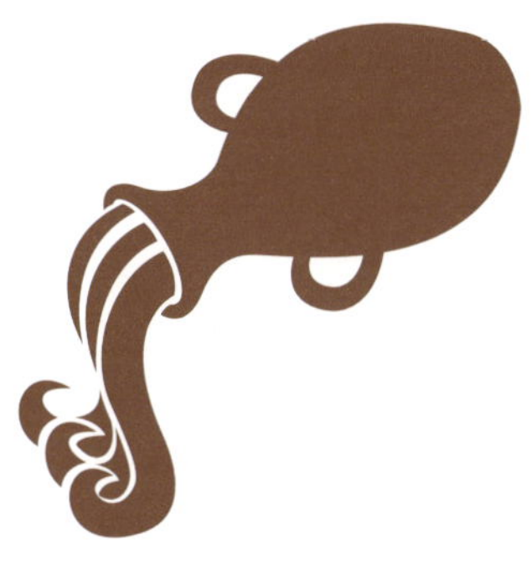
Aquarius the Waterbearer

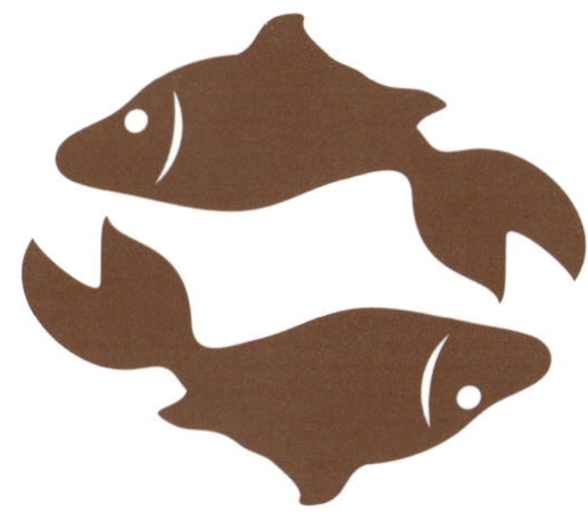
Pisces the Fish

OTHER SYMBOLS OF ANCIENT GREECE

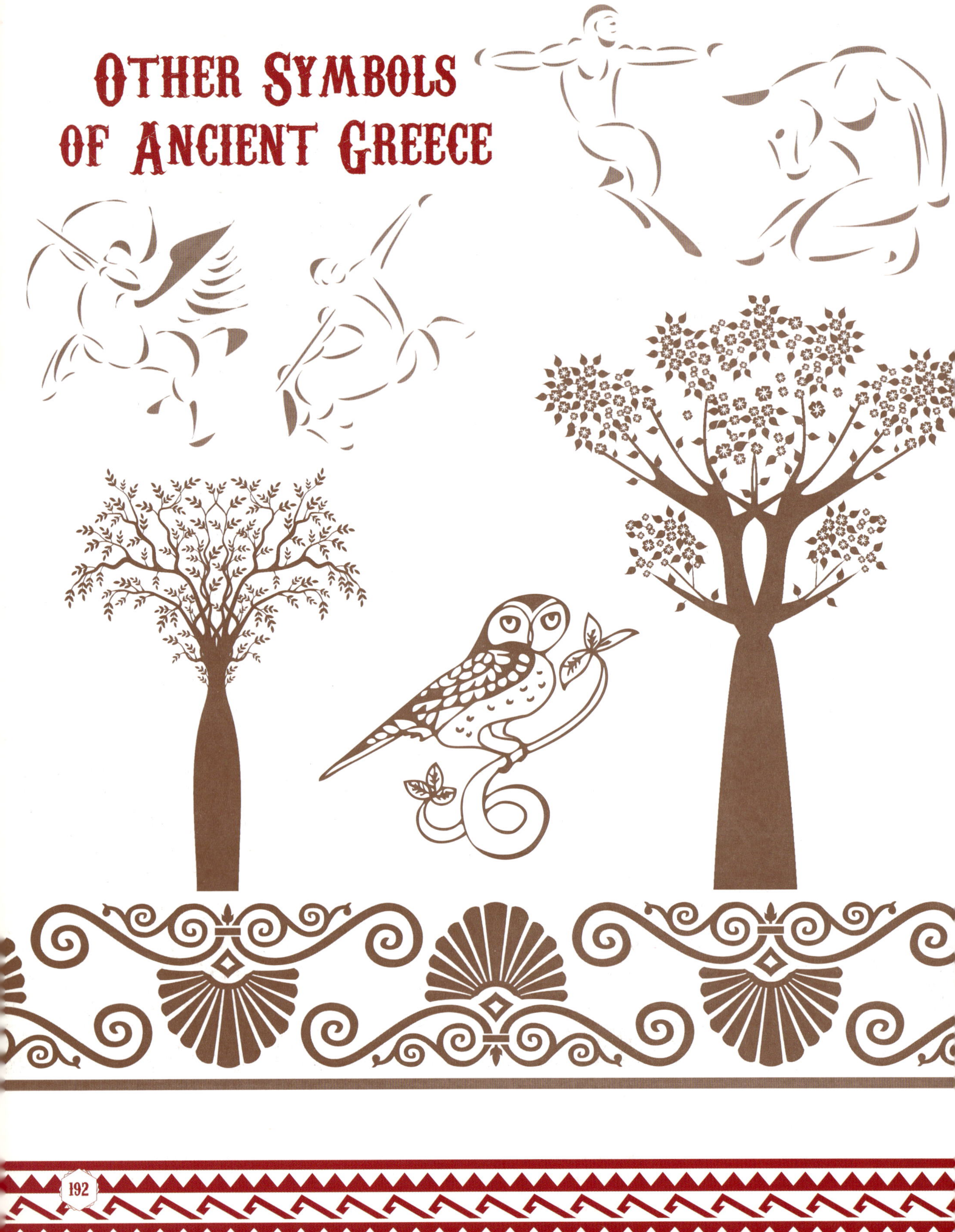

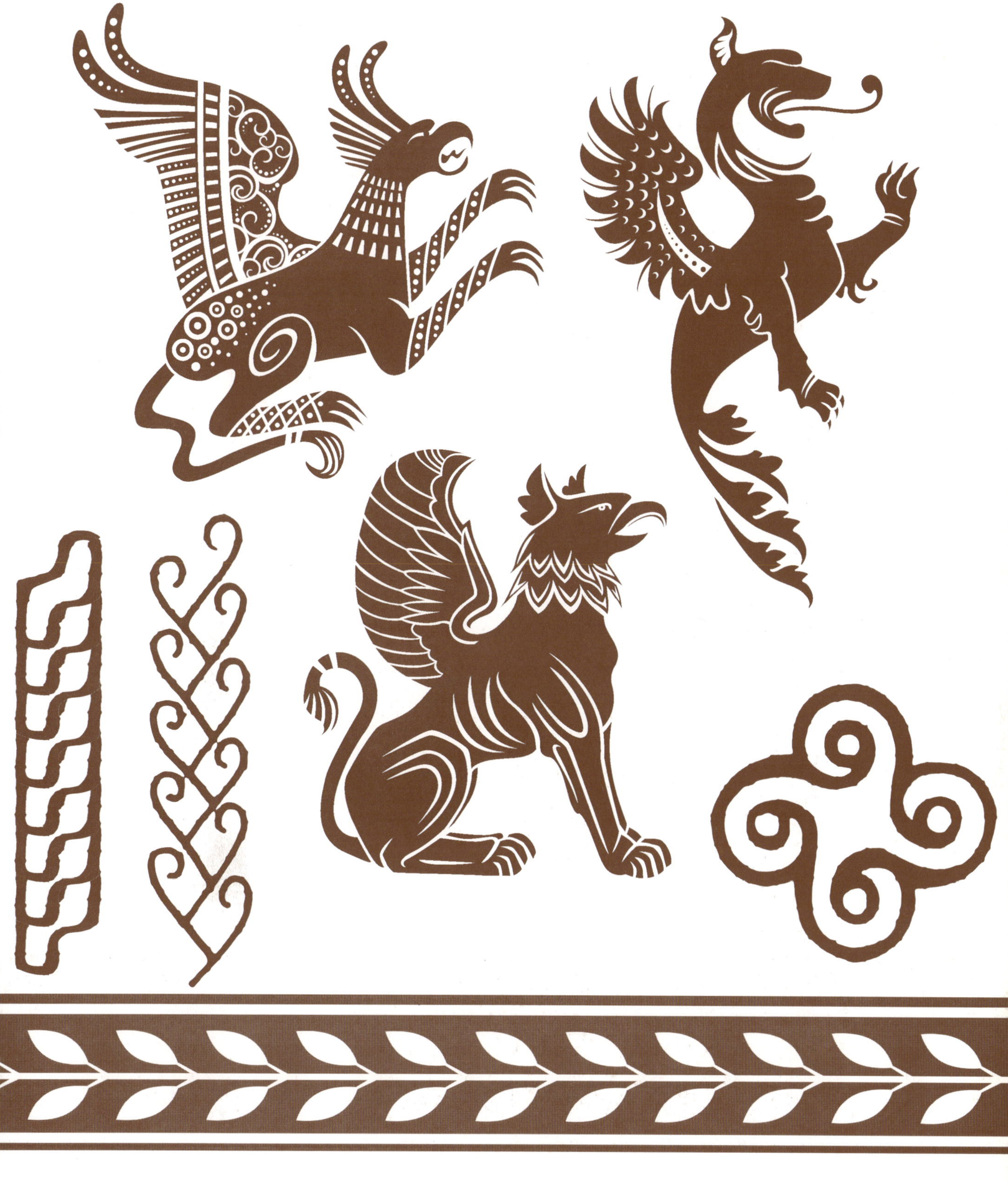

Nordic Runes and Images

Both the Vikings and the Anglo-Saxons believed that runes were invested with magic that would protect them from calamity. Today vestiges of the art of these ancient peoples can be seen carved on stones still scattered throughout Great Britain and Scandinavia.

Image from a Runestone

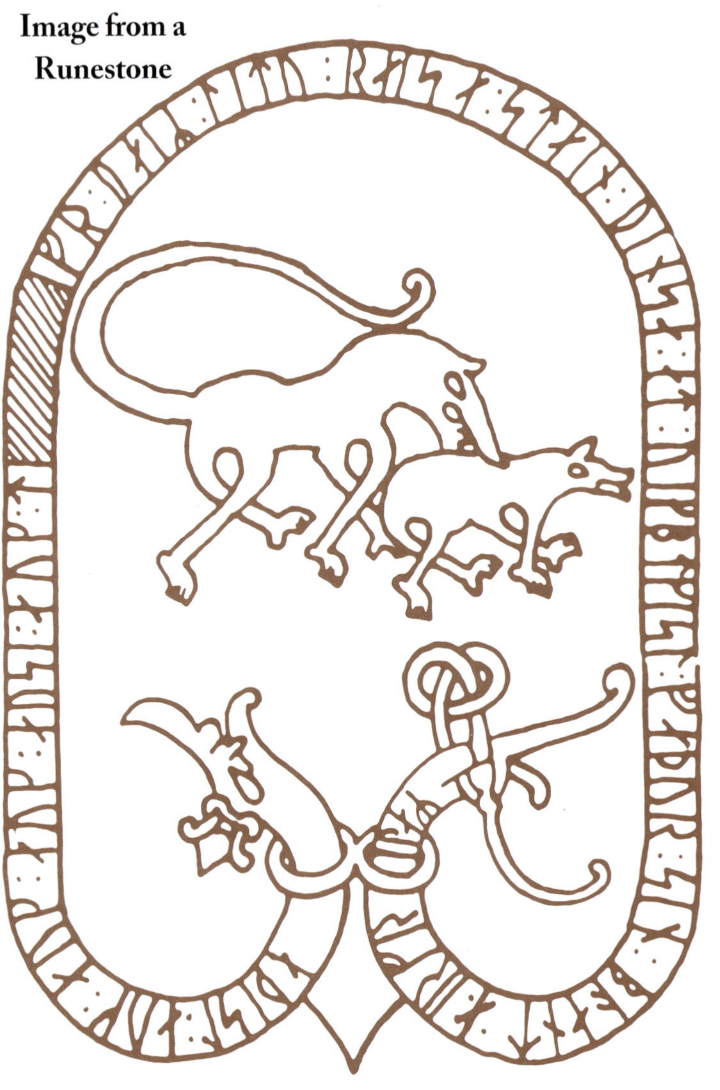

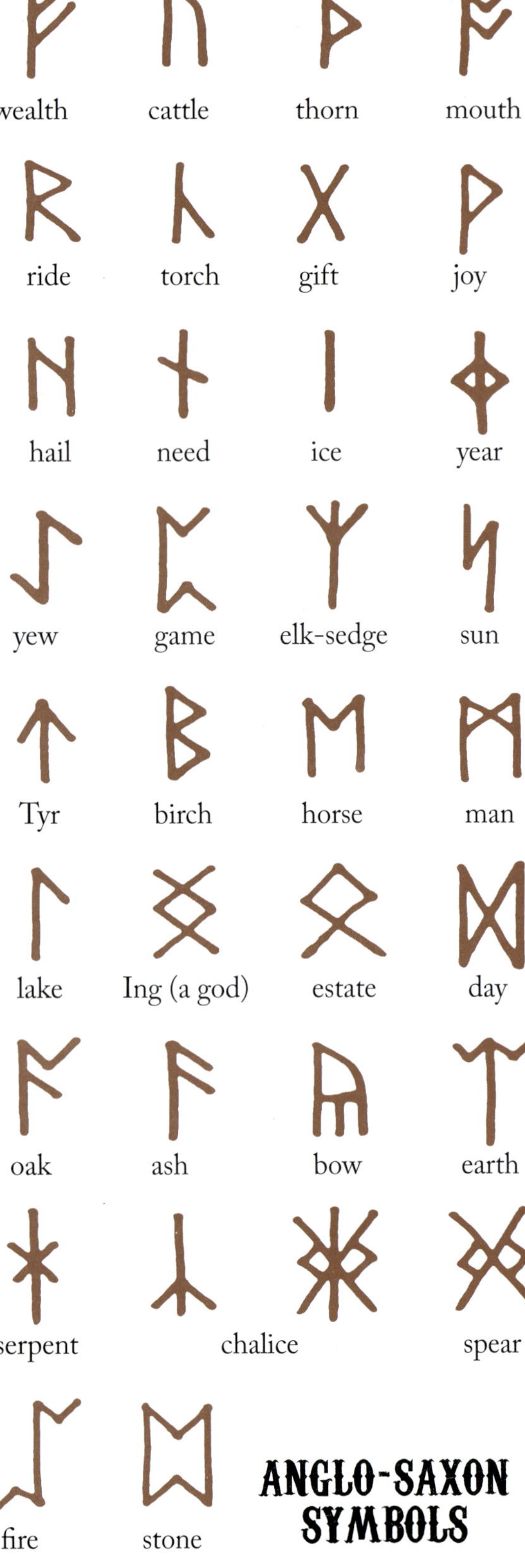

ANGLO-SAXON SYMBOLS

VIKING ALPHABET

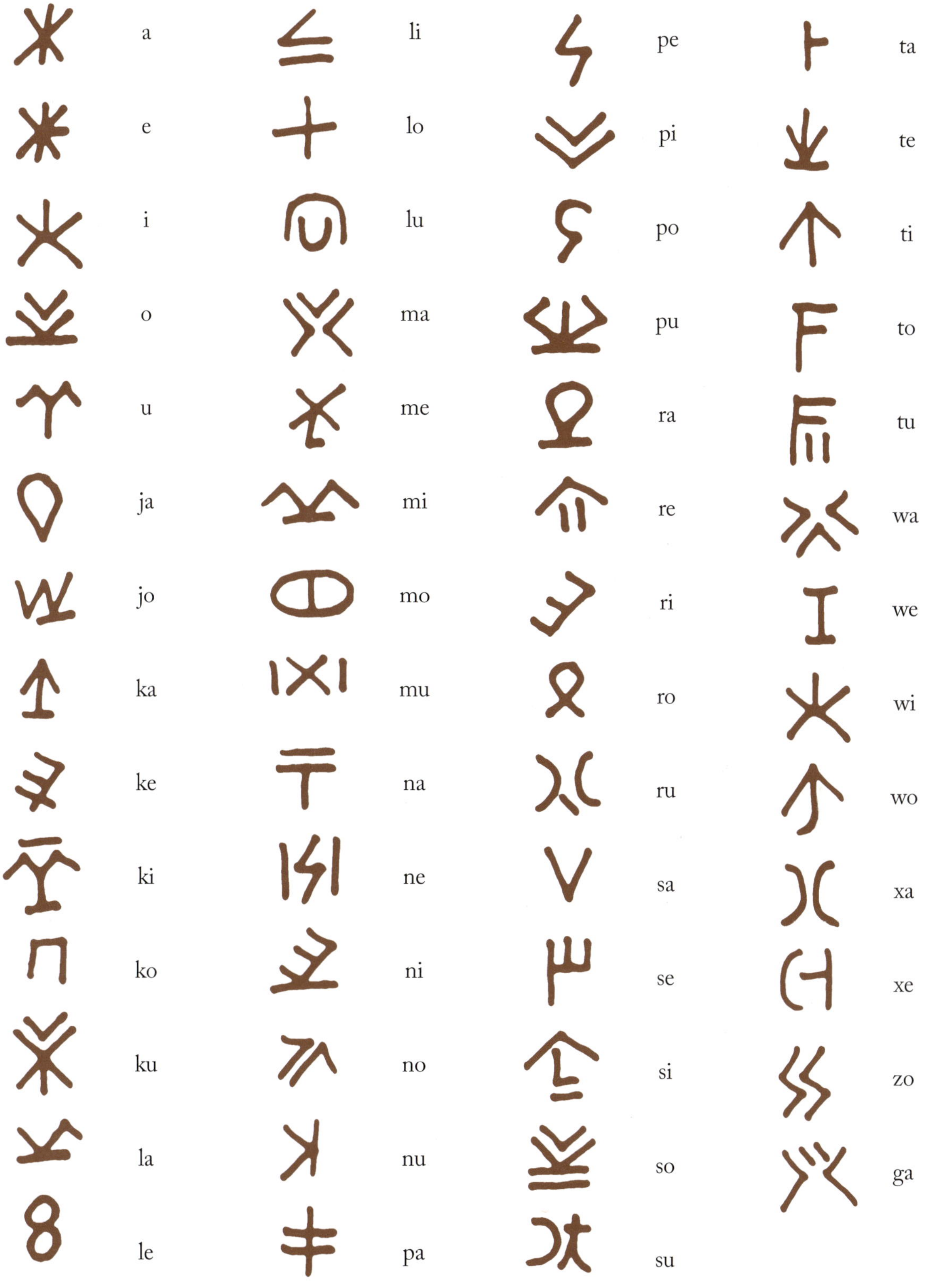

a
e
i
o
u
ja
jo
ka
ke
ki
ko
ku
la
le

li
lo
lu
ma
me
mi
mo
mu
na
ne
ni
no
nu
pa

pe
pi
po
pu
ra
re
ri
ro
ru
sa
se
si
so
su

ta
te
ti
to
tu
wa
we
wi
wo
xa
xe
zo
ga

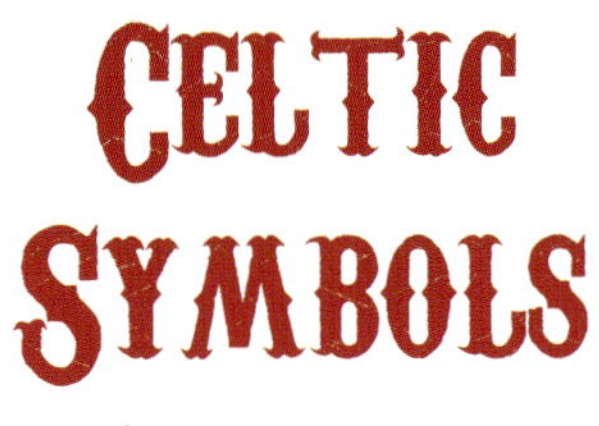

Celtic Symbols

Found on ancient artifacts in Ireland, Celtic symbols have been around for a very long time and are subject to many interpretations

A Celtic knot is one such symbol. It has no beginning or end. Perhaps that is why these lovely symbols have come to represent the timeless nature of the spirit.

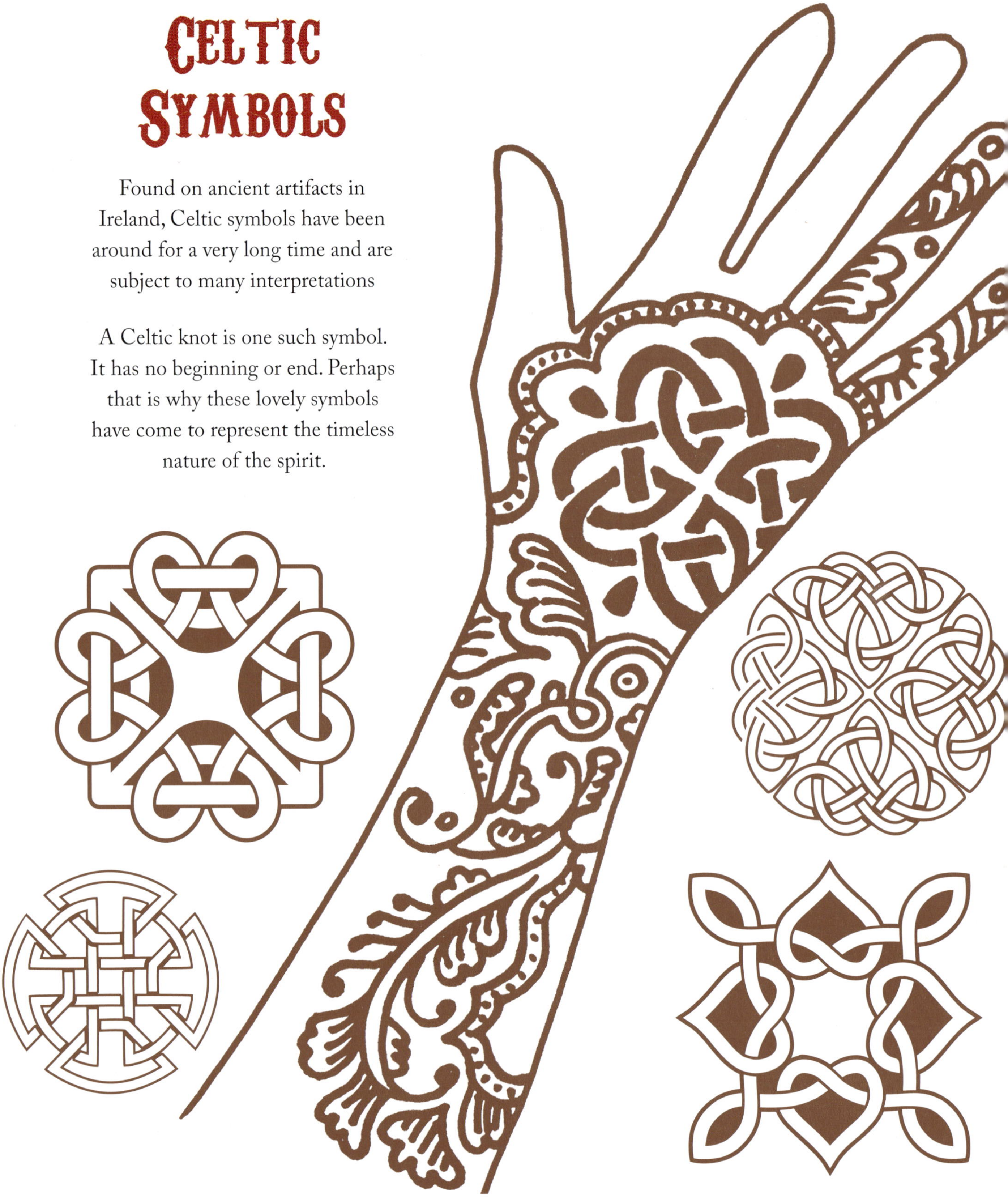

Images from North America

The love of nature inherent in all Native American cultures is reflected in the signs and symbols featured in their art.

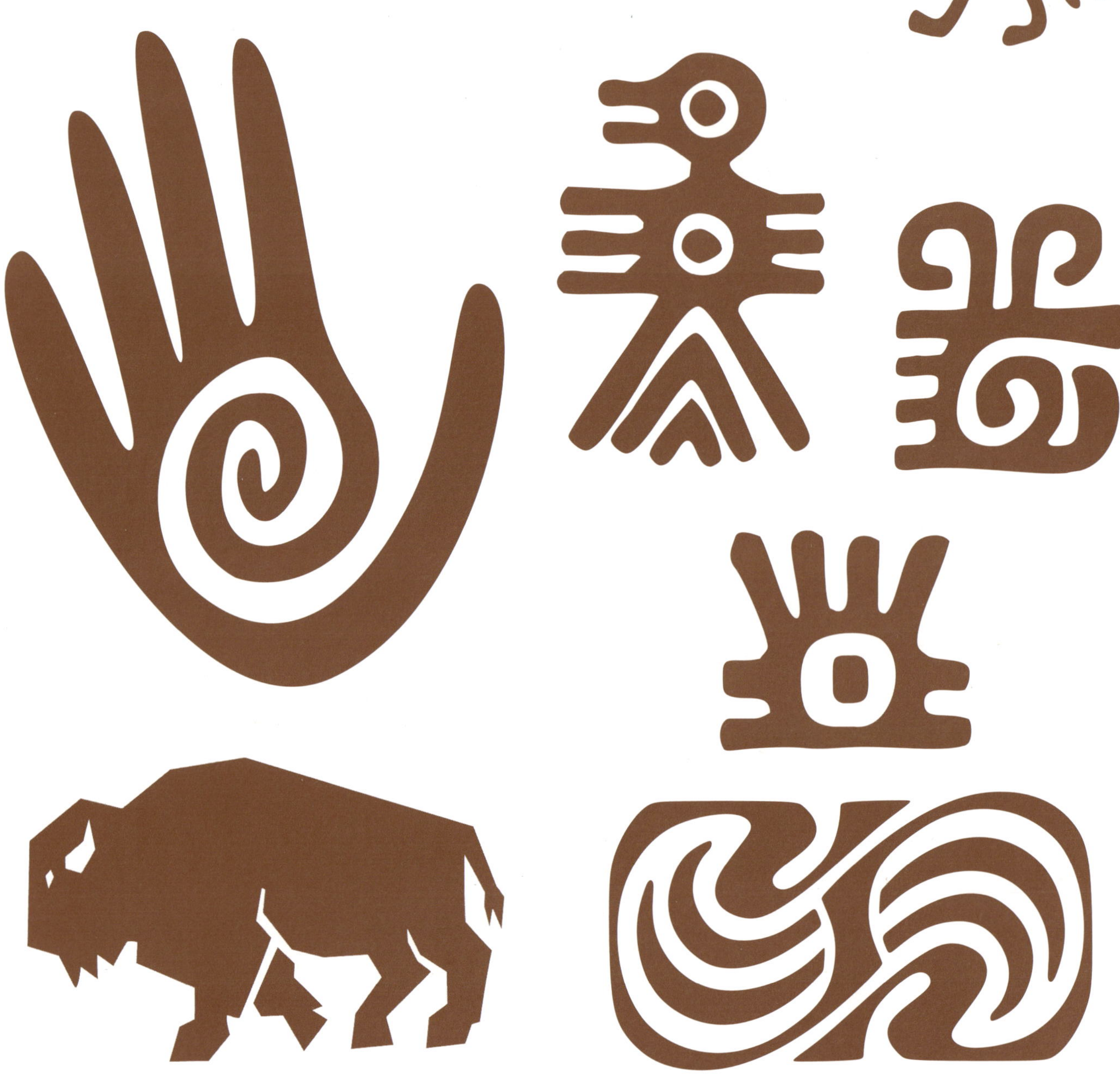

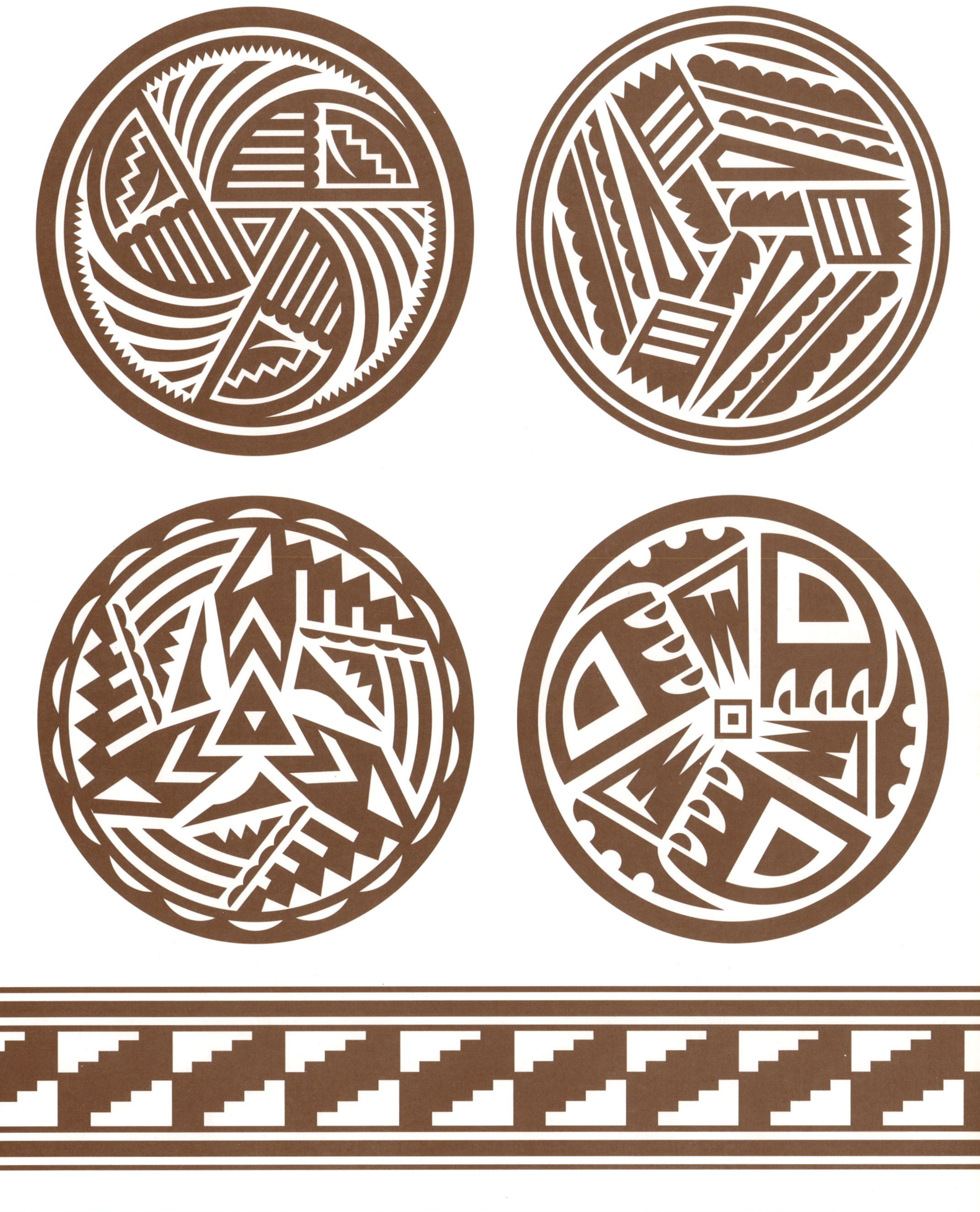

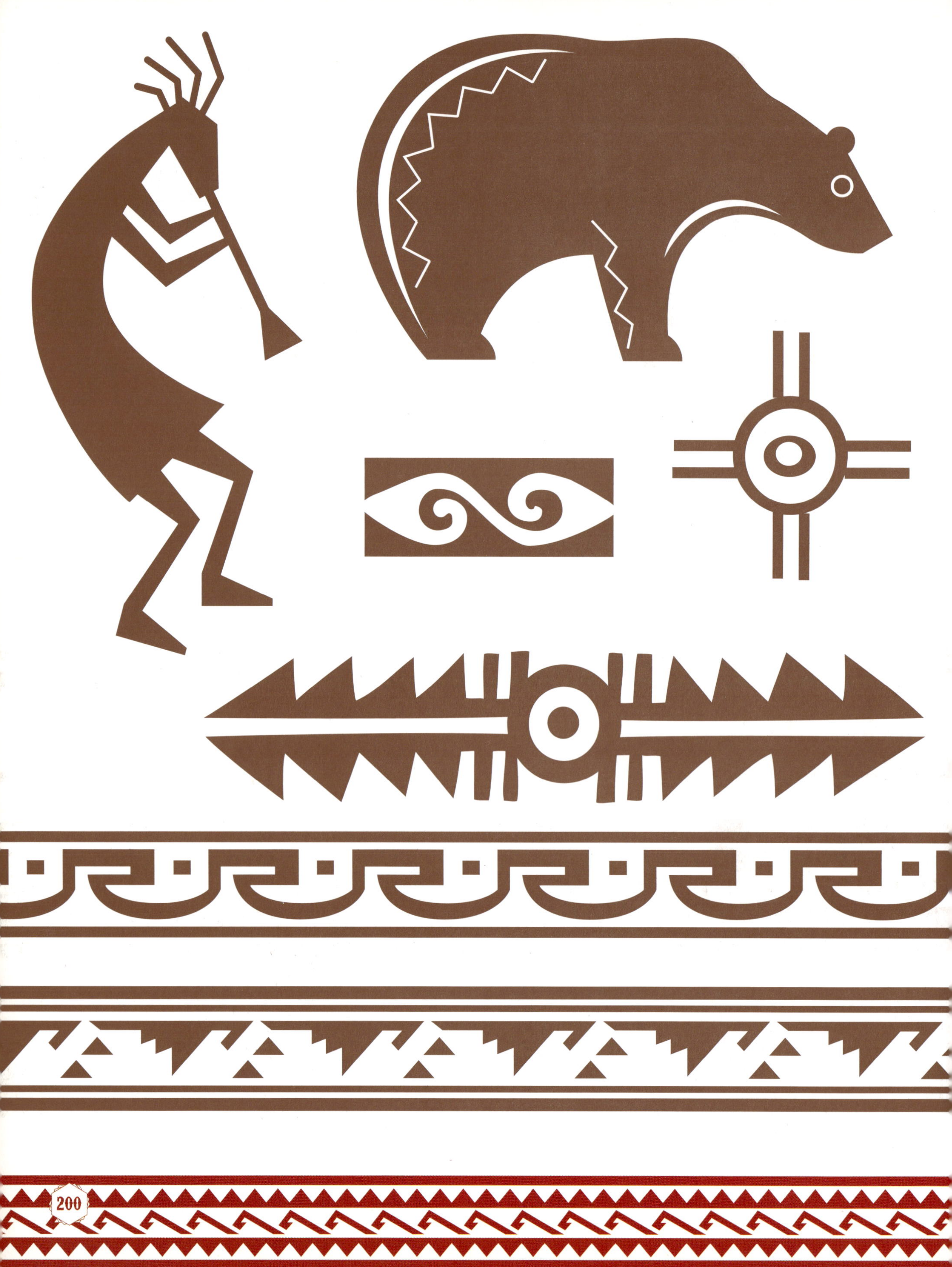

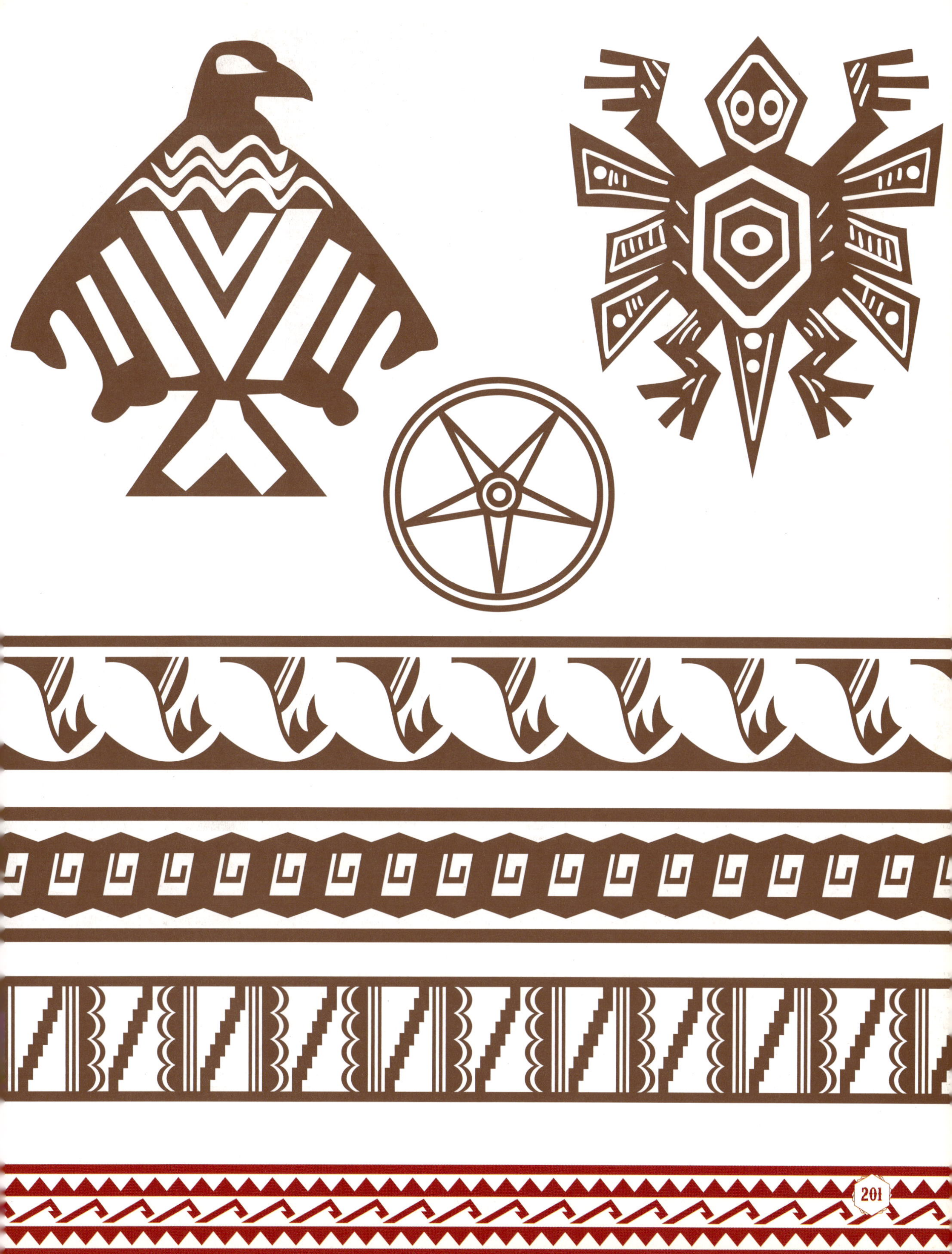

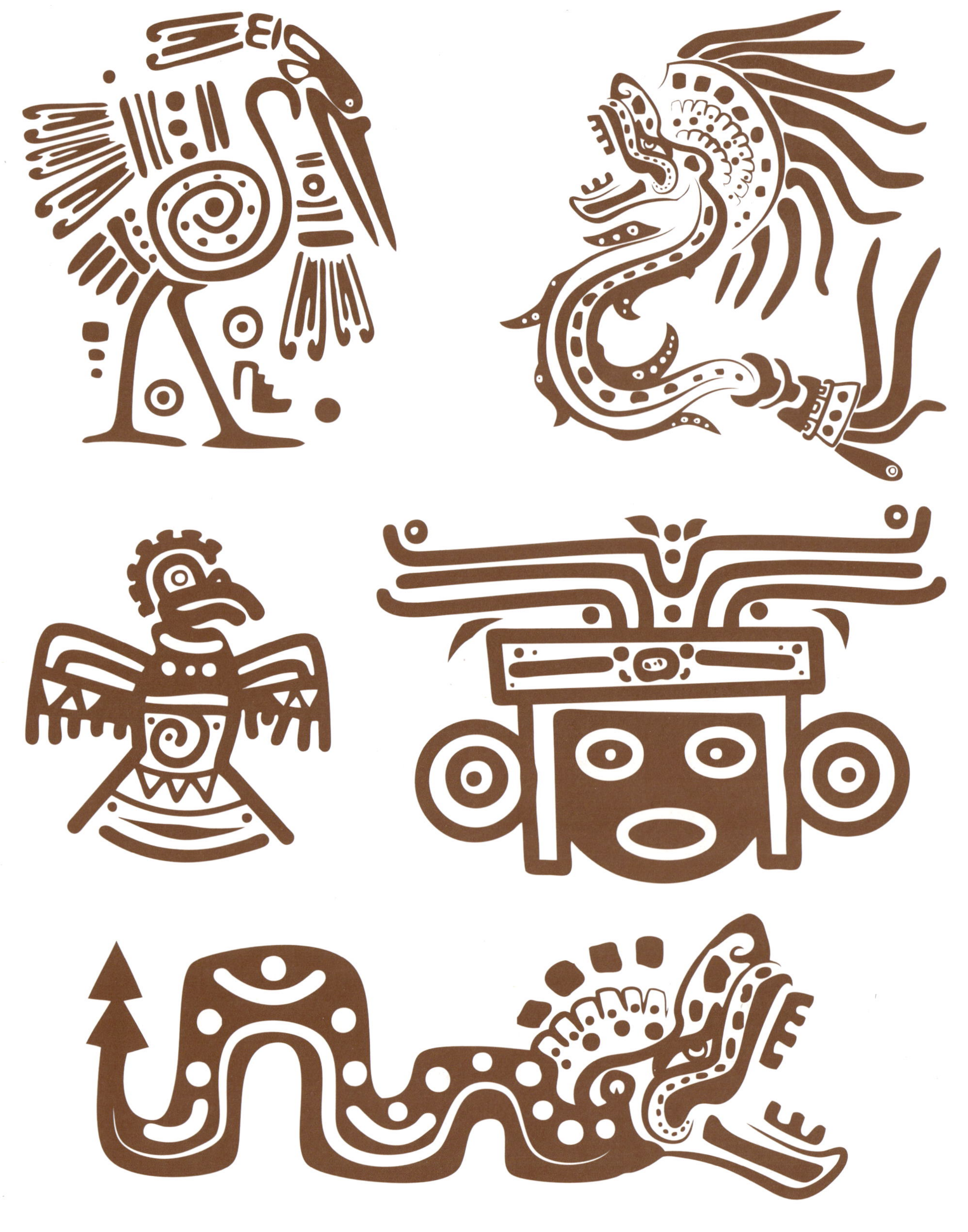

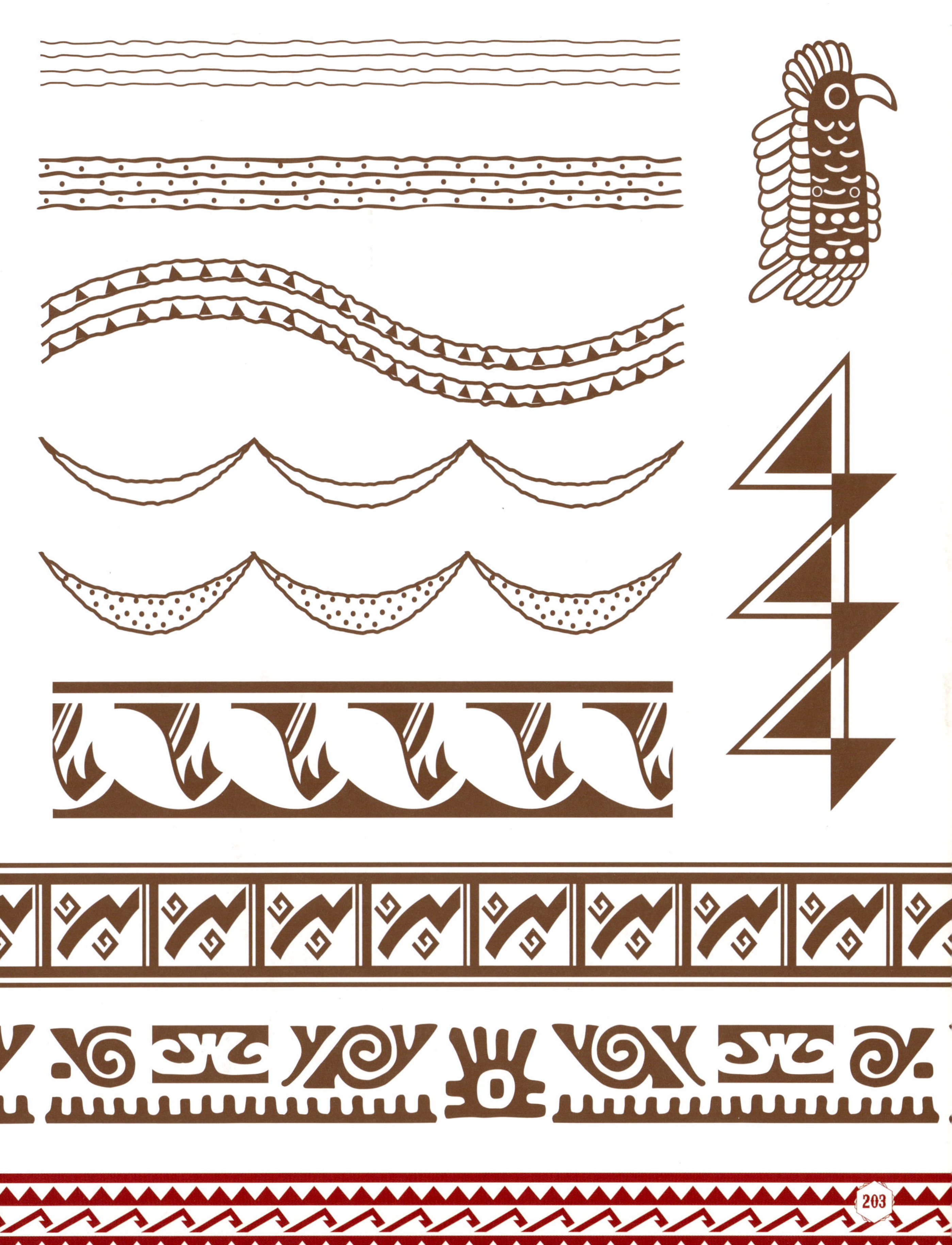

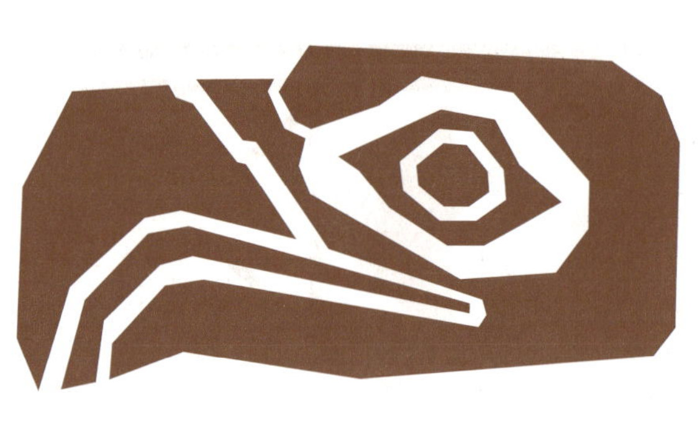
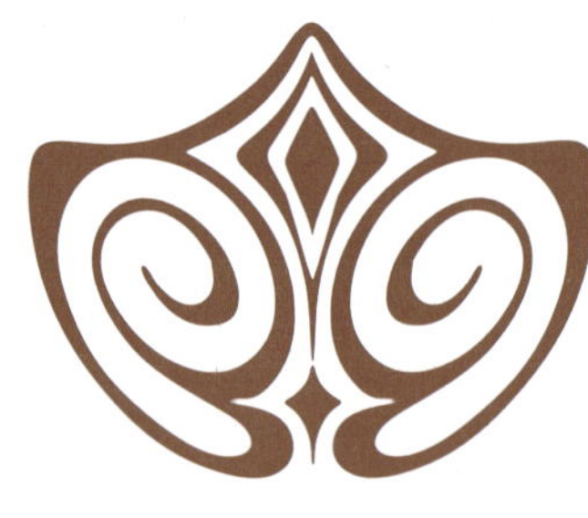
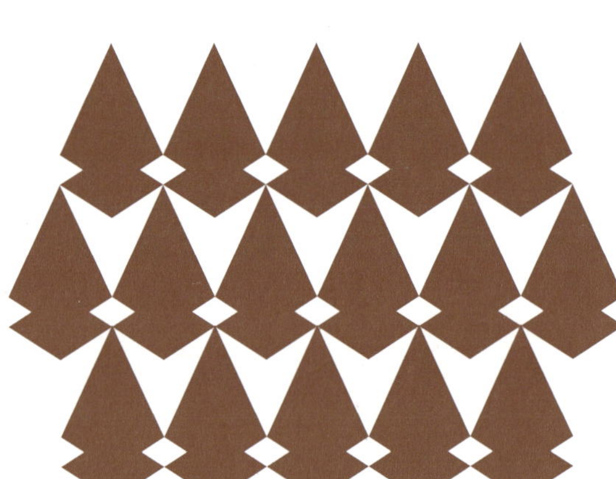
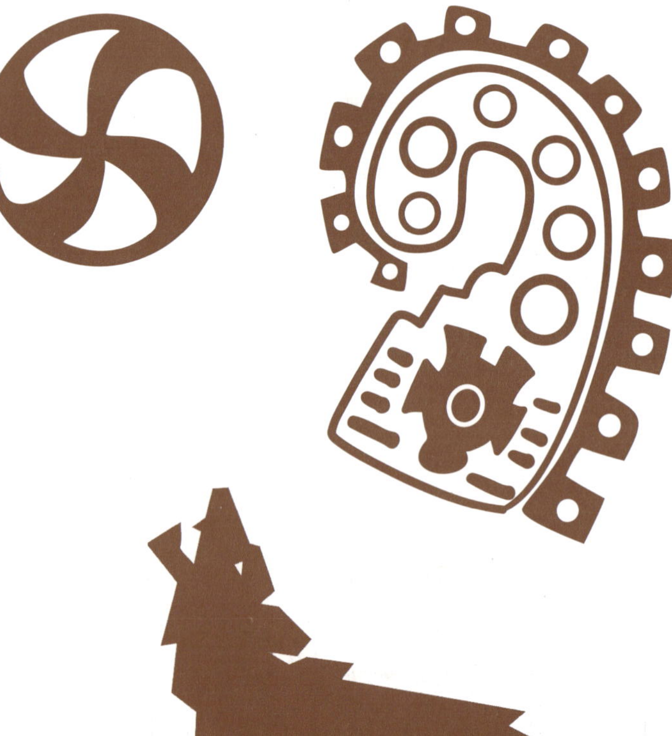
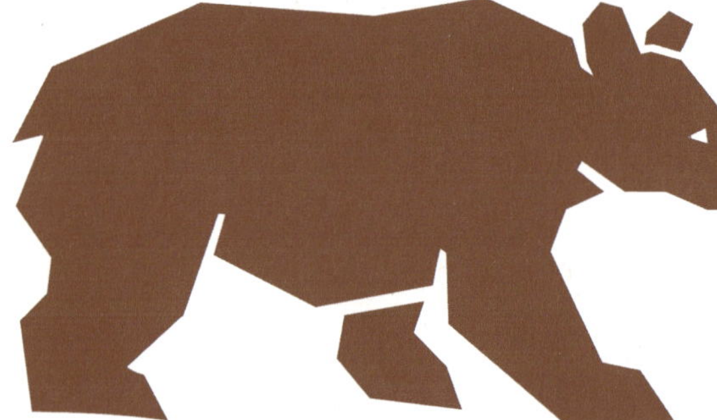

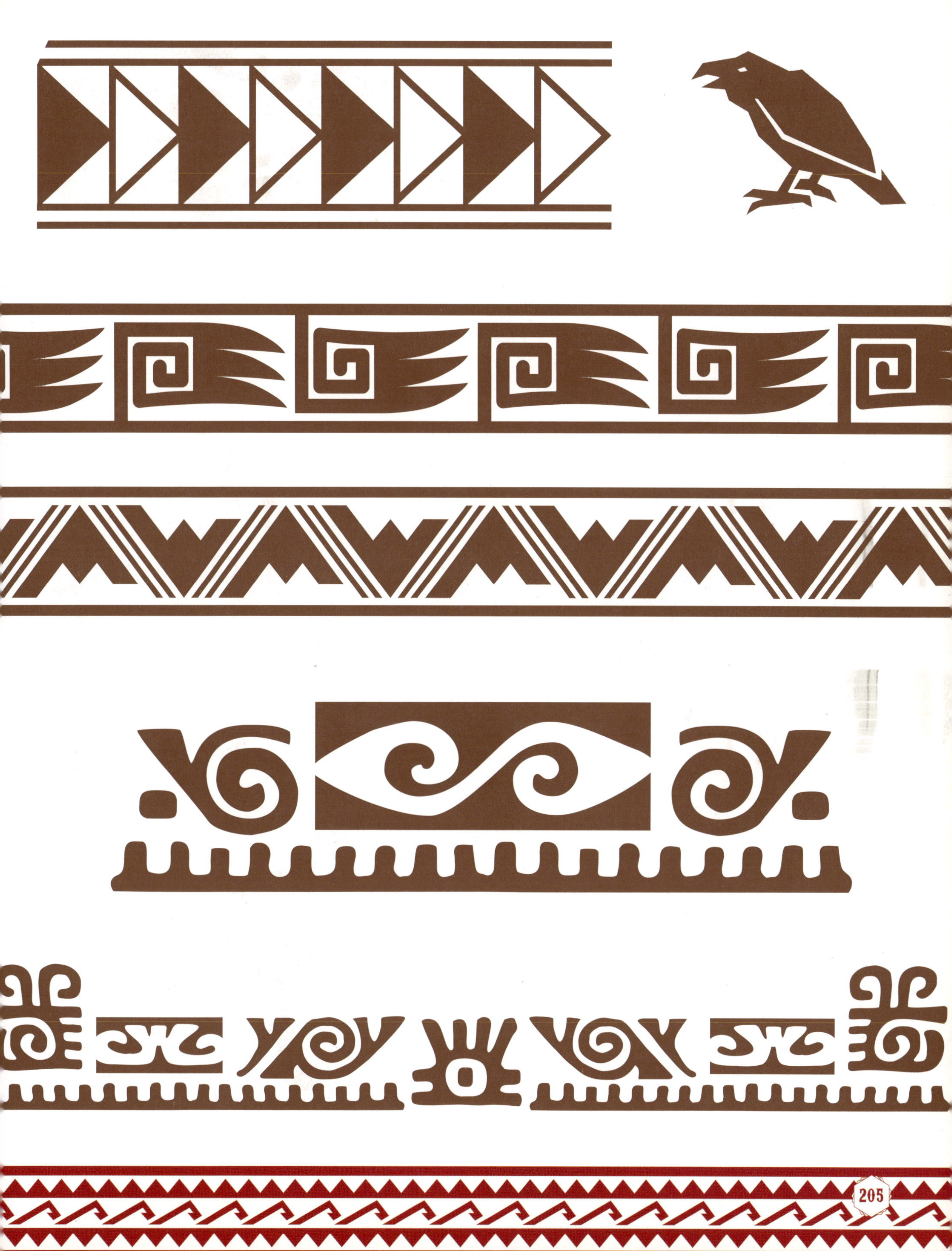

MODERN INTERPRETATIONS

Is there anyone who does not wish to embellish his or her natural-born gifts? And who among us would not wish to invite good fortune into our lives? Perhaps it's not so astonishing, then, that a 3,000-year-old art identified with beauty and luck should find a resurgence among the people of today.

Symbolic of joy, blessings, love, and fertility, in addition to beauty and luck, henna body art is now more popular than ever. Talented henna artists command princely sums to adorn guests at festive occasions such as weddings, birthday parties, bat mitzvahs, and graduations.

It is also not at all unusual to find mainstream celebrities proudly sporting traditional henna designs or wearing a more contemporary henna motif. Modern henna designs offer interpretations of serious spiritual symbols, mythical beasts and gargoyles, of fanciful butterflies, seashells, and dolphins. No matter what one's style or inclination, the choices for personal expression are limitless, allowing new twists on this ancient style of body adornment.

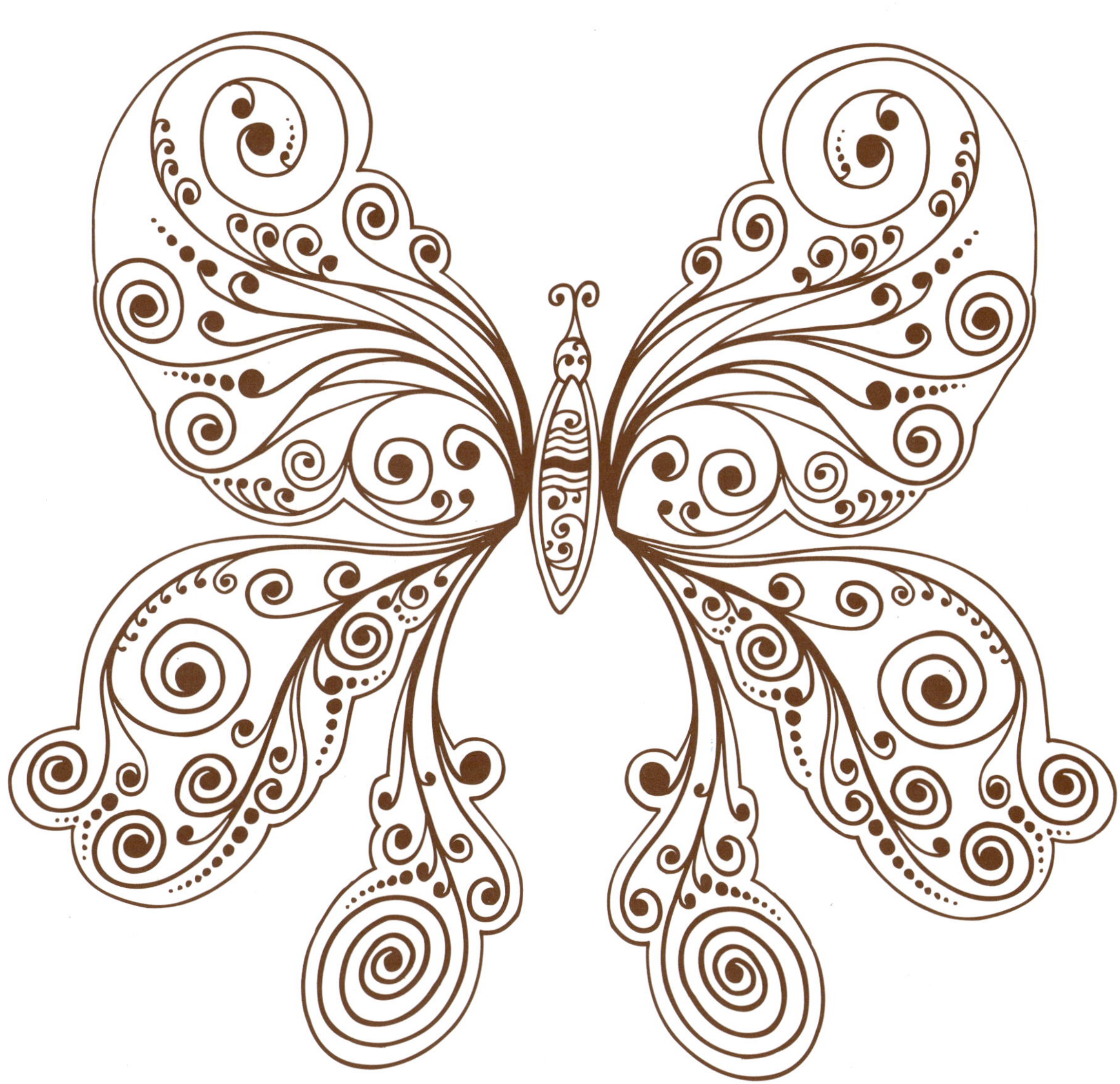

Yoga Motifs, Buddhist Symbols and the Seven Chakras

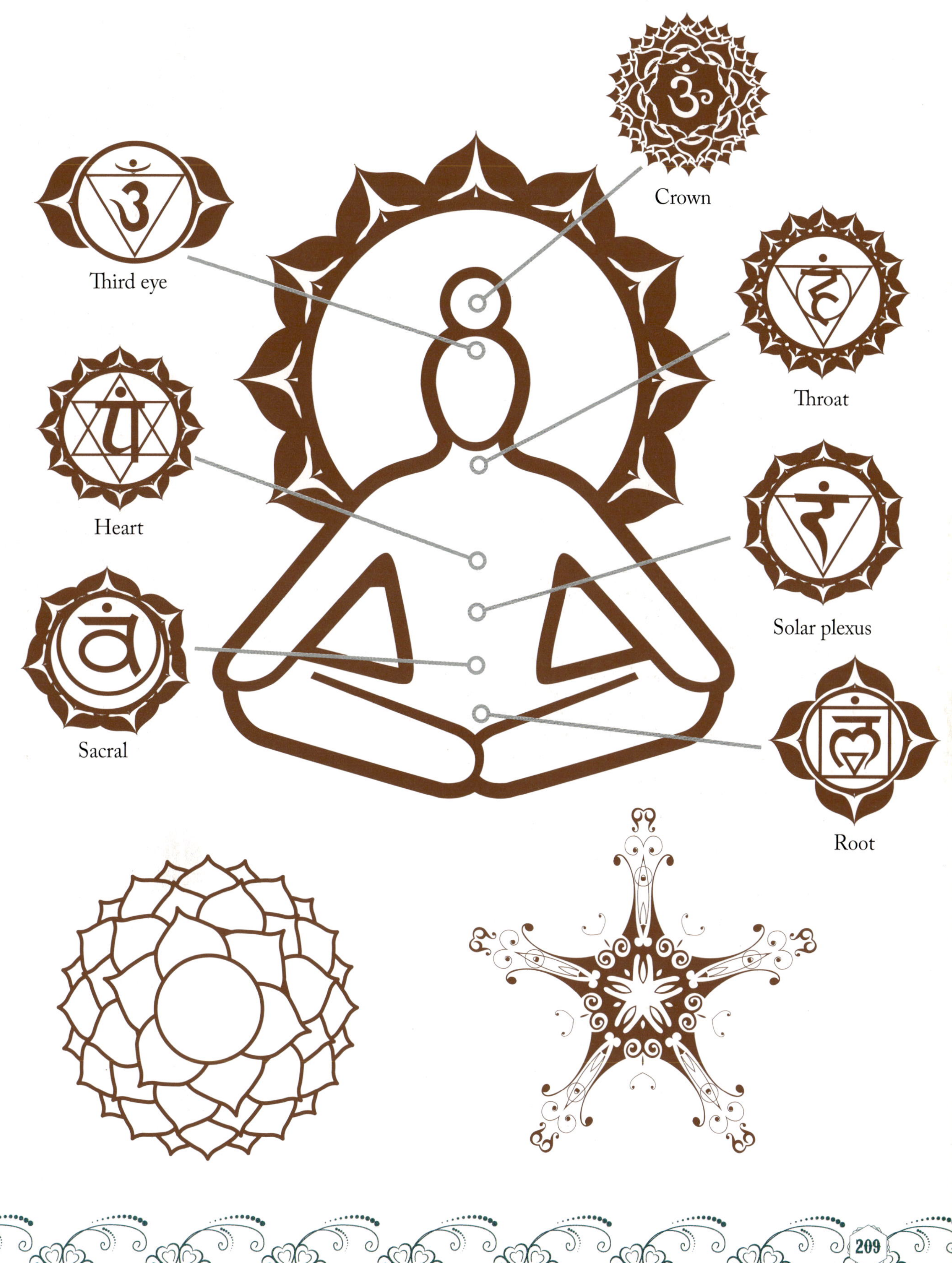
Crown
Third eye
Throat
Heart
Solar plexus
Sacral
Root

Symbols and Sayings of World Faiths

CHRISTIANITY

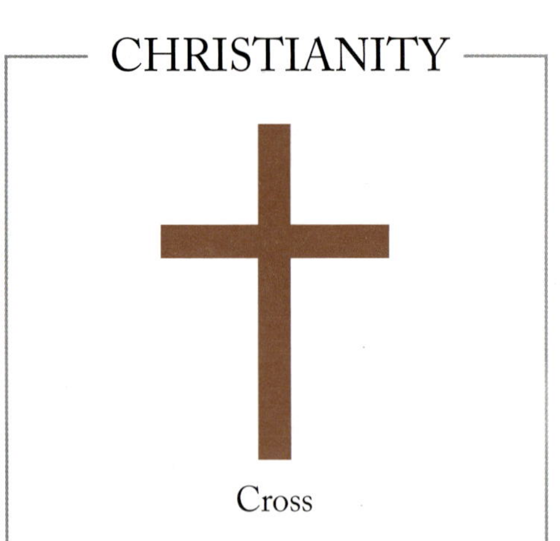
Cross

JUDAISM

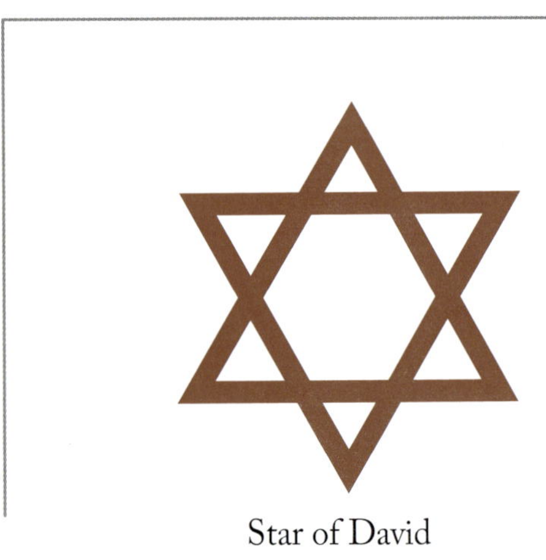
Star of David

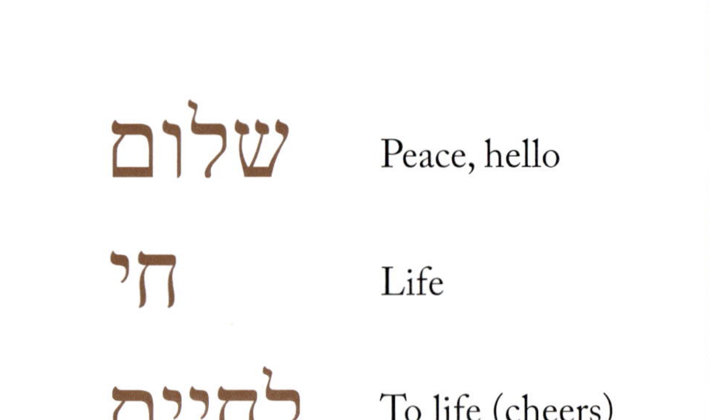

שלום	Peace, hello
חי	Life
לחיים	To life (cheers)

BUDDHISM

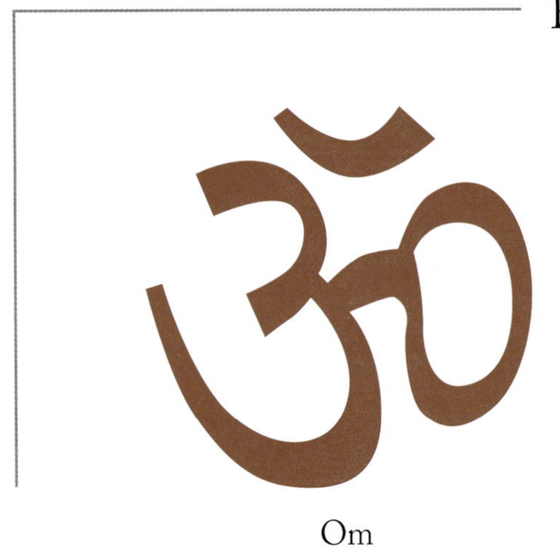
Om

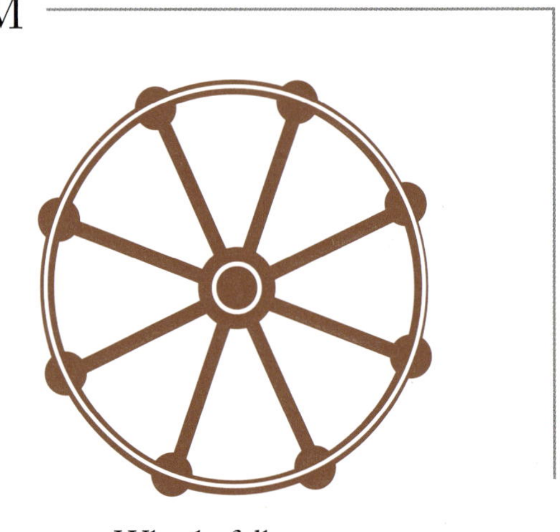
Wheel of dharma

ISLAM

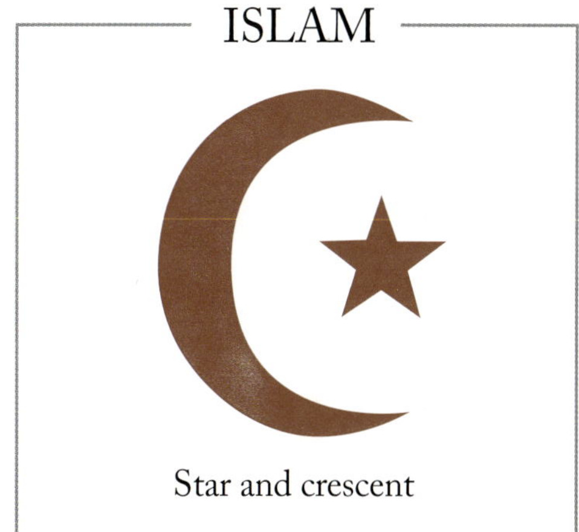

Star and crescent

SIKH

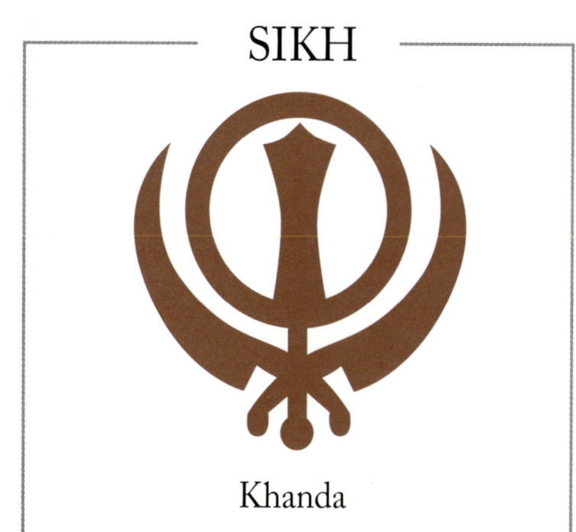

Khanda

TAOISM

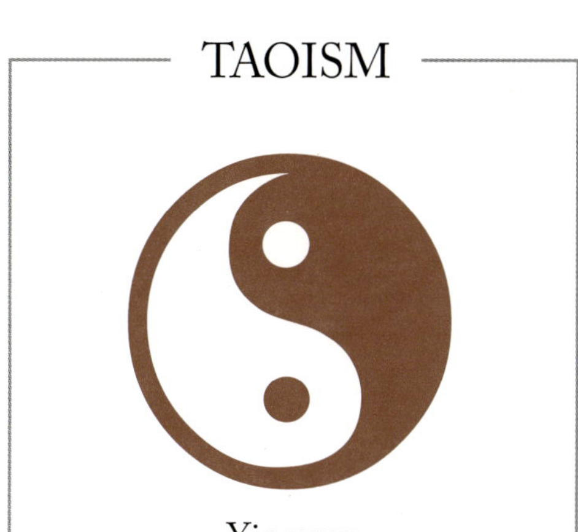
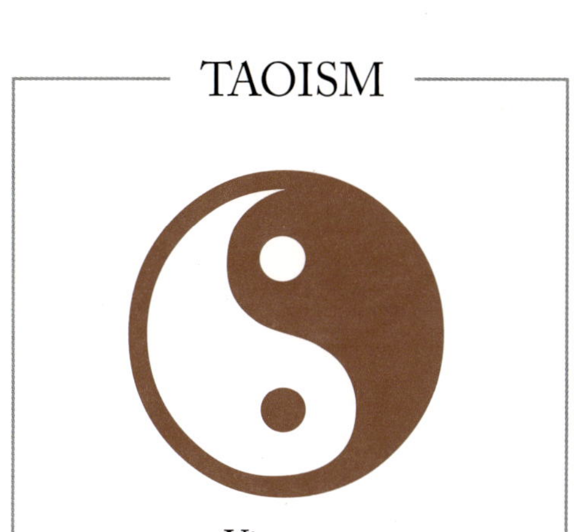

Yin yang

BAHAI

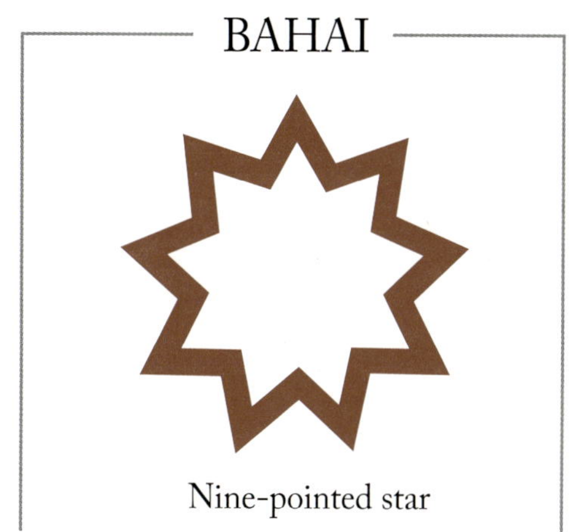

Nine-pointed star

JAIN

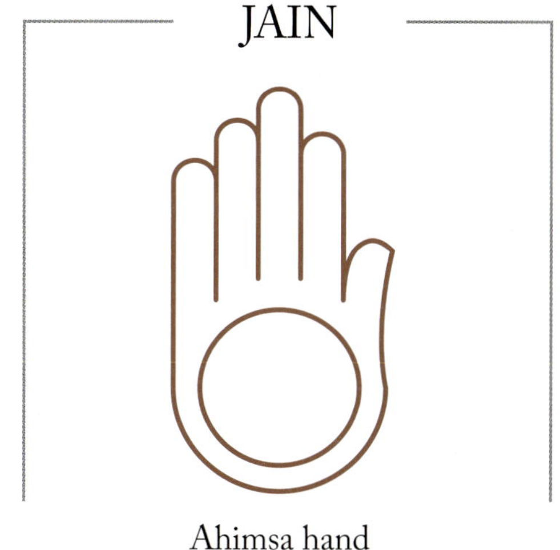

Ahimsa hand

SHINTO

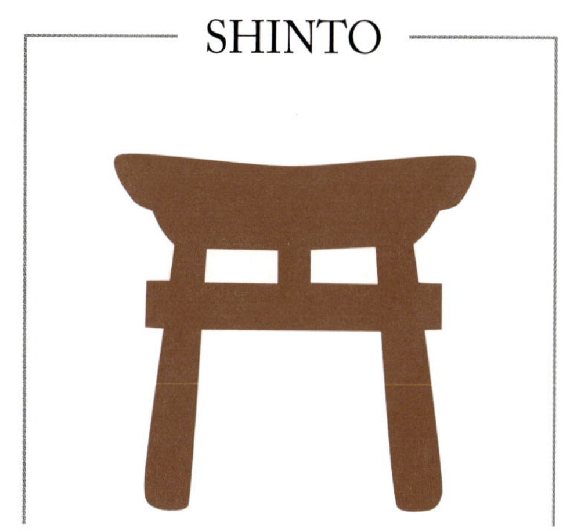

Torii gate

VINES AND CURLS

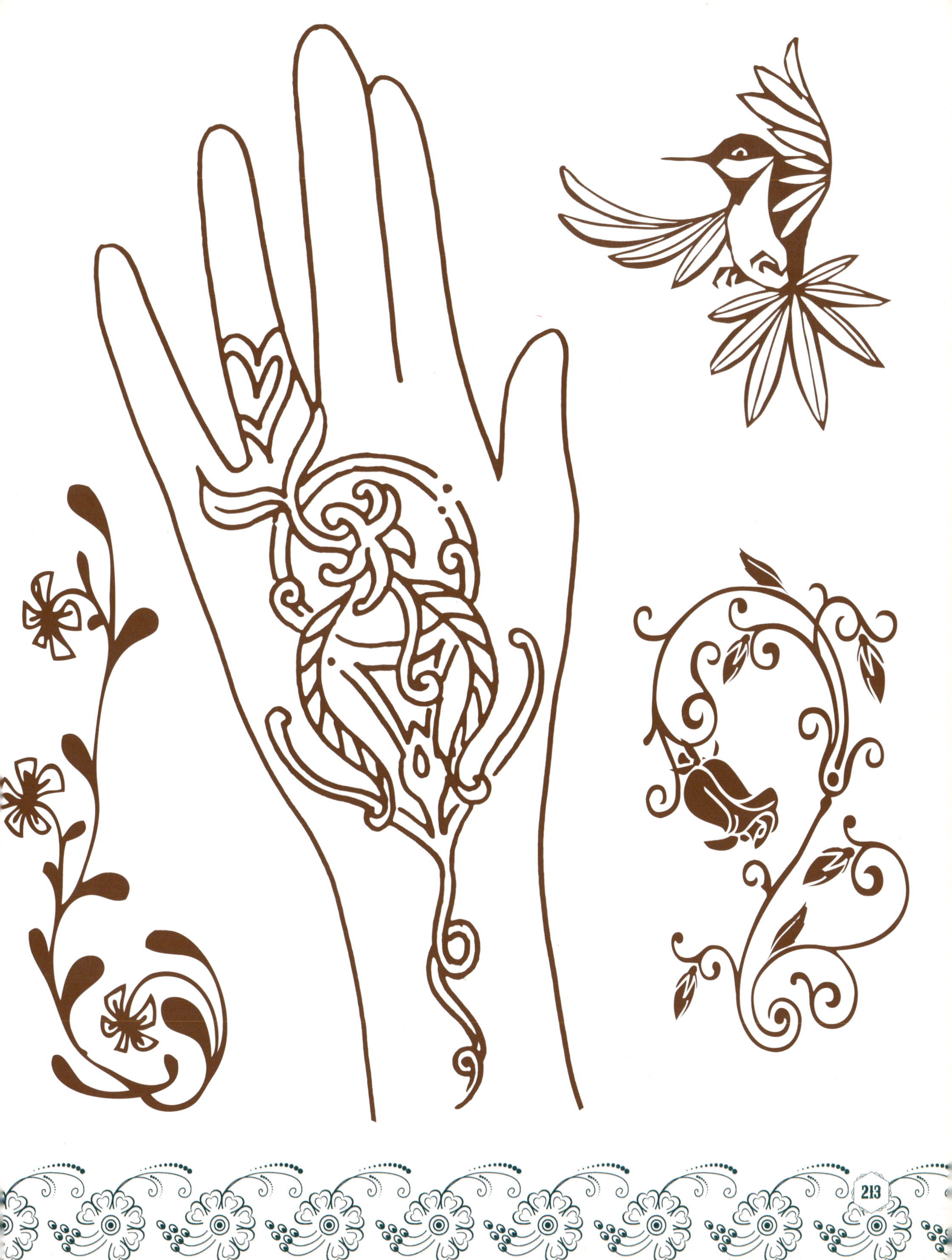

Butterflies

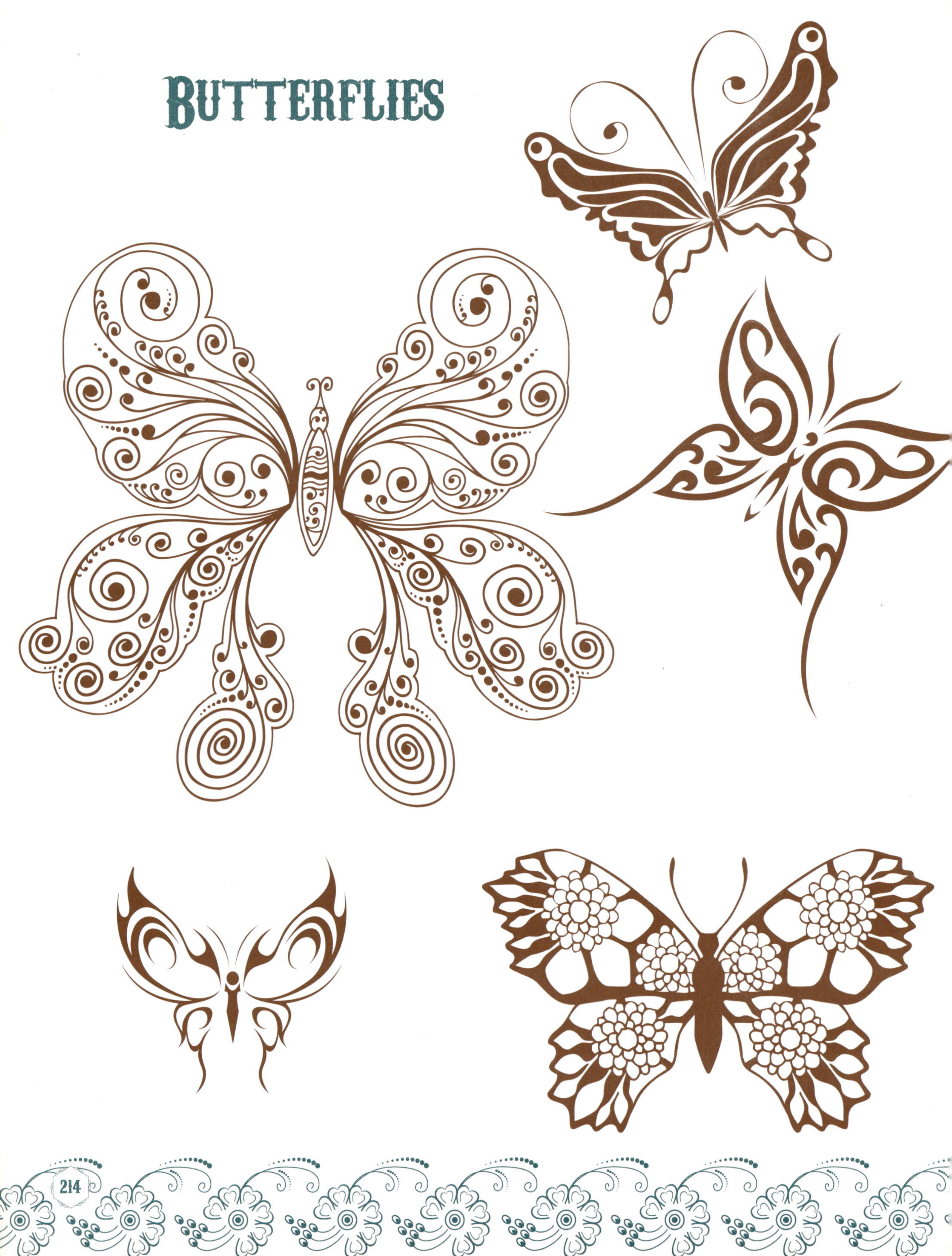

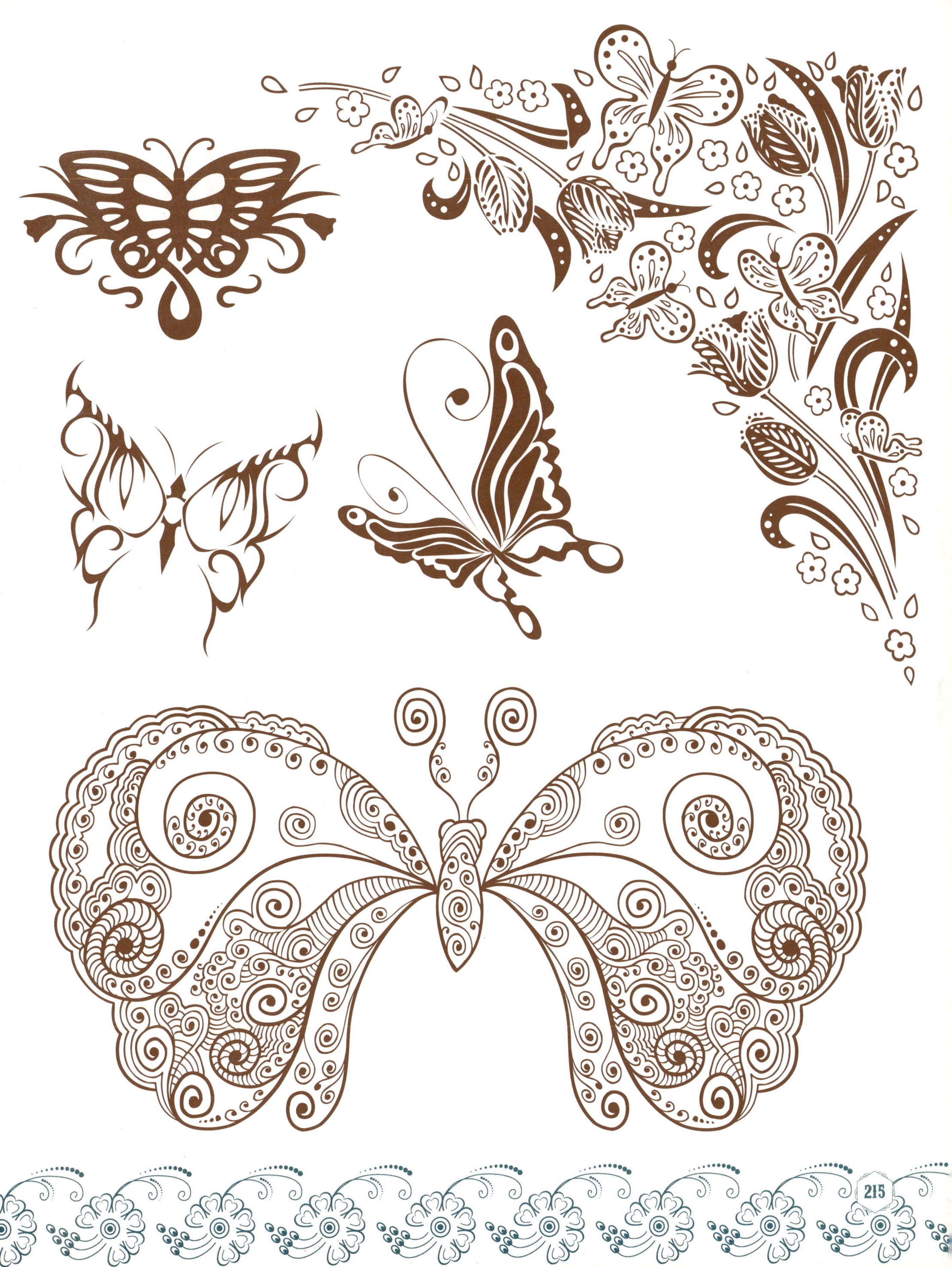

Hearts, Diamonds and Tiaras

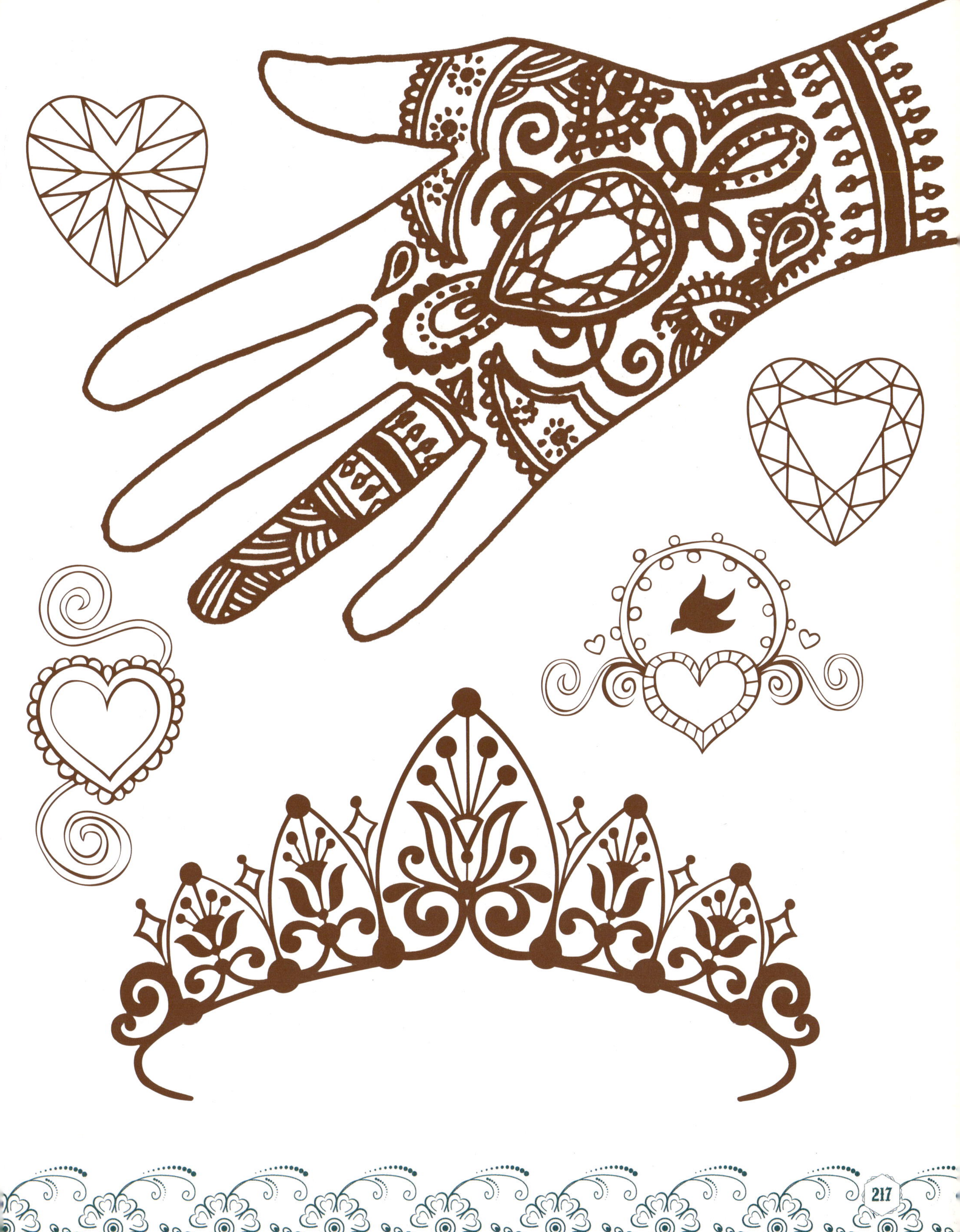

Dinosaurs, Dragons and Other Beasts

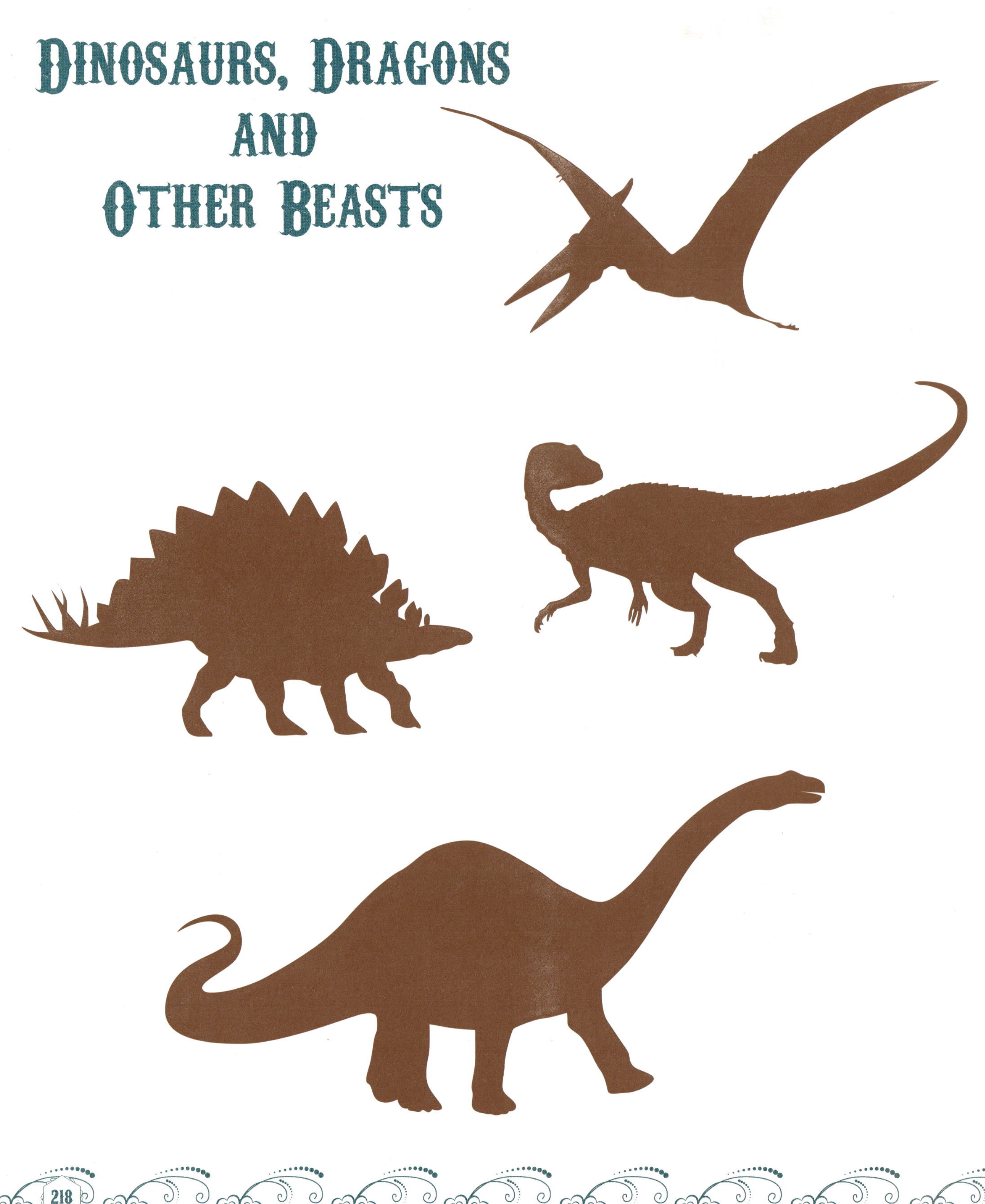

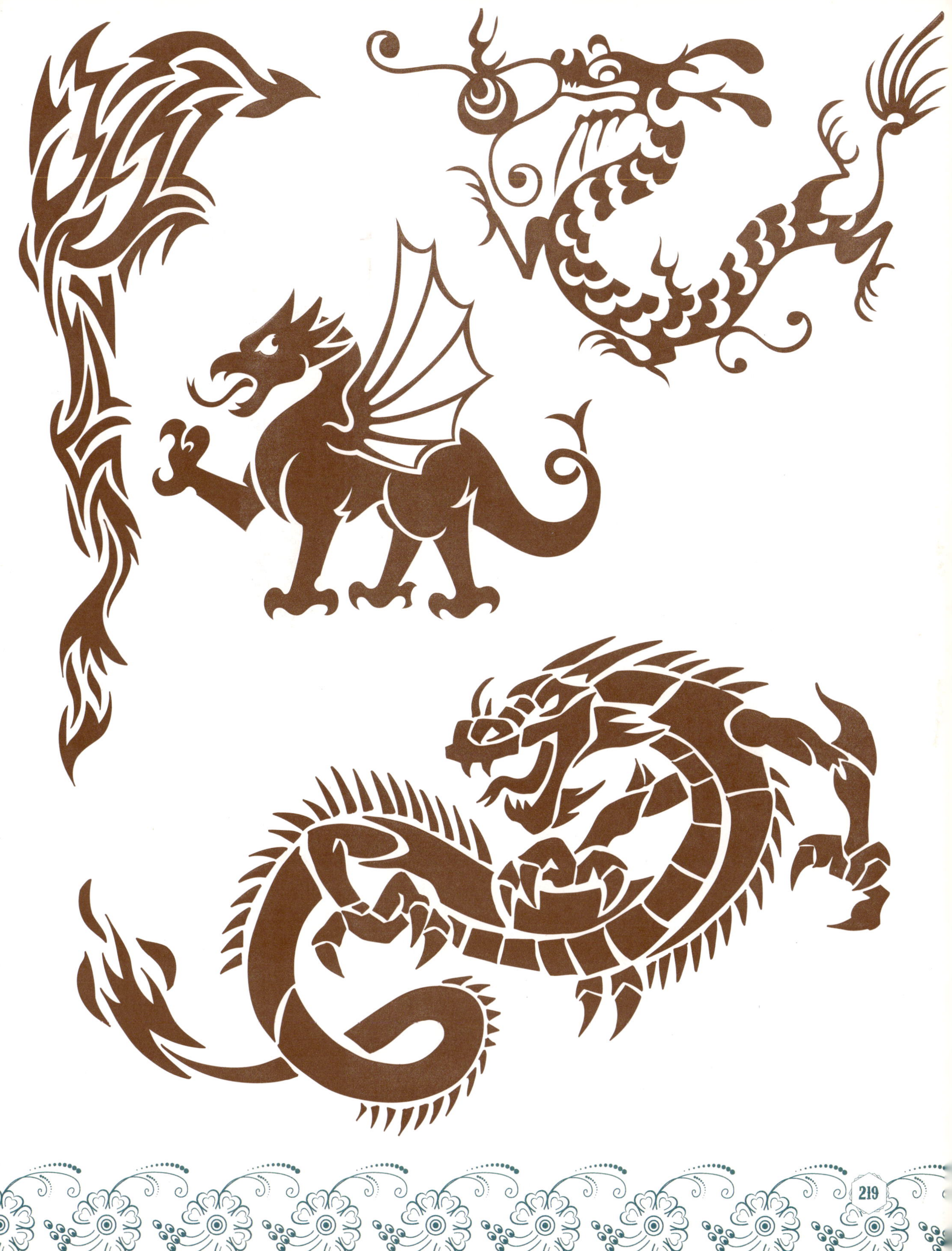

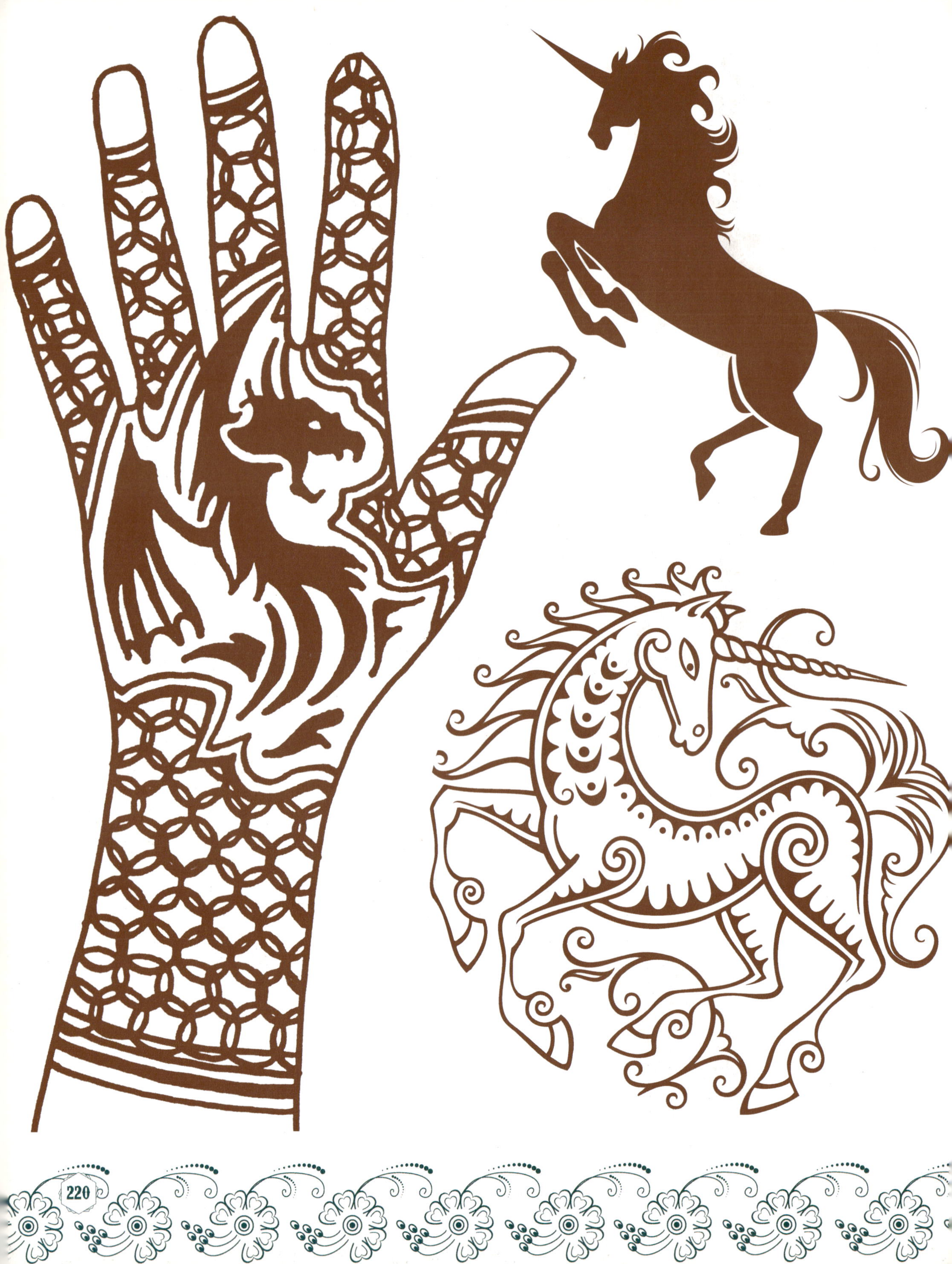

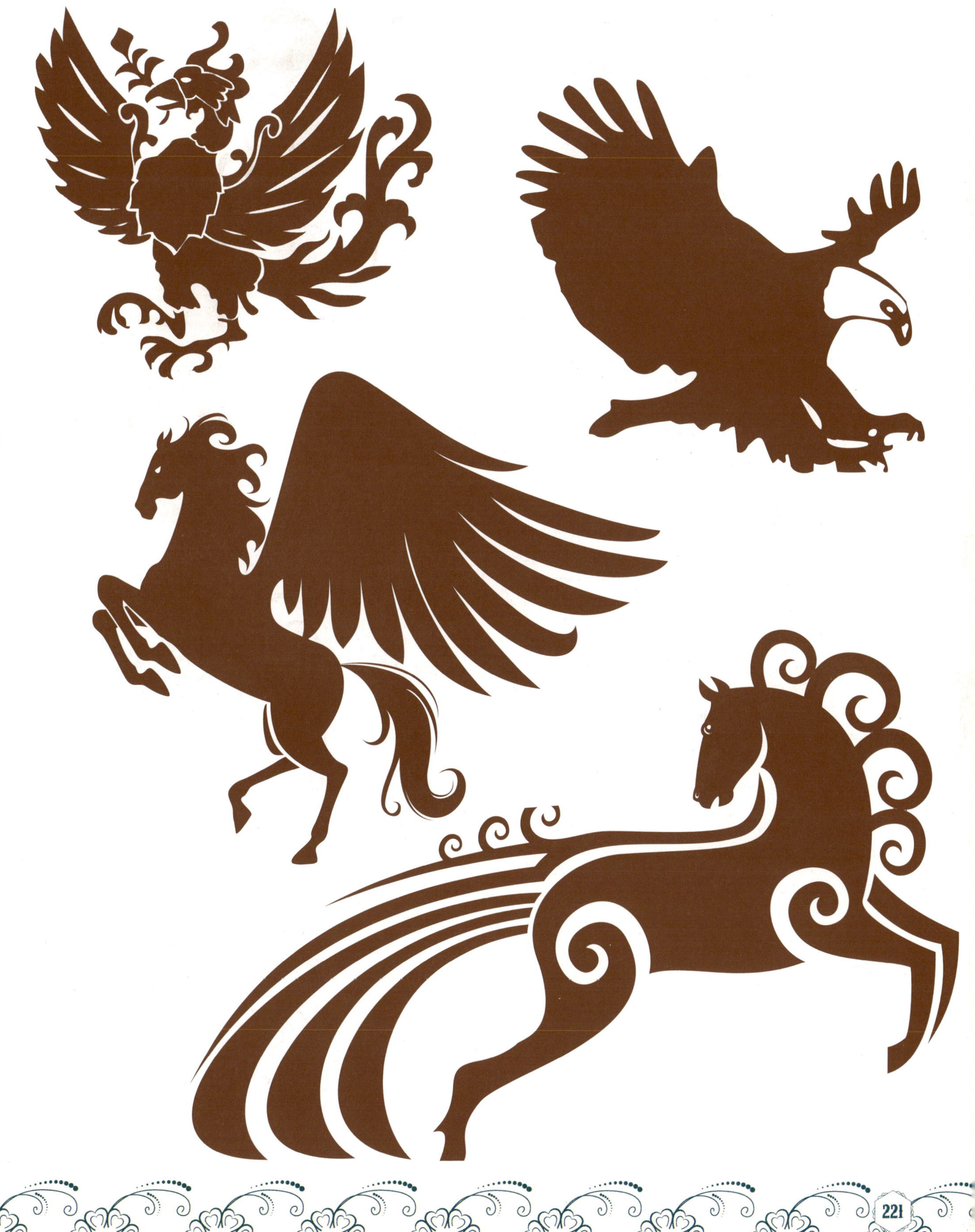

Creatures of the Sea

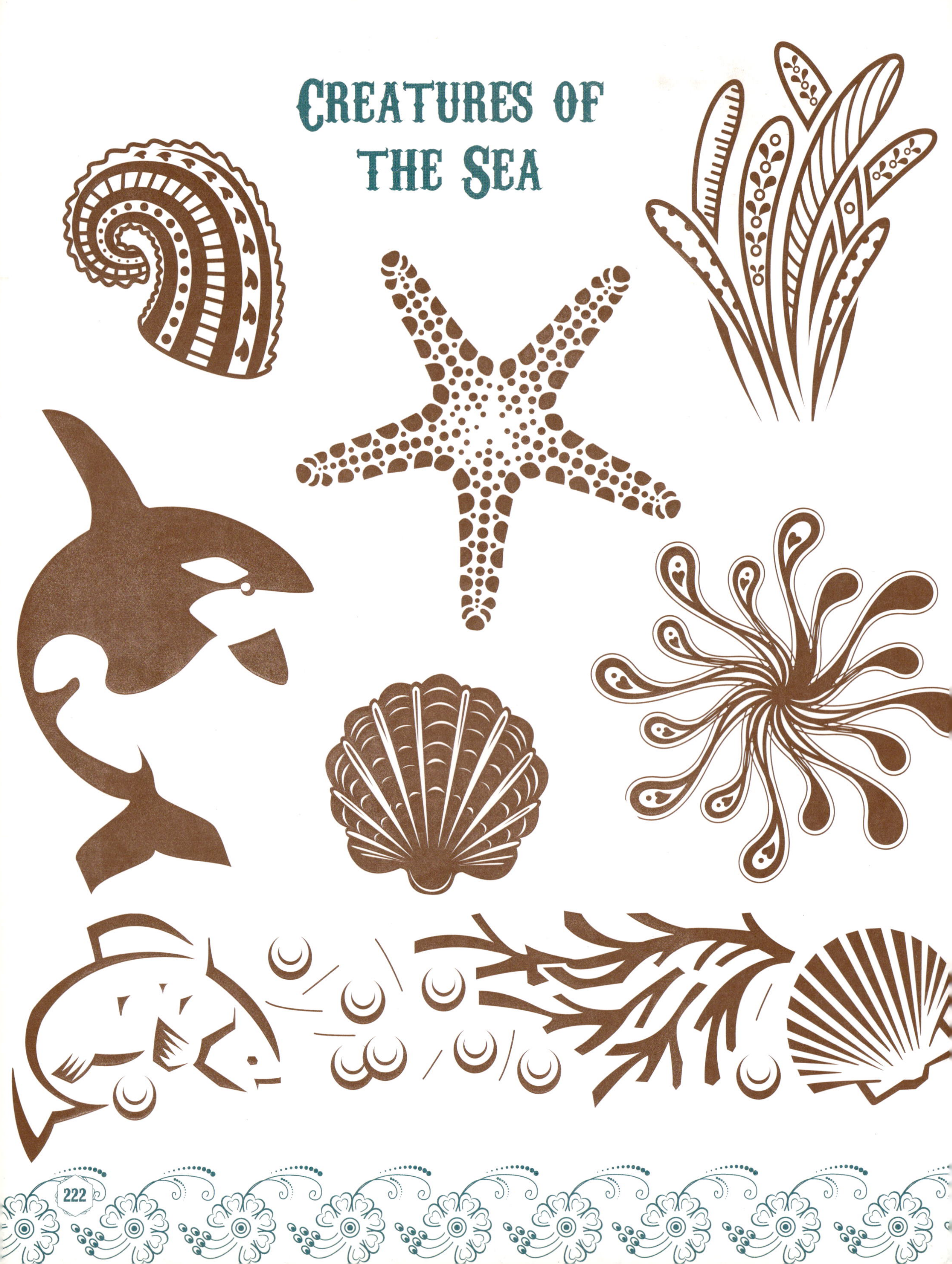

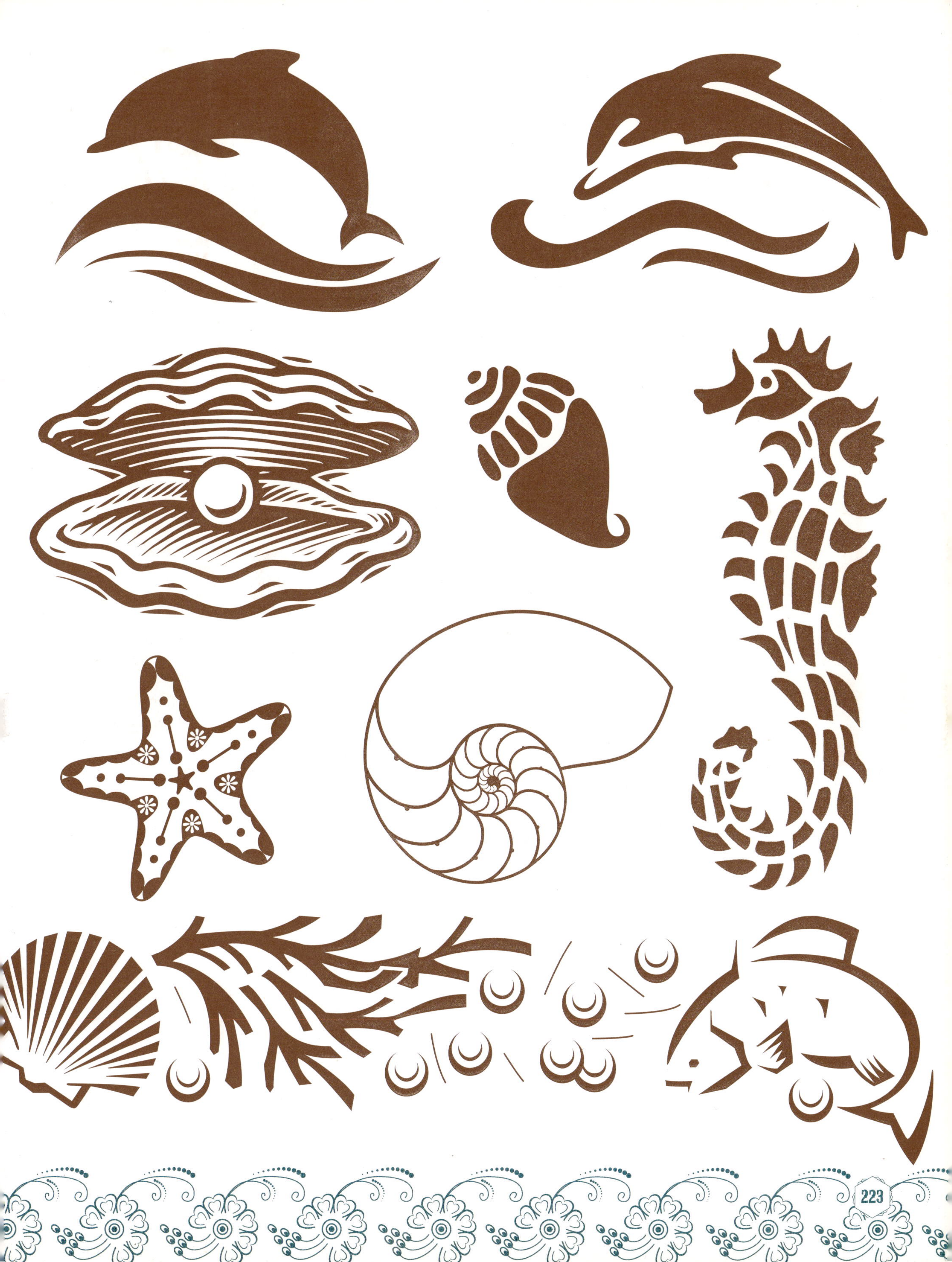

ACKNOWLEDGMENTS

The author would like to thank Sandhya Patangay of Henna Studio in New York City for her generous support, as well as her beautiful and delicious mehndi cakes!

The Book Shop, Ltd. would like to thank the following organizations and individuals for permission to reproduce their images in this book:

Pages 2–3, 6, 18 (top), 19–24, 26, 35, back cover—iStockphoto

Page 8—Alfredo Dagli Orti, The Art Archive at Art Resource, New York

Page 9—Werner Forman Archive/Oriental Collection, State University Library, Leiden

Page 12—Art Resource, Metropolitan Museum, Rogers Fund, 1955

Page 14—Art Resource, Metropolitan Museum, Fletcher Fund, 1996

Page 15—Werner Forman Archive/Formerly Philip Goldman Collection

Pages 16–17, 18 (bottom)—Hemera

Pages 32–33, 35, 37–38—Eleanor Kwei